From Samarqand to Toledo

Islamic History and Civilization

STUDIES AND TEXTS

VOLUME 201

The titles published in this series are listed at *brill.com/ihc*

From Samarqand to Toledo

Greek, Sogdian and Arabic Documents and Manuscripts from the Islamicate World and beyond

Edited by

Andreas Kaplony
Matt Malczycki

TUTA SUB AEGIDE PALLAS · 1683 ·

BRILL

LEIDEN | BOSTON

Cover illustration: Signatures of witnesses from the sale of a vineyard in Lorita, district of Toledo (P.Arch.Hist.Nac., Clero-secular regular, inv. Car. 3000 4 recto = P.Mozarab. 22; 1134)

The Library of Congress Cataloging-in-Publication Data is available online at https://catalog.loc.gov
LC record available at https://lccn.loc.gov/2022050819

Typeface for the Latin, Greek, and Cyrillic scripts: "Brill". See and download: brill.com/brill-typeface.

ISSN 0929-2403
ISBN 978-90-04-52786-7 (hardback)
ISBN 978-90-04-52787-4 (e-book)

This book is printed on acid-free paper and produced in a sustainable manner.

Contents

List of Figures VII
Notes on Contributors VIII

Introduction 1
Andreas Kaplony and Matt Malczycki

1 Who Did What in Eighth-Century Aphrodito? P.Würzb. Inv. 122–127, Greek Tax Documents, and Some Observations on Prosopography 4
Janneke de Jong

2 Thinking in Arabic, Writing in Sogdian: Arabic-Sogdian Diplomatic Relations in the Early Eighth Century 67
Said Reza Huseini

3 Reconstructing Dhū l-Rumma's Poetry with the Help of Muqātil b. Sulaymān's *Tafsīr* (P.Cair.Arab. Inv. 1235 Verso and Recto) 88
Hazem Hussein Abbas Ali

4 A Prisoner's Fate in Fatimid Egypt: The Late Coptic Paitos Dossier 104
Vincent Walter

5 The *Book of Twitches of Shem, Son of Noah*, and Other Manuals of Palmomancy from the Cairo Genizah and al-Quṣayr 139
Gideon Bohak

6 Scientific Textbooks and Their Application in Practice: Interdependencies of Literary and Documentary Evidence of Scientific Activities 162
Johannes Thomann

7 Christian and Islamic Documents in Arabic: The Concept of *Sunna*. (Appendix: On the Sale of a Mosque) 183
Rocio Daga Portillo

Quoted Editions 225
Index 232

Figures

1.1 Top-down communication of tax demands and relative hierarchies of people involved 10
2.1 Arabic Letter from Dēwāshtīč to al-Jarrāḥ b. ʿAbd Allāh dated 718–719 CE (P.Petersb.Acad. inv. B 12 = P.Kratchkovski) 70
2.2 Document 1.I, Letter to Dēwāshtīč. Dated to 721 C.E. (Livshits 2015: 90) 76
3.1 P.Cair.Arab. inv. 1235 recto: Dhū l-Rumma, A-*min Dimna* (Macartney, ed., poem no. 46) 102
3.2 P.Cair.Arab. inv. 1235 verso: Muqātil b. Sulaymān, *Tafsīr* (Shiḥāṭa, ed., vol. 3: 189.7–192.2) 103
4.1 P.Lond.UniColl. inv. 71024 recto. 114
4.2 P.Stras. inv. Kopt. 332(D) recto. 118
4.3 P.Stras. inv. Kopt. 332(D) verso. 119
4.4 P.Col. inv. 594 recto. 123
4.5 P.Col. inv. 594 verso. 124
4.6 P.Col. inv. 597 recto. 130
4.7 P.Col. inv. 597 verso. 131
4.8 P.Lond.UniColl. inv. 71026 recto. 134
4.9 P.Lond.UniColl. inv. 71026 verso. 135
5.1 P.Cair.IslArt inv. Quseir82 1016 b recto 155
5.2 P.Cair.IslArt inv. Quseir82 1016 b verso 156
6.1 Number of Greek authors on astronomy and astrology (per 35 years) 171
6.2 Number of Arabic authors on astronomy and astrology (per 35 years) 172
6.3 Number of Sanskrit works on astronomy and astrology (per 50 years) 174
6.4 A Geomantic Tableau (P.Vind. inv. A.Ch. 8516). 18.0 cm high × 8.6 cm wide. Twelfth–thirteenth centuries. Egypt 176
6.5 Reconstruction of the geomantic part of P.Vind. inv. A.Ch. 8516 177
7.1 First document on buying a mosque (P.Arch.Hist.Nac.inv. Clero-Secular_Regular, Car. 3036, N.15_1 recto = P.Mozarab. 82; 1205). 210
7.2 First document on buying a mosque (P.Arch.Hist.Nac.inv. Clero-Secular_Regular, Car. 3036, N.15_1 verso = P.Mozarab. 82; 1205) 211
7.3 Second document on buying a mosque (P.Arch.Hist.Nac.inv. Clero-Secular_Regular, Car. 3037, N.4_1 recto = P.Mozarab. 92; 1208). 215
7.4 Second document on buying a mosque (P.Arch.Hist.Nac.inv. Clero-Secular_Regular, Car. 3037, N.4_1 verso = P.Mozarab. 92; 1208). 216

Notes on Contributors

Hazem Hussein Abbas Ali
PhD (2010), Habilitation (2016), is an associate professor at Beni-Suef University, Egypt and head of Records Management and Archival Studies Department at Middle East College, Oman. He has published on Arabic papyri and archival science, most recently, "Casting Discord: an Unpublished Spell from the Egyptian National Library."

Gideon Bohak
PhD (1994), holds the Jacob M. Alkow Chair for the History of the Jews in the Ancient World at Tel Aviv University. His main field of research is the history of Jewish magic. His most recent books include *A Fifteenth-Century Manuscript of Jewish Magic* (2014, in Hebrew), *Magie, anges et démons dans la tradition juive* (2015, with Anne Hélène Hoog), and *Thābit ibn Qurra On Talismans and Pseudo-Ptolemy On Images 1–9* (2021, with Charles Burnett).

Rocio Daga Portillo
PhD (1990), is a lecturer at the Department of Arabic and Islamic Studies at LMU München. She has published over thirty Artikels on Islamic law, the history of al-Andalus, and Christian Arabic literature. Currently, she is working on Arabic legal documents from Toledo and the Fayyum.

Janneke de Jong
studied Classics at Radboud University Nijmegen, specializing in Greek papyrology. After receiving her PhD from the same university (2006), she worked at various Dutch universities as lecturer and (postdoc)researcher. She is currently employed as a high school teacher of Classics.

Said Reza Huseini
is a Junior Research Fellow at King's College, Cambridge University. He works on the Turko-Mongolians' understanding of diverse society between 1200–1600 in Iran, Central Asia, and India.

Andreas Kaplony
PhD (1986), Habilitation (2001), is Chair of Arabic and Islamic Studies at LMU München and co-director of the Arabic Papyrology Database. He has widely published on Arabic-Islamic history, including The *Ḥaram of Jerusalem* (2002) and "Hybrid Judeo-Persian and Arabic Correspondence: Eight Documents from

the Cairo Genizah" (in press, with Ofir Haim, Maximilian Kinzler, and Ludwig Paul). Currently, he is working on Arabic documents from the Fayyum.

Matt Malczycki
PhD (2006), is the Joseph A. Kicklighter Professor of History at Auburn University (USA) where he teaches Islamic history and Arabic.

Johannes Thomann
PhD (1992), is a visiting scholar at the Institute of Asian and Oriental Studies (IAOS) of the University of Zurich. He has published on the history of science, Arabic astronomical documents, and Arabic folk literature. Most recently appeared "The Foundation of al-Manṣūr's Palatial City and Its Horoscope" (2022, in *Baghdād*, ed. Jens Scheiner and Isabel Toral).

Vincent Walter
is currently a researcher in the field of Coptic papyrology at Leipzig University Library and a PhD student at Free University of Berlin. His main research interests are the language and diplomatics of Coptic documentary texts, particularly letters from early Islamic and medieval Egypt, as well as the Coptic literature produced in the Fayyum.

Introduction

Andreas Kaplony and Matt Malczycki

As the title states, the articles contained in this volume discuss places as diverse as Central Asia and western Europe. The research languages of the papers include Arabic, Coptic, Greek, Hebrew, Latin, and Sogdian. The topics vary widely and include tax assessment, poetry, incarceration, and palmomancy. What brings the apparently disparate papers together is that each one fills in small lacunae left in the historical records of the medieval Islamicate world. In different ways and to varying degrees each one does this by using documents or manuscripts to answer questions left unanswered by the historical record.

Janneke de Jong's article, "Who Did What in Eighth-Century Aphrodito? P.Würzb. Inv. 122–127, Greek Tax Documents, and Some Observations on Prosopography," offers the reader crucial background information to the organization and administration of taxes in early Islamic Egypt. Through her detailed onomastic study she offers a prosopography of the tax assessors and their world. Her work is an important contribution that builds on earlier studies by Bell, Morimoto, and Simonsen. "Who Did What?" gives the reader a glimpse of who the tax assessors were as a social group and thus offers some help in understanding who they were as people. Her appendices shed light on the connections among tax assessors in early eighth-century Aphrodito.

Said Reza Huseini's "Thinking in Arabic, Writing in Sogdian: Arabic-Sogdian Diplomatic Relations in the Early Eighth Century" is a study of conquest-era language politics. In the early second/eighth century in the time of Caliph al-Walīd (d. 96/715), Umayyad forces undertook the conquest of Sogdia. Over the next two decades, through conversion, warfare, and diplomacy, this region became part of the Muslim world. Huseini takes a new look at evidence first gathered in the 1930s at Mount Mugh in Tajikistan. By applying the "building block" method of Eva Grob, the author demonstrates that the introduction of Arabic imperial epistolary into Sogdiana reveals much about politics and power in the conquest period. Choosing which language to compose a letter in and choosing which elements of the other language to include in that letter can tell us much about how correspondents viewed each other and how they manipulated the epistolary style to achieve political ends.

In "Reconstructing Dhū l-Rumma's Poetry with the Help of Muqātil b. Sulaymān's *Tafsīr* (P.Cair.Arab. Inv. 1235 Verso and Recto)," Hazem Hussein Abbas Ali offers new insight into some very old poetry. The focus of the article is P.Cair.Arab. inv. 1235, which contains a poem by Dhū l-Rumma (d. ca. 117/735).

 | DOI:10.1163/9789004527874_002

Dhū l-Rumma was a Bedouin poet of the Umayyad era whose work harkened back to the Jāhiliyya. This poem was edited by Carlile Henry Hayes Macartney in 1919, although Macartney relied on other manuscripts. Ali argues that the Macartney edition contains lines that were not present in older copies of the poem. His evidence is the other side of P.Cair.Arab. inv. 1235, which contains a fragment of the *Tafsīr* of Muqātil b. Sulaymān (d. 150/767).

Vincent Walter's "A Prisoner's Fate in Fatimid Egypt: The Late Coptic Paitos Dossier" includes five new text editions. Walter uses a dossier of Coptic letters from the tenth century written by a man named Paitos. Paitos was a small landowner who found himself in jail for failing to pay his taxes. His incarceration came just when his crops were ready for harvest and transport, which was a particularly bad time for a Fayyumic landowner. Among other things, Walter's article examines various ways in which Arabic words and structures infiltrated Coptic in this period.

"The *Book of Twitches of Shem, Son of Noah,* and Other Manuals of Palmomancy from the Cairo Genizah and al-Quṣayr" by Gideon Bohak takes up the topic of divination as practiced in the seventh/thirteenth century. The specific kind of divination studied in this article is palmomancy (i.e., divination through the interpretation of involuntary body movements such as twitching). Bohak's article provides a description of this forgotten practice that was quite common among the peoples of the premodern Middle East. The article contains a survey of the available literature on the topic as well as an edition of a previously misidentified Arabic text from al-Quṣayr.

Johannes Thomann's "Scientific Textbooks and Their Application in Practice: Interdependencies of Literary and Documentary Evidence of Scientific Activities" takes the reader to a time when many of the arts modern scholars would describe as "pseudoscientific" were as highly regarded as any formally researched in the world's universities today. Thomann attempts to create a typology for published Arabic scientific documents using the historically appropriate (pre-Enlightenment) definitions of science. From a historical perspective, it seems that these arts had died out in Egypt in the centuries leading up to the Arab-Islamic era. Thomann suggests India as the source for a scientific renaissance in the eastern Mediterranean.

Rocio Daga Portillo's, "Christian and Islamic Documents in Arabic: The Concept of *Sunna*. (Appendix: On the Sale of a Mosque)," sheds light on the development of legal language and norms by exploring the use of Arabic among non-Muslims in Christian Spain. Toledo was the Visigothic capital of Iberia until the Muslims conquered it in 92/712. Muslims ruled the city until 478/1085, when King Alfonso VI captured and occupied it. Although one might have expected the legal language of the city to revert to Latin or a Romance language, it did not, at least not for another three centuries. Instead, Muslims, Jews, and Christians used Arabic for legal documents. The reason they were able to do so was that *sunna* (law) was much more flexible than modern law and more fluid than modern scholars have supposed.

Acknowledgements

The work contained in this volume was part of Documents and Manuscripts in the Arab-Islamic World: The Seventh International Society for Arabic Papyrology (ISAP) Conference (Berlin, 20–23 March, 2018). The organizers were Lajos Berkes (New Testament Studies, Humboldt-Universität zu Berlin), Beatrice Gruendler (Arabic Studies, Freie Universität Berlin), Konrad Hirschler (Islamic Studies, Freie Universität Berlin), Andreas Kaplony (Arabic and Islamic Studies, Ludwig-Maximilians-Universität München; International Society for Arabic Papyrology), Verena Lepper (Egyptology, Humboldt-Universität zu Berlin; Egyptian Museum and Papyrus Collection, National Museums Berlin), Michael Marx (Corpus Coranicum, Berlin-Brandenburg Academy of Sciences and Humanities), Johannes Niehoff-Panagiotidis (Byzantine Studies, Freie Universität Berlin), and Tonio Sebastian Richter (Egyptology, Freie Universität Berlin).

Generous material, financial, and human support was provided by a number of benefactors. As a result, the 2018 ISAP conference was able to take place in several venues throughout Berlin. Portions of the conference took place in Staatliche Museen zu Berlin Preussischer Kulturbesitz (specifically the Gobelinsaal of the Bodemuseum and the reading room of the Egyptian Museum and Papyrus Collection), the Holzlaube of the Freie Universität Berlin, the Grimm-Zentrum of the Humboldt Universität zu Berlin, the Einsteinsaal of the Berlin-Brandenburg Academy of Sciences and Humanities, and the Orientabteilung of the Staatsbibliothek zu Berlin. Ludwig-Maximilians-Universität München and the International Society for Arabic Papyrology also provided general support.

CHAPTER 1

Who Did What in Eighth-Century Aphrodito? P.Würzb. Inv. 122–127, Greek Tax Documents, and Some Observations on Prosopography

Janneke de Jong

Abstract

The late seventh- and early eighth-century archive from Aphrodito, preserving more than 400 documents in three languages (Greek, Coptic, Arabic), offers a unique glimpse into the fiscal administration and the linguistic landscape on the local level in Egypt under Umayyad rule. Apart from detailed fiscal registers, the papyri contain thousands of names, which have not yet been thoroughly studied. Their onomastic value aside, these names may have the potential to be investigated for understanding social relations in Aphrodito. In this contribution, I will discuss whether and how the fiscal documentation can be used to study social relations underlying Aphrodito's fiscal-administrative management, focusing on the identification of tax assessors, both as individuals and as a group, and on connections between the texts in which they appear. This discussion will function as a case study illustrating the possibilities and limitations of a prosopographical study of late seventh- and early eighth-century Aphrodito. The bigger goal of such an approach is to assess the relative place of individuals and groups that can be distinguished in Aphrodito and in this way get a better understanding of the functioning of Aphrodito as a (tax) community.

1 A Fiscal-Administrative Archive[1]

In 1901, local villagers in Kom Ishgau in Egypt decided to dig a well.[2] When they did so, they discovered a substantial number of papyri written in various languages. Through merchants, the papyri were sold to interested parties on the antiquities market, and as a result, documents belonging to this find found

1 Abbreviations of papyrological editions according to John F. Oates and William H. Willis (founding editors), *Checklist of Editions of Greek, Latin, Demotic, and Coptic Papyri, Ostraca, and Tablets*. I would like to thank Olivier Hekster for his comments on this contribution.

2 Becker 1907: 68.

 | DOI:10.1163/9789004527874_003

their way into various papyrological collections. Since the first decade of the twentieth century many of these documents have been published. Up to the present, Bell and Crum's monumental edition (Bell 1910) of Greek and Coptic papyri from late seventh- and early eighth-century Aphrodito remains a major work of reference, even if a substantial number of Greek, Coptic, and Arabic texts from the same archive have been published elsewhere.[3] Also, occasionally new documents turn up in collections where it was unknown (or had been forgotten) that their inventories included material from late seventh- and early eighth-century Aphrodito.

So far, these documents have mainly attracted attention for the information they offer on Aphrodito's fiscal-administrative organization. However, as thousands of individuals are attested in the documents, it seems to be worthwhile to also study the material from a prosopographical perspective.[4] The aim of this contribution is to examine whether and how the documentary papyri from Aphrodito are relevant for such a prosopographical approach in order to study what I would like to label "the social organization of the tax system in eighth-century Aphrodito." By this I mean the way in which the people mentioned in the papyri from Aphrodito in the late seventh and early eighth century were involved in its tax system and how this related to their position in the local community and—in some instances—outside their community, more specifically in their relation to central authorities. The question of whether and how names may provide clues for this social composition and its administrative functioning will be addressed using a selection of names attested in (the majority of) Greek papyri from Aphrodito.

To explain it rather simply, the prosopographical method collects as much data as possible for each individual in order to make more generalized observations about the bigger group or community that these individuals were part of.[5] Much data are already available for eighth-century Aphrodito. Further-

3 The most elaborate publications of papyri from late seventh- to early eighth-century Aphrodito are P.Heid.Arab. I; P.Lond. IV; P.Ross.-Georg. IV; P.Qurra; P.World. See the list of published texts provided by Richter 2010 and the overview in Trismegistos Archives, Arch ID 124 (https://www.trismegistos.org/arch/detail.php?arch_id=124), noting that the list is not yet complete.

4 On prosopography in general, see for instance Cameron 2003; Smythe 2008; Verboven, Carlier, and Jan Dumolyn 2007. On prosopography in sixth-century Aphrodito, see Ruffini 2008; Ruffini 2011. See also the observations made to this work by Papaconstantinou 2013.

5 Information to be collected includes name and patronymic, matronymic, profession or other designation (e.g., priest), function in the text, date of the document, residency, landholdings, attestations in other texts, and other relevant points if applicable. Accumulation of these details of individual information may facilitate distinguishing between groups and trying to assess the individual's and the group's position in society. Examples of groups to

more, as documents from the archive continue to be published and additional information may be expected, work on Aphrodito's individuals may be a fruitful new direction. Finally, technological developments enable and facilitate new approaches. One could think of the availability of databases that can be mined for names and of software programs that facilitate the creation of datasets and allow visualizations of social or other networks.[6]

The papyri from Aphrodito offer a good place of departure for such a project, as they preserve names and other data on persons with differing positions in early Islamic Egypt's society. Even if these data pose many challenges (such as their incomplete nature, to name just one), the fiscal documentation of seventh- and eighth-century Aphrodito offers insight in a differentiated palette of individuals' roles, duties, privileges, and obligations, varying from being registered as a taxpayer to transporting the collected money to al-Fusṭāṭ, or to receiving allowances out of the taxes collected. In other words, the individuals attested all occupied a specific place in society, which defined their relations with others. As one's relative place in society depends on multiple factors, such as one's position in the political-administrative structure, one's gender, and one's cultural background, assembling and analyzing the data available for the people attested in the Aphrodito papyri might provide deeper insight in the distribution of power and authority, the ways in which women are visible next to men in the documentation and active in the management of land, and issues such as onomastic practices and language use.[7] Moreover, thanks to Aphrodito's nature as a delimited fiscal-administrative community, which directly communicated with the provincial authorities in al-Fusṭāṭ, its documentation is not only relevant for its fiscal-administrative functioning on the local level but also ties it in with the bigger state structures. In other words, the

be distinguished are men/women, officials (people acting on behalf of the authorities)/taxpayers, landholders/nonlandholders, people from Aphrodito/people residing elsewhere but having land in or having fled to Aphrodito, *mawālī* (converts to Islam)/Muslims, and Muslim Arabs/Christian Arabs. However, unfortunately the evidence does not always provide such detailed information on individuals.

6 E.g., the *Papyrological Navigator* (PN). For names, obviously *Trismegistos* (TM) *People* is indispensable. However, as TM is a work in progress, the material for the seventh and eighth century has not yet been arranged in the same level of completeness and accuracy as the pre-fifth-century Greek texts; see the remarks on "Quality Control," https://www.trismegistos.org/ref/about_qc.php.

7 An onomastic study focusing on whether names can be identified as Greek, Coptic, or Arabic should also deal with the question of to what degree these names can be assumed to reveal the identity of the persons having these names. Even if it may be difficult to draw conclusions on the basis of the Aphrodito papyri, the resulting corpus of names may be used as a point of reference to be compared with other *corpora* of names.

bigger question to be addressed is how the data on persons preserved in the papyri may serve to reconstruct a more dynamic picture of a local society and its embedding in the larger state structure. A concomitant question, of course, is to what degree the results for Aphrodito can be representative for seventh- and eighth-century Egypt.

As the majority of documents concern fiscal obligations, it is self-evident that the fiscal liability on the individual level will be one focus point. Indeed, Simonsen (1988) already offers an analysis of individual tax assessments in which he demonstrates the wide-ranging differentiation in types of taxes and amounts of taxes demanded from the tax payers. He also made some observations on the corpus of tax payers: "In a number of instances, more than one person stands liable for the given amount of *dêmosia* (sc. *gês*, public tax on land), *diagraphê* (poll tax) or *embolê* (corn tax) and, thus, none of these taxes can be regarded as personal taxes. Both men and women appear in the lists, and in a number of instances the taxpayers' business is stated too."[8] Simonsen's formulation is rather general, and I think it is worthwhile to pursue this further quantitatively and qualitatively. It appears, for instance, that only a few women or certain professions are mentioned, and this raises the question of why they feature in these texts, what this implies for female landownership or the divisions of tasks within Aphrodito, and how representative these women or occupations are. If individuals are encountered in documents from different years, it may even become possible to assess how they fared: clues may arise from comparison between several years and which taxes they paid, whether the amounts remained the same, and whether the assessments related to the same plots of land. The establishment of professions and functions gives insight in labor division and might be contrasted with what is not stated: most likely all taxpayers who are otherwise unlabeled (if it comes to profession/activity) were landholders and/or farmers.[9]

The ultimate goal of analyzing the data on people is to assess the relative place of individuals and groups that can be distinguished in Aphrodito and in this way get a better understanding of the functioning of Aphrodito as a (tax) community. Establishing the officials and their activities, moreover, is import-

8 Simonsen 1988: 88.

9 Landless people appear to have been listed separately in assessment documents. However, people, whose confessions are indicated, sometimes also possessed land. An unedited papyrus, Lond. 1480 B (de Jong forthcoming b), for example, lists three individuals who are further qualified as carpenters (ll. 22; 98; 100), one as a doctor (l. 96), one as a digger (l. 103), and one as a shipwright (l. 118, if the abbreviation is solved correctly), who are all registered to have paid land tax.

ant for the relation between Aphrodito and the central authorities in al-Fusṭāṭ and Alexandria. Connecting such an approach to other studies of Aphrodito, for instance Aphrodito's landholding system or its situation in the sixth century, may facilitate comparisons.[10]

In what follows, a case study will be presented in order to show the possibilities and limitations of such a "people's approach," focusing on the people/individuals who are attested in the papyri. The advantage of a case study is that it is limited in scope, and yet may illustrate the possibilities and limitations of the approach. The first step is to identify a specific group of individuals, after which other questions may be asked, such as how the individual members of that group appear elsewhere in Aphrodito's documentation, what this may or may not tell us about these individuals and about their community, and what specific and general observations can be made about this group. The result of this limited case will of course be far from a proper prosopography. Rather, my aim is to demonstrate that such a project is worthwhile and, in my view, offers possibilities for further exploration.

Before discussing the case study, however, it is necessary to briefly sketch Aphrodito's tax system. This will serve not only as a general background but also make clear how several administrative levels were involved in the enactment of Aphrodito's tax collection.

2 The Tax System: Communication and Collection

The basic principles of Aphrodito's tax system have already been explained by Bell in 1910 (= P.Lond. IV). In the 1980s two studies of early Islamic Egypt's fiscal system appeared, one by Kosei Morimoto (1981), the other by Jørgen Simonsen (1988). Both used Aphrodito's Greek fiscal documents in order to get a clearer understanding of the specifics of the early Islamic tax system. Their studies, like Bell's, are fundamental, but at the same time they are based on relatively few documents, which relate to different districts of Aphrodito and are dated to different years. In other words, it is difficult to assess whether the information they preserve is generally valid for the whole of Aphrodito during a longer period or whether they only apply to some specific districts, and this for the limited span of time to which they are attributed. All the same, the documents are important sources for various aspects of the fiscal-administrative organization of Aphrodito's tax system, e.g., for the way in which the central authorities com-

10 Zuckerman 2004; Ruffini 2011; Marthot 2013.

municated with the local authorities over fiscal matters, for the way in which the tax amounts demanded from Aphrodito's population were established and collected, and for people involved in the tax system in various roles.

The generally accepted view, set out by Bell, Morimoto, and Simonsen on the basis of the papyrological documentation, is that the central authorities in al-Fusṭāṭ, headed by the governor, each year established a lump sum to be paid by Aphrodito, including further specification of the quota (*zêtoumena*) for its subdivisions. Official orders to pay (*entagia*) addressed to the communities of the subdivisions were provided by the central authorities so that the local officials could pass these on to these communities of taxpayers per subdivision. These data and instructions were communicated to the *dioikêtês* (administrator), the financial head of the *dioikêsis* (administrative district). He was a key figure and would pass on the governor's instructions to the men in charge of the smaller fiscal-administrative units of the *dioikêsis*, who were subordinate to him. The *dioikêtês* instructed the leading men of the individual subdivisions to select men—most likely from among their subcommunity—who would be responsible for distributing the sums demanded over the individual tax payers, i.e., assess each individual taxpayer for the taxes applying to him or her. These selected men, *epilechthentes*, will be discussed further in the case study presented below. Figure 1.1 illustrates the top-down communication of the tax demands and the relative hierarchies of the people involved in the different stages of this procedure.[11]

The practical collection of the demands would then take place, but the information on the exact method is scarce. Probably the method varied according to the circumstances. Perhaps the liable taxpayers would go to the collectors to pay their contribution or the tax collectors went to the taxpayers' houses to collect the amounts. If taxpayers went to pay their taxes, they might do so at a public place or in a public building especially designed for the collection of taxes within an indicated period of time. Another possibility, perhaps especially in case of untimely payment, is that the collector undertook action himself, sometimes putting the taxpayer under pressure or even using

11 In this table, the named monasteries are left out. They do not appear in P.Würzb. inv. 122–127. Their relation to *kômê Aphroditô* remains somewhat unclear, see Bell 1910: xvi–xvii. The earliest dated attestations of these monasteries in early Islamic Aphrodito are dated to 709 CE (SB I 5650; SB I 5651; W.Chr. 256). Other documents in which one or more of them appear are of later date: P.Lond. 1413 (716–721). Of uncertain date are P.Lond. 1414; 1416; 1419; 1434; 1436; 1442; 1445; 1552; P.Ross.Georg. IV 19; 20. Perhaps an administrative change in or before 709 CE explains their inclusion in documents from that year onwards, but the matters remains to be settled.

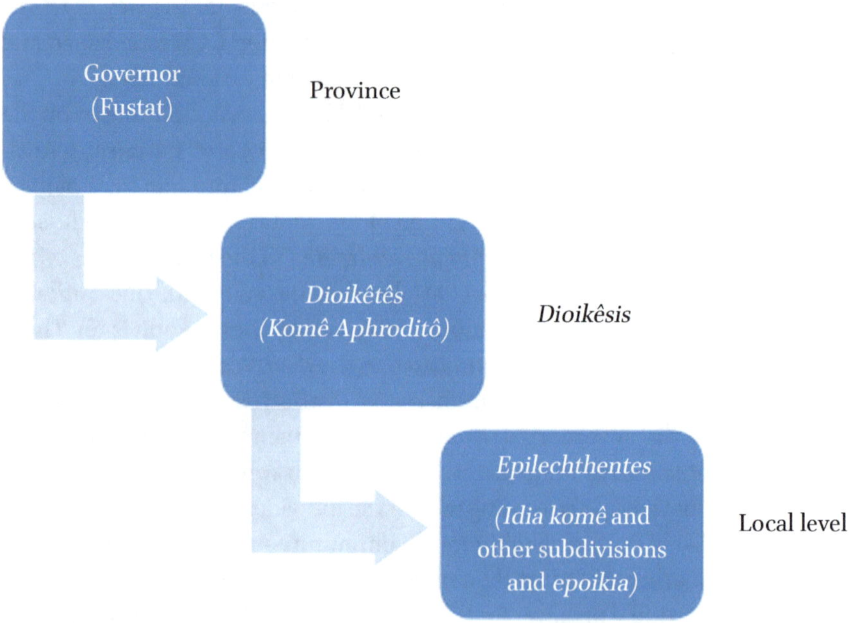

FIGURE 1.1 Top-down communication of tax demands and relative hierarchies of people involved

force.[12] Whether a tax collector would be waiting for the taxpayer to come and bring in their taxes or whether he would actively go round the houses may also have depended on the collector himself, on the size of the community, or on other reasons that remain undocumented. The evidence suggests that it was not always possible for the liable taxpayers to pay the tax in person, as in some cases we see that people are assessed or pay on behalf of others.[13] However, in order to keep good track of each person's obligations, this needed to be administrated carefully.

12 A well-known example is *PSR* I 11, which contains reference to an oral petition by a local villager to Qurra about having been violently treated by a village headmen. Letters by Qurra warn Basileios to keep an eye on fair and peaceful collection, e.g., P.Lond. 1338, where Qurra urges Basileios "not to give any ground of complaint or cause of displeasure whatsoever against yourself" (translation by Bell), P.Lond. 1345.29–37. P.Lond. 1356.24–31 contains a warning not to assess a village (*chôrion*) too heavily or lightly. Declarations of fair assessments of taxes are also found in Coptic documents, e.g., P.Lond. 1552.

13 E.g., P.Lond. 1420.39; 46. In l. 39, the assessment is registered "through/by the children of Herakleios, priest." In line 46: "through/by the wife of Kyrillos." This probably implies that the children and the wife of Herakleios and Kyrillos, respectively, were assessed on behalf of these named men.

However this may be, the tax organization produced several types of documentation, reflecting various stages and the involvement of various parties in the procedure,[14] and preserving information on landholdings and taxpayers. One can think of the letters by the governor to the *dioikêtês* ordering the collection or transfer of collected taxes. Another type of documentation is tax registers, where the contributions of taxes or of individual taxpayers are listed. Yet another type is assessment documents. These are the documents in which the tax assessors (*epilechthentes*) have assessed the taxes to which he or she was liable for each taxpayer. These assessment documents thus show the results of the distribution of the lump sum per local unit over the individual taxpayers per local unit.

To date, a dozen such assessments, *merismos* documents, have been published from among the Greek papyri from seventh- and eighth-century Aphrodito.[15] Together with one unpublished papyrus codex, which is kept in Würzburg, these assessment documents constitute the corpus for this contribution's modest case. This Würzburg codex, P.Würzb. inv. 122–127, in several respects differs from the other (published) assessments due to its different purpose and function, but it shares some of their structural features. The structural features in the other published assessments comprise a heading line mentioning the fiscal-administrative district concerned, information on the data concerned, the names of the assessors, and a brief summary of the total amounts. They then continue with the individual registrations of the taxpayers, indicating which amounts they have to pay for which tax. At the bottom of the page, the total sums of the page concerned are given. At the end of the document, the totals of the pages are collected in a table and the totals are given.

The Würzburg codex is a somewhat different assessment type in which the tax amounts are assessed as lump sums for the individual fiscal-administrative subdivisions of Aphrodito; no individual assessments were made, that is, they contain no separate entries for individual taxpayers residing or registered in these subdivisions, only the total sums per subdivision. It seems clear that the type of assessment preserved in the Würzburg codex is about the collective amounts of the subdivisions rather than about the people. An interesting point is that the text is divided into two sections: the first part presents the assessments of the fiscal-administrative subdivisions of *kômê Aphroditô*; in the

14 Documents relating to the central authorities, local administrators, and the tax paying locals all appear in the archive. Even the sociocultural background of each of these groups may be reflected in the use of language, see Richter 2010; Delattre and de Jong 2014.

15 A fuller discussion of the *merismos* documents is given in the introduction to my edition of P.Würzb. inv. 122–127. Edition of this codex: de Jong forthcoming a.

second part, the assessments of the individual *epoikia* (hamlets) are given. This ordering in two parts may reflect the geographical-fiscal-administrative organization of the *dioikêsis*, as I discuss elsewhere.[16] The important point for the first case study presented below is that the Würzburg codex offers new names of tax assessors and may provide new information on their place in the community of Aphrodito.

3 Case Study: The Tax Assessors (*Epilechthentes*)

As mentioned above, the term ἐπιλεχθέντες *epilechthentes*, "selected men," (sing. *epilechtheis*) is used as a designation for the men who were responsible for making the assessment of individual taxpayers on the local level.[17] The procedure by which the *epilechthentes* were selected is referred to in one of the letters by the governor of Egypt, Qurra b. Sharīk, to the local financial administrator named Basileios:

> And gather together the headmen and leading men of each fiscal-administrative unit (*chôrion*) and order them to choose (*epilegomai*) trustworthy and intelligent men; and when they are chosen [under oath?] order them to draw up the assessment of each fiscal-administrative unit to the best of their ability, seeing to it that you are found a faithful overseer of the pagarchy and (that you cause them) to make the said assessment under oath, and when it is completed send it to us, taking a copy of it, and keeping it with you, writing to us the name and patronymic and the specific fiscal-administrative unit of the persons who have made the said assessment.[18]

The governor instructs his local contact person to gather the leading men of Aphrodito's fiscal-administrative units who would then select assessors.[19] These men would compose the assessments, by which they would distribute the tax demands over the individual taxpayers. When making the assessments of the individual fiscal-administrative units, the *epilechthentes* were expected

16 De Jong forthcoming a.

17 It is not clear whether *epilechthentes* should be considered a technical term. It seems not to have been used consistently in all (types of) documents, as for instance in P.Würzb. inv. 122–127 the term is occasionally left out. Yet, the specific task of the *epilechthentes* is clear not only from P.Würzb. inv. 122–127 but also from other documents.

18 P.Lond. 1356.15–24. Translation slightly adapted from Bell 1911: 282.

19 Statements that these assessors had been selected are found in fragmentary Coptic declarations P.Lond. 1543; 1578; 1579.

to take notice of each individual taxpayer's financial capacity. As members of their local communities, they probably had direct knowledge of or access to the relevant data, for instance on personal status and professions (hence tax liability), land holdings, and agricultural productivity.[20]

This role of distributing the taxes over the individuals is confirmed by some of the published assessment documents, which preserve the names of the assessors, further qualified by the term *epilechtheis*, or its plural *epilechthentes*, in the heading.[21] It is furthermore illustrated by P.Würzb. inv. 122–127, where the names of the assessors are noted at the bottom of the assessment of the various subdivisions.[22] In most cases, the term *epilechtheis/epilechtenthes* is added. It is missing for the *epoikia* Bounôn, Kerameiou, Poimên, Hagios Pinoutiôn, and Sakoore, but given the document's overall layout, there can be no doubt that the names of the individuals written underneath the assessments imply their function as assessor. In P.Würzb. inv. 122–127, the *epilechthentes* who made the assessment for the subdivisions of *kômê Aphroditô* (the subdivisions listed in P.Würzb.inv. 123) are identified by name and patronymic (or function) and furthermore by reference to their *origo*: the *epilechthentes* from the same fiscal-administrative unit are identified and grouped together, after which their provenance (*origo*) is stated. The assessments for the *epoikia* were made by different *epilechthentes*, whose provenance is not specifically indicated. The question arising here is whether this implies that they were registered in the fiscal-administrative unit for which they drew up the assessment.

With 21 assessors named, the assessment preserved in P.Würzb. inv. 122–127 constitutes an important addition to our knowledge of the handful of assessors known from other documents from seventh- and eighth-century Aphrodito (see table 1.A below). P.Lond. 1420.1 (706 CE) mentions Theodoros and Phoibammon, sons of Victor, from *Hagios Pinoutiôn*, as having produced the assessment of *Pente Pediades*. In line 154 the assessment for *Duo Pediades* starts, but there the information on the *epilechthentes* is lost. P.Lond. 1424.1 (714 CE?) again preserves an assessment for *Pente Pediades*, drawn up by at least three men. Only the name of Pekusios son of Hermaôs is certain. The selected men named in the fragmentary assessment P.Lond. 1428.20 (date uncertain) are [Sen]outhios son of Georgios and Abraham son of Stephanos. Their provenance is not indicated. Likewise fragmentary is P.Lond. 1429.20 (date uncertain), which mentions [Theod]oros son of Pêsoos as *epilechtheis*. In the assessment for an indiction year 3 for Kerameiou, P.Lond. 1475, Hermaôs son of Kollô(s)

20 Bell 1910; Simonsen 1988.
21 See appendix A for attestations of the term in P.Lond. IV.
22 See the table in appendix B for attestations of the term in P.Würzb. inv. 122–127.

is mentioned as *epilechtheis*. P.Lond. 1554.3 mentions Theodosius son of Philotheos, *epilechtheis*. Furthermore, Bell makes a convincing case that the individuals attested in P.Lond. 1434.51–53 and 1441.87 are also *epilechthentes*.[23]

Interestingly, some of the assessors appear to be attested elsewhere in documents from the Aphrodito archive. However, it is not always certain that persons with the same name are one and the same person. In spite of its limited scope, an evaluation of the data known for these "known" *epilechthentes* and the ones making their appearance in P.Würzb. inv. 122–127 serves as an indication of how a prosopographical study of the people of seventh- and eighth-century Aphrodito might be helpful in revealing more about the identities behind the names or their function. Before I get to this analysis of individuals, I will broadly indicate how the *epilechthentes* are indicated in P.Würzb. inv. 122–127.

P.Würzb. inv. 122–127 can be divided into two sections: one part of the assessment comprised the fiscal-administrative units *idia kômê, ta monastêria* (the monasteries), "those who are in Babylon," *Pente Pediades, Treis Pediades, Duo Pediades*, and "the people of St. Mary's"; a second part contains assessments for individual *epoikia*.[24] The assessors for the first section of P.Würzb. inv. 122–127 are nine individuals from three different fiscal-administrative units' subdivisions: five assessors were from *Pente Pediades*, two from *Treis Pediades*, and two from *Duo Pediades*. Seven men are identified with a name and patronymic, while one man has no patronymic but is specified as a priest (Andreas, priest, from *Duo Pediades*). For one man, his patronymic or function designation is lost (Jakob, from *Treis Pediades*).

In the second section of the assessment, where the individual *epoikia* are registered one after another, 12 different *epilechthentes* are mentioned; the names of eleven of these can be read. Seven of these are identified by name and patronymic, four by means of name and function designation. One name is largely lost but seems to have been of the name and patronymic type. Six *epilechthentes* drew up the assessment for the *epoikion* Pakauneôs. Three of these are identified by means of their ecclesiastic function instead of a patronymic. No provenance is indicated. Given the relative quota and amounts assessed

23 In both documents, see Bell's note to the line. As the term *epilechtheis* or *epilechthentes* is not added to these individuals' names, these cases are left out of the present overview, but they remain to be discussed. Also, in this contribution, my point of departure are the Greek texts. This contribution, therefore, offers no exhaustive discussion of the *epilechthentes* but rather aims to examine the possibilities of the approach taken.

24 As I have proposed elsewhere, this division may reflect the geographical division of the *dioikêsis*, with a relatively densely populated nucleus, and a peripheral zone where the *epoikia* were located; see de Jong forthcoming a.

for this *epoikion*, it would be expected that several *epilechthentes* would have been responsible for *epoikion* Emphyteutôn's assessment. Yet, no *epilechthentes* are mentioned. Possible explanations are that the scribe or copyist forgot to insert the names of the assessors or—less likely—that the record on which this copy was based was handed in incompletely. Another possibility may be that the assessments for Pakauneôs and Emphyteutôn were made by the six *epilechthentes* mentioned for Pakauneôs. However, in that case, the order of the assessments of Pakauneôs and Emphyteutôn may have been expected to be reversed. This is unlikely for two reasons: One is the hypothetical order of the pages, based on the direction of the fibers and physical condition of the codex. The other is that in other documents Pakauneôs always precedes Emphyteutôn. For each of the other *epoikia* (Bounôn, Kerameiou, Poimên, Psyrou, Hagios Pinoutiôn, Sakoore) only one *epilechtheis* is mentioned, never with an indication of his provenance (*origo*).

4 Results

Based on the quantitative (the number of attestations) and qualitative (the nature of the attestations) discussion of the corpus of names that is presented in the appendix, some observations about the *epilechthentes* can be made, which I will summarize here.

First, the number of assessors seems to relate to the size of the fiscal-administrative division assessed. In P.Würzb. inv. 122–127, this is clear for the *epoikia*: whereas six *epilechthentes* drew up the assessment for *epoikion* Pakauneôs, only one is stated for the smaller *epoikia*, where the assessment work was less elaborate. This principle may also apply to the first section, naming nine assessors. If P.Lond. 1420 can be taken as a representative example, two assessors were responsible for assessing 124 taxpayers; if this is extrapolated to 21 assessors for the whole of Aphrodito, the number of taxpayers would be 1,302. However, this number can only be a rough indication, for which a multiplier can be brought in to guesstimate the total population.[25] As numbers of people will have varied per fiscal district and as we have no other secure clues for the numerical relation between assessors and taxpayers, no claim to exactitude in establishing the number of inhabitants can be made.

25 Taking a multiplier of 4 would result in a total population of some 5,200. Taking a multiplier of 5 results in some 6,500 inhabitants. These multipliers are based on the average household size as established by Bagnall and Frier 1994. A more detailed attempt to guesstimate the relative sizes of the fiscal-administrative districts is in preparation (de Jong).

A second point relates to the registration of the provenance of the assessors. Is it significant that the provenance (*origo*) of the *epilechthentes* is stated in the first part of the Würzburg codex, relating to *kômê Aphroditô*, whereas it is lacking in the second part, relating to the *epoikia*? Several explanations may be given for the absence of this. For instance, it might imply that P.Würzb. inv. 122–127 was not yet completed, or that this version was not intended to be sent to the central authorities. Another possibility is that the *epilechthentes* themselves were registered in the *epoikion* for which they made the assessment, so their provenance was not required to be stated explicitly here. However, at least one case—that of Hôrouogchios the *logographos*—suggests this explanation is not always applicable. Also, the first section of the codex (the assessment of *kômê Aphroditô*) shows that nine men from three different subdivisions were responsible for the assessment of its seven subdivisions. So, here we see that the assessors sometimes had to deal with other subdivisions than those in which they were registered themselves. Furthermore, the assessors relating to *Pente Pediades* mentioned in P.Lond. 1420.1 are stated to be from Hagios Pinoutiôn. It seems, therefore, that there were no strict regulations for the provenance of the assessors and the subdivisions for which they were responsible. Nevertheless, it also seems that it was not uncommon that the assessors were "registered members" of the fiscal-administrative subdivisions they were assessing.[26]

The third, and most important point, however, relates to the identification of individuals and establishing connections between texts. This may be helpful for finding answers to the uncertainties raised so far and also in settling issues related to the identification of the individuals. This relates to the chosen methodology, as a prosopographical approach to the Aphrodito documents will bring possibilities but also problems. To start with an obvious question: are persons with the same name always the same individual? Going through the Aphrodito archive's documentation, it appears that several of the assessors' names are attested in other texts. In some cases it is highly likely that the same person is implied. In others, however, it seems that they may have been different persons. In quite a few cases, establishing certainty in identifying namesakes remains difficult.[27] In some cases, looking at the data both quantitatively and

26 Perhaps they were even assessing themselves, if this is a correct interpretation for Theodosius son of Philotheos, who seems to have assessed himself in P.Lond. 1554.18.

27 The same individuals were not always referred to in the same way (both within the same texts as in different texts). However, it seems reasonable to assume that—to the people involved—there was no confusion in establishing someone's identity. See furthermore the discussion in appendices A and B.

qualitatively, may help solve the questions. Hence, a detailed discussion of the attestations of all the names of the *epilechthentes* who appear in P.Lond. IV and P.Würzb. inv. 122–127 is presented in appendices A and B in order to examine whether (some of) the *epilechthentes* can be identified with namesakes appearing in other documents.

Identification is not always straightforward: whether identification of namesakes is probable, possible, uncertain, or unlikely largely depends on the frequency of the name and the contextual evidence. Certain names are so common that it is conceivable that multiple people had the same name. The practice of having a double name is well-known from Ptolemaic and Roman Egypt. Some examples are also found in Coptic texts from the seventh and eighth centuries.[28] However, a comprehensive onomastic study of papyri in the seventh and eighth centuries is a desideratum. Also within the late seventh- to early eighth-century archive from Aphrodito, individuals may be referred to in different ways, as will be demonstrated below, even if, to my knowledge, double names—of the types found in the Graeco-Roman periods—have not (yet) appeared in the Greek Aphrodito texts. Other names may be rarer, so that identification in these cases may become easier. However, both in cases of common or rarer names, the practice of using further identifiers, such as a patronymic, a (formal or informal) function designation, or an epithet, contributes considerably to identifying individuals.[29] Nevertheless, these additions do not always result in unique (in the sense of identifiable as one and the same individual) persons. Some examples indicate that in the case of people sharing name and patronymic caution is also needed, as persons with these same names may be different people. This probably is the case for, e.g., Papnouthios son of Ptêron (in different chronological contexts) and Senouthios son of Georgios (*epilechtheis* in P.Lond. 1428 and appearing as a fugitive in P.Lond. 1460). Therefore, as many clues as possible should be collected for identification, such as the identifiers just mentioned, but also, if possible, chronological (the date of a document), geographical (the fiscal-administrative unit and/or names of land plots with which the individuals can be associated), or textual connections, which may be confirmed by shared appearances. This latter circumscription reflects my assumption that, if individuals who are attested together in the same text also appear

28 See Broux and Coussement 2014: 129, footnote 4.

29 Even if both the personal name and the father's name were common, their combination in name and patronymic drastically reduced the number of unique individuals. See the name entries in Bell's Index of Personal Names. Adding a function designation may have been the usual practice when a patronymic was lacking.

with the same individuals in a different document, the chance that the individuals are the same is higher.[30] Nevertheless, as in most cases complete certainty is lacking, I have chosen to qualify identification as likely, possible, uncertain, and unlikely.[31] Arguments for these evaluations will be provided in the discussion of the names in appendices A and B. Ultimately, if certain identification is impossible, namesakes should be considered as different individuals until identification is confirmed, perhaps from future data collection.

Apart from demonstrating that a combined quantitative and qualitative analysis of names can be helpful in identifying individuals, I would like to test whether and how several of the documents from Aphrodito can be linked to each other. This means that careful and detailed consideration and discussion of all the material is necessary, even if its relevance will not be immediately clear. However, as I noticed when I was collecting the data on the *epilechthentes*, the web of connections seemed to broaden continuously and my dataset was quickly piling up, almost becoming too large for the present purpose.[32] Also, although I suspect relations between several other texts in which their names are mentioned, further examination of this issue goes beyond the scope of this contribution. Even so, I think a case can be made for stating that some individuals and documents appear to stand out; that is, some persons and some documents appear, as it were, to be hubs where the same names turn up in close proximity.[33] What this means in terms of fiscal and social prominence

30 To define the commonality or rarity of a name, I have (rather arbitrarily) labeled 20 or more attestations as common; between 10–19 attestations as frequent; between 4–9 attestations as occasional; and 3 attestations or less as rare.

31 For a study on the difficulty of identifying individuals, see Ruffini 2011: xi–xii, who in his prosopography of Byzantine Aphrodito identified homonymous individuals if they shared two further "loosely applied criteria," which he clarifies as "a title, a patronym, a role (such as witness or lessor) in a text, and at times even something as broad as a time-period, if other characteristics were sufficiently suggestive."

32 That is why the discussion of the *epilechthentes* is offered in an appendix, and why the dataset under scope is limited to the names listed in Bell's Index of Persons in P.Lond. IV. Documents from the seventh- and eighth-century archive from Aphrodito that were published later and in other volumes or journals have not been included in the present case study.

33 Examples are P.Lond. 1433; 1434.51–53; 1549; 1553 and others (see the discussion of the assessors in appendices A and B), where various people, who in P.Würzb. inv. 122–127 are qualified as assessors, are attested together. However, note that the function and the role of the people appearing in it differs in each of these documents. In further work on the people of Aphrodito, it is my intention to make visualizations of connections between individuals and texts.

remains to be determined, which can only be achieved in relation to the bigger picture. Thus, the bigger picture and the detailed analysis of data are two sides of the same medal.

5 Some Further Questions

Whereas the discussion so far has intended to show that the prosopographical method may be useful in identifying individuals, guesstimating the population size, and establishing connections between documents, there are also questions that need to be addressed, but they can only be answered tentatively. These questions concern the practical implications of being appointed as assessor. What did it mean to the people involved: how did it affect their social position, and how did they do their job? Was it a difficult task people tried to avoid, or did it imply opportunities for personal gain? (How) were the assessors facilitated by their authorities?

To start with the practical side, assuming that assessors started working from existing lists and registers, it can be postulated that an important aspect of the job was to control whether all data were still valid or—if changes had occurred—to make sure that the data were updated. In this respect, their task would be to keep the system going. Their own behavior in the actual collection of money was controlled by the authorities, as appears in the numerous statements that the amounts demanded were just.

Another point is whether or how being appointed as a tax collector may have affected the new appointees, both individually and as a group. A question here is whether the assessors can be considered as a group. Their joint appearance in the documentation may be taken as an argument in favor of this. It appears from the Würzburg codex that some 20 to 25, or perhaps 30, assessors were active for one fiscal year's assessment for the whole of Aphrodito. From the evidence available, it cannot be ascertained whether they had to do this task for one year, or perhaps for several years. If Qurra's letters were formal and sent out each year as part of the tax procedure, it may be assumed that the assessors were chosen each year. It is conceivable that this was done in a formal setting, as the headmen of the fiscal-administrative districts seem to have received their instructions to select the assessors in a collective meeting. This also implies that the leading men were acquainted with one another. The same may go for the assessors. The assessors responsible for the same fiscal-administrative division clearly had to cooperate and coordinate. But assessors from different fiscal-administrative divisions perhaps did not necessarily meet in person. Yet, these, too, may have been acquainted with their colleagues, as they all became part of the network involved in Aphrodito's fiscal administration. This meant being in the network of local headmen, who were in the network of the *dioikêtês* and his staff.

Were they recognized by others and distinguished as a group or in their function, and if so, how? It is quite possible that they were. As taxes affected every member of the local society, to the taxpayers it must have been clear that the assessors were performing a task that they were officially authorized to do. Also, to their own superiors it must have been known who exactly were involved in the fiscal administration and which tasks they were responsible for. Documents in which the assessors and tax collectors declare under oath that they performed their duty honestly, or that they would be liable to punishment,[34] demonstrate that, on the one hand, the authorities tried to guarantee the correct cooperation of the assessors by imposing these oaths and uttering threats and applying punishments in cases of misbehavior. It seems conceivable that the authorities would, on the other hand, somehow offer compensation for their task to ensure the assessors' willingness to comply. But I have found no certain evidence for this. An alternative form of compensation could be the social distinction resulting from being an assessor. In terms of social power, being involved in the tax system would elevate these persons above the group of common taxpayers, as they had become (temporary) participants in the tax administration. This may have been effected by visible symbols or in language. In this respect, the question is how value laden the term *epilechtheis* was. Was it merely a word to indicate the selected assessors, or can it also be considered to have carried authority? Even if it cannot be established that this was a technical term or an official designation, it seems plausible that it had an authoritative connotation. Whether or not this would bring prestige to the assessors or whether it would have a positive or negative effect on their social reputation can only be speculated about and may have varied according to each individual's personal case and context.[35]

---

34 These punishments could be fiscal and physical, so it seems from various documents.

35 For negative perceptions of tax collectors—albeit in relation to the Gospels, and hence at a much earlier period than is discussed here—as "one of the most socially despised segments of that time," see Nave 2002: 153–154 and footnotes 37 and 38. Cf. also Green 1997: 669, noting (again about the New Testament's depiction of a tax collector) that Zacchaeus "would have belonged to a circle of persons almost universally despised."

6 Conclusion

It was the aim of this contribution to sketch some of the possibilities (and constraints) of studying the people from seventh- and eighth-century Aphrodito through a prosopographical approach. Such an approach allows us to get a deeper understanding of the practical functioning of the village.[36] The case of the *epilechthentes* shows how studying individuals on the basis of names and further designations is not only helpful in identifying these individuals but also offers new insights into the connection between the documents from seventh- and eighth-century Aphrodito. Furthermore, such an approach may lead to raising new questions, which hopefully results in a new way of looking at Aphrodito from a social point of view. After all, the fiscal administration could only exist because of the people who organized it.

Appendix A: The *epilechthentes* in P.Lond. IV

In the majority of cases, the names of the assessors are lost in the assessments published in P.Lond. IV. No names have been preserved where they would be expected on the basis of the assessments' structure in P.Lond. 1420.154 (*Duo Pediades*, 706 CE); 1421.2 (*Treis Pediades*, 720 CE?); 1422 (*chôrion* uncertain, date uncertain); 1423 (*chôrion* uncertain, date uncertain); 1425 (perhaps *Treis Pediades*, cf. P.Lond. 1421.138; or *Pente Pediades*, cf. P.Lond. 1420.90);[37] 1424.34 (date uncertain); 1426 (*chôrion* uncertain,[38] date uncertain); 1427 (*Duo Pediades*?, date uncertain).

In a few other documents the names of the assessors have been preserved, amounting to some ten individual assessors. Unfortunately, not all of them are identifiable by name. These assessors will be discussed first, before looking at the assessors attested in P.Würzb. inv. 122–127.

36 For village life in early Islamic Egypt, see Wilfong 2002; Cromwell 2017; Ruffini 2011. Ruffini 2018 also offers some broad remarks on Aphrodito in the post-conquest period, but he mainly focuses on pre-Islamic Aphrodito.

37 In P.Lond. 1420.90 Pesate son of Hôrouogchios and his brother are assessed for a part of *topos Sasnoeit*. In P.Lond. 1424.34, Basileios son of Hôrouogchios is assessed for a part of the same *topos*. It is tempting to identify the unnamed brother of Pesate in P.Lond. 1420.90 with Basileios son of Hôrouogchios.

38 Or perhaps relating to several *choria*, as, e.g., Kollouthos son of Abraham who is also attested in P.Lond. 1421.154 (*Treis Pediades*). However, Hermaôs son of Joannes is attested in P.Lond. 1420.130; 1552.10, which rather relate to *Pente Pediades*.

The epilechthentes *in P.Lond. 1420.1*

P.Lond. 1420 (706 CE) is described by Bell as a "book, at present containing 12 folios or parts of folios."[39] It contains two assessments for two different subdivisions: for *Pente Pediades* (ll. 1–153) and for *Duo Pediades* (ll. 154–275). It is not clear whether the assessments were originally separate books or whether they were already joined. After the heading line, summarizing the document's contents, date, and the assessors, the grand totals for the various taxes assessed are given. The assessment proper starts on the next page. Each taxpayer is registered, provided with the plot(s) of land for which (s)he was assessed, and the taxes with the amounts for which (s)he was assessed.

In the assessment for *Pente Pediades*, two *epilechthentes* are stated. The assessment seems to have contained 124 different entries. If the insertion of only one patronymic ("son of Victor") and of only one indication of provenance ("from *Hagios Pinoutiôn*") accompanying "Theodoros and Phoibammon" implies that the patronymic and place of provenance apply to both individuals, this would mean that **Theodoros and Phoibammon, sons of Victor**, are brothers from *Hagios Pinoutiôn*. As the name Theodoros is so commonly attested in P.Lond. IV, identification with other attestations of the same name is impossible.[40] The name Phoibammon son of Victor is also attested in P.Lond. 1420.77; 1431.45. The Phoibammon son of Victor, attested in P.Lond. 1420.77 is assessed together with a Jacob, priest, for part of the *topos Abba Taurinou*, which was located in *Pente Pediades*. It is interesting that they are assessed for land tax and *embolê* but not for the poll tax. Were they exempt, because they were registered for paying the poll tax elsewhere? In the case of Phoibammon—if he is the same person as the assessor listed in l. 1—he could have been registered for poll tax in *Hagios Pinoutiôn*. Or was he exempt from poll tax because he was an assessor? The name Phoibammon son of Victor also appears in P.Lond. 1431.45, a list of arrears of *embolê* contributions. As he is listed in the section relating to *Pente Pediades* (ll. 39–49), he may well be identified with the individual in P.Lond. 1420.77. The question, however, is whether the Phoibammon son of Victor, appearing in assessments related to *Pente Pediades*, is the same as the *epilechtheis* in P.Lond. 1420.1 who is stated to be from *Hagios Pinoutiôn*. Both names, Phoibammon and Victor, are common, so even if the combination as name and patronymic is only attested three times, this is no convincing argument for identification. Moreover, there are some indications in the assess-

39 Bell 1910: 231.

40 Bell 1910 did not include Theodoros son of Victor in his Index of Persons, only the name Theodoros.

ments that people who are assessed and who are from a different division than that to which the assessment relates were noted as such. Compare, for instance, P.Lond. 1420.181 and 192, where the individuals assessed are noted to be from Kerameiou. They do pay other taxes, but no poll tax? Could it be the case that they were registered for poll tax in Kerameiou? Analogous to these examples, it could be argued that if Phoibammon son of Victor, assessed in P.Lond. 1420.77, was the same as the *epilechtheis* who drew up the assessment and came from *Hagios Pinoutiôn*, where he perhaps was registered for poll tax, he would have been added. Identification cannot be ascertained on the basis of the present evidence available.

The epilechthentes *in P.Lond. 1424.1*

This assessment for *Pente Pediades* (714 CE) was made by at least three men. From the name of the first one, only the last letter of his patronymic has been preserved, which obstructs identification.

The name of the second *epilechtheis* is readable: **Pekusios son of Hermaôs.** Both names are common. Their combination as personal name and patronymic is also attested in another two texts. An individual of the same name appears in P.Lond. 1420.58, where he is assessed together with a J[oan]n(es) for various plots of land (*ktêmata*) in *Pente Pediades* for 6 *nomismata* of land tax, 2 1/2 *nomismata* for poll tax, and 6 *artabai* of corn. In P.Lond. 1562.8 an individual of the same name is registered for payment of a tax; the document probably concerns *Pente Pediades*, as many of the individuals listed in P.Lond. 1562 are attested in other documents relating to *Pente Pediades*.[41] As all three attestations of Pekusios son of Hermaôs may be linked to *Pente Pediades*, identification is likely.

41 E.g., Hermaôs son of Apa Têr in l. 1, is also attested in P.Lond. 1420.131. Makarios son of Pkame, registered in line 2, also occurs in P.Lond. 1420.132. Line 3 registers Daniel son of Theososius, who is also assessed in P.Lond. 1420.133. Line 6 has Elias son of Barous, who is also assessed for poll tax in P.Lond. 1420.136. Line 7 registers Theodosios son of J⌊os⌋eph, who is also attested in P.Lond. 1420.134 and Kollouthos son of Mia, who is also assessed P.Lond. 1420.138; l. 8 registers Pnei son of Georgios, who appears as *lashane*, "headman," of *Pente Pediades* in P.Lond. 1521 and 1626 (only *lashane*). Could he be the same as Pnei, the *elaiourgos*, mentioned twice in P.Lond. 1420 (in line 134 assessed together with his son for poll tax and in l. 142 as father of Leontios, who is assessed for poll tax)? Psalos son of Dianês is attested in P.Lond. 1562.1; in P.Lond. 1420.132 a "son of Dianês" is assessed for poll tax. Given the context and the overlap with the other names, it is probable that he is the same person. Note that, except for Pekusios son of Hermaôs, all the individuals listed in P.Lond. 1420; 1562 are landless, i.e., they are only assessed for poll tax. The scribe of P.Lond. 1562 is from Pakauneôs.

The name of the third assessor is largely lost. It seems to have been **Pkaloos** (for which name Bell in his Index of Persons mentions Pkaroos or Pkarous as alternatives). Both Pkaloos and Pkaroos are attested in P.Lond. 1420.20; 120. Line 20 registers Pkaloos as father of a Bethanias, who is assessed for 1/3 of a *nomisma* and 1/3 of an *artabê* of corn for a part of *topos* Pkaroou; in line 120 Anna, daughter of Philotheus son of Pkaroos, is assessed 1/2 of a *nomisma* for a part of *topos* Pkaroou, also in *Pente Pediades*. It looks as if the same plot of land is concerned and as if both people assessed were related to Pkaloos. Bethanias may have been his son, Anna his granddaughter. If this is correct, this may be an example of shared family holdings, but we cannot be certain. Other questions arise: were the individuals assessed owners or leasers of the part of the plot for which they were assessed? And is the Pkaloos mentioned as assessor in P.Lond. 1424.1 indeed the same individual, and could the plot of land be named after him? If this is the case, does this imply that Pkaloos was the owner or had been in previous times? What does this imply for the relation between his son and granddaughter and the parts of the plot they were assessed for? In any case, the plot of land named after Pkaroou was shared (whatever this sharing implied) between four people in 706 CE, as appears from its attestations in P.Lond. 1420.20; 21; 101; 120.[42] There may have been a family link between Bethanias and Anna, but this is only hypothetical given the present state of evidence. Even if this was the case, there is no clue in P.Lond. 1424 that this shared (family) landownership was still applicable to this *topos* in 714 CE, when new names are attested in relation to the plot of land. The main link between Pkal[ ] in P.Lond. 1424.1 and the other texts in which the name occurs is that the texts relate to *Pente Pediades*. This may make identification possible, but not certain.

The epilechthentes *in P.Lond. 1428.20*

P.Lond. 1428 (733 CE?) consists of two fragments of a book, identified by Bell as an assessment: although the term *merismos* is not preserved, fragment 2, line 20 gives the names **[Sen]outhios son of Georgios** and **Abraham son of Stephanos**, *epil*[*echthentes*]. Fragment 2 recto concerns the *embolê*, and it seems only to have preserved the totals of the fiscal subdivision concerned; its verso, however, has preserved some names of individual taxpayers and columns relating to the poll and land tax. However, this is too fragmentary to be certain of the exact relation or contents of the fragment. Fragment 1 is interesting, as

42 Attestations in assessments or fiscal registers of later date (P.Lond. 1419+SB 15099 (716/717); 1424 (714); P.Ross.Georg. IV 23 (date uncertain)) seem to demonstrate that the parts of the plot had gotten new landowners or leasers.

its verso concerns an assessment of landless people, whereas its recto refers to poll tax, land tax, maintenance (*dapanê*), and *embolê*, with further specification of the surface of the land and its state as irrigated or unirrigated. The *dapanê* required in money is further qualified as "with and without *entagia*."[43]

All four names (the main names and patronymics) are common. For the combinations as names and patronymics, however, the case is different. An individual named Senouthios son of Georgios is further attested in P.Lond. 1420.141; 1430.113; 1460.9. The question is whether this is one and the same man. In P.Lond. 1420.141 a Senouthios son of Georgios is assessed for poll tax. As this person is listed in the section of landless people, he did not possess or lease land.[44] There is no reason to confirm or deny identification of this Senouthios son of Georgios with the *epilechtheis* of P.Lond. 1428. Yet, this is interesting for the question of whether *epilechthentes* were only selected from among landholders. Perhaps well-to-do craftsmen might also have taken up such tasks. If that is the case, the question of whether Senouthios son of Georgios can be identified in P.Lond. 1430.113 gains importance. P.Lond. 1430 is a fragmentary tax register, in which in line 113 a Senouthios son of Georgios is further designated as a carpenter. Unfortunately, no further information can be deduced here. Again, there is no reason to confirm (nor to deny) identification with the *epilechtheis* of P.Lond. 1428. But his designation as a carpenter (*tektôn*) may qualify him for identification with the landless namesake in P.Lond. 1420.141. An argument against this, however, is that other landless individuals listed in this section (P.Lond. 1420.129–143) sometimes have further designations.[45] Most likely Senouthios son of Georgios, who is registered in a list of fugitives in P.Lond. 1460.9 (ca. 709 CE) and who is stated to be from *Tria Kastra*, is a different individual. It seems unlikely that this man should be identified with the assessor in P.Lond. 1428.20 and/or the individual(s) listed in P.Lond. 1420.141 and 1430.113.

Abraham son of Stephanos is only attested in his capacity as *epilechtheis* in P.Lond. 1428. As he is not attested elsewhere, nothing more is known about him. Nevertheless, his involvement in the assessment of taxes implies that he enjoyed a somewhat elevate position in his local community.

---

43 According to Bell 1910, introduction to P.Lond. 1428, this implies that this *dapanê* was intended for local officials, not for those at the central level.

44 However, there is an assignment of a *topos* Tsament to Senouthios son of Georgios here. According to Bell, this is to indicate the man's provenance. However, whose provenance would this indicate, Senouthios' or Georgios'? As in l. 23 Georgios son of Taam is assessed for *topos* Tsament, it might be the case that this refers to Georgios and that Georgios was the father of Senouthios.

45 E.g., P.Lond. 1420.129 Stephanos, *poimên*, "shepherd"; 134 Pnei, *elaiourgos*, "oil producer."

The epilechtheis *in P.Lond. 1429.20*

P.Lond. 1429 consists of four fragments of a book, identified by Bell as an assessment: although the term *merismos* is not attested on the preserved fragments, fragment 3, line 20 gives the name [Theo]**doros son of Pesoos**, *epil*[*echtheis*]. This fragment is concerned with payments in corn. A first column seems to give a total amount for *embolê*, which is divided between numbers of *artabai* of corn for the granary and for the maintenance (*dapanê*) tax, each listed in a column.[46] The other fragments also refer to land tax and poll tax, preserving a few personal names and references to plots and types of land.

The name Theodoros is common, whereas Pesoôs is occasionally attested. The combination of these names as name and patronymic is rare.[47] One further attestation of a Theodoros son of Pesoôs is preserved in P.Lond. 1426 fragment 2.39. As the first line of this fragment states, this is an assessment of gold taxes, concerning the poll tax contributions of landless people. Unfortunately, the fragmentary state does not allow us to define whether, apart from the poll tax, maintenance tax (*dapanê*) and *embolê* were also assessed, as is the case in fragment 1, which Bell attributed as belonging to the same book and which also relates to landless people. There may be a connection between the two texts (P.Lond. 1426; 1429) in that they show some similarity in their rendering of *embolê* assessments. Apart from a contribution for *dapanê* in money, a contribution was also assessed in kind. Just as in P.Lond. 1429, the number of *artabai* of corn is divided between payments for the granaries and payments for *dapanê*, as fragment 1^r seems to demonstrate. Among the landless people assessed for at least a poll tax, and possibly also for *dapanê* and *embolê*,[48] Theodoros son of Pesoôs is listed. It cannot be ascertained whether or not he is or is not the same person as the *epilechtheis* mentioned in P.Lond. 1429.20.

---

46 Cf. *epilechtheis* in P.Lond. 1429 fragment 2. This would imply that the *dapanê* could—apart from a tax in money—also be required as a part of the *embolê*. However, given the fragmentary nature of the papyrus, this is far from clear. The same seems to be the case in P.Lond. 1426 fragment 1^r; 1428 fragment 2.

47 It should be checked whether the fragment could have been part of the same book. The handwriting was labeled by Bell as "neat, round, rather large minuscule, in ink of a reddish tint" (1426) and as "neat, round miniscule of medium size in reddish ink" (1429). If Theodoros son of Pesoôs is one and the same person, and if P.Lond. 1426 and P.Lond. 1429 belonged to the same book, this raises the question of whether he had been assessing himself. Also, if the landless Theodoros son of Pesoôs is the same person as the assessor in P.Lond. 1429 fragment 3.20, he might be another example of a nonland-possessing *epilechtheis*.

48 Bell 1910, introduction to P.Lond. 1426 and fragment 1.

An epilechtheis *in P.Lond. 1432.1?*

The first line of P.Lond. 1432 seems to demonstrate that this document is a *merismos*, see Bell's introduction to the text. Only the first letter of the name of (one of) the assessor(s) has been preserved. Hence, it is impossible to identify the person. Furthermore, it cannot be ascertained if he would have been designated as *epilechtheis*, although it is reasonable to assume that this would have been the case.

The epilechtheis *in P.Lond. 1475 (descr.)*

According to Bell, the heading of one of the fragments of a book of assessments relating to the *epoikion* Kerameiou contains a reference to **Hermaos son of Kollô(s)** *epil(e)chth(eis)*. This combination of names is only attested once. Whereas the names Hermaos and Kollouthos are common, the name Kollôs is only attested once, as patronymic in this text.

The epilechtheis *in P.Lond. 1554.3*

Line 3 of this bilingual document preserves the name **Theodosios son of Philotheos**, *epil*[*ech*(*theis*)] in a part written in Greek script and preserving the assessment proper. Lines 6–7 preserve his name in Coptic script. Further lines contain a statement by this man that he made the assessment fairly and correctly. The name of the *epoikion* to which this document relates is lost. However, this fragment of an assessment only preserves four names of individuals who are assessed for 1/6 of a *nomisma*, resulting in a total assessment of 2/3 of a *nomisma*. In a further fragment, line 19, a man of the same name is among the individuals assessed. The question is whether this Theodosios son of Philotheos is the same man. If this was the case, he was himself assessed by others, whose names appear in the Coptic declaration in lines 29–34.

Both names are common. In this specific combination, they are attested in other texts nine times. However, it is difficult to be certain whether all these attestations refer to the same individual. P.Lond. 1420.250 contains the assessment for Theodosios son of Philotheos in the section relating to *Duo Pediades*. A man of the same name is assessed in P.Lond. 1427.6. Bell notes in the introduction to the text that the fragment relates to one of the *Pediades* but that the qualification *Duo*, *Treis*, or *Pente* is missing. The same individual as the Theodosios son of Philotheos is likely to appear in the assessment for *Duo Pediades* in P.Lond. 1432.101. P.Lond IV 1544 preserves a declaration in Coptic, in which 14 men seem to declare to have received money. In line 17, the declaration is made by Theodosios son of the deceased (*makarios*) Philotheos. Crum suggests the document may relate to fugitives, but it also could be a declaration for taxes collected. The same individual makes a statement in P.Lond. 1545, where he appears, again with the addition *makarios*, preceding the patronymic in lines 2 and 15 (partly restored). This addition is left out on the verso of the document in line 16, where the subject line summarizes the contents of the document. Here, his provenance is indicated as Pakauneôs. As this fiscal-administrative unit is mentioned as Theodosios' provenance, this individual is probably not the same man who turned up in the assessments for *Duo Pediades*, as in that case an indication of his provenance from a different administrative unit would be expected there. Probably the same Theodosios son of Philotheos turns up in P.Lond, IV 1548.9, a sworn declaration written in Coptic, where his role may again be tax-collection related. The document is witnessed by six individuals and was written by the scribe Apollo son of Psoios from Pakauneôs, as the Greek subscription states. That again the same individual is listed among the guarantors in P.Lond. 1549 seems highly likely, resulting from the addition that he was from Pakauneôs. In P.Lond. 1591.6, a man with the same name is again attested as a witness to a declaration document. As one of the other witnesses is stated to be from Pakauneôs, the same may go for Theodosios son of Philotheos mentioned here as well.

To conclude, if the appearance of Theodosios son of Philotheos in documents related to *Duo Pediades*, without further indication of his provenance, implies that he was linked to that fiscal-administrative unit, it can be assumed that he was a different individual from his namesake, who was stated to be from Pakauneôs and who turns up in five documents. It is interesting to note that the Theodosios son of Philotheos associated with *Duo Pediades* is registered as a taxpayer in assessments written in the Greek script, whereas the Theodosios son of Philotheos associated with Pakauneôs seems to have had a prominent role in his *epoikion*. This would make the identification with Theodosios son of Philotheos, *epil*[*echtheis*], attested in P.Lond. 1554.3; 6 plausible. It may also have been that this same man assessed himself in P.Lond. 1554.18.

Appendix B: The *epilechthentes* in P.Würzb. Inv. 122–127

After this discussion of the assessors known from the previously published texts, attention will now be given to the names of the assessors stated in P.Würzb. inv. 122–127 (de Jong forthcoming a). The assessment for *kômê Aphroditô*, which is given in the first section, is made by nine individuals from three subdivisions. In the section related to the *epoikia*, a total of 12 assessors is registered. For each *epoikion* (except for Emphyteutôn) the assessors are specified. The fragment relating to *Hagios Pinoutiôn* is too damaged to preserve the name of an *epilechtheis*. The assessors for *kômê Aphroditô* are listed as a group, clustered by means of their provenance. After the names, the word *epil(echthentes)* indicates their involvement in this assessment.

Pente Pediades (*Line 35*)

Mentioned are **Psoios son of Mênas, Makarios son of Athanasios, Phoibammon son of Thakore, Georgios son of Hermaôs,** and **Mênas son of Kollouthos.**

Treis Pediades (*Line 36*)

These are **Jakob [ ]** and **Papnouthios son of Ptêron.**

Duo Pediades (*Line 36*)

Mentioned are **Andreas, priest** and **Pachumios son of Taurinos.** In contrast to the collective assessment for *kômê Aphroditô*, the assessors for the *epoikia* are given for each *epoikion* individually and without indication of their provenance.

***Pakauneôs* (*Line 57*)**

Six *epilechthentes* drew up the assessment for Pakauneôs: **Psatês, priest, Philoteos son of Makarios, Enoch son of Victor, Philotheos, deacon, Senouthios son of Daniel,** and **Pekusios, deacon.** Three of these are identified by means of their ecclesiastic function instead of a patronymic. After the names, the word *epil(echthentes)* indicates their involvement in this assessment. No provenance is indicated.

Emphyteutôn

Given the relative quota and amounts assessed for this epoikion, we would expect that several *epilechthentes* would have been responsible for Empyteutôn's assessment. Yet, no *epilechthentes* are mentioned. Did the scribe forget to insert the names of the assessors, or was his record incomplete?

***Bounôn* (*Line 87*)**

For Bounôn, we find **Joannes son of Georgios.** The word *epilechtheis* is lacking. No provenance is indicated.

***Kerameiou* (*Line 102*)**

The name of **Panesnêu son of Adam** is given at the bottom of the assessment for Kerameiou. The word *epilechtheis* is lacking. No provenance is indicated.

***Poimên* (*Line 117*)**

Petros son of Phêu is mentioned at the bottom of the assessment for Poimên. The word *epilechtheis* is lacking. No provenance is indicated.

Psyrou (Line 132)

For Psyrou, we find **Apollô son of Christos**, *epilechth(eis)*. No provenance is indicated.

Hagios Pinoutiôn (Line 146)

The name of one *epilechtheis* was stated here but is lost. The word *epilechtheis* is lacking. No provenance is indicated.

Sakoore (Line 160)

Hôrougchios, *logographos*. The word *epilechtheis* is lacking. No provenance is indicated.

Kômê Aphroditô (*Lines 35–36*)

Starting with the assessors for *kômê Aphroditô*, five out of the nine assessors are identified by means of their provenance from *Pente Pediades*.

(1) The first one is **Psoios son of Mênas**. The name Mênas is common, whereas Psoios is attested for some dozen individuals. The combination as name and patronymic exists in another ten attestations in eight different texts, in P.Lond. 1432.38; 1435.129; 1454.2; 1459.22; 23; 28; 1494.38; 1549; 1561.20; 1587.12 The question is whether all these instances refer to the same individual.

A Psoios son of Mênas is attested as a taxpayer in P.Lond. 1432.38. The heading of this document identifies this text as the assessment of *embolê* for Aphrodito and its fields for a third indiction. Perhaps the part where Psoios son of Mênas is listed relates to the *idia kômê* (village itself): the total amount of *artabai* listed on the first folio is 444 (cf. folio 1^{b}.22; folio 2^{b}.79). It should be noted that this cannot be ascertained, as the number constitutes the sum of a page. However, lines 114–121 give the total for all fiscal-administrative units of Aphrodito, which suggests that these would have been included in P.Lond. 1432. The only clearly distinguished unit is *Duo Pediades*, whose assessment is preserved in two columns on folio 3^{b}.93–104. This implies that the preceding lines relate to *idia kômê*, *Pente Pediades*, or *Treis Pediades*. This makes for a possible, but not a certain, identification of Psoios son of Mênas, the assessor.

P.Lond. 1435 contains an account of requisitions relating to *kômê Aphroditô*. In l. 129, Psoios son of Mênas is listed in relation to—as it seems—the price of writing material (τι(μῆς) χαρτίω(ν), "price of papyrus"). Perhaps he is compensated for his expenses for the price of blank papers he needed for official fiscal-administrative business. However, as the nature of the fragment starting on folio 6 is very unclear, so is the identity and role of Psoios son of Mênas on line 129.

A further attestation is found in P.Lond. 1454.2. This document contains a fragmentary list, added to a Coptic guarantee of surety, with the names of 16 men out of a list of 31 men. According to Bell in his introduction to the text, the list represents men required as sailors or workmen, but no details that give further information on this have been preserved. It is subscribed by the notary Theodoros. In l. 2, a Psoios son of Mênas is listed. No specification is given of the provenance of the men listed. Identification with the assessor is possible, but not certain. If he was the same man, and if this indeed is a list of requisitioned workmen, this would imply that the same individuals could be assessors and requisitioned workmen.

P.Lond. 1459.22; 23; 28 also attest a Psoios, with addition of the patronymic Mênas in line 22. The patronymic is left out in lines 23 and 28, but this may be explained if the Psoios is the same person as the one mentioned in l. 22. The text, which according to Bell once was a book, contains an account of amounts paid in, perhaps to the local treasury or financial office, by various subdivisions of Aphrodito, as contributions of an installment of a third indication year.[49] The state of the book is fragmentary, but perhaps the second column of folio 1^{b}, relating to *Treis Pediades*, gives an impression of its original layout. A heading line stated the name of the fiscal-administrative division concerned and the names of two persons who may have been responsible for making the account, and perhaps also for collecting the total sums. The next line states the total amount brought in. This is followed by an overview, arranged by date, of amounts brought in, also stating the names of the persons who brought in the amounts. Yet, it is unclear why and what they exactly paid in, and on whose behalf: considering that Psoios is listed three times, it seems that he may have brought in the amounts on behalf of or collected from (several) other taxpayers. If that is the case, Psoios son of Mênas pays amounts for *Treis Pediades* (ll. 22 and 23, a total of 15 *nomismata*) and for the *epoikion* Bounôn (l. 28, amount lost). Although the identification with the assessor cannot be certain, it is possible, as the Psoios son of Mênas in P.Lond. 1459 seems involved in bringing in collected amounts of money.

In several Coptic documents Psoios son of (late) Mênas is also attested. P.Lond. 1494.38 is a guarantee declaration, written in Coptic and Greek, by officials of *Treis Pediades*. Four local men, whose names are listed in ll. 41–46 in Greek script, declare to the governor Qurra b. Sharīk, through the *dioikêtes*

49 P.Lond. 1459.35–37 preserve the word *katabolê* and give the total amount of 2,500 *arithmia nomismata*; lines 63–65 list two *epoikia* otherwise unattested in Aphrodito's documentation from the eighth century; see Marthot 2013: 182, 249. The *chôrion* Pernaidos is also otherwise unattested.

Basileios, that they will deliver three sailors, whose names are listed in Greek script in lines 21–26, for the military expedition (*cursus*) in the following year. Among the witnesses to the sworn declaration, Psoios son of *makarios* (late) Mênas is listed. That no provenance is indicated for him here may imply that he is from *Treis Pediades*, which suggests that he is not the same individual as the assessor who is listed among the assessors from *Pente Pediades* in the Würzburg assessment.

Perhaps a more positive case for identification is found in P.Lond. 1549. This document preserves a list of guarantors by the notary Theodoros, now naming 25 individuals, and for some of these their provenances. It is unclear whether several of the individuals listed in a series without provenance should all be ascribed to the provenance following the last individual of that series. If this is the case, Psoios son of Mênas is listed as one of several individuals from *Pente Pediades* and, as such, to be identified with the assessor attested in P.Würzb. inv. 122–127.35. Interestingly, Mênas son of Kollouthos, and fellow assessor in P.Würzb. inv. 122–127.35, is also among the guarantors in P.Lond. 1549, where he is moreover designated as *hypodektes*.

Whether the Psoios son of *makarios* Mênas attested in a Coptic declaration at the foot of a tax register, P.Lond. 1561.20, is the same as the one in in P.Lond. 1494 is uncertain: the tax register relates to the *epoikion* Kerameiou.

P.Lond. 1587.12 also lists Psoios son of Mênas making a declaration, in Coptic, to the governor, together with others, concerning an undertaking related to four *nomismata*. There is no certainty in establishing this man's identity.

(2) **Makarios son of Athanasios** is the second name listed among the *epilechthentes* from *Pente Pediades*. Although both names are common, their combination as name and patronymic results in only one further attestation, in P.Lond. 1455.2. This fragment preserves a list of ten names, probably originally at the foot of a Coptic document, which seems to be comparable to P.Lond. 1454 and whose purpose remains obscure. The document was also written by the notary Theodoros, who is known from other lists, such as the just mentioned P.Lond. 1454; 1549. Identification of Makarios son of Athanasios with the assessor is possible, but not certain.

(3) The name **Phoibammon son of Thakore** is not yet attested in the eighth-century Greek papyri. Nor is (a variant of) the name Thakoris. The combination Phoibammon son of Th[is only attested a few times in the Aphrodito documents:[50] in P.Lond IV 1453.15 (date uncertain) a Phoibammon son of Th[is

50 There are quite a few possibilities for a father's name starting with a *theta*, e.g., Theodo-

attested as a surety. He is registered in the section relating to *kômê Aphroditô*. An individual named Phoibammon son of Thakore is attested as a taxpayer in P.Cair.Masp. II 67138 (545–546 CE), folio 2 line 15 and folio 3 line 43, and in P.Cair.Masp. II 67139 (542–546 CE), folio 2 line 8 (Pathakore) and folio 4 line 6, but both documents predate the present fragment by almost two centuries. These sixth-century attestations are the only attestations of the name Thakore. It would be too bold to speculate that this Phoibammon son of Thakore was a faraway predecessor of the present *epilechtheis*. But it is clear that this is a different person.

(4) **Georgios son of Hermaôs**. Taken separately, the names Georgios and Hermaôs are both commonly attested. Combined as name and patronymic, however, only two other attestations are found. A Georgios son of Hermaôs is attested in P.Lond. 1449.12. This is a list of the names of 13 individuals who are requisitioned to serve as sailors, probably during a *cursus*, a naval assault on Constantinople, and therefore, they will be sent to Anatolê. The *epoikia* Pakauneôs and Keramiou jointly provide one sailor: Georgios son of Hermaôs. Given this provenance, this Georgios is probably a different person than his namesake, the *epilechtheis* from *Pente Pediades* in P.Würzb. inv. 122–127.35. In P.Lond. 1552.22, a Georgios son of Hermaôs features as one of the six subscribers of a tax assessment for the *xenon* ("hospitality tax" (?)[51]) who declare that they did their duty honestly. Again, as provenance is missing here, identification is possible, but not certain. If the same man is concerned, his appearance between assessors other than those in the Würzburg assessment suggests that he served more than once. The list could relate to a quite substantial community, if six subscribers can be taken as evidence for that.[52]

(5) **Mênas son of Kollouthos.** With Mênas and Kollouthos, again two common names are encountered, whose combination as name and patronymic drastically decreases the number of attestations in other texts to four. These references possibly all concern one and the same individual, as the provenance

sios, Theodoros, Theophilos, Thermouthios, Thomas (see P.Lond. IV Index of Persons under *Theta*: 550–551). But in combination with the name Phoibammon, the only result is Phoibammon son of Theodoros, who is attested in P.Lond. 1499.14; 1558.15.

51 On the *xenon* tax, see Bell 1910, P.Lond. 1433, footnote to line 20.

52 Cf. the registrations of two small communities in the same document, which are only subscribed by one person (who is the same person who is registered as having paid the money). Ll. 28–31 concern the *horos* (monastery) of St. Mary, with Phoibammon, *proestôs* as representative and subscriber; ll. 32–35 the monastery of Hagios Barbaros, with Meôs, *proestôs* as representative and subscriber.

of the man, himself from *Pente Pediades*, or the connection of the document to *Pente Pediades* imply. Mênas son of Kollouthos appears in P.Lond. 1416v D.30 (ca. 732–733), where he is listed as paying tax for a plot of land (*topos*) in *Pente Pediades*. In P.Lond. 1432 (date uncertain), an assessment for *embolê* for Aphrodito and its *Pediades*, a Mênas son of Kollouthos, is listed on the first page in the second column, line 28. He is again listed in line 90, where he is assessed for 7 *artabai*. It seems that a new assessment starts here, as it follows a summary (*anakephalaiôsis*). Given the fact that line 94 starts with *Treis Pediades*, it may well be that lines 82–93 concern *idia kômê*, *Pente Pediades*, and *Treis Pediades*. A Mênas son of Kollouthos appears as one of the assessors for the *embolê* of the *dioikêsis* in P.Lond. 1434.52, where he is specified to be from *Pente Pediades*.[53] It is highly likely that this is the same person as the assessor in P.Würzb. inv. 122–127.35. Note that in P.Lond. 1434.52 Mênas is listed alongside Andreas, priest from *Duo Pediades*, who is also among the *epilechthentes* listed in P.Würzb. inv. 122–127.36. The connection may further be confirmed by the attestation of Panisnêu in P.Lond. 1434.53; an *epilechtheis* of that name appears in P.Würzb. inv. 122–127.102 for the assessment of *epoikion* Kerameiou. Mênas son of Kollouthos features again in P.Lond. 1549, a list following a Coptic declaration of guarantee. In the list, which is appended to the Coptic declaration and written in Greek, Mênas is listed among the guarantors and qualified as *hypodektes* ("financial official, tax collector") from *Pente Pediades*. The list, drawn up by the notary Theodoros, names 25 individuals and their provenances, among whom are also Psoios son of Mênas from *Pente Pediades* (see above and table 1.B1) and Senouthios, son of Daniel (see below and table 1.B14). Although these documents are certainly not all equally conclusive, all attestations of Mênas son of Kollouthos may well point to one and the same individual.[54]

(6) One of the two assessors from *Treis Pediades* is named **Jacob**. His patronymic is lost. Also, the name's common attestation obfuscates possible identification.

---

53 Cf. P.Lond. 1434, note to lines 51–53, where Bell speculates that the individuals listed here are assessors. Although the designation *epilechtheis* is lacking here, the correctness of Bell's assumption is confirmed by the explicit reference to Menas son of Kollouthos as *epilechtheis* from *Pente Pediades* in P.Würzburg inv. 122–127.35. The date of P.Lond. 1434 is uncertain. The occurrence of both *epilechthentes* Menas son of Kollouthos and Andreas, priest, who are also mentioned in P.Würzb. inv. 122–127 seems to suggest that assessors could be involved in assessing taxes in different years.

54 The same Menas son of Kollouthos is furthermore listed in another assessment document P.Lond. 1480 (b) = D40105 (8) (de Jong, in preparation).

(7) The other assessor from *Treis Pediades* is **Papnouthios son of Ptêron**. The name Papnouthios is frequently attested in P.Lond. IV, but not (yet) in combination with Ptêrôn. The name Ptêron or Ptêronos attested in P.Würzb. inv. 122–127 may be a variant of the name Ptêros, if this is the correct solution of the name that occasionally was abbreviated by suspension of omicron, and which is occasionally attested, cf. P.Lond. IV, 570.

(8) Coming to the assessors from *Duo Pediades*, the name **Andreas** is commonly attested in eighth-century Aphrodito. Usually, it is used in a combination of name and patronymic. In a few other attestations it is used without further specification, or with the addition of the qualification *dioikêtes* or *presbyteros* ("priest"). An Andreas, *presbyteros* is attested in P.Lond. 1419.528;[55] 665; 668;[56] 1105[57] as paying taxes in various contexts. There is no clue that in these cases the Andreas, priest is the same as the assessor in P.Würzb. inv. 122–127.36 or that these references indicate the same Andreas, priest—except in P.Lond. 1419.665; 668.

P.Lond. 1420.36 names Andreas, priest in the context of the assessment of Hôrouogchios son of Onnophrios. This Hôrouogchios was assessed for various plots of land, some of which were specified to be "on the name of," followed by the name of a person. This assessment concerns *Pente Pediades*. The phrasing of line 36 is: "for part of the same (= the *topos* St. Mary's, mentioned also in the preceding line) on the name of Andreas, priest." It is unclear what this means: according to Bell (note to line 29) it would mean that Hôrouogchios pays on behalf of Andreas, perhaps because Andreas was absent. But why would Hôrouogchios pay for various absent people? The question arises how this relates to the ownership of the plots here. Perhaps Andreas was a tenant of this specific plot owned by Hôrouogchios, and this is the reason for this way of registration. However this may be, Hôrouogchios is assessed for various landholdings of which he may have been the owner. In any case, he seems to have had some form of fiscal-administrative responsibility over the people mentioned in the plots for which he was assessed. Whether the priest Andreas referred to in this context is the same as the assessor in P.Würzb. inv. 122–127.36 is uncertain.

55 Andreas appears to represent the *ekklesia Apostolôn*.

56 In P.Lond. 1419.665; 668 Andreas, priest, pays half of an amount for part of the plot of Tsamêt and Papkalernei and for a part of the plot of land of Piah Palei and Ankoore; the other amount is paid in both instances by a Theofilos. These payments are registered within a registration of a certain]p Ponnitos.

57 Andreas, priest pays 1/12 in a joint assessment/registration, which is listed under the name of Pilatos, who pays 1/2 of that total registration relating to the plot of Ppin. The others involved in the shared payment are Pkas (4/12) and Papos (1/12).

A different case is offered in P.Lond. 1434.52, where Andreas, priest from *Duo Pediades* is listed alongside Mênas son of Kollouthos from *Pente Pediades*. The addition of their respective provenance and the fact that they are registered as cooperating in this context probably indicates that both individuals can be identified with the *epilechthentes* listed in P.Würzb. inv. 122–127.35–36. If, as Bell notes to P.Lond. 1434.51–53, these lines list the local assessors for the *embolê* tax, the two men again acted as assessors in the year 716. Indeed, lines 50–56 relate a *diastolè* ("order, payment, assessment") of 2,000 *artabai* of corn for the *embolê* for the *dioikêsis kômês Aphroditô* on 3 Pachôn in an indiction year 13, for an indiction year 14. Does this mean a payment proper or an assessment? Could it imply that on 3 Pachôn, the payment of 2,000 *artabai* was reported to the tax office and registered there?[58] Interestingly, the distribution of these 2,000 *artabai* over the different subdivisions is also registered, in lines 54–57.

In the Coptic-Greek tax register P.Lond. 1553v.29 he is listed among several other taxpayers.[59] In the Coptic declaration below the Greek list, which relates to *Duo Pediades*, he features again: in 33–34 as declarant of fair taxation and in l. 38 as the scribe. In both cases, in Coptic he is designated as "Andreas, *elachistos presbyteros*." Identification with the man registered as a taxpayer in l. 29, therefore, is possible. If a different person was intended, the scribe (Andreas himself) would have taken an effort to distinguish between himself and the taxpayer.[60] This, then, would indicate that tax assessors could assess themselves.

In P.Lond. 1555^{v}.35, Andreas, *presbyteros* is listed among individuals paying taxes, but it is unclear for which fiscal-administrative unit. Reference is made in l. 23 to a *meris* of Hagios Henoch, and in the subscription at least one of the declarants is indicated to be from Pakauneôs.[61] It is not clear whether this

58 The word *diastolê* means "specification," "order," "payment." It may imply the actual payment or the transfer of the collected *artabai* of corn, even if the assessment concerns the next year. Practically, however, it would be unlikely that all assessors/collectors would transfer their collected items on the same date. Another enigma in these lines is the meaning of the word *apo* in this context. Does it refer to the assessors' provenance or does it refer to the provenance of the collected payment? The two provenances may go together, of course.

59 *R.* line 2 lists an Andreas p[… However, it can only be speculated whether the word *presbyteros* has been lost.

60 Further confirmation that the document concerns *Duo Pediades* is provided, e.g., Pekusios son of Pkoore (l. 28), who is also attested in P.Lond. 1420.225, the assessment relating to *Duo Pediades*.

61 So, in this case, further comparison with names and texts is desirable.

man is to be identified with Andreas, priest, who was assessor in P.Würzb. inv. 122–127.36 and identified in P.Lond. 1434.52; 1453[v], and is probably also to be identified with Andreas son of Solomon, priest in the texts discussed below. In P.Lond. 1573.28, an Andreas, priest is found among eleven other men writing a declaration about their involvement in the tax collection, perhaps in making the assessment.[62] According to Crum, the document relates to Pakauneôs. A connection can be seen with Philotheos son of Makarios, who is listed as one of 12 declarants in P.Lond. 1573.30 (710 CE) and who may be the assessor attested in P.Würzb. inv. 122–127.57 (see below). If Philotheos son of Makarios and Andreas, priest, listed in P.Lond. 1573 are indeed the assessors also listed in P.Würzb. inv. 122–127, it might seem that Andreas, priest is connected to both *Duo Pediades* and Pakauneôs. However, this question remains open.

Several other texts attest an Andreas son of Solomon, priest, who may be the same man as the Andreas, priest just discussed. A clue for identification is provided by the designation *presbyteros* and by the connection to *Duo Pediades*. Andreas son of Solomon, priest, is attested in P.Lond. 1432.104, where he is listed among the individuals assessed in the section for *Duo Pediades*. The register 1432 is the assessment for *embolê* for Aphrodito and its *Pediades* for a third indiction. Andreas is assessed for 10 *artabai* of corn. This document can be related to P.Lond. 1560, a tax register, probably concerning people from *Duo Pediades*. In P.Lond. 1560.19, an Andreas son of Solomon, *p*[*resbyter*] is listed as having paid 1/6 of a *solidus* for an unknown tax. However, note that *presbyteros* is partly restored. Interestingly, P.Lond. 1560.18 attests a Petros son of Apa Kyros. A man of this name appears in P.Lond. 1432.100, near line 104 where Andreas, Solomon's son is referred to. Moreover, P.Lond. 1432.102 attests a Kollouthos son of Pkoui. He might be identified with [A]pa Kollouthos son of Pa]koui (sic in line 16 of the edition) in P.Lond. 1560.17. Interestingly, Kollouthos son of Pkoui is also attested in the document P.Lond. 1549, where he is stated to be from *Duo Pediades*.

P.Lond. 1453 (probably connected with CPR XXII 56 and 59, see Morelli 2001: 266) gives a list of names or people who may be appointed in an official function of tax collector, with other persons acting as guarantors. Line 7 presents Andreas son of Solom[on pr]i(est), who is further qualified as *pistô*( ), to which term Bell remarks in a footnote to line 3 that the meaning of this word is obscure. The word may be linked to the act of guaranteeing that the tax collectors appointed will do their jobs properly (πιστόω means to "confirm," so the

62 Note the reference to him.

word may well be related to this). It remains unclear, however, whether Andreas son of Solomon, priest, in this text is guaranteeing that someone else is reliable or whether it is guaranteed by someone else that Andreas son of Solomon, priest, is reliable. Either way, this text shows the prominent involvement of Andreas son of Solomon, priest, in his local community.

In P.Lond. 1495.13, Andreas son of Solomon, *elachistos* priest, acts as witness in a Coptic declaration by two officials from *Duo Pediades* that two requisitioned sailors will be produced and sent north. Probably the same man again acts as witness in a document relating to the delivery of 46 sailors and perhaps concerning the whole *dioikêsis* in P.Lond. 1497.27, subscribing the document in Coptic in his own hand and designating himself as "Andreas son of Solomon, with God *presbyteros*."

To conclude the discussion of texts featuring Andreas, priest, it seems safe to identify a man of this name with Andreas son of Solomon, priest (in Coptic documents sometimes further qualified as *elachistos*), who is connected to *Duo Pediades*. This person would then be attested in P.Lond. 1432.104; 1434.52; 1453.7; 1495.13; 1497.27; 1553^{v}.; 1560.19 and as the assessor in P.Würzb. inv. 122–127.36.

(9) **Pachumios son of Taurinos** is the other assessor stated to be from *Duo Pediades*. The name Pachumios is occasionally attested, Taurinos frequently. The combination as name and patronymic is only attested elsewhere once. The assessor probably is the same individual as the Pachumios son of Taurinos who is attested in P.Lond. 1420.229, as this document also relates to *Duo Pediades*. In this assessment for the fiscal-administrative unit *Duo Pediades*, Pachumios son of Taurinos is assessed to pay, together with Stephanos, 16 2/3 *arithmia nomismata* and 8 *artabai* of corn for parts of several land plots.[63]

63 Perhaps there is also a connection between P.Würzb. inv. 122–127 and P.Lond. 1481 descr. In P.Lond. 1481 descr. the name Pachumios appears; however, according to Bell, in this case it concerns the name of a *topos*. P.Lond. 1481 descr. starts with the sums of contributions for various taxes, then lists names, probably of land plots. Among some of the *topoi* Bell lists Pach[umiou?]. An edition of the fragment may give clarity as to whether this concerns a land plot or whether it could also be a personal name. Given the total numbers in the heading, the assessment in P.Lond. 1481 descr. probably concerns *Duo Pediades*, perhaps for an indiction year 2: it has the same phrase as the assessment P.Würzb. inv. 122–127 uses throughout, including the word *tablin*: "to be collected and transferred to the *tablin nomismata* 211 ½ 1/3." This amount, in *arithmia nomismata*, is the amount that *Duo Pediades* paid for *chrusika dêmosia* in the second indiction year (CE 704), cf. P.Lond. 1412.481. Furthermore, the fragment P.Lond. descr. 1481 gives the amount of 60 *nomismata* for a third indiction year. This looks like the amount assessed for maintenance (*dapanê*), which would also compare to the amount of 64 *arithmia nomismata* assessed for *Duo Pediades* for this tax post in P.Würzb. inv. 122–127.26.

The epoikia (*"Hamlets"*)

Pakauneôs (line 57)

Continuing with the *epilechthentes* for the *epoikia*, six *epilechthentes* are listed for Pakauneôs.

(10) The first one is **Psate**. The name Psate, with variants Psatēs or Psote, is commonly attested, usually in combination with another name, as the main name or patronymic. A Psatês, priest, is not found in Bell's Index of Persons to P.Lond. IV. However, an individual referred to in that way is attested in SB XX 15099.105 (belonging to P.Lond. 1419) as paying tax for a part of the plot Lakkos. If this Psatês is the same person, his connection to the land plot Lakkos raises the question as to what fiscal-administrative subdivision the plot belonged and where Psatês himself was registered. The data are confusing.[64]

(11) The next assessor listed in P.Würzb. inv. 122–127.57 is **Philotheos son of Makarios**. Both names are common, and this specific combination as name and patronymic is attested in eight other texts in P.Lond. IV. In P.Lond. 1421.112 (assessment relating to *Treis Pediades*, 720?), the heirs of Philotheos son of Makarios are assessed for 7 1/3 *arithmia nomismata* for land tax, not for poll tax, and for 8 1/2 *artabai* of corn for the *embolê*. The assessment relates to four plots of land, one of which is part of the *topos Abba Iakob*.

In P.Lond. 1422.20 (assessment probably relating to *Treis Pediades*, date uncertain), [Phi]l[o]theos son of Makarios is assessed for 1 *arithmia nomisma* for land tax, 1/6 *nomisma* for poll tax, and 3 *artabai* of corn. This assessment relates to a part of the plot of Abba Jakob, which was also among the plots of land in P.Lond. 1421.112. As the name is largely damaged, identification cannot be irrefutably ascertained. However, given the connection to *Treis Pediades* and the land plot of Anna Iakob, identification with Philotheos son of Makarios in P.Lond. 1421.112 is possible.

In P.Lond. 1431.67 (assessment of *embolê* for Aphroditô, 706–707 CE) again the heirs of Philotheos son of Makarios are assessed for 8 1/2 *artabai* of corn in the section for *Treis Pediades*. Here, identification with the heirs of Philotheos son of Makarios in P.Lond. 1421.112 is probable.

64 The land plot is also attested in P.Lond. 1420.235 (assessment relating to *Duo Pediades*) and P.Lond. 1422.46 (date uncertain and *chôrion* uncertain, perhaps *Treis Pediades*, cf. Philotheos son of Makarios). Or this is an example of landownership beyond one's registered domicile. However, in that case it would be expected that Psatês' domicile would be indicated.

It seems that the Philotheos son of Makarios appearing in the three texts just discussed is one and the same person. Whether he is also the assessor attested in P.Würzb. inv. 122–127.57 remains to be established. In the texts just discussed there are no clues that would corroborate such an assumption. Two other attestations of the same name are likewise difficult to identify.

In P.Lond. 1433.265 (706–707 CE, list of expenses), Philotheos son of Makarios is listed as recipient of a payment of 1/6 of a *nomisma* on 5 Pauni for his employment as a workman (*aggareutês*). This is listed in the section relating to "people of St. Mary's." Whereas it can be assumed that this work was required labor, it cannot be ascertained whether this is the same Philotheos son of Makarios as the individual attested in the documents discussed so far. Also, clear indications of identification with the assessor in P.Würzb. inv. 122–127.57 are lacking.

In P.Lond. 1449.72 (710–712 CE), Philotheos son of Makarios, grandson of Phez (?) is listed among 23 people who were probably required from Aphrodito for the military expedition (*cursus*). He seems to be listed among 14 people from *kômê Aphroditô*. After the names of the required individuals, amounts are given. The exact meaning of these remains unclear.[65] Similarly, the question whether this individual is the same or a different Philotheus son of Makarios as in P.Würzb. inv. 122–127.57 remains unanswered. The addition of the grandfather's name Phez does not clarify this attestation.

More clues for identification with the assessor Philotheos son of Makarios in P.Würzb. inv. 122–127.57 can be derived from three documents written in Coptic and Greek, with a clear connection to the *epoikion* Pakauneôs.

In the Coptic-Greek tax register P.Lond. 1555, on line 25, Philotheos son of Makarios is registered for payment of one *nomisma*. This register relates to Pakauneôs, which may be a clue for identification with the assessor in P.Würzb. inv. 122–127.57.

In P.Lond. 1573.30 (709–710 CE), a Philotheos son of Makarios is listed as one of 12 declarants who subscribes a guaranteeing agreement. Although Philotheus' name has not been preserved in the Greek list at the foot of the Coptic declaration, it most probably had been there (cf. the heading in l. 33: *diastalm*( ), 12 names, but only eight names have been preserved). The document refers to Pakauneôs and is clearly related to taxation. It may be speculated that this document was an official acknowledgement that these individuals were responsible for making the assessment for Pakauneôs or perhaps for collecting the taxes. Given this text's fiscal character and relation to Pakauneôs, it is

65 P.Lond. 1449 note to line 21.

entirely possible that the Philotheus son of Makarios appearing here among the declarants is the assessor attested in P.Würzb. inv. 122–127.57.

A further attestation of a Philotheos son of late Makarios is P.Lond. 1610.54. In this text, Philotheos appears as a witness in a declaration addressed to the governor through Basileios by a husband and his wife, who are from Pakauneôs. It is a very interesting document in which a woman seems to have had fled and in which the couple and a certain Phoibammon son of Kyriakos declare that their property was restored to them and that they had no further claims with the authorities. Not only does this document demonstrate women as active participants in the local community's life, but its official (juridical?) and personal character gives us a glimpse into the inhabitants' daily worries. Given this text's relation to Pakauneôs, it is well possible that the Philotheus son of Makarios appearing here among the declarants is the assessor attested in P.Würzb. inv. 122–127.57.

(12) **Enoch son of Victor.** The names Enoch and Victor again are both very common. Their combination as name and patronymic, however, is only attested in three documents. The question is whether this sharp decrease in the number of attestations enhances the chances of identification.

The assessor in P.Würzb. inv. 122–127.57 is likely to be identified with the Enoch son of Victor who is attested over many times in P.Lond. 1433, where he is further qualified as *pistikos* ("trustworthy person") from Pakauneôs.[66] Both the relation to Pakauneôs and his active involvement in the fiscal administration are indications that the same man is implied. In P.Lond. 1433, a register of requisitions of various kinds, Enoch son of Victor is referred to in various ways. The most elaborate designation is as: "Enoch son of Victor, *pistikos* from Pakauneôs" (e.g., in lines 70; 78; 134), but in other lines the reference to him is shorter: "Enoch son of Victor *pistikos*" (e.g., in lines 75; 84; 142), "Enoch son of Victor from Pakauneôs" (e.g., in line 188), "Enoch from Pakauneôs" (as in line 236), "Enoch, *pistikos*" (lines 191; 237; 238), "the same Enoch" (line 71), and just "Enoch" (line 79). He is listed in relation to the transfer of money for several posts on 19 and 21 Pauni, 8 Epeiph, 15 and 25 Mesore, 1 Epagomenê, and 21 Thôth, and recurring throughout the document in sections relating to the different fiscal-administrative divisions.

66 Bell 1910: 547. In his Index of Persons, Bell gives two separate entries for Enoch son of Victor. One entry lists P.Lond. 1455.4; 1518.33, another one the references in P.Lond. 1433. In the same index, p. 544, only one entry is given for Victor father of Enoch, listing all three texts. As has been argued above, the individual attested in P.Lond. 1433 is likely the same man as the assessor in P.Würzb. inv. 122–127 and also to be identified with the witness appearing in P.Lond. 1518.33.

An Enoch son of Victor is also attested in P.Lond. 1455.4. Due to the fragmentary state of the document, which most probably originally contained a Coptic part, only the list of 10 names in Greek script subscribed by the notary Theodoros has been preserved. The document resembles P.Lond. 1454, although the exact function of the list remains unclear. No indication of a *chôrion* (fiscal-administrative unit) is given. Interestingly, in P.Lond. 1455.2, one of the *epilechthentes* registered in P.Würzb. inv. 122–127.35 as one of the assessors from *Pente Pediades* turns up: Makarios son of Athanasios. If the Enoch son of Victor in P.Lond. 1455.4 and the Makarios son of Athanasios in P.Lond. 1455.2 are indeed the same people as the homonymous assessors from the Würzburg codex, then we might conclude that P.Lond. 1455 probably refers to men from the whole *dioikêsis*.

Another identification of Enoch son of Victor seems possible in the third text in which he is attested. In P.Lond. 1518.33 Enoch son of *makarios* Victor acts as witness in a surety for six families of fugitives who had been arrested. As the document relates to Pakauneôs, this Enoch son of Victor may well be the same man as the assessor in P.Würzb. inv. 122–127.

Yet another attestation of Enoch, son of the late (*makarios*) Victor is found in P.Lond. 1548.11. Enoch is listed here as a witness in a guarantee declaration. There are two clues for identification with the assessor. The first is that the document's scribe is from Pakauneôs. The other is that in line 12 "Philotheos, son of the late *makarios* Menas, *diakonos* (deacon)" appears as another witness. This person may be the same as the assessor in P.Würzb. inv. 122–127, where he is listed next to Enoch (see below, no. 13).

An Enoch son of Victor is clearly actively involved in the fiscal administration of Aphroditô in P.Würzb. inv. 122–127.57; 1433; 1518; 1548, and it is likely that in these texts we deal with one and the same person. Less clear is his identity in P.Lond. 1455.4. However, the appearance of another man who also acts as assessor in P.Würzb. inv. 122–127 leaves open the possibility that the same Enoch son of Victor is also implied in P.Lond. 1455.4.

(13) The name Philotheos is commonly found among the residents of Aphrodito. The name is mostly further qualified by means of a patronymic, and in a few instances by another designation, such as in the case of **Philotheos**, *diakonos* (deacon), who is listed among the assessors for Pakauneôs in P.Würzb. inv. 122–127. It is possible, but not certain, that the man with the same name and designation is encountered in P.Lond. 1599.12, the only other attestation of Philotheos, *diakonos* (deacon). This Coptic-Greek document, written by the scribe Theodoros, concerns fugitives. A fragmentary list of eleven persons is included in Greek script. Philotheos, deacon, is one of the witnesses to the

declaration, the purpose of which may be that the families will stay in place. The reference to amounts of money, according to Crum, may be related to some kind of fine for fugitives.[67] Apart from the combination of name and designation, there is no certainty that this is the same man. However, the fact that he is involved in this document concerning fugitives in a somewhat authoritative function may be an argument for his prominent position, which would match his appearance in P.Würzb. inv. 122–127 as an assessor.[68] Another clue may be provided by P.Lond. 1548. In line 12, "Philotheos, son of the late *makarios* Menas, *diakonos* (deacon)" appears as a witness in a guarantee declaration, which is written by a scribe from Pakauneôs. In the previous line of this document, Enoch, son of the late Victor (discussed above, no. 12) is mentioned as another witness. The proximity of Philotheos and Enoch in this document, its link to Pakauneôs, and their joint appearance as assessors in P.Würzb. inv. 122–127 all favor their identification.

If this identification is accepted, a further step can be taken. Philotheos, son of Menas may also be identified with the four other namesakes, who are all separately registered in Bell's Index of Persons, probably because their designation is different in different texts. Therefore, it should be examined whether all these attestations concern the same individual.

In P.Lond. 1549, Philotheos, son of Menas, is listed as *meizôn* ("village headman") from Pakauneôs in a Coptic declaration containing 25 names of guarantors. As other assessors appearing in P.Würzb. inv. 122–127 also appear in this declaration, Philotheos, son of Menas, is probably one and the same person.

The Philotheos frequently mentioned in P.Lond. 1433 is probably also the same person. In this text, Philotheos is designated in various attestations in various ways, with one or more of the designations "son of Menas," *presbyteros* ("priest"), and *pistikos* ("trustworthy person"). This text was discussed above, in relation to Enoch, son of Victor, who is prominently present in this document, also as a *pistikos*. The *logographos* Horouogchios, another assessor in the Würzburg codex (see below, no. 21), also features in this text. That in this text, Philotheos is sometimes designated a *presbyteros* may indicate that at a certain point his ecclesiastical position changed.

If the shift in ecclesiastical designation from *diakonos* to *presbyteros* is conceded, the reference to Philotheos, son of Menas, *presbyteros* in P.Lond. 1558.25 may also concern the same individual. This tax register may relate to the whole

67 Crum, introduction to the text. A further document registering fugitives is, e.g., P.Lond.1518.

68 Comparison with other individuals listed as witnesses may help.

dioikêsis. Philotheos, son of Menas, *presbyteros* is registered for the payment of 1/12 of a *nomisma*.

Finally, a Philotheos, son of Menas, without further designations, is encountered in P.Lond. 1495.15; 1536.11; 1565.41; 1570.7; 27; 1610.48. Again, the question is whether there are any additional clues to be found in these text that are helpful for identifying this man as one and the same person.

P.Lond. 1495 is a Coptic-Greek guarantee declaration by two officials from *Duo Pediades* that two requisitioned sailors will be produced and sent north. In line 13 of the same document, Andreas son of Solomon, *elachistos* priest (see above, no. 8) acts as a witness. The proximity of these men acting as witnesses in the same document may be a clue that they are the same persons attested as assessors in the Würzburg codex.

P.Lond. 1536 is a Coptic declaration by some 20 guarantors for a priest Hermias. The document's provenance is not indicated. The Philotheos, son of Menas mentioned in line 11 may be the same as the previous ones, but identification cannot be ascertained.

In P.Lond. 1565, three village officials make a declaration to the governor through Basileios about their payment of taxes and contributions, probably on behalf of their *chôrion* (fiscal-administrative unit). The document may relate to the whole *dioikêsis*. One of the other declarants, appearing in lines 3, 40, and 60, is Ezekias, son of Gamoul. This man also features in P.Lond. 1549, where not only Philotheos, son of Menas but also several other assessors mentioned in P.Würzb. inv. 122–127 appear (see discussion of assessors nos. 1, 5, and 14). The joint appearance of Philotheos, son of Menas and Ezekias, son of Gamoul in both P.Lond. 1565 and P.Lond. 1549 may support their identification.

A similar declaration is preserved in P.Lond. 1570, where Patermoutis is the declarant. It seems that Philotheos, son of Menas signed on his behalf ("Philotheos, son of Menas, asked, has written") in lines 7 and 27. Interestingly, in line 26, Hôrougchis, *logographos* appears. This man is also attested as assessor in the Würzburg codex (see below, no. 21). Again, the joint appearance of Philotheos, son of Menas and one of the assessors attested in the Würzburg codex seems to favor their identification.

Yet one other attestation of Philotheos is to be discussed. He is listed as Philotheos, son of *makarios* ("late") Menas signing on behalf of the three declarants in P.Lond. 1610.48, which seems to relate to Pakauneôs. Interestingly, line 54 of the same document preserves the name of one of the witnesses, who is Philotheos, son of *makarios* Makarios. This individual, as was argued above, may well be identified with the assessor of the same name (see above, no. 11).

(14) The fifth assessor listed for Pakauneôs is **Senouthios son of Daniel.** Whereas the name Senouthios is common, Daniel is attested less often. As a personal name in combination with patronymic, Senouthios son of Daniel is attested seven times in P.Lond. IV.

Senouthios son of Daniel is attested in P.Lond. 1436.71 in a section relating to *Pente Pediades*, but the nature of him being listed is unclear. The papyrus book is very fragmentary and seems to have contained registrations of various kinds. Fragment 5r (lines 66–82) perhaps concerned required workmen, as is suggested by lines 75, 77, 80. That the provenance of Senouthios son of Daniel was also mentioned appears from the addition *apo* after his name. However, the papyrus breaks off there, so this provenance cannot be established. Identification, thus, remains questionable.

Another attestation of the name Senouthios son of Daniel (spelled Daunêl) is preserved in P.Lond. 1460.148, where he is stated to be from Thlagran. As this is a list of fugitives, this Senouthios is very likely not the same person as the assessor.

A further attestation of the name appears in P.Lond. 1549. This is a Coptic declaration, containing signatures of guarantors and witnesses (no edition is provided of the Coptic text), followed by a list, repeating the names of the 25 guarantors in Greek script. Some of the individual guarantors are further qualified by a designation (*meizôn*, "village headman"; *hypodektês*, "tax collector"; *hêgoumenos*, "leader"), demonstrating that they belonged to the group of locally prominent men. With some men, their provenance is indicated. The document was written by the scribe Theodoros. However, what was the purpose of this document? It would be reasonable to suspect a financial link here. Could it be that these 25 men were the assessors for the whole *dioikêsis*, who had declared that they would do or had fulfilled their jobs properly? The number of 25 individuals listed here is not so far off the number of 21 assessors encountered in P.Würzb. inv. 122–127. Moreover, names of the other assessors attested in P.Würzb. inv. 122–127 also appear in P.Lond. 1549.[69] This may be a coincidence, or it may be an argument for a connection between the documents P.Würzb. inv. 122–127 and P.Lond. 1549. In this case, identification of Senouthios son of Daniel in both texts is possible.

The Coptic-Greek financial register P.Lond. 1553 lists a Senouthios son of Daniel, who had been assessed and/or had paid half a *nomisma*, in line 40. His payment is registered in the section relating to *epoikion* Emphyteutôn. Interestingly, in line 42 of the same section the heirs of a Pekusios, deacon, are

---

69 Psoios son of Mênas and Mênas son of Kollouthos.

registered with 1/3 of a *nomisma*. It is tempting to identify this deacon Pekusios with the assessor who is mentioned immediately after Senouthios son of Daniel in P.Würzb. inv. 122–127.57 on the grounds that both men are also listed in close proximity in P.Lond. 1553. If they are to be identified with the assessors, P.Lond. 1553 demonstrates that they had fiscal liability in Emphyteutôn, although it remains unclear whether this was also their provenance.

P.Lond. 1557 preserves a list of names and amounts in Greek script. As Crum observes, the names are preceded by oblique strokes in a different ink. This probably indicated that the payments were done or checked. Verso line 22 lists a Senouthios son of Daniel. The amount he was due has not been preserved.[70] There are no clues that confirm identification with the assessor attested in P.Würzb. inv. 122–127.57.

The fragment P.Lond. 1564 preserves a Coptic declaration in which three men, among whom is Senouthios son of Daniel, declare not to have "laid aught upon (any) beyond that which we had fixed." The edited text has the title "tax-receipt," but maybe this is the declaration of fair procedure by which tax registers were usually subscribed by the tax assessors or collectors? Identification with the assessor attested in P.Würzb. inv. 122–127.57 remains unconfirmed, but is possible.

P.Lond. 1569.3 refers to Senouthios son of Daniel, adding his function as *hypodektes*, "tax collector." This fragment preserves the beginning of a declaration in Coptic by two local officials to the *dêmosios logos* through the *pagarch*. The indication that this Senouthios son of Daniel was a tax collector is interesting. His role in the tax collection may be taken as an argument for identification with the Senouthios son of Daniel attested in P.Lond. 1549. Involvement in the fiscal administration is also apparent in P.Würzb. inv. 122–127.57, so the assessor listed there may also be the same man as the one listed in P.Lond. 1569.3. If this identification is correct, it appears that the individuals who were appointed as assessors were also active as tax collectors. Unfortunately, the Coptic declaration has no date, so it cannot be definitively established whether Senouthios son of Daniel would assess and collect the taxes in the same year.

(15) The name of the last assessor listed for Pakauneôs is again commonly attested. Whereas a patronymic is missing, the addition of his function may give some clue. The name **Pekusios**, deacon is attested in P.Lond. 1553.42. The line refers to the "heirs of Pekusios, deacon," who are registered for payment of 1/3 *nomisma*. These are registered under the *epoikon* Emphyteutôn. As

70 Most people paid 1/12, some 1/6, 1/24, and one person 1/2.

already observed above, identification of Pekusios, deacon with the assessor in P.Würzb. inv. 122–127 cannot be ascertained. However, it is interesting that in P.Lond. 1553.40, Senouthios son of Daniel is listed among the taxpayers, next to the registration of Pekusios, deacon. Although coincidence cannot be excluded, if their appearance in the same document is taken as a clue to their social and fiscal proximity, it is at least a possibility that the two taxpayers in P.Lond. 1553.40; 42 are to be identified with the two assessors for Pakauneôs in P.Würzb. inv. 122–127. Given the fact that in P.Lond. 1553.42 the heirs of Pekusios are registered for the payment, the *terminus post quem* of this tax register is 702–703 CE.

Bounôn

(16) **Joannes son of Georgios** drew up the assessment for Bounôn. Both names are fairly common, but there are only three attestations in which the names appear in the combination of name and patronymic. P.Lond. 1460 is a list of fugitives. In line 5, a Joannes son of Georgios, from Psimate in the Panopolite *nome* is registered. The *chôrion* in which he was residing when the list was drawn cannot be established. Line 41 of the same document contains a reference to another Joannes son of Georgios. This man's provenance was Akôm, also in the Panopolites. These men, then, turn out to be different individuals, and it seems unlikely that one of them is to be identified with the assessor in P.Würzb. inv. 122–127. A third attestation is listed in Bell's Index of Names for P.Lond. 1468 descr. This probably is an assessment for the gold taxes for several *chôria*, among which is Bounôn. However, in his description of the text, Bell does not include the name Joannes son of Georgios. Publication of the text may throw light on the matter.

Kerameiou

(17) **Panesnêu son of Adam** is registered in P.Würzb. inv. 122–127.102 as the only assessor for Kerameiou. His provenance is not indicated, perhaps implying that he was from Kerameiou. He is not explicitly designated by means of the term *epilechtheis*. His name is interesting, as both the name Panesnêu and the name Adam are relatively little attested: the name Adam is only attested twice, in both cases in P.Lond. 1553 and as patronymic. This might imply that the man identified as "son of Adam," Panesnêu (l. 10), and Simon (l. 41) were brothers. However, Simon son of Adam is mentioned in a section relating to *epoikion* Emphyteutôn, whereas Panesnêu son of Adam is attested in a section concerning Keramiou. This latter observation may be an indication that this Panesnêu son of Adam is the same person as the tax assessor for Kerameiou in P.Würzb. inv. 122–127.102.

One other attestation is interesting, even if identification is problematic. Spelled Πανι̣σνη̣υ (but without a patronymic) in P.Lond. 1434.53, one wonders whether this individual may be identified with the assessor mentioned in the Würzburg codex. An argument for identification would be that two of the other assessors already discussed are also attested in that same text, in the preceding line.[71] However, the Panisnêu mentioned in P.Lond. 1434.53 is stated to be from Poimên, not from Kerameiou. For other attestations of the name Panesnêu, identification is impossible or excluded.[72]

Poimên

(18) P.Würzb. inv. 122–127.117 mentions **Petros son of Phêu** as the only assessor for Poimên. He is referred to without indication of provenance, and without explicitly designating him as *epilechtheis*. Whereas the name Petros is common in P.Lond. IV, the name is not attested with the patronymic Phêu, if this is the correct reading of the patronymic. The last letter of the patronymic could be read as β or υ. Neither the name Phēb nor Phē is listed in Bell's Index of Names. P.Lond. 1421 preserves an assessment relating to *Treis Pediades*.[73] Line 116 reads: …]*phēu*. Unfortunately, it cannot be established how much of the preceding name, and perhaps of the patronymic, is lost. With so little to hold onto, it seems unlikely that the individual listed here would have been the assessor Petros son of Phêu. Perhaps the patronymic might also be a spelling variant of Phep or Phib, of which there are few attestations in eighth-century Aphrodito,[74] but still not as patronymic combined with the name Petros.

71 P.Würzb. inv. 122–127.35: Mênas son of Kollouthos; P.Würzb. inv. 122–127.36: Andreas, *presbyteros*. Although the word *epilechtheis/epilechthentes* is lacking in P.Lond. 1434.51–53, the individuals listed here are probably assessors; see Bell's footnote to lines 51–53.

72 A Panesnêu is attested without patronymic in P.Lond. 1430.70, where the son of Panesnêu is registered for paying 1/3 *nomisma*. The phrasing of the entry suggests that the son pays on behalf of his father. In P.Lond. 1432.101, a Panisnêu is assessed for an unknown number of *artabai* of corn together with Theodosios. Again, Panisnêu appears without a patronymic; the papyrus breaks off after the name Theodosios. The section where they are listed relates to *Duo Pediades*. A patronymic is likewise lacking in P.Lond. 1435.166. This individual is further designated as an oil producer. Different individuals, as they have a different father, are: P.Lond. 1460.127 (son of Senouthios); 1553.25 (son of Kaus …); 1557.15 (son of Makarios).

73 The individual here is assessed for part of the land plot Pchichit(os) (also Chichitos), see Marthot 2013: s.v. Χιχόϊτος, Chichoïtos.

74 Phep: P.Lond. 1419.313. Phib: P.Lond. 1421.38; 1431.52.

Psyrou

(19) The assessor for Psyrou attested in P.Würzb. inv. 122–127.132 is **Apollô son of Chrêstos.** No provenance is indicated, but the term *epilechth*(*eis*) is added. The name Apollôs is common, the name Chrêstos and its variable spellings (Chrêsse, Chruse) are few. No Apollô son of Chrêstos is listed in Bell's Index of Persons. However, an Apollô son of Chruso is attested in the Greek-Coptic tax register P.Lond. 1553v.1, so the question is whether this person could be the same person as the tax assessor in P.Würzb. inv. 122–127.132. The difficulty to come up with a certain identification is caused by the difference of the spelling of the patronymic. At the same time, variant spellings of the same name are common enough so that a different spelling need not exclude identification.

An example may be provided by Pachumios son of Chrêstos. The name Chrêstos is included once in Bell's Index of Names, as the father of Pachumius in P.Lond. 1431.48, where he is registered for an arrear of 3 *artabai* of corn for the *embolê* tax. The section in which he is registered relates to *Pente Pediades*. A particular attestation of the name Chruse is interesting in this connection. A Chruse, father of Pachumius is registered in P.Lond. 1420.71. In this assessment for *Pente Pediades*, Pachumios is assessed for money taxes and for 3 *artabai* of corn for the *embolê*. Given the roughly same date of the documents, the relation to *Pente Pediades*, and the number of *artabai* of corn, it seems likely that these two texts imply the same Pachumius but that his patronymic was spelled differently in each case. This parallel variability of spelling may be one argument for identification of the Apollô in P.Würzb. inv. 122–127.132 with the Apollô in P.Lond. 1553ᵛ.1, whose patronymic is spelled Chruse and who is registered for 1 1/6 *nomisma*. The name of the fiscal-administrative unit for which he is listed is not clear. What is notable, however, is that in this document five (or possibly six) names are attested of individuals who have the same name as, and who perhaps can also be identified with, assessors in P.Würzb. inv. 122–127. In that case, a suspected connection between P.Würzb. inv. 122–127 and P.Lond. 1553 can be corroborated by means of the relatively high number of shared names.

Hagios Pinoutiôn

(20) In P.Würzb. inv. 122–127.146, a gap impedes the reading of the name of the *epilechtheis* who drew up this assessment for *Hagios Pinoutiôn*. What can be made out is that no provenance was indicated but that the person was designated as **priest**. The designation *epilechtheis* is lacking. Perhaps Phullô or Apollô could be a possible restoration. A Phullô, priest is only attested once, in P.Lond. 1419.33, without further clarity of context. An Apollôs, priest is attested in several texts, among which P.Lond. 1553v.12 may be of interest. Here, Apollôs is registered, in a section relating to *Hagios Pinoutiôn*, for 1/2 and 1/3 *nomisma*.

As was pointed out above, five other assessors attested in P.Würzb. inv. 122–127 may be attested in P.Lond. 1553 as well: Andreas, priest; Senouthios son of Daniel; Pekusios, deacon; Panesnêu son of Adam; Apollô son of Chrêstos; [Apoll]ô, priest (?).[75] This could be a hint for identification with the assessor in P.Würzb. inv. 122–127.146, although because of the insecure reading of the name this hypothesis cannot be confirmed.

Sakoore

(21) The only *epilechtheis* mentioned for Sakoore, without indication of provenance and without use of the designation *epilechtheis*, is **Hôrouogchios.** Furthermore, he is indicated without patronymic, but the designation *logographos* is added to his name. The name is attested regularly, occurring both as name and as patronymic. The assessor in P.Würzb. inv. 122–127.160 is known from a number of other documents, too, where he is also qualified as *logographos*. Hence, in these cases, identification with the assessor in P.Würzb. inv. 122–127.160 is probable. These texts will be discussed first.

In P.Lond. 1412.136, Hôrouogchios, *logographos* appears in a fiscal register bringing in or transferring taxes collected from the group of "those in Babylon."[76] In P.Lond. 1413.[15]; 118 he is attested as one of the officials transferring collected tax money to the treasury on three different dates in an indiction year 1. He is also referred to, but merely as "the same," in the same documents in lines 16, 17, 119, and 120.

Hôrouogchios, *logographos* is also attested in P.Lond IV 1433.34; 106; 158; 206; 249; 290; 376; 416; 505; 531 (706–707 CE). Here, Hôrouogchios is mentioned as recipient of wages in money (*misthos*) and maintenance (*dapanê*), clearly for his employment as *logographos* for a period of 12 months. Interestingly, he seems to have been transferring the money to himself, as this is the correct interpretation of line 34 concerning the register of *kômê Aphroditô*. Contributions for his wages and maintenance are proportionally extracted from every fiscal-administrative subdivision listed. The dates on which this transfer was done in all cases is noted on 8 Tybi.

---

75 Names of the assessors attested in P.Würzb. IV inv. 122–127 and also appearing in P.Lond. 1553 are: Andreas, priest; Senouthios son of Daniel; Pekusios, deacon; Panesnêu son of Adam; Apollô son of Chrêstos.

76 Note that the transfers done for the other fiscal-administrative subdivisions that were done on the same date (Pauni 17, indiction 15), were registered as "prepayments through the most famous dux." The question is whether the reference to Hôrouogchios, *logographos* here is a scribal mistake, especially as his name does not turn up any further in the document; see Bell's note to the line. Nevertheless, that his name is mentioned indicates that the scribe was familiar with the name.

The same Hôrouogchios, *logographos* appears in P.Lond IV 1570.26 in the subscription of a declaration by the headman of *Hagios Pinoutiôn*, Patermoutis. Hôrougchios' role is not completely clear. He seems to assist Patermoutis. In lines 7 and 27 of the same document, Philotheos, son of Menas is attested, probably signing on behalf of Patermoutis. This man is also attested as assessor in the Würzburg codex (see above, no. 13). This joint appearance of Philotheos, son of Menas and Hôrougchios, who also appear together as assessors in the Würzburg codex, favors their identification.

The name Hôrougchios features a few times in P.Lond IV 1424 (relating to *Pente Pediades*, 714?).[77] Line 66 is interesting, where Hôrouogchios is further designated as *ge erg*. However, perhaps here the patronymic Georgiou is to be read, as a Hôrouogchios son of Georgios is attested in several other documents. In P.Lond IV 1416.31 (date uncertain), Hôrouogchios son of Georgios is listed for *topos* Taplam( ) and *topos* Amm(a) Mari(a) in *Pente Pediades*. Bell remarks in the note to this line that he doubts whether the reference to a *topos* Amm(a) Mari(a) is correct, saying: "It would seem that either this tax-payer held no land at Taplam( ), the insertion of this name being a mistake, or that the extent of his holding, and consequently the amount of his quota, were unknown to the clerk."[78] Nevertheless, even if this name was inserted by mistake, the patronymic and the association with *Pente Pediades* (indicated in line 27) for this individual are notable. In P.Lond IV 1432.91 (date uncertain), Hôrouogchios son of Georgios is assessed for 20 *artabai* of corn for the *embolê* in a section relating to one of the *Pediades*, so it seems. In P.Lond IV 1549, Hôrouogchios son of Georgios, from *Pente Pediades*, appears as one of the 25 guarantors at the bottom of a guarantee declaration. Interestingly, this document contains the names of some other persons who may be identified as assessors in P.Würzb. inv. 122–127: Psoios son of Menas (no. 1); Menas son of Kollouthios (no. 5); Philotheos, son of Menas (no. 13); and Senouthios son of Daniel (no. 14). The question is whether this could imply that Hôrouogchios, the *logographos*, is to be identified with Hôrouogchios son of Georgios. The connection to *Pente Pediades* in P.Lond. 1416.31; 1432.91; 1549 supports the identification of Hôrouogchios son of Georgios. His joint appearance in P.Lond. 1549 with four of the assessors mentioned in P.Würzb. inv. 122–127 also favors his identification with the *logographos*.

P.Lond IV 1445.6 (date uncertain) relates to expenses. Hôrougchios, *chartoularios* seems to receive 3 *nomismata*. However, his exact role and identity

77 P.Lond IV 1424.34 (relating to *Pente Pediades*, 714?) mentions a Basileos son of Hôrouogchios, assessed for part of the *topos* Sasnoeit. The assessment concerns *Pente Pediades*. In line 61, a Hôrouogchios son of Philotheos is assessed for 1 1/2 *nomismata*.

78 Bell 1910:162.

remain obscure. The function of *chartoularios* seems to have been quite high in P.Lond. 1447.137; 139; 141, being preceded by the epithet *endoxos* or *endoxotatos*. It cannot be established with certainty whether this Hôrouogchios is the same person as the assessor in P.Würzb. inv. 122–127.160, but this may well be the case given the next document.

P.Lond IV 1448 (703?) preserves an account of expenses of and produced by "me Hôrouogchios, *notarios*, for the months Thôth until Pharmouthi," as the heading in line 1 makes clear. He may well be the *logographos*, as his involvement in the fiscal registration of Aphrodito, which seems to have had a more general character rather than being connected to one specific locality.

Identification of the assessor in P.Würzb. inv. 122–127.160 with Hôrouogchios, *logographos* in other documents seems certain on the basis of the designation used. Less certain, but possible, is the identification of this man with the *notarios* and the *chartoularios*. He may also be identified with Hôrouogchios son of Georgios. If this is the case, Hôrouogchios, *logographos* was registered in *Pente Pediades*. If the other identifications also apply, his case shows that the role in which an individual functions in a text may affect the way he is identified. Where he is attested as a tax-paying subject, he is registered under his name and patronymic; whereas in his function as servant of the financial administration, his patronymic is replaced by his designation as *logographos*, *notarios*, and *chartoularios*. Moreover, the variation in terminology may furthermore imply that a rough indication of his tasks or responsibilities would be enough, rather than using a strict qualification.

The results from the discussion above are presented in tables 1.A and 1.B showing all attestations known to date of *epilechthentes* from seventh- and eight-century Aphrodito.

TABLE 1.A Attestations of *epilechthentes* in P.Lond. IV

#	Text	Date	Assessment for subdivision	Assessor	Provenance of assessor	Attestations in other texts	Qualification	Division/plot of land	Identification with assessor in P.Würzb.
1	P.Lond. 1420.1	706	*Pente Pediades*	**Theodoros son of Victor**	Hagios Pinoutiôn	none			
2	P.Lond. 1420.1	706	*Pente Pediades*	**Phoibammon son of Victor**	Hagios Pinoutiôn				
						P.Lond. 1420.77		*Pente Pediades*	uncertain
						P.Lond. 1431.45		*Pente Pediades*?	uncertain
3	P.Lond. 1420.154	706	*Duo Pediades*	**lost**	lost				
4	P.Lond. 1424.1	714	*Pente Pediades*	**[...]o**	lost				
5	P.Lond. 1424.1	714	*Pente Pediades*	**Pekusios son of Hermaos**	lost				
						P.Lond. 1420.58		*Pente Pediades*	likely
						P.Lond. 1562.8		*Pente Pediades*	likely
6	P.Lond. 1424.1	714	*Pente Pediades*	**Pkal[...]**	lost				
						P.Lond. 1420.20		*Pente Pediades*	possible
						P.Lond. 1420.120		*Pente Pediades*	possible

TABLE 1.A Attestations of *epilechthentes* in P.Lond. IV (*cont.*)

#	Text	Date	Assessment for subdivision	Assessor	Provenance of assessor	Attestations in other texts	Qualification	Division/plot of land	Identification with assessor in P.Würzb.
7	P.Lond. 1428.20	uncertain	uncertain	**[Sen]outhios son of Georgios**	not indicated			unknown	
			Pente Pediades			P.Lond. 1420.141		*topos* Tsament (*Pente Pediades*)	uncertain
						P.Lond. 1430.113	*tekton*	unknown	uncertain
						P.Lond. 1460.9		Tria Kastra (outside of the *dioikêsis* of Aphrodito)	unlikely
8	P.Lond. 1428.20	uncertain	uncertain	**Abraham son of Stephanos**	not indicated				
9	P.Lond. 1429.20	uncertain		**[Theod]oros son of Pêsoos**	not indicated				
						P.Lond. 1426.39			uncertain
10	P.Lond. 1432	uncertain; indiction 3	Aphroditô and its *Pediades*, including the *epoikia*	**A[ ]**	lost				
11	P.Lond. 1475 descr.		Kerameiou	**Hermaos son of Kollô(s)**	not indicated				

TABLE 1.A Attestations of *epilechthentes* in P.Lond. IV (*cont.*)

#	Text	Date	Assessment for subdivision	Assessor	Provenance of assessor	Attestations in other texts	Qualification	Division/plot of land	Identification with assessor in P.Würzb.
12	P.Lond. 1554.3; 6; 18	uncertain	Various *epoikia*, including Sakoore? Cf. note to line 25	**Theodosios son of Philotheos**	not indicated				
						P.Lond. 1420.250		*Duo Pediades*	unlikely
						P.Lond. 1427.6		? Pediades	unlikely
						P.Lond. 1432.101		*Duo Pediades*	unlikely
					Pakauneôs	P.Lond. 1544.17	*makarios* Philotheos		probable
					Pakauneôs	P.Lond. 1545.2; [15]; v16	*makarios* Philotheos		probable
					Pakauneôs	P.Lond. 1548.9			probable
					Pakauneôs	P.Lond. 1549			probable

TABLE 1.B Attestations of *epilechthentes* in P.Würzb. inv. 122–127

#	Text	Date	Assessment for subdivision	Assessor	Provenance of assessor	Attestations in other texts	Qualification	Division/plot of land	Identification with assessor in P.Würzb.
1	P.Würzb. inv. 122–127.35	Indiction 1	Kômê Aphroditô	**Psoios son of Menas**	*Pente Pediades*				
						P.Lond. 1432.38		*idia kôme, Pente Pediades* or *Treis Pediades*	possible
						P.Lond. 1435.129		*Kômê Aphroditô*	uncertain
						P.Lond. 1454.2			uncertain
						P.Lond. 1459.22; 23; 28		several subdivisions	possible
						P.Lond. 1494.38		*Treis Pediades*	unlikely
						P.Lond. 1549		*Pente Pediades*	likely
						P.Lond. 1561.20		Kerameiou	uncertain
						P.Lond. 1587.12			uncertain
2	P.Würzb. inv. 122–127.35	Indiction 1	Kômê Aphroditô	**Makarios son of Athanasios**	*Pente Pediades*				
						P.Lond. 1455.2			possible
3	P.Würzb. inv. 122–127.35	Indiction 1	Kômê Aphroditô	**Phoibammon son of Thakore**	*Pente Pediades*				

TABLE 1.B Attestations of *epilechthentes* in P.Würzb. inv. 122–127 (*cont.*)

#	Text	Date	Assessment for subdivision	Assessor	Provenance of assessor	Attestations in other texts	Qualification	Division/plot of land	Identification with assessor in P.Würzb.
4	P.Würzb. inv. 122–127.35	Indiction 1	*Kômê Aphroditô*	**Georgios son of Hermaôs**	*Pente Pediades*				
						P.Lond. 1449.12		Pakauneôs and Kerameiou	unlikely
						P.Lond. 1552.22			uncertain
5	P.Würzb. inv. 122–127.35	Indiction 1	*Kômê Aphroditô*	**Menas son of Kollouthos**	*Pente Pediades*				
						P.Lond. 1416*v.* D. 30		*Pente Pediades*	possible
						P.Lond. 1432.28; 90		*Pente Pediades* (?)	possible
					Pente Pediades	P.Lond. 1434.52			likely
						P.Lond. 1549	*hypodektes*	*Pente Pediades*	likely
6	P.Würzb. inv. 122–127.35	Indiction 1	*Kômê Aphroditô*	**Jakob [ ]**	*Treis Pediades*				
7	P.Würzb. inv. 122–127.36	Indiction 1	*Kômê Aphroditô*	**Papnouthios son of Ptêron**	*Treis Pediades*				

TABLE 1.B Attestations of *epilechthentes* in P.Würzb. inv. 122–127 (*cont.*)

#	Text	Date	Assessment for subdivision	Assessor	Provenance of assessor	Attestations in other texts	Qualification	Division/plot of land	Identification with assessor in P.Würzb.
8	P.Würzb. inv. 122–127.36	Indiction 1	*Kômê Aphroditô*	**Andreas, priest**	*Duo Pediades*				
						P.Lond. 1419.528	*presbyteros*	assessment for church Apostolos. Paid through Andreas priest and others	uncertain
						P.Lond. 1419.665	*presbyteros*	*topos* Tsamêt and Papkalernei	uncertain
						P.Lond. 1419.668	*presbyteros*	*topos* Piah Palei and Ankoore	uncertain
						P.Lond. 1419.1105	*presbyteros*	*topos* Ppin	uncertain
						P.Lond. 1420.36		*Pente Pediades*, part of plot St. Mary's	uncertain
					Duo Pediades	P.Lond. 1434.52	*presbyteros*		likely
						P.Lond. 1553v.29		*Duo Pediades*	possible
						P.Lond. 1553v.33–34	*elachistos presbyteros*	*Duo Pediades*	likely
						P.Lond. 1553v.38	*elachistos presbyteros*	*Duo Pediades*	likely

TABLE 1.B Attestations of *epilechthentes* in P.Würzb. inv. 122–127 (*cont.*)

#	Text	Date	Assessment for subdivision	Assessor	Provenance of assessor	Attestations in other texts	Qualification	Division/plot of land	Identification with assessor in P.Würzb.
						P.Lond. 1555v.35	*presbyteros*	Pakauneôs	uncertain
						P.Lond. 1573.28	*presbyteros*	Pakauneôs	uncertain
				Andreas son of Solomon, p[resbyter]					
						P. Lond. 1432.104			
						P.Lond. 1453.7	*presbyteros, ôs pistô( )*	one of the Pediades	likely
						P.Lond. 1495.13	*elachistos presbyteros*	*Duo Pediades*	likely
						P.Lond. 1497.27	with God, *presbyteros*	the whole dioikêsis?	likely
						P.Lond. 1560.19	*presbyteros*	probably *Duo Pediades*	likely
9	P.Würzb. inv. 122–127.36	Indiction 1	*Kômê Aphroditô*	**Pachumios son of Taurinos**	*Duo Pediades*				
						P.Lond. 1420.229		*Duo Pediades*	likely
10	P.Würzb. inv. 122–127.57	Indiction 1	*Epoikion Pakauneôs*	**Psatês, priest**	not indicated	SB XX 15099.105	*presbyteros*		uncertain

TABLE 1.B Attestations of *epilechthentes* in P.Würzb. inv. 122–127 (*cont.*)

#	Text	Date	Assessment for subdivision	Assessor	Provenance of assessor	Attestations in other texts	Qualification	Division/plot of land	Identification with assessor in P.Würzb.
11	P.Würzb. inv. 122–127.57	Indiction 1	*Epoikion Pakauneôs*	**Philoteos son of Makarios**	not indicated	P.Lond. 1421.112	heirs of Philotheos son of Makarios	*Treis Pediades*, Abba Iakob and other plots	uncertain
						P.Lond. 1422.20		*Treis Pediades*, Abba Iakob	uncertain
						P.Lond. 1431.67	heirs of Philotheos son of Makarios	*Treis Pediades*	uncertain
						P.Lond. 1433.265		people of St. Mary's	unlikely
						P.Lond. 1449.72		Kômê Aphroditô	uncertain
						P.Lond. 1555.24		Pakauneôs	possible
						P.Lond. 1573.30		Pakauneôs	possible
						P.Lond. 1610.54	Philotheos son of makarios Makarios	Pakauneôs	possible
12	P.Würzb. inv. 122–127.57	Indiction 1	*Epoikion Pakauneôs*	**Enoch son of Victor**	not indicated				
						P.Lond. 1433 *passim*	*pit* (*pistikos*)	Pakauneôs	likely

TABLE 1.B Attestations of *epilechthentes* in P.Würzb. inv. 122–127 (*cont.*)

#	Text	Date	Assessment for subdivision	Assessor	Provenance of assessor	Attestations in other texts	Qualification	Division/plot of land	Identification with assessor in P.Würzb.
						P.Lond. 1455.4		*dioikêsis*?	possible
						P.Lond. 1518.33		Pakauneôs	likely
						P.Lond. 1548.11	Enoch, son of *makarios* Victor	Pakauneôs	likely
13	P.Würzb. inv. 122–127.57	Indiction 1	*Epoikion Pakauneôs*	**Philotheos, deacon**	not indicated	P.Lond. 1599.12	*diakonos*		possible
				Philotheos, son of *makarios* Menas, deacon		P.Lond. 1548.12	*diakonos*	Pakauneôs	likely
				Philotheos, son of Menas, village headman		P.Lond. 1549	*meizôn*	Pakauneôs	likely
						P.Lond. 1433 *passim*	*presbyteros, pistikos*		likely
				Philotheos, son of Menas		P.Lond. 1558.25	*presbyteros*	*dioikêsis*?	possible
				Philotheos, son of Menas		P.Lond. 1495.15		*Duo Pediades*	possible
						P.Lond. 1536.11			uncertain
						P.Lond. 1565.41			possible
						P.Lond. 1570.7; 27		Hagion Pinoutiôn	possible
						P.Lond. 1610.48		Pakauneôs	possible

TABLE 1.B Attestations of *epilechthentes* in P.Würzb. inv. 122–127 (*cont.*)

#	Text	Date	Assessment for subdivision	Assessor	Provenance of assessor	Attestations in other texts	Qualification	Division/plot of land	Identification with assessor in P.Würzb.
14	P.Würzb. inv. 122–127.57	Indiction 1	*Epoikion Pakauneôs*	**Senouthios son of Daniel**	not indicated				
						P.Lond. 1436.71		*Pente Pediades*	uncertain
						P.Lond. 1460.148		Thlagran	unlikely
						P.Lond. 1549		*dioikêsis*?	possible
						P.Lond. 1553.40		Emphyteutôn	uncertain
						P.Lond. 1557.22			uncertain
						P.Lond. 1564.2			uncertain
						P.Lond. 1569.3	*hypodektes*		possible
15	P.Würzb. inv. 122–127.57	Indiction 1	*Epoikion Pakauneôs*	**Pekusios, deacon**	not indicated				
						P.Lond. 1553.42	deacon	Emphyteuton	possible
16	P.Würzb. inv. 122–127.87	Indiction 1	*Epoikion Bounôn*	**Joannes son of Georgios**	not indicated				
						P.Lond. 1460.5		Psimate, Panopolites	unlikely
						P.Lond. 1460.41		Akôm, Panopolites	unlikely
						P.Lond. 1468 descr.			

TABLE 1.B Attestations of *epilechthentes* in P.Würzb. inv. 122–127 (*cont.*)

#	Text	Date	Assessment for subdivision	Assessor	Provenance of assessor	Attestations in other texts	Qualification	Division/plot of land	Identification with assessor in P.Würzb.
17	P.Würzb. inv. 122–127.102	Indiction 1	*Epoikion Kerameiou*	**Panesnêu son of Adam**	not indicated				
						P.Lond. 1553.10		Kerameiou	likely
				Panisnêu	from Poimên	P.Lond. 1434.53		Kerameiou	uncertain
18	P.Würzb. inv. 122–127.117	Indiction 1	*Epoikion Poimên*	**Petros son of Phêu**	not indicated				
19	P.Würzb. inv. 122–127.132	Indiction 1	*Epoikion Psyrou*	**Apollô son of Christos**	not indicated				
						P.Lond. 1553v.1		various	possible
20	P.Würzb. inv. 122–127.146	Indiction 1	*Epoikion Hagios Pinoutiôn*	**…ô, *presbyteros***	not indicated				
				Apollô, *presbyteros*		P.Lond. 1553v. 12	*presbyteros*	Hagios Pinoutiôn	possible
21	P.Würzb. inv. 122–127.160	Indiction 1	*Epoikion Sakoore*	**Hôrougchios, logographos**	not indicated				
						P.Lond. 1412.136	logographos	Those who are in Babylon	likely

TABLE 1.B Attestations of *epilechthentes* in P.Würzb. inv. 122–127 (*cont.*)

#	Text	Date	Assessment for subdivision	Assessor	Provenance of assessor	Attestations in other texts	Qualification	Division/plot of land	Identification with assessor in P.Würzb.
						P.Lond. 1413.[15]. 16; 17	[*logographos*]		likely
						P.Lond. 1413.118; 119; 120	*logographos*		likely
						P.Lond IV 1424.66	son of Georgios		possible
						P.Lond IV 1433.34 etc.	*logographos*	*dioikesis*	likely
						P.Lond. 1570.26	*logographos*		likely
						P.Lond. 1448.1	*notarios*		possible
						P.Lond. 1445.6?	*chartoularios*		possible
				Hôrouogchios, son of Geôrgios		P.Lond. 1416.31		*Pente Pediades Topos Taplam*( ); *topos* Amm(a) Mari(a)	possible/likely
						P.Lond. 1432.91		One of the *Pediades*?	possible/likely
						P.Lond. 1549		*Pente Pediades*	likely

Bibliography

Abbott, Nabia. 1938. *The Ḳurrah Papyri from Aphrodito in the Oriental Institute*. Studies in Ancient Oriental Civilisation 15. Chicago: University of Chicago Press. [P.Qurra]

Bagnall, Roger S., and Bruce W. Frier. 1994. *The Demography of Roman Egypt*. Cambridge: Cambridge University Press.

Becker, Carl H. 1907. "Arabische Papyri des Aphroditofundes." In *Zeitschrift für Assyriologie und verwandte Gebiete* 20: 68–104.

Bell, Harold Idris. 1910. *The Aphrodito Papyri: With an Appendix of Coptic Papyri*. Edited by W.E. Crum. Volume 4 of *Greek Papyri in the British Museum: Catalogue, With Texts*. London: British Museum.

Bell, Harold Idris. 1911. "Translations of the Greek Aphrodito Papyri in the British Museum." In *Der Islam* 2: 269–283.

Broux, Yanne, and Sandra Coussement. 2014. "Double Names as Indicators of Social Stratification in Graeco-Roman Egypt." In *Identifiers and Identification Methods in the Ancient World*, edited by Mark Depauw and Sandra Coussement. Orientalia Lovaniensia Analecta 229. Leuven: Petters, 119–139.

Cameron, Averil, ed. 2003. *Fifty Years of Prosopography: The Later Roman Empire, Byzantium and Beyond*. Proceedings of the British Academy 118. Oxford: Oxford University Press.

Cromwell, Jennifer A. 2017. *Recording Village Life: A Coptic Scribe in Early Islamic Egypt*. Ann Arbor: University of Michigan Press.

de Jong, Janneke H.M. 2019. "A New Assessment From Eighth Century Aphrodito." In *Proceedings of the 28th International Congress of Papyrology: Barcelona 1–6 August 2016*, edited by Alberto Nodar and Sofía Torallas-Tovar. Publicacions de l'Abadia de Montserrat. Barcelona: Universitat Pompeu Fabra, 600–608.

de Jong, Janneke H.M. Forthcoming a. "A Concise Tax Assessment from Eighth Century Aphrodito." In *P.Würzb. II*, edited by Holger Essler.

de Jong, Janneke H.M. Forthcoming b. "People and Payments: Fragments of a Tax Assessment (?) from Eight Century Aphrodito."

Delattre, Alain, and Janneke H.M. de Jong. 2014. "Greek as a Minority Language." In *The Late Antique History of Early Islam: Muslims Among Christians and Jews in the East Mediterranean*, edited by Robert G. Hoyland. Studies in Late Antiquity and Early Islam 25. Princeton: Darwin, 37–62.

Green, Joel B. 1997. *The Gospel of Luke: The New International Commentary on the New Testament*. Grand Rapids: Eerdmans.

Grohmann, Adolf. 1952. *From the World of Arabic Papyri*. Royal Society of Historical Studies. Cairo: Al-Maaref Press. [P.World]

Marthot, Isabelle. 2013. *Un village égyptien et sa campagne: étude de la microtoponymie du territoire d'Aphroditê* (*VIe–VIIIe s.*). PhD diss., Paris, École Pratique des Hautes Études.

Morelli, Federico. 2001. *Documenti greci per la fiscalità e la amministrazione dell'Egitto arabo*. Corpus Papyrorum Raineri 22. Griechische Texte 15. Vienna: Hollinek.

Morimoto, Kosei. 1981. *The Fiscal Administration of Egypt in the Early Islamic Period*. Asian Historical Monographs 1. Kyoto: Dohosha.

Nave, Guy D. 2002. *The Role and Function of Repentance in Luke-Acts*. Academia Biblica 4. Leiden: Brill.

Papaconstantinou, Arietta. 2013. Review of Giovanni Roberto Ruffini, *A Prosopography of Byzantine Aphrodito*. In *Bryn Mawr Classical Review*, March 33. http://bmcr.brynmawr.edu/2013/2013-05-33.html (last access March 8, 2019)

Richter, Tonio S. 2010. "Language Choice in the Qurra Dossier." In *The Multilingual Experience in Egypt, from the Ptolemies to the Abbasids*, edited by Arietta Papaconstantinou. Farnham: Ashgate, 189–220.

Ruffini, Giovanni R. 2008. *Social Networks in Byzantine Egypt*. Cambridge and New York: Cambridge University Press.

Ruffini, Giovanni R. 2011. *A Prosopography of Byzantine Aphrodito*. American Studies in Papyrology 50. Durham, NC: American Society of Papyrologists.

Ruffini, Giovanni R. 2018. *Life in an Egyptian Village in Late Antiquity: Aphrodito Before and After the Islamic Conquest*. Cambridge and New York: Cambridge University Press.

Simonsen, Jørgen B. 1988. *Studies in the Genesis and Early Development of the Caliphal Taxation System, with Special References to Circumstances in the Arab Peninsula, Egypt, and Palestine*. Copenhagen: Akademisk Forlag.

Smythe, Dion. 2008. "Prosopography." In *The Oxford Handbook of Byzantine Studies*, edited by Elizabeth Jeffreys et al. Oxford: Oxford University Press, 176–181.

Verboven, Koenraad, Myriam Carlier, and Jan Dumolyn. 2007. "A Short Manual to the Art of Prosopography." In *Prosopography Approaches and Applications: A Handbook*, edited by Katharine S.B. Keats-Rohan. Prosopographica et genealogica 13. Oxford: University of Oxford Press, 35–70.

Wilfong, T.G. 2002. *Women of Jeme: Lives in a Coptic Town in Late Antique Egypt*. Ann Arbor: University of Michigan Press.

Zuckerman, Constantin. 2004. *Du village à l'Empire: autour du registre fiscal d'Aphroditô (525/526)*. Monographie [du] Centre de Recherche d'Histoire et civilisation de Byzance Monographies 16. Paris: Association des Amis du Centre d'Histoire et Civilisation de Byzance.

CHAPTER 2

Thinking in Arabic, Writing in Sogdian: Arabic-Sogdian Diplomatic Relations in the Early Eighth Century

Said Reza Huseini

Abstract

This paper discusses the relations between Arabs and Sogdians as reflected in some letters found in Mount Mugh in modern Tajikistan in 1933. It argues that their relations were more complex than the image given in the Arabic historical narratives. It maintains that both the Arabs and the Sogdians consciously used each other's languages in certain circumstances as a kind of diplomatic technique to support their requests, made effective by showing their awareness of their addressee's language and cultural elements and to highlight their own political and cultural values. Similarly, it shows that the Arabs and the Sogdians were flexible in adopting each other's administrative practices for official communication.

The study of Arab[1] military expansion in Sogdiana[2] is usually based on Arabic historical narratives such as al-Balādhurī's (d. 279/892) *Futūḥ al-buldān*[3] and

---

1 To complete this article, I have benefited from the help of several scholars in the field, especially Petra M. Sijpesteijn. She kindly reviewed this paper and gave important comments that helped me to have a better understanding of the Arabic documents. Thanks to Werner Diem for his help with the correction of my translation of the Arabic document. I am grateful to Ilya Yakubovich, who kindly sent me his copy of Kračkovskij's Russian article on the Arabic letter and his valuable comments on the Sogdian one. Thanks to Flora Roberts for helping me with reading the relevant Russian articles and also thanks to Ankita Hoellen for her review and useful suggestions. I am grateful to Jonathan Lee for his precise review of this paper and his comments, especially on the importance of these documents in understanding the process of the political, cultural, and ideological transition in early eighth-century Sogdiana. For the period under study, the term "Arab" seems to have been already formed as an identity; see Webb 2016: 140–151; Webb 2018.

2 I use "Sogdiana" instead of the Arabic "Mā warāʾ al-Nahr" and its translation "Transoxiana," as both terms only refer to geographical regions beyond the Oxus River, while "Sogdiana" covers the geography, languages, cultures, and people of that region. Moreover, Sogdian documents called this region *Sogd*; hence in this article this indigenous and historic designation is preferred to what are essentially terms imposed by foreigners.

3 Al-Balādhurī 2000.

 | DOI:10.1163/9789004527874_004

al-Ṭabarī's (d. 310/923) *Tārīkh al-rusul wa-l-mulūk*,[4] both compiled during the early Abbasid period. These narratives highlight Arab military triumphs over the Sogdians but engage less with their relations beyond the battlefields. However, a number of Sogdian documents and an Arabic letter (P.Kratchkovski) discovered from Mount Mugh in modern Tajikistan in 1933 show that relations between Arabs and Sogdians were more complex than the image given in the Arabic historical narratives.[5]

These documents are highly significant, as they come from the archive of Dēwāshtīč (d. 721), the Sogdian ruler of Panjikant and the last king of Sogdiana, whose diplomatic relations with the Arabs are the subject of this paper. The themes of these documents vary from administrative, economic, and legal documents to private letters. They are important from both a linguistic and historical perspective. Linguistically, they present original Sogdian compositions produced in Sogdiana, and historically they reflect the sociopolitical situation during the Arab conquest of Sogdiana in the early eighth century.[6]

The Sogdian Mount Mugh documents have already received scholarly attention. Similarly, the Sogdian king Dēwāshtīč is a well-known historical character.[7] The Sogdian documents were translated and published in Russian by Vladimir Aaronovich Livshits in 1962, then in a revised edition translated into English in 2015. However, this double translation resulted in a number of errors, which were recently discussed and corrected by Ilya Yakubovich.[8]

In contrast, the Arabic letter from Mount Mugh, known as P.Kratchkovski, has been greatly studied, but not really understood, and its relation to the Sogdian letters, particularly Mount Mugh Document 1.I. has been neglected. The present paper discusses these two letters and argues that both the Arabs and the Sogdians consciously used each other's languages in certain circumstances as a kind of diplomatic technique to support their requests, make them effective by showing their awareness of their addressee's language and cultural elements, or to highlight their political and cultural values.

4 Al-Ṭabarī 1960–1977. Along with the Arabic text, the Persian translation (al-Ṭabarī 1375/1996) was also used for this paper.

5 Livshits 2015.

6 Livshits 2015; reviewed by Yakubovich 2017. See also Yakubovich 2002: 232.

7 Several work are written in Russian, French, English, and Persian on Dēwāshtīč; Marshak 1994 has provided a good list of readings. In today's Tajikistan, Dēwāshtīč is considered a national hero and a statue has been made in Panjikant, in Tajikistan, in his honor.

8 Yakubovich 2017: 413–426; see also Yakubovich 2002.

1 The Arabic Letter (P.Kratchkovski)

The Arabic letter was found in 1933 at the fortress of Mount Mugh in the Zarafshan valley during an excavation led by Alexandr Arnoldovich Freiman. It was first published by V.A. Kračkovskaja and Ignatij J. Kračkovskij in 1934, with some discussion about its chronology and historical context, but without reference to its significance in Arab-Sogdian diplomatic relations.[9]

The letter is written with black ink on leather by an anonymous scribe. It is 26 cm high × 19 cm wide. Apart from some lines, the letter is readable. It was issued by Dēwāshtīč, the Sogdian ruler of Panjikant, to al-Jarrāḥ b. ʿAbd Allāh al-Ḥakamī, the *amīr* of Khurasan in 99–101/718–719. In the letter Dēwāshtīč asks the Arab *amīr* to return Ṭarkhūn's sons, who were kept by the Arabs. Ṭarkhūn was an ally of Dēwāshtīč.

The Arabic text reads as follows:

١ بسم الله الرحمن الرحيم
٢ للامير الجراح بن عبد الله من مولاه ديوا
٣ ستى السلم عليك ايها الامير
٤ ورحمت الله فانى احمد اليك
٥ الله الذى لا اله الا هو
٦ اما بعد .... اصلح الله الامير وامتع
٧ به فانى (كتبت اذكر/انهى)
٨ للامير حاجتى وحاجة ابنى طرخون وان الا
٩ مير امتع الله به ذكر ابني طرخون بخير
١٠ فان را الامير من الراى ان يكتب
١١ الى سليمان ابن ابى السرى فيبعث بهما الى الامير
١٢ فليفعل او يامر لى الامير بدابة من دواب
١٣ البريد فابعث عليها غلامى يات بهما
١٤ الامير فان الله جعل قدم الامير لاهل
١٥ المط...... غياث ورحمة
١٦ اسل الله لـ.....والسلم عليك ايها الامير ورحمت الله

9 Kračkovskaya and Kračkovskij 1934/1955; Kračkovskij 1946/1955.

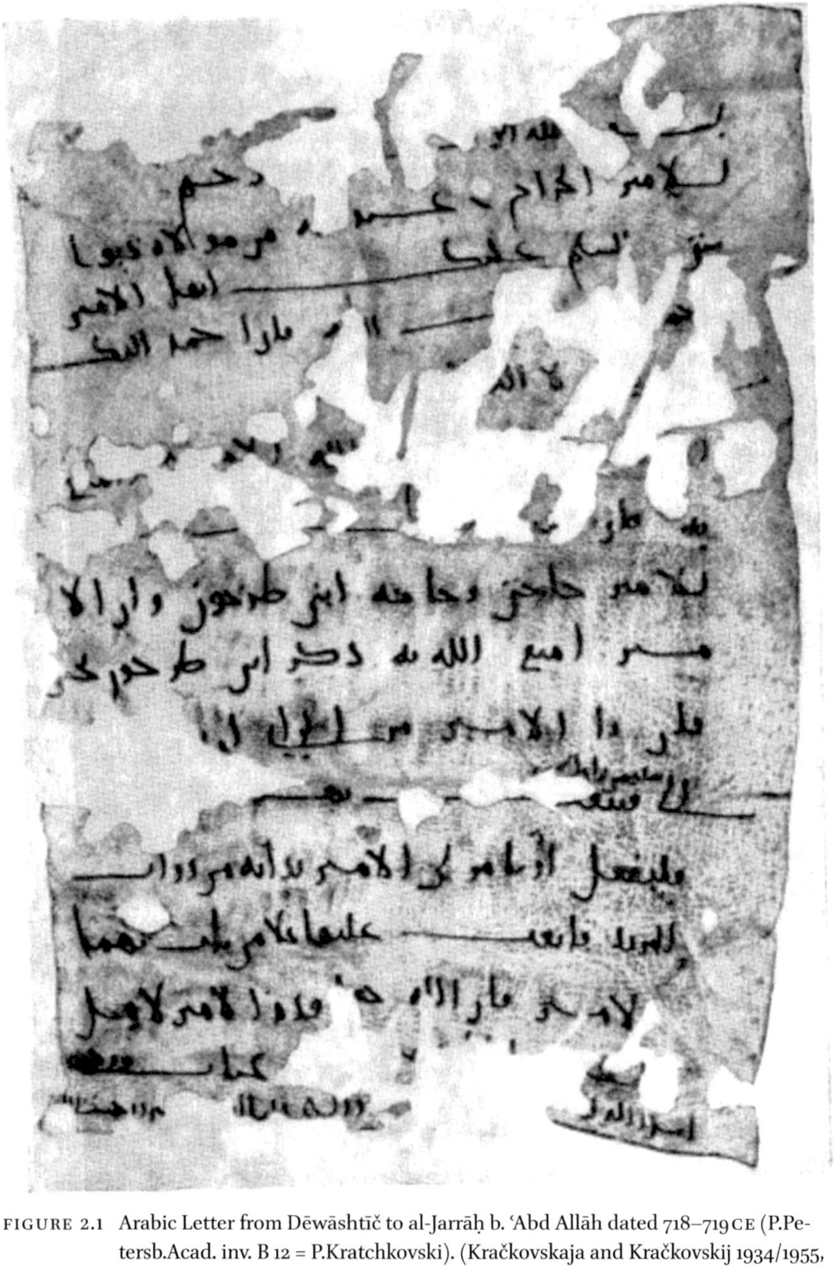

FIGURE 2.1 Arabic Letter from Dēwāshtīč to al-Jarrāḥ b. ʿAbd Allāh dated 718–719 CE (P.Petersb.Acad. inv. B 12 = P.Kratchkovski). (Kračkovskaja and Kračkovskij 1934/1955, plate)
© HERMITAGE

(1) In the name of God, the Merciful and the Compassionate!
(2) To the *amīr* al-Jarrāḥ b. ʿAbd Allāh, from his *mawlā* Dīwāstī
(3) Peace be upon you, O *amīr*,
(4) and God's mercy. I praise for your sake to
(5) God, besides Whom there is no (other) God.

(6) Further, [...], may God keep the *amīr*'s behaviors correct and may
(7) he grant enjoyment through Him
(8) [I wrote to the *amīr* about] my need and the need of the two sons of Ṭarkhūn. And that
(9) the *amīr*, may God grant him enjoyment, remembers the two sons of Ṭarkhūn well.
(10) If the *amīr* sees fit, to write
(11) to Sulaymān b. Abī al-Surī to send the two of them to the *amīr*,
(12) then he (the *amīr*) should do so or the *amīr* should order for a horse from the horses
(13) of the courier, and I will send my servant on it to bring the two of them to the *amīr*.
(14) For God made the *amīr*'s arrival to the people
(15) of ʾLM ... a bounty and mercy
(16) I ask God for [...] Peace be upon you, O *amīr* and God's mercy.

Using Eva Mira Grob's analysis of letters consisting of "building-blocks," with each block containing units, "whose boundaries to other units are marked," we can analyze this letter in detail.[10] Structurally, the letter follows the model of similar letters from the same period as preserved on papyrus from Egypt[11] and paper documents from Sanjar Shāh close to Mount Mugh.[12] The opening, address, greeting, and blessing follow the same formulary structure, and Kračkovskij suggests that the word *ʾilayka*, "for your sake," in the blessing of line 4 is unique to this letter.[13] However, this type of blessing is commonly used in Arabic letters from this period when addressed to Muslims, which is the case here.[14] Geoffrey Khan, who argues that the same epistolary formula appears in documents from Egypt and Khurasan in the Umayyad period, also suggests that "the Arabs brought with them to the conquered territories their own letter

10 Grob 2010: 25.
11 Khan 2008: 890.
12 Haim, Shenkar, and Kurbanov 2016.
13 Kračkovskaja and Kračkovskij 1934/1955: 78–82.
14 Diem 2008: 856.

formulae and did not take them from the local practices in the various places where they settled."[15] The Sogdian Arabic letter therefore provides further confirmation of Khan's assertion.

Interestingly, there are some elements that are unique to this letter and that differ from other Arabic documents. To understand them, an analysis of the letter from the perspectives of linguistic strata and the hierarchical use of languages is required.

First, close attention should be paid to the language of this letter. It has been issued in Arabic by the Sogdian ruler to the Arab governor. This can be assumed to be an example of language accommodation and an example of superstratum influence, in which the language of the superior is adopted by the inferior as a result of political or economic dominance.[16] Indeed, here Dēwāshtīč uses Arabic—the language of his superior, the *amīr*—as he describes himself in the letter as being on a lower status as *mawlā*. Posing as a supplicant, moreover, he also puts himself in an inferior status. On the other hand, by addressing the Arab *amīr* in Arabic, Dēwāshtīč increases his chances of securing his request for the return of Ṭarkhūn's sons.

Second, by choosing Arabic, Dēwāshtīč projects that he is prepared for convergence through communication. Linguistically, convergence means that two languages structurally resemble one another as a result of language contact. Usually, some elements of the superior's language are borrowed by the inferior under certain economic or political circumstances.[17] Politically, Dēwāshtīč's convergence possibly points to his wish for collaboration and establishing good relations with the *amīr*—something for which we also have evidence from other sources.[18]

Another unique feature of this communication is that, unlike most of the Arabic letters from this period, this letter starts with *li-l amīr* instead of *ilā al-amīr* and repeats *al-amīr* in the letter eleven times.[19] In addition, a shorter form

15 Khan 2008: 890–891.

16 Crystal 2008: 465.

17 Pearce 2007: 3; Crowley and Bowern 2010: 269–272.

18 A certain *mrw'n* (Marwān) mentioned in document A-14:31 carried letters from Fatūfarn to Dēwāshtīč; al-Ṭabarī 1375/1996: 9:4021. Though the name is Arabic, the person may have been a convert; see Smirnova 1970: 214–223; Lurje 2008: 42; Livshits 2015: 65–68. Azarpay (1981: 66) suggests that this good relation is reflected even in Sogdian paintings from Panjikant.

19 The most similar letter to our case in terms of opening is P.DonnerFragments 3, an Arabic letter from Egypt dated 742 and written to the governor al-Qāsim b. ʿUbayd Allāh. Though it begins with *li-l amīr* and has the same blessing formulae, it does not repeat *al-amīr*; Donner 2016: 37. Recently, Petra M. Sijpesteijn discussed an unpublished petition written

of the blessing *wa-raḥmatu llāhi* plus the address *ʾayyuhā l-amīr* are added to the greeting formulae, which is absent in contemporary letters from Egypt.[20] Could this be an influence from Sogdian? A close reading of other Sogdian documents from the Mount Mugh collection suggests that this is the case. For instance, the Sogdian Mount Mugh Document B-10 repeats the Sogdian terms *xuw* and βγ, both meaning "lord," 13 times. Also, Mount Mugh Document Nov-2 repeats these words in almost every line.[21] Both of these letters are written to Dēwāshtīč by his local rulers and appointed officials. If we assume that Dēwāshtīč introduced this Sogdian element into the Arabic letter, then it could be counted as an example of substratum influence. From a sociolinguistic point of view, this happens "when a language is imposed on a community, as a result of political or economic superiority," and as a consequence, it incorporates some characteristics from the inferior language.[22]

The analysis above raises the question as to whether Dēwāshtīč's action is a conscious linguistic strategy. In the letter, Dēwāshtīč asks for the return of Ṭarkhūn's sons. Ṭarkhūn was the ruler of Samarqand in 709–710.[23] He had concluded a treaty with the Arab general Qutayba b. Muslim al-Bahīlī (d. 96/715), which included the payment of an annual tribute.[24] The Sogdian elites of Samarqand, unsatisfied with this arrangement, organized a coup lead by Ḡūrak and killed Ṭarkhūn, and so Ḡūrak became the ruler of Samarqand.[25] This event indicates the degree to which powerful Sogdian nobility could change the situation at their will. Subsequently, Qutayba marched towards Samarqand to avenge Ṭarkhūn. He was assisted by troops sent by the rulers of Bukhara, Khwarezm, and perhaps Dēwāshtīč from Panjikant. In a letter sent to the Chinese emperor Xuánzōng (d. 762) six years later in 718–719, Ḡūrak explained that a large Arab army besieged the city and put pressure on the city by dig-

on papyrus (P.Vind.inv. A.P. 669) dated to the third/ninth century that uses the title *amīr* repeatedly. In the letter a widow asks the *amīr* for help, and repetition of *amīr* as part of a blessing or separately creates a needy tone to secure the request. A parallel pattern can be seen in Bactrian document *cq*, dated 465 CE from Rob, in which a person addresses a higher official to help him. These letters suggest that the more the sender is in need, the humbler the language used; Sims-Williams 2007: 96–97.

20 Sijpesteijn 2013: 299–452.

21 Livshits 2015: 85–87; 82–85.

22 Crystal 2008: 463–464.

23 Here, Ṭarkhūn is a personal name and not the title Ṭarkhān, a military rank, also mentioned in the Bactrian document; Sims-Williams 2001: 134–135; Livshits 2015: 53. Al-Ṭabarī (1375/1996: 9: 3825–3828) mentions Ṭarkhūn as king of Sogd and Nizak Ṭarkhān as a general.

24 Al-Ṭabarī 1375/1996: 9: 3825.

25 Al-Ṭabarī 1375/1996: 9: 3846.

ging trenches and using battering rams.[26] Fragments of wall paintings from Dēwāshtīč's palace at Panjikant show that he had access to wheeled battering rams and perhaps offered them to Qutayba for the siege of Samarqand.[27]

Ṭarkhūn and Dēwāshtīč were allies, while Dēwāshtīč considered Ḡūrak a usurper and opposed him by helping the Arabs.[28] Ḡūrak, faced with defeat, was forced to make a peace treaty and to accept Qutayba's conditions. In return, Qutayba recognized him as king of Samarqand. It is not known if Ṭarkhūn's two young sons were taken under the protection of Dēwāshtīč, who was ruler of Panjikant at this time, or kept by the Arabs in Samarqand.[29] So far, apart from this letter, there is no other evidence to explain who had Ṭarkhūn's sons at that time. Six or seven years later, when Dēwāshtīč issued this Arabic letter, Qutayba was already dead, but Ḡūrak was still king of Samarqand. Knowing the conditions in Samarqand, Dēwāshtīč did not want to see Ṭarkhūn's sons separated from himself—possibly he had ulterior motives since his guardianship of Ṭarkhūn's sons would have increased his chances for the throne of Samarqand.[30] However, in the letter, Dēwāshtīč asks the *amīr* al-Jarrāḥ to write to Sulaymān b. Abī al-Surī indicating that he knew where and who kept the sons, but he himself did not have access to them. By asking the *amīr* to intervene, Dēwāshtīč may have known that the *amīr* would send the sons to him once he received them, particularly after he clearly requested them, and the *amīr* remembered them well.

Indeed, Dēwāshtīč's linguistic and political strategies as displayed in the Arabic letter stress that Dēwāshtīč wanted to secure control of Ṭarkhūn's sons. The use of the Arabic language and his self-presentation as a *mawlā* in the service of the *amīr* are therefore clever diplomatic ploys to support his request. Dēwāshtīč even proposes to send a servant to retrieve the children if that makes this transaction easier. Ilya Yakubovich and Pavel Lurje suggest that the Arabic language used in the letter implies that Dēwāshtīč declared himself a Muslim.[31] However, using the Arabic language, Islamic terminology, and a self-presentation as a *mawlā* are not sufficient reasons to assume he had converted. Rather, Dēwāshtīč uses these phrases not necessarily from a sense of piety or because he is a Muslim but simply because he was familiar with the standard form of an Arabic letter written to an Arab official widely used in the second–

26 Livshits 2015: 49.
27 Azarpay 1981: 65.
28 Grenet and de la Vaissière 2002: 156–157.
29 Marshak 1994.
30 Yakubovich 2002: 245.
31 Yakubovich 2002: 245; Lurje 2008: 31.

third/eighth–ninth centuries, yet he modified the form of the letter specifically for his own purpose.

Likewise, the letter does not prove that Arabic had become the official language in Sogdiana. Indeed, all other Mount Mugh documents are written in Sogdian. Arabic was one language among others used by a multilingual administration, in which bilingual people also worked in the service of the Sogdian ruler. This was simply out of a need to rule over a large multilingual population and was very practical. There was no need to change this by imposing an imperial (and foreign) language.

The discovery of P.Kratchkovski at Mount Mugh raises another important question. It was found as part of Dēwāshtīč's archive, or possibly part of his official administration. Thus, this letter had not been sent to the *amīr*. Kračkovskij suggests that either there were two letters, one of which was kept by Dēwāshtīč, or that it had not been sent off because al-Jarrāḥ had been summoned from Khurasan to Iraq before the letter could be sent.[32] So far, no Arabic document in duplicate has been found from the region. Furthermore, al-Jarrāḥ's period of governorship over Khurasan lasted only 17 months, and he spent most of his time in Marw, which is far from Sogdiana.[33] Hence, the second suggestion may be assumed possible unless new evidence appears.

2 The Sogdian Letter (Mount Mugh Document 1.1)

The second letter I want to discuss is written in Sogdian and known as Mount Mugh Document 1.1. It was the first Sogdian document found on Mount Mugh—by local farmers in the spring of 1932. After its discovery it was passed from hand to hand among villagers for a year. It eventually came to the attention of Soviet scholars who began systematic excavations at Mount Mugh in 1933. Another 90 documents and other materials were discovered during the excavation. Mount Mugh Document 1.1 was handed over to a local official in 1933 and sent to Dushanbe, but shortly after that it disappeared and has remained lost up to the present. The photograph of the letter sent to Leningrad that Freiman used for his study was also lost. Fortunately, another photograph of this unique document survived, and the document was later identified by Livshits as an authentic Sogdian document and published by him in 1962.[34]

32 Kračkovskaya and Kračkovskij 1934/1955: 70.
33 Shaban 1970: 85–87; Yakubovich 2002: 246.
34 Yakubovich 2002: 232; Livshits 2015: 88–92.

Though this unique document has already been read and interpreted by several scholars, it remains the subject of debate. Recently, Ilya Yakubovich produced a new translation that settled some of the problems faced by earlier scholars: he explained its difficulties and gave better historical context.[35] My analysis and interpretation of the letter is based on his new reading and translation.

The letter is written with black ink on pale gray Chinese silk paper that is 29.8 high × 28.2 cm wide. The document has been folded four times, probably to put it in a bag carried by a courier. The letter was sent by ʿAbd al-Raḥmān b. Ṣubḥ, an important administrator who worked with Saʿīd b. ʿAbd al-ʿAzīz, *amīr* of Khurasan in 102/721. It addresses Dēwāshtīč and speaks about the *amīr*'s satisfaction with him. Then it introduces two persons, one is a Zoroastrian priest (*βγnptw*), whom Dēwāshtīč knows and who carries the *amīr*'s letter and an additional verbal message to Dēwāshtīč. ʿAbd al-Raḥmān continues and says that the *amīr* praised Dēwāshtīč's letters and asks Dēwāshtīč to send him similar letters. At the end he asks Dēwāshtīč not to delay in executing the *amīr*'s orders otherwise quite different orders will come, and they may not be friendly.

The letter reads as follows:

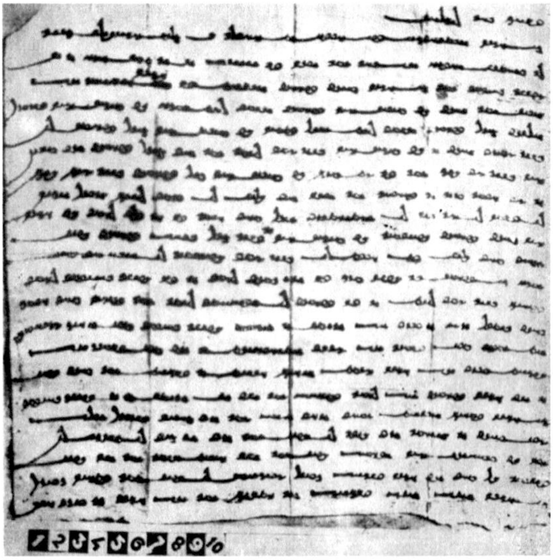

FIGURE 2.2 Document 1.I, Letter to Dēwāshtīč. Dated to 721 C.E.
LIVSHITS 2015: 90

35 Yakubovich 2002.

(1) *prnʾm βγy δʾmδnʾk*
(2) *MN xmyr ʾʾβtrxwmʾn pwn swpx ʾt sγwδy-k MLKʾ smʾrknδc MRʾY*
(3) *δy-wʾštyc ʾspʾs ZKn βγy rty nwkr py-ʾʾnʾkh ZK ny-z-tk ʾʾys ZY ZK*
(4) *kwrcy βγnptw rty MN xmyr wʾnʾkw pwstkw ʾʾβʾrnt pr xmyr xwsʾnty-ʾkh*
(5) *cʾβʾk rty cʾnkw kw tʾβvk sʾr pwstkw ʾkrtw δʾrt rtms kw tʾmʾk sʾr prywy-δ*
(6) *ʾnδykw mʾyδ pwstk(w) ʾkrtw δʾrt rtkδ ptsʾr kw tʾβʾk sʾr mʾyδ pwstk Lʾ*
(7) *βrʾy-štʾyw cʾnkw ZY kw tʾmʾk sʾr βrʾy-štw δʾrty rty ʾzw mʾyδ pwstkw ʾkw tʾβʾk*
(8) *sʾr βrʾy-šw kʾm rty py-št tym kw tʾβvk sʾr wyδ pwstkw βrʾy-šʾm kʾm*
(9) *ZY šw xwty wy-ny ZY ptγwšy rty nwkr ʾzw kδʾc Lʾ wytw δʾrm cywyδ nʾmʾk*
(10) *Lʾ prtr Lʾ šy-ʾ_tr Lʾ ʾstʾrstryw rtkδ tγw xwty pr xy-pδw δstw kw xmyr*
(11) *sʾr wʾnkw pwstkw kwnʾwtʾy kw tʾmʾk sʾr ZY prʾy-myδ βrγh pwstkw kwnʾ*
(12) *rtšw tγw kδʾc wʾxwpt Lʾ βrʾy-štw kwnʾwtʾy Lʾ ʾnβx-tw kwnʾ*
(13) *rtms MN pwstk βy-kpʾr tym pr ny-z-ytkw δstw ZY pr kwrcy βγnptw δstw*
(14) *ptγʾm βrʾy-štw δʾrt ZY pr pwstkw Lʾ npʾxtw δʾrty rty ptsʾr tγw xšwty*
(15) *wʾnkw βrtpδ ʾy-š ZY wβy-w ZNH ny-z-tk ZY ZNH kwrcy βγnptw twʾ ʾz-γʾm*
šyrxwz-ʾkt
(16) *ʾnt rtp(rw) twʾ prtry-ʾkh šyr-rw ʾntʾxwsʾkt ZY ZKw twʾ prtry-ʾkh*
(17) *kʾmʾnt wβyw ZKn xmyr sytt ʾzγʾm xyʾ_rt ʾt prmʾnt rty wʾnkw kwnʾ*
(18) *ZY ZKw xmyr pwstkw ZNH δsty ptcxš rty ʾcw ZK nyztk ZY ZK kwrcy βγnptw*
(19) *MN xmyr ptγʾm ʾʾβrʾnt rtšw nyxw nγʾwš rty ʾyw mγwnw prywyδ rʾδh*
(20) *šwʾ wʾnkw ZY cnʾγty ʾy-w knpy Lʾ kwnʾ rty ʾyw ʾz-mnw Lʾ βrkyn Lʾ*
(21) *nwr kw wtʾšʾkʾ sʾr ʾpstnh kwnʾ rty ʾcw sʾcʾt ʾkrty rty nwr kwnʾ*
(22) *pʾrwty kδ tγw ZKw xmyr prmʾnh ywnyδ šwʾmʾntk Lʾ kwnʾ rty ptsʾr y-wnyδ*
(23) *MN xmyr ʾnyh ʾnyh prmʾnh ʾʾy-stkʾm rty ZKh xmyr ZY wz-y-z γrβ*

(1) In the name of God, the Creator.
(2–3) From the *amīr* ʿAbd al-Raḥmān b. Ṣubḥ to Dēwāshtīč, the king of Sogdiana and the ruler of Samarqand.
(3) Praise be to God!
(3–5) Now (?), yesterday there came Nižtak and the priest Kurči, and they brought from the *amīr* a letter about the *amīr*'s satisfaction with you.
(5–6) When he wrote a letter to you, he also wrote this letter to me in the same terms.
(6–8) If, then, he had not sent this letter to you, as he had sent it to me, I would [still] have sent this [present] letter to you.
(8–9) But [now] I shall also send that letter [from the *amīr*] to you, that you may see and hear it.
(9–10) Now, I have never seen [a letter that would be] better, or finer or more sublime (?) than that letter.

(10–11) And if you write such a letter to the *amīr* yourself, with your own hand, then write also a letter to me in the same way.

(12) You would never be able to send it so well [written], you will not be able to articulate [so well your thoughts]!

(13–14) Also, in addition to the letter, he sent you a message through Nižtak and the priest Kurči and did not write it in the letter.

(14–17) But then you know yourself that, on the one hand, Nižtak and the priest Kurči are your true friends, caring much for your well-being (and they want your well-being) and, on the other hand, they are true assistants and faithful [servants] of the *amīr* Saʿīd.

(19–20) Follow it in everything, so as not to fall short [of your obligations] at all.

(20–21) Do not waste time and do not delay from today to tomorrow, but do today what needs to be done.

(22–23) Because if you do not carry out the *amīr*'s order immediately, then immediately a very different order will come from the *amīr*, and the *amīr* and *wzyz* much ....[36]

At first look, this letter compares very well with other contemporary Sogdian documents. However, it includes unique elements that vary from standard Sogdian official letters. These differences are unique linguistic elements that, on the one hand, show linguistic interaction between the two population groups and, on the other hand, point to a similar use of language that we encountered in the Arabic letter. I will return to that, but first I will describe what features stand out.

The letter opens with the formulae *prn'm βγy δ'mδn'k*, "In the Name of God the Creator," in the first line above the rest of the text. This is not a common Sogdian formula and layout, but certainly a variant on the Arabic *basmala*.[37] The suggestion that this is a Sogdian innovation under Arabic (Islamic) influence can be attested by comparing it with other documents from the eighth century. Among the Middle Persian documents found from the Qom region (in the northern part of present-day Iran), document Berk. 187 has the opening formula *pad nām ī yazd ī kardakkar*, "In the name of God who is powerful," although not on a separate line. Using *yazd* instead of *yazdān* is a reference to one God instead of Gods and can be interpreted as a tendency towards monotheism. The fact that the sender of this letter was inspector of the *mazgitān*,

36 Yakubovich 2002: 234–235. I have modified Arabic names and titles mentioned in his translation, for instance, changing *Emir* to *amīr*.

37 Yakubovich 2002: 235.

"mosques," makes clear that this opening formula was the Middle Persian equivalent to the Arabic *basmala*.[38] Further Arabic influence can be seen in another Middle Persian letter written on papyrus, perhaps in Egypt in the second half of the seventh or even the first half of the eighth century. Dieter Weber, who published this letter in 2005 and recently has revised it, suggests that the letter was written by a Muslim merchant to his brother. It opens with *pad nām ī yazd*, "In the name of God," on a separate line above the rest of the text and refers to the term *ahlaw*, "righteous," suggesting the sender's conversion to Islam.[39] The thesis of the Arabic influence on Middle Persian is also supported by the fact that the earlier Middle Persian documents discovered in the Qom region do not have this opening formula. These documents were written by local administrators addressing local figures.[40] Likewise, in the Bactrian letter (document Y. 771/2, Kadagstan) πιδο ναμο ειζιδασο, "In the name of God," is clearly a translation of the *basmala*, since no other preserved Bactrian document has a similar opening formula.[41] Similarly, two Judeo-Persian documents from Khotan open with *pa nām Ized Khuda*, "In the name of God the Lord."[42]

The letter continues with *MN xmyr ʾʾβtrxwmʾn pwn swpx*, "from the *amīr* ʿAbd al-Raḥmān b. Ṣubḥ," *ʾt sγwδy-k MLKʾ smʾrknδc MRʾY δy-wʾštyc*, "to Dēwāshtīč, king of Sogdiana and ruler of Samarqand." Though it is written in Sogdian, the letter follows the common Arabic construction *min … ilā …*, "from so-and-so," used in letters from this period, and which Grob calls the internal address. This internal address indicates the relation between the sender and the addressee, namely from a superior to an inferior. Yakubovich suggested that a Sogdian influence could be seen in *ʾβtrxwmʾn*, as there is a Sogdian personal name ending in *-xwmʾn*, like *βrxwmʾn*, the king of Samarqand in the middle of the seventh century CE.[43] The double *aleph* (ʾʾ) in *ʾʾβtrxwmʾn* is used for the Arabic *ʿayn* and the *x* for the Arabic *ḥāʾ*.[44]

Interestingly, in the name itself we can see Arabic influence. The name is written with *pwn*, which means "son of," an equivalent for Arabic *bin* in between the *amīr*'s name and that of his father. Lurje argued that the *w* in *pwn* "may have

38 I am thankful to Dieter Weber who helped me to understand the relevant Middle Persian documents. Weber 2008: 219; Weber 2020: 144.

39 Weber 2005: 225–231

40 Weber 2020: 143–144.

41 Sims-Williams 2001: 144–145.

42 First document published in Margoliouth 1903, with some misinterpretation, particularly the misreading of the Persian *Ized* for Arabic *Yazīd*; republished with new readings by Salemann 1904. The second document was published by Zhan and Guang 2008.

43 Yakubovich 2002: 236.

44 Lurje 2008: 37.

resulted from a regressive metathesis of *ū* in *bnū* 'son' resulting in *bun*, or from the rule whereby a vowel between *p* and any dental is articulated as *u*."[45] This constitutes a breakaway from Sogdian practice, where the name is followed by the father's name and only then by the word son.

The letter includes *ʾspʾs ZKn βγy*, "Praise be to God," the Sogdian equivalent of the Arabic *al-ḥamdu li-llāh*.[46] This is another element that is unique to this Sogdian letter. It is obviously due to an Arabic influence. In my view, it was consciously added to emphasize the Muslim identity of the sender, otherwise it would have been possible to simply add some common Sogdian honorific phrases.

The main text also includes some Arabizations. Instead of the common Sogdian term *xuw*, "Lord," we find the term *xmyr* repeated nine times. *Xmyr* is certainly the Sogdian form of the Arabic *amīr*, though it is not known how or why *x* was used to write *amīr*. Lurje suggests that it could be that it is under the influence of the frequency of *x* in Sogdians terms for rulers, as in *xuw*, *xutaw*, and *ixshid*,[47] but this is not very convincing. In any case, *xmyr* can be regarded as an Arabic loanword in Sogdian,[48] and the rest of them are not loanwords but, as we have discussed, a conscious usage of Arabic for specific aims in certain situations. Still, compared to other Sogdian letters, the references to "lord" are fewer than what would be expected. Also, we find no equivalent to the blessings or greetings in Arabic letters that generally follow the mention of the addressee, when he/she is of a higher rank than the addressee. Another striking element is the use of the *ʾt*, "to [you]," to address Dēwāshtīč. In Sogdian, this is a very impolite form of addressing the king of Sogd. Sogdian authors would typically have used some honorifics and a polite form of address.[49]

Why then did ʿAbd al-Raḥmān write his letter in this way, using Sogdian and the expressions influenced by Arabic discussed above? Linguistically, the use of Arabic elements in this Sogdian letter could be explained as a case of style shifting, but more likely the change has a cultural dimension, namely the difference of religions and the relation between the sender and the addressee.[50] Equally

45 Lurje 2008: 37.

46 Yakubovich (2002: 236) agrees that this phrase is the equivalent of the Arabic *al-ḥamdu li-llāh*, but nevertheless considers it an unsettled issue.

47 Lurje 2008: 49–50.

48 Yakubovich 2002: 50.

49 An example can be seen in Mountain Mugh Document A-14 in which Dēwāshtīč is addressed as *ʾt βγw xwβw RBch ʾnwth sγwδy-ʾnk* MLK-ʾ *smr-knδc* MRY *δy-wʾštyc*, "to the lord and sovereign, the great support, the king of Sogd and sovereign of Samarqand Dēwāshtīč"; Livshits 2015: 56–67.

50 Pearce 2007: 3.

important is the fact that the letter is written in Sogdian, yet it does not follow the Sogdian letter structure completely. Thus, it assumes a kind of linguistic divergence. While writing in the language of the addressee, specific Arabic elements were added to highlight the cultural, religious, and political differences between the Arab sender and the Sogdian addressee. Using the Sogdian language shows (as in the Arabic letter discussed above) a sign of respect to the Sogdian addressee and perhaps a hierarchical dependency, while the Arabic and Islamic elements, as well as the informal way of addressing the Sogdian king, suggests that ʿAbd al-Raḥmān wanted to make a point about his religion and position.

The layout, structure, and the fine handwriting suggest that the letter was written by a professional scribe trained in the Sogdian chancery. It is not known if the scribe translated an Arabic letter or wrote down an oral message he had received. The translation of the Arabic phrases into Sogdian indicate that whoever did this understood their meaning well. Yakubovich claims that the writer was a sympathetic Arab official, but he offers no evidence or further explanation.[51] In any case, this letter suggests that after the Arab conquest, the local administrators remained in place working for the new masters, as was the case in other places, most notably Egypt and Sasanian Iran.[52]

A contextual analysis of the second letter highlights how the Arab-Sogdian relations had changed in comparison to the first letter. ʿAbd al-Raḥmān's choice of the Sogdian language for this letter indicates Dēwāshtīč's importance for the Arabs. He is recognized as king of Sogd and sovereign of Samarqand[53] and not described as *mawlā*. The Sogdian letter was issued during the governorship of Saʿīd b. ʿAbd al-ʿAzīz.[54] Saʿīd was known as Khuzayna, "Mistress," for his soft treatment of non-Arabs. This supports the idea that this letter shows him recognizing the superior position of the Sogdian king.[55] In the letter ʿAbd al-Raḥmān writes that the *amīr* praised Dēwāshtīč for the well-crafted letters he has been sending him. In fact, the *amīr* had never seen letters better composed, finer, or more sublime than those of Dēwāshtīč. Unfortunately, none of these letters appear to have survived, and we cannot know whether this was also an appreciation of the Arabic used by Dēwāshtīč's administration.[56]

51 Yakubovich 2002: 231; in a personal communication, however, Yakubovich added that the letter was dictated rather than actually written by an Arab official.

52 Sijpesteijn 2013: 49–81.

53 Grenet and de la Vaissière 2002: 156–157; Yakubovich 2002: 247.

54 Kennedy 2001: 46.

55 Al-Ṭabarī 1375/1996: 9: 4013–4014.

56 The letter suggests that Dēwāshtīč was not able to write a flattering letter to the *amīr*

Generally, the tone of the letter is friendly, with the *amīr* Saʿīd b. ʿAbd al-ʿAzīz expressing his "satisfaction" with Dēwāshtīč. Yakubovich suggests that this satisfaction is the key to understanding the whole letter, as it was written with good intentions.[57] However, ʿAbd al-Raḥmān also implies his dissatisfaction with Dēwāshtīč because the latter has been contacting the *amīr* without going through him. Whether officially recognized or not, ʿAbd al-Raḥmān considered himself the *amīr*'s advisor and wanted to be recognized by Dēwāshtīč and be kept informed about his relation with the *amīr*.[58] In the letter, he calls himself the *amīr*, but certainly he was not the actual *amīr* of Khurasan, and Dēwāshtīč must have been aware of this. Dēwāshtīč consciously ignored him, as he wanted to depict himself as equal to the Arab *amīr* of Khurasan, and hence not required to communicate with an inferior intermediary. ʿAbd al-Raḥmān further tells Dēwāshtīč to read the *amīr*'s letter and to listen to the verbal message that the messenger delivers to him. At the end, he politely warns Dēwāshtīč not to delay in following the *amīr*'s orders lest quite different and less amicable orders soon follow.

The mixed respect and superiority that ʿAbd al-Raḥmān displays in this letter can be explained in several ways. Perhaps the Arabs recognized Dēwāshtīč as a powerful king whom they had to negotiate with—a diplomatic technique to express a more subtle and complicated relationship. At this time Sogdiana was under pressure by the Turks, and Dēwāshtīč might possibly have united with the Turks to dominate Sogdiana.[59] Yakubovich suggests that this letter was written in order to convince Dēwāshtīč to remain on good terms with the Arabs and to keep him on their side and that, for this reason, the Arabs generously called him "king of Sogdiana" and were willing to cooperate. Conversely, it might have been the case that ʿAbd al-Raḥmān's attempt to flatter and establish personal contact with Dēwāshtīč shows that the Arabs were keen to engage in local politics.[60]

Equally important is the relation between the *amīr* and the Zoroastrian priest and its reflection on Arab diplomacy towards Dēwāshtīč. The very fact that the *amīr* sent Kurči, a Zoroastrian priest (*kwrcy βγnptw*) accompanied by Nižtak, perhaps another Zoroastrian character, means that he was aware

himself. However, he could have had bilingual people in his service who could. His good relationship with the Arabs was well-known and that could have attracted such people to his court; Yakubovich 2002: 239.

57 Yakubovich 2002: 241.

58 Yakubovich 2002: 243.

59 Al-Ṭabarī 1375/1996: 9: 4017; see Grenet and de la Vaissière 2002: 158; Yakubovich 2002: 247.

60 Yakubovich 2002: 231–253.

that Dēwāshtīč was Zoroastrian.[61] Mentioning the priest's name at the beginning of the letter and speaking about his mission would definitely attract the addressee's attention because he knew him. Emphasizing their concern about Dēwāshtīč's well-being while at the same time demonstrating their faithfulness to the *amīr* could increase their respect in the addressee's eyes, as they were the *amīr*'s official representatives.[62] Clearly, Zoroastrian priests were respected local dignitaries who performed political missions for the Arabs, as they represented powerful local forces who served well as powerbrokers for the new rulers. At the same time, the *amīr*'s close relation with the Zoroastrian delegates would have raised the *amīr*'s standing in the eyes of Dēwāshtīč.

We do not know much about how or when the relation between the *amīr* and the Zoroastrian priests was formed, but there is evidence to suggest that the *amīr* directly contacted the head of Zoroastrian priesthood of Samarqand in 721 CE. The evidence appears in a fragment of a letter written on paper with handwriting similar to Mount Mugh Document 1.1. This fragmentary letter was found among other objects from Mount Mugh and is now in the Hermitage's Oriental Division. The letter was subsequently used to line a dagger scabbard and as such it is heavily damaged. However, the Sogdian equivalent to the Arabic *basmala* is visibly written in a separate line above the text, as is the name of the *amīr* Saʿīd b. ʿAbd al-ʿAzīz (*xm'yr s'ytt pwn ''btr''zyz*). The letter itself is addressed to a certain Wakhshu, chief priest of Samarqand (*wxwšw sm'rknδc βγ'tyn* [*βγn*]*ptw*). The rest of the text is not readable, but perhaps the two priests mentioned in the Sogdian letter were sent by Wakhshu to serve the *amīr*.[63]

Friendly relations between the Arab and the Sogdians did not last long. In 103/722 the new Arab governor of Khurasan, Saʿīd al-Ḥarashī (possibly died 115/735), had a very different approach to regional relations. His predecessor's diplomatic relationship with Sogdian leaders was set aside as he sought to ensure Arab domination over Sogdiana at any cost. Dēwāshtīč's presence as king of Sogdiana was not tolerated by al-Ḥarashī, who recognized Ğūrak as the legitimate ruler. Ğūrak retained his status as vassal king and sought to exploit this relationship against his old enemies. The Arab preference for Ğūrak over Dēwāshtīč sealed the latter's fate.[64] Politically isolated and possibly recognized as a rebel,

61 Thanks to Jonathan Lee who drew my attention to this very important point. He suggests that the two parties were aware of each other's religious traditions, as they showed this in their communications. He correctly states that one may look at these documents in order to study how Arabs and Sogdians adapted each other's languages to this end.

62 Yakubovich 2002: 242.

63 Livshits 2015: 37–39.

64 Yakubovich 2002: 248.

Dēwāshtīč remained at Abgār Fort or Mount Mugh and communicated with his allies in the hope of reversing this situation. However, no help reached him. In 103/722, Dēwāshtīč was surrounded by an Arab army under Sulaymān b. Abī al-Surī (the person already mentioned in the Arabic letter), who was supported by local allies. Possibly, Dēwāshtīč's earlier relations with Sulaymān could save him for a short time, as he was captured and imprisoned for a while. Later, however, al-Ḥarashī executed him without any order from Iraq. Following his death, Sogdiana formally submitted to the Umayyad caliphs, and from this point forward Arab Muslim control of the region increased.[65]

3 Conclusion

The two letters discussed above highlight a number of key elements in Arab-Sogdian relations during the first three decades of the eighth century CE and how epistolary rhetoric was used. The first (Arabic) letter shows how the Sogdian ruler used Arabic together with Sogdian elements to secure his request, yet still recognizing Arab-Muslim political superiority. It suggests that he was well aware of the addressee's linguistic and cultural ideals. The Arabic letter was written on parchment, while almost all other letters exchanged between Dēwāshtīč and other Sogdian officials are on Chinese paper, a choice that might possibly be another sign of respect.

The second (Sogdian) letter clearly shows a different mode of relations between the Sogdian king and the Arabs. The king's fine letters were appreciated by the *amīr*, which may suggest that the king successfully used letters as a diplomatic technique to establish his position in the eyes of the Arabs. The second letter, written in Sogdian but with some striking Arabic and Islamic elements, shows that the Arabs emphasized their cultural and religious identity. They recognized the Sogdian superiority while emphasizing their own political power and authority and hierarchical superior position vis-à-vis the Sogdian king. This letter was written on Chinese paper, the common material used when addressing the Sogdian king. It shows the Arabs' flexibility in adopting local traditions or using them to show their awareness of the addressee's administrative practices.

Much remains unclear. However, a careful analysis of the language and content of the two letters offers us important insights into the political relations between Arabs and Sogdians. Even more interesting, however, are the dynamic

65 Marshak 1994.

cultural relations that they display, as scribal, linguistic, and cultural elements are used, adopted, and introduced to serve specific purposes.

Bibliography

Azarpay, Guitty. 1981. *Soghdian Painting: The Pictorial Epic in Oriental Art*. Berkeley: University of California Press.

al-Balādhurī, Aḥmad b. Yaḥyā. 2000. *Futūḥ al-buldān*. Edited by ʿAbd al-Qādir Muḥammad ʿAlī. Beirut: Dār al-Kutub al-ʿIlmiyyah.

Crowley, Terry, and Claire Bowern. 2010. *An Introduction to Historical Linguistics*. New York: Oxford University Press.

Crystal, David. 2008. *A Dictionary of Linguistics and Phonetics*. The Language Library. 6th ed. Malden, MA and Oxford: Blackwell.

Diem, Werner. 2008. "Arabic Letters in Pre-Modern Times: A Survey with Commented Selected Bibliographies." In *Documentary Letters from the Middle East: The Evidence in Greek, Coptic, South Arabian, Pehlevi, and Arabic (1st–15 c CE)*, edited by Eva Mira Grob and Andreas Kaplony. Special issue, *Asiatische Studien* 62: 843–883.

Donner, Fred. 2016. "Fragments of Three Umayyad Official Documents." In *The Heritage of Arabo-Islamic Learning: Studies Presented to Wadad Kadi*, edited by Maurice A. Pomerantz and Aram A. Shahin. Islamic History and Civilization 122. Leiden: Brill, 30–47.

Grenet, Franz, and Étienne de la Vaissière. 2002. "The Last Days of Panjikent." In *Silk Road Art and Archaeology* 8: 156–157.

Grob, Eva Mira. 2010. *Documentary Arabic Private and Business Letters on Papyrus: Form and Function, Content and Context*. Archiv für Papyrusforschung und verwandte Gebiete. Beiheft 2. Berlin and New York: de Gruyter.

Haim, Ofir, Michael Shenkar, and Sharof Kurbanov. 2016. "The Earliest Arabic Documents Written on Paper: Three Letters from Sanjar-Shah (Tajikistan). (With an Appendix by Anna-Grethe Rischel and Michelle Taube, National Museum of Denmark)." In *Jerusalem Studies in Arabic and Islam* 43: 141–189.

Kennedy, Hugh. 2001. *The Armies of the Caliphs: Military and Society in the Early Islamic State*. Warfare and History. London and New York: Routledge.

Khan, Geoffrey. 2008. "Remarks on the Historical Background and Development of Early Arabic Documentary Formulae." In *Documentary Letters from the Middle East: The Evidence in Greek, Coptic, South Arabian, Pehlevi, and Arabic (1st–15 c CE)*, edited by Eva Mira Grob and Andreas Kaplony. Special issue, *Asiatische Studien* 62: 885–906.

Kračkovskaja, V.A., and I[gnatij] J. Kračkovskij. 1934/1955. "Drevnejškij arabskij dokument iz Srednej Azii." In *Sogdijskij Sbornik*: 52–90. Reprint in Kračkovskij, I[gnatij]

J. *Izbrannye sočonenija*. Vol. 1. Moscow: Izdat. Akad. Nauk SSSR, 182–212. [P.Kratchkovski]

Kračkovskij, I[gnatij]J. 1946/1955. "Nad arabskimi rykopisjami" [Among Arabic Manuscripts]. In Kračkovskij, I.J. *Izbrannye sočonenija*. Vol. 1. Moscow: Izdat. Akad. Nauk SSSR, 110–115. [Partial reprint of the book of the same title, published in 1946, Moscow: Akad. Nauk SSSR.]

Livshits, Vladimir A. 2015. *Sogdian Epigraphy of Central Asia and Semirech'e*. Translated by Tom Stableford. Edited by Nicholas Sims-Williams. Corpus Inscriptionum Iranicarum, part 2, 3. London: School of Oriental and African Studies.

Lurje, Pavel. 2008. "Khamir and Other Arabic Words in Sogdian Texts." In *Islamisation de L'Asie Centrale: processus locaux d'acculturation du VIIe au XIe sičcle*. Cahiers de Studia Iranica 39. Paris: Association pour l'avancement des études iraniennes, 29–57.

Margoliouth, David S. 1903. "An Early Judaeo-Persian Document from Khotan, in the Stein Collection, with Other Early Persian Documents." In *Journal of the Royal Asiatic Society of Great Britain and Ireland* 35: 735–760 and plates.

Marshak, Boris. 1994. "Dēwāštīč." In *EIr* 7: 334–335 (last accessed February 2018).

Pearce, Michael. 2007. *The Routledge Dictionary of English Language Studies*. Routledge Dictionaries. London: Routledge.

Salemann, Carl. 1904. "Po povodu Jevrejsko-persidskago otryvka iz' Xotana" [On a Judeo-Persian Fragment From Khotan]. In *Zapiski vostočnago otdelenija Imperatorskago Russkogo Arheologičeskago Obščestva* 16: 46–57.

Shaban, Muhammad A. 1970. *The ʿAbbāsid Revolution*. Cambridge: Cambridge University Press.

Sijpesteijn, Petra M. 2013. *Shaping a Muslim State: The World of a Mid-Eighth-Century Egyptian Official*. Oxford Studies in Byzantium. Oxford: Oxford University Press.

Sims-Williams, Nicholas, 2001. *Bactrian Documents from Northern Afghanistan*. Volume 1: *Legal and Economic Documents*. Corpus inscriptionum Iranicarum 2, 6, 1. Studies in the Khalili Collection 3, 1. Oxford: Nour Foundation.

Sims-Williams, Nicholas, 2007. *Bactrian Documents from Northern Afghanistan*. Volume 2: *Letters and Buddhist Texts*. Corpus inscriptionum Iranicarum 2, 6, 2. Studies in the Khalili Collection 3, 2. Oxford and New York: Nour Foundation.

Smirnova, Ol'ga. I. 1970. *Očerki iz istorii Sogda* [Essays on the history of Sogdiana]. Moscow: Nauk.

al-Ṭabarī, Muḥammad b. Jarīr. [1960–1977]. *Tārīkh al-umam wa-l-mulūk*. Edited by Muḥammad Abū l-Faḍl Ibrāhīm. 11 vols. Cairo: Dār al-Maʿārif.

al-Ṭabarī, Muḥammad b. Jarīr. 1375/1996. *Tārīkh-i Ṭabarī yā Tārīkh al-rusul wa-l-mulūk*. Edited and translated by Abulqasim Payanda. 11 vols. Tehran: Intishārāt Asāṭīr.

Webb, Peter. 2016. *Imagining the Arabs: Arab Identity and the Rise of Islam*. Edinburgh: Edinburgh University Press.

Webb, Peter. 2018. "Identity and Social Formation in the Early Caliphate." In *Routledge Handbook on Early Islam*, edited by Herbert Berg. New York: Routledge, 129–158.

Weber, Dieter. 2005. "A Pahlavi Papyrus from Islamic Times". In *Bulletin of the Asia Institute* 19: 225–231.

Weber, Dieter. 2008. *Berliner Pahlavi-Dokumente: Zeugnisse spätsassanidischer Brief- und Rechtskultur aus frühislamischer Zeit. Mit Beiträgen von Myriam Krutzsch und Maria Macuch*. Wiesbaden: Harrassowitz.

Weber, Dieter. 2020. "Living Together in Changing Iran: Pahlavi Documents on Arab and Christians in Early Islamic Times." In *Acts of Protection in Early Islamicate Societies*, edited by Edmund Hayes and Eline Scheerlinck, Special issue, *Annales Islamologiques* 54: 139–164.

Yakubovich, Ilya. 2002. "Mugh 1.I. Revisited." In *Studia Iranica* 31: 231–253.

Yakubovich, Ilya. 2017. Review of Livshits 2015. In *Indo-Iranian Journal* 60: 413–426.

Zhan, Zhang, and Shi Guang. 2008. "Yijian xinfaxian Youtai-Bosiyu xinzha de duandai yu shidu" [A newly discovered Judeo-Persian letter]. In *Journal of the Dunhuang and Turfan Studies* 11: 71–99.

CHAPTER 3

Reconstructing Dhū l-Rumma's Poetry with the Help of Muqātil b. Sulaymān's *Tafsīr* (P.Cair.Arab. Inv. 1235 Verso and Recto)

Hazem Hussein Abbas Ali

Abstract

P.Cair.Arab.inv.1235 contains on verso a poem by the Umayyad poet Dhū l-Rumma (ca. 77–117/696–735). Upon comparing the text with the text edited by Carlile Henry Hayes Macartney (1919: 341–352, poem no. 46) and Muṭīʿ Bābilī (1964: 431–440, poem no. 46), I found a number of differences, both in the number of verses and in their sequence as well as in the reading of individual words. Starting from the text on recto, which is part of the *Tafsīr* by Abū l-Ḥasan Muqātil b. Sulaymān al-Balkhī (d. 150/767), (ed. Shiḥāṭa: 3: 189.7–192.2) this paper presents a newly arranged edition of Dhū l-Rumma's poem.

1 Establishing the Authenticity of the Text and the Sequence of Verses

Umayyad poetry dynamically developed and registered, obliquely and directly, the deeper changes in the spiritual condition of the times. This period of rapid development was flanked by more settled periods of poetic creativity: on the one hand, pre-Islamic, on the other, Abbasid poetry, and there can be no doubt that Umayyad poetry stems from a powerful poetic tradition of high achievement.[1]

The text contains a poem by Abū l-Ḥārith Ghaylān b. ʿUqba (ca. 77–117/696–735), the great Bedouin poet of the Umayyad era who was given the nickname Dhū l-Rumma, "the one with the frayed cord," most probably due to an amulet he wore as a child. He belonged to the ʿAdī tribe of the Ribāb confederation, which lived in the Yamāma and the adjacent desert of al-Dahnāʾ in the eastern part of the Arabian Peninsula. There, he was born and spent most of his life, although he made frequent visits to Basra and Kufa.[2]

1 Jayyusi 1983.
2 Papoutsakis 2011; see also al-Muttalibi 1960; Montgomery 1998; van Gelder 2005.

 DOI:10.1163/9789004527874_005

The greatest challenge a specialist in Arabic poetry can face is the attribution of verses to their author and the sequence of verses. In 1911, Muṣṭafā Ṣādiq al-Rāfiʿī seemed to contest the authenticity of our poem in his *Taʾrīkh ādāb al-ʿArab*,[3] but he actually just summarized the ideas and opinions of earlier scholars. In 1926, Ṭāhā Ḥusayn, who was influenced by the ideas of David Margoliouth, added fuel to the discussion in his *al-Shiʿr al-jāhilī*, a book that aggravated many of the more radical Islamists and scholars, yet in 1927, in his *Fī l-adab al-jāhilī*, he did not question the authorship of Dhū l-Rumma.[4] However, when we read the text of our document and compare it to the ones edited and published by Macartney (1919: 341–352, poem no. 46) and Muṭīʿ Bābilī (1964: 431–440, poem no. 46), we find differences, not only in the order of verses but also in their number and in individual words. Our document, obviously, is much older (end of the first/seventh to beginning of the second/eighth centuries).

Now, to check the text on verso for sequence and, eventually, for space allowing for missing parts, we can rely on the text on recto. In our case, we are in the lucky situation that the recto contains part of the well-known *Tafsīr* of Muqātil b. Sulaymān, i.e., his commentary on Q 24: 11–20 (*Sūrat al-Nūr, Āyāt al-ʾIfk*).[5] In the last few years, Muqātil's *Tafsīr* has attracted the attention of scholars, most probably due to the fact that this is the earliest *tafsīr* extant today. Kees Versteegh describes Muqātil's *Tafsīr* as "by far the most independent and interesting of the early commentaries." Elsewhere, he calls this *tafsīr* "one of the earliest products of Qurʾānic scholarship in Islam."[6]

Muqātil's text is definitely in good condition. This is a complete commentary, not just a collection of quotations like later commentaries, and Versteegh suggests that the kind of exegesis it represents belongs to the most primitive form of commentary on the Quran.[7] Muqātil belongs to a generation of exegetes whose main purpose was to explain the text of the Quran for common believers. In most cases he supplies glosses and explanatory notes for words or expressions that might not be immediately understood by the reader. His primary device of clarification is the simple adjacent of text and paraphrase, sometimes introduced by explanatory notes such as *yaʿnī*, "it means" (i.e., "the intention is") and *yaqūlu*, "he says." In some cases, Muqātil does not limit his comments or explanations to the individual verse but extends his observations

3 For convenience, I used the reprint al-Rāfiʿī 2000: 1: 284.

4 Mazrae, Tabar, and Reisi 2013.

5 Muqātil b. Sulaymān 1979–1989/2002: 3: 189.7–192.2.

6 Versteegh 2012.

7 Sirry 2012.

to the rest of the Quran. In later *tafsīr* literature, this type of explanation is known as *tafsīr al-Qurʾān bi-l-Qurʾān*, "explaining the Quran by the Quran."

Often, we find no relationship between the texts on recto and on verso, but in our case, there are some. (1) Dhū l-Rumma (d. ca. 117/735) and Muqātil (d. 150/767) lived in the same period, at the turn from the Umayyad to the Abbasid Caliphate. (2) Given the given sequence of Muqātil's text, I think that Dhū l-Rumma's text is in the right order. (3) However, a bad restoration caused a wrong reading: both on recto and verso, there are four single lines missing and two lines, right and left, have been combined wrongly. (4) The two texts were written in a similar type of script.

If we rearrange the document according to Muqātil's text, Dhū l-Rumma's verses do not have the same order as in the editions of Macartney and Muṭīʿ Bābilī. The number of verses in both editions is 48, yet in our text there are only 37 (for four of them, we have no text), with no space left to insert the remaining ones.

2 Date of the Document on Verso

P.Cair.Arab. inv. 1235 verso (unpublished) uses the Kufic letters *alif*, *ḥāʾ*, *jīm*, *kāf*, and *yāʾ* with tail bent to the right. By comparing the way of writing these letters with dated papyri, we can date it to the end of the first/seventh or the beginning of the second/eighth century. It is written on fine brown papyrus. The beginning and the end of the text is complete, yet the document has been damaged in many parts. The text is mostly preserved except for the middle part, where a restoration was attempted and where a few parts are missing.

3 Diplomatics

Upon comparing the writing of verso and recto with papyri from the first–second/seventh–eight centuries, especially those dated to 90/709,[8] we find similarities with the final *alif*, the final *yāʾ*, the ligature *mīm*-final *nūn*, the ligature *lām*-intermediate *jīm*/*ḥāʾ*/*khāʾ*, the intermediate *kāf*, the ligature *ʿayn*-*jīm*/*ḥāʾ*/*khāʾ*, the ligature *mīm*-final *ʿayn*, the ligature *jīm*/*ḥāʾ*/*khāʾ*-*rāʾ*,[9] and the verse divider:

8 Grohmann 1934–1962: 3: pls. 1–7, 13, 19.

9 There is a similar description of papyrus P.Utah 280 (dated by 225–228/840–843) by Muehlhaeusler 2014.

TABLE 3.1 Comparison of the writing in Dhū l-Rumma, Muqātil, and Grohmann

Grohmann (1st–2nd/7th–8th centuries)	Recto (Muqātil)	Verso (Dhū l-Rumma)	
			final *alif*
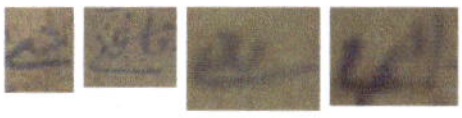			final *yāʾ*
			ligature *mīm-nūn*
			ligature *lām-jīm/ḥāʾ/khāʾ*
			intermediate *kāf*
			ligature *ʿayn-jīm/ḥāʾ/khāʾ*
			ligature *mīm*-final *ʿayn*
			ligature *jīm/ḥā/khāʾ-rāʾ*
			verse divider

4 Checking the Text on Verso through the Text on Recto

By flipping the verso horizontally and putting the recto on front of it, I identified the missing parts and found out where space was missing. I first read Muqātil's text on recto and found that in between there are four lines missing (lines 11; 14; 19; 22); thus, on verso, the same space is also missing (lines 4;

9; 17; 22). Obviously, there had been a mistake in restoration, and we need to move up the left part of lines 17 and 18 of Dhū l-Rumma's poem (marked below in grey), as they belong to the right part of lines 16 and 17.

As the following comparison shows, our document and Macartney's edition have the same 31 verses (lines 1–10; 12–13; 15–18; 20–21; 23–26; 28–36 of our document), although not in the same order and with some different readings; five verses are found in our document but not in the Macartney edition (lines 11; 14; 19; 22; 27 of our document), and 15 verses are found in the Macartney edition but not in our document. Were they latter added from another poem? Or are they missing from the older document?

TABLE 3.2 Comparison of verses in the unpublished document and Macartney's edition

Document (unpublished)			Macartney (published)		
١	وَشَارِعِ الْقِلاَةَ بَيْنَ دِمْنَةٍ أَمِنْ	تدمعُ العينُ ظلَّتِ حتّى تصابيتَ	١	وَشَارِعِ الْقِلاَتِ بَيْنَ دِمْنَةٍ أَمِنْ	تدمعُ العينُ ظلَّتِ حتّى تصابيتَ
٢	وزعتُها ما إذا ظلَّتْ عبرةً نعمْ	تترَّعُ عواصٍ منها أبتْ بحلمي	٢	وزعتُها ما إذا ظلَّتْ عبرةً نعمْ	تترَّعُ عواصٍ منها أبتْ بحلمي
٣	حاجةٌ منكَ لها واهتاجتْ تصابيتَ	تُقطَّعُ ألا أقرانُها أبتْ ولوعٌ	٣	حاجةٌ منكَ لها واهتاجتْ تصابيتَ	تُقطَّعُ ما أقرانُها أبتْ ولوعٌ
٤	تَعَرُّضُ مَيٍّ دُونَ مِنْهَا حَانَ إذَا	مولعُ بالصَّبابةِ قلبٌ حنَّ لنا	٤	تَعَرُّضُ مَيٍّ دُونَ مِنْهَا حَانَ إذَا	مولعُ بالصَّبابةِ قلبٌ حنَّ لنا
٥	مَضَىا الذِي الزَّمَانَ الْوَجْدُ يَرْجِعُ وَمَا	مجزعُ الدارِ دمنةِ في للفتا وما	٥	مَضَى الذِي الزَّمَانَ الْوَجْدُ يَرْجِعُ وَمَا	مجزعُ الدارِ دمنةِ في للفتى وما
٦	وشارعِ القلاة أيامَ ليتَ ألا	أجمعُ العيشُ انقضا ثمَّ لنا رجعنَ	١٣	أنَّني غيرَ حيلةٌ لي ما عشيَّةَ	مُولَعُ التُّرْبِ فِي وَالخطِّ الْحَصى بِلَقْطِ
٧	ـا(مَزَارُهَـ بَعِيدٌ مَيٌّ لاَ لَيَالِي)	(متشيَّعُ الهوى شتَّى ـلبه)ق ولا	١٥	أُعِيدُهُ ثُمَّ انْخَطَّ وأمْحُو أَخُطُّ	وُقَّعُ الدَّارِ فِي وَالْغِرْبَانُ بِكَفِّيَّ

TABLE 3.2 Comparison of verses in the unpublished document and Macartney's edition (*cont.*)

Document (unpublished)			Macartney (published)		
٨	النّوَا طَايرُ ولا لَنَا مَشْؤُومٌ نَحْنُ وَلاَ	المُرُوَّعُ الفؤادُ بالبينِ ذلَّ ولا	١٦	أصابني فارسيًّا سنانًا كأنَّ	أوجعُ الحبِّ لوعةُ بلْ كبدي على
٩	غُرُوبه كَأَنَّ عَذْبٍ عَنّ وَتبَسِم	أجرعُ الرَّملِ منَ تردَّاها أقاح	٦	وشارعِ القلاتِ أيامَ ليتَ ألا	أجمعُ العيشُ انقضى ثمَّ لنا رجعن
١٠	مُطَرَّفٍ بِطَفْلٍ الأَحْوَى الإِسْحِلُ جَرَى	نصَّعُ فهي أنيابِها منْ الزُّهرِ على	٧	مَزَارُهَا بَعِيدٌ ميٌّ لاَ لَيَالِي	متشيَّعُ الهوى شتَّى قلبهُ ولا
١١	[...]	[...]	٨	النَّوى طَائرُ لَنَا مَشْؤُومٌ نَحْنُ وَلاَ	المُرَوَّعُ الفؤادُ بالبينِ ذلَّ وما
١٢	قرونه كَأَنَّ مَيَّالٍ وَأَسْحَمَ	وخروعُ ضالٌ واراهنَّ أساودُ	٩	غُرُوبه كَأَنَّ عَذْبٍ عَنّ وَتبَسِم	أجرعُ الرَّملِ منَ تردَّاها أقاحي
١٣	أنّني غيرَ حيلةٌ لي ما عشيَّةَ	مولَعُ التُّربِ في وَانخطّ الحَصى بِلَقْطِ	١٠	مُطَرَّفٍ بِطَفْلٍ الأَحْوَى الإِسْحِلُ جَرَى	نصَّعُ فهي أنيابِها منْ الزُّهرِ على
١٤	[...]	[...]		طَعْمُهُ مِنْهُنَّ المَحْضَ السُّلافَ كَأَنَّ	تضجعُ الكواكبِ أيدي جعلتْ إذا
١٥	أُعِيدُهُ ثُمَّ الخطَّ وأمحُو أَخُطُّ	وُقَّعُ الدَّارِ فِي وَالْغِرْبَانُ بِكَفّي		هجعةٍ بعدَ المستقى خصراتٍ على	فتنقعُ الصَّوادِي تَرْوَى بِأَمْثَالِهَا
١٦	أصابني فارسيًّا سنانًا كأنَّ	أوجعُ الحبِّ لوعةُ بلْ كبدي على	١٢	قرونه كَأَنَّ مَيَّالٍ وَأَسْحَمَ	وخروعُ ضالٌ واراهنَّ أساودُ
١٧	راعها المُحَصَّبِ عندَ ناقتي أرى	المُرَجَّعُ والهديلُ اليماني رواحُ	١٧	شاقها المُعَسَّبِ عندَ ناقتي أرى	المُرَجَّعُ والهديلُ اليماني رواحُ
١٨	ركابنا فإنَّ قرِّي : لها فقلتُ	نزَّعُ تهوينَ حيثُ مِنَ وركبانها	١٨	لها : ركابنا فإنَّ قرِّي[] فقلتُ	نزَّعُ تهوينَ حيثُ مِنَ وركبانها

TABLE 3.2 Comparison of verses in the unpublished document and Macartney's edition (*cont.*)

Document (unpublished)			Macartney (published)		
١٩	[...]	[...]		بالبُرى يُعكسنَ الأكوارِ لدى وهنَّ	وُقَّعُ ومنهنَّ منّا غرضٍ على
	لَيْلَةَ الْمُثَنِّينَ بَعْدَ مَضَتْ فَلَمَّا	أَرْبَعُ الشَّهْرِ مِنَ عَشْرٍ عَلَى وَزَادَتْ	٢٠	لَيْلَةَ الْمُثَنِّينَ بَعْدَ مَضَتْ فَلَمَّا	أَرْبَعُ الشَّهْرِ مِنَ عَشْرٍ عَلَى وَزَادَتْ
٢٠	فأصبحتْ الظَّلامِ جنحَ منيً منْ سرتْ	تملَعُ الفجرِ معَ أيديها ببسيانَ	٢١	فأصبحتْ الظَّلامِ جنحَ منيً منْ سرتْ	تملَعُ الفجرِ معَ أيديها ببسيانَ
٢١	[...]	[...]	٢٧	وَدِيقَةٍ ذَاتِ شَهْبَاءَ وَهَاجِرَةٍ	يتصدَّعُ حَميها من الحصى يكادُ
٢٢	عِظَامِهِ فِي دَبَّبَت قَفَرَاتٍ أَخِي	أَخْضَعُ وَهْوَ الْكَرَى أَعْجَازِ شُفَافَاتُ	٢٨	بعدما وأطلالَ وجهي لها نصبتُ	المُولَّعُ اللَّياحُ واكتنَّ الظِّلُّ أزى
٢٣	رؤوسهم أضحتْ الظَّلماءُ انجابتِ إذا	ظلَّعٌ وهيَ الكرى طولِ من عليهنَّ		وَالْتَقَتْ عَثَانِينَ ذُو نَحْسٌ هَاجَ إِذَا	يَمْصَعُ الآلَ بِهَا أَشْبَاهٌ سَبَارِيتُ
٢٤	وتنتحي حالًا بالجهدِ يقيمونها	فيركعُ أخرى الإدلاجِ نعسةٌ بهم		مهيبةٍ كلَّ الصَّدعِ اعتسافَ عسفتُ	تصوَّعُ عنّي الآجالُ بها تظلُّ
٢٥	بِنَيِّهَا أَزْرَى الأَرْجاءِ بِمُخْطَفَةٍ	هَجَّعُ والطَّيرُ بالقومِ السُّرى جذابُ		نَهَاؤُهُ اسْتَحَارَتْ الآلُ إِذَا وَخَرْقٍ	يَنْجَعُ السَّيرَ جَوْزِهِ فِي يَكَدْ لَمْ بِهِ
٢٦	وَدِيقَةٍ ذَاتِ شَهْبَاءَ وَهَاجِرَةٍ	يتصدَّعُ حَميها من الحصى يكادُ		كَأَنَّهُ السَّرَابِ وَرَقْرَاقُ قَطَعْتُ	تَتَرَيَّعُ أَرْجَائِهِ فِي سَبَائِبُ
٢٧	بعدما وأطلالَ وجهي لها نصبتُ	المُولَّعُ اللَّياحُ واكتنَّ الظِّلُّ أزى		وَارْتَقَى الأَيَادِيمَ الآلُ أَلْبَسَ وَقَدْ	مقنعُ حوافيهِ منْ نشزٍ كلِّ على
٢٨	مُغْوَرٍ فِي سَاعَةً إِلَّا قِلْنَ وَمَا	أَدْرَعُ وَالصُّبْحُ تِلْكَ إِلاَّ بِتْنَ وَمَا	٢٦	بِنَيِّهَا أَزْرَى الأَرْجاءِ بِمُخْطَفَةٍ	هَجَّعُ والطَّيرُ بالقومِ السُّرى جذابُ

TABLE 3.2 Comparison of verses in the unpublished document and Macartney's edition (*cont.*)

Document (unpublished)			Macartney (published)		
٢٩	أمَّهاتِه عنْ الشَّمسُ تزلُّ وهامٍ	تَقَعْقَعُ الْمَثَانِي فِي وَأَلْجِ صِلاَبٍ	٢٤	رؤوسهم أضحتْ الظَّلماءُ انجابتِ إذا	ظلَّعُ وهيَ الكرى طولِ من عليهنَّ
٣٠	كأنَّها حرف قادتهن هَين إذا	أقرعُ الظَّنابيبِ عار الشَّوا أحمُّ	٢٥	وتنتحي حالًا بالجهدِ يُقيمونها	فتركعُ أخرى الإدلاجِ نشوةُ بها
٣١	رَوَافِعًا إلَّا يُصْبِحْنَ مَا قَلآئِصُ	تَزَعْزَعُ أَعْنَاقُهُنَّ سِيرةً بِنَا		كَأَنَّهُ يَمِيدُ مَغْلُوبٍ كُلَّ تَرَى	يَتَبوَّعُ مَشْطُونَةٍ فِي بِحَبْلَيْنِ
٣٢	بِالْقِرَا الْقَيْسِ امْرِئِ أَيْدِي أَبْطَأَتْ إِذَا	تُقَنَّعُ لا حَاسِرًا جَاءَتْ الرَّكْبِ عَنِ	٢٣	عِظَامِهِ فِي دَبَّت قَفَراتٍ أَخِي	أَخْضَعُ وَهْوَ الْكَرَى أَعْجَازِ شُفَافَاتُ
٣٣	يقودُها الثّيابِ طلساءُ السُّودِ من	مشيَّعٌ قلبُ الظَّلما في الرَّكْبِ إلى		شَفَّهَا شَغَامِيم مُسْلَهِمَّاتٍ عَلَى	بلقعٍ ويهماءُ حاجاتٍ غرِيباتُ
٣٤	بَنَاتِكُمْ عَارَ أَنْ إِلاَّ اللّهُ أَبَى	أَشْسَعُ الْقَيْسِ امْرَأَ يَا مَكَانٍ بِكُلِّ		بُدَّنٌ وَهْيَ أَهْلِنَا مِنْ بِهَا بَدَأْنَا	تَضْرَعُ اللَّيلِ آخِرِ فِي جَعَلَتْ فَقَدْ
٣٥	القِرَى الْمُبْتَغِي الرَّاكِبِ مُنَاخَ كَأَنَّ	بَلْقَعُ الْقَيْسِ امْرَأً إلاّ يَجِدْ لَمْ إِذَا	٢٩	مُغْوَّرٍ فِي سَاعَةً إلاَّ قِلْنَ وَمَا	أَدْرَعُ وَالصُّبْحُ تِلْكَ إلاَّ بِتْنَ وَمَا
	غيلان واسمه الرمة[...]		٣٠	أمَّهاتِه عنْ الشَّمسُ تزلُّ وهامٍ	تَقَعْقَعُ الْمَثَانِي فِي وَأَلْجِ صِلاَبٍ
				مُسْتَرَادِهَا فِي الطَّيْرَ وَرَاقَ تَرَامَتْ	موضَّعٌ وسخلٌ حوافيها في دمٌ
				بِهِ رَقَعَتْ إِذَا نَازٍ مُسْتَوٍ عَلَيَّ	المُرَقَّعُ النَّعيلُ طارَ دياميمُهُ
				وغُودرتْ المهارى منهُ نجتْ سمامُ	الْهَمَلَّعُ والْمَاطِلِيُّ أَرَاحِيبُهَا

TABLE 3.2 Comparison of verses in the unpublished document and Macartney's edition (*cont.*)

Document (unpublished)	**Macartney (published)**		
	٣٢	رَوَافِعًا إلاَّ يُصْبِحْنَ مَا قَلآئِصُ	تَزَعْزَعُ أَعْنَاقُهُنَّ سِيرَةً بِنَا
	٣١	كَأَنَّهَا حرفًا بارينَ إذا يخدنَ	أقرِعُ الظَّنابيبِ عاري الشَّوى أحمُّ
		جَدِيلَهَا يَمْطُو شَدْفَاءُ جُمَالِيَّةٌ	أَتلَعُ الحرقَ اجتابتِ ما إذا نهوضُ
		الْـ وَيَبْعُدُ الْبَعِيدُ يَدْنُو مِثْلِهَا عَلَى	المتنعُ النّازحُ ويُطوى قريبُ
	٣٣	بِالْقِرَى الْقَيْسِ امرِئِ أَيْدِي أَبْطَأَتْ إذَا	تُقَنِّعُ لا حَاسِرًا جَاءَتْ الرَّكْبِ عَنِ
	٣٤	يقودُها الثّيابِ طلساءُ السُّودِ من	مشيّعٌ قلبُ الظّلماءِ في الرَّكبِ إلى
	٣٥	بَنَاتِكُمْ عَارَ أَنْ إلاَّ اللّهُ أَبَى	أَشْسَعُ الْقَيْسِ امْرَأً يَا مَكَانٍ بِكُلِّ
	٣٦	القِرَى الْمُبْتَغِي الرَّاكِبِ مُنَاخَ كَأَنَّ	بَلْقَعُ الْقَيْسِ امْرَأً إلاّ يَجِدْ لَمْ إذَا

5 Conclusion

Muqātil's well known *Tafsīr* on recto helps us to reconstruct Dhū l-Rumma's poem on verso: Dhū l-Rumma's poem consists of 37 verses, not 48, and bad restoration led to an erroneous text. The meanings of the new reading are in good sequence. The following 16 verses are not found in our document and possibly were added from another poem?

6 Edition

P.Cair.Arab. inv. 1235 recto: Muqātil b. Sulaymān, *Tafsīr* (corresponding with Šihāṭa, ed., vol. 3: 189.7–192.2)

١ [على] قدر ما خاض [فـ]ـيه من أمرها [والذي تولى كبره منهم يعني]
٢ عظمة منهم يعني من العصبة وهو عبد الله [بن أبي رأس]
٣ المنافقين وهو الذي قال ما برئت منه وما بر[ئ منها]

٤ [له عذاب عظيم وما برئ منها أي شديد]
٥ [ففي الآية] عـ[ـبـ]ـر[ة لجميع] المسلمـ[ـين إذا كانت] بينهم خطيئة
٦ [فمن أعلن عليها بـ]ـفعل أو كلام أو عرض بها أو أعجبه ذلك أو رضـ[ـي]
٧ [به فهو شريـ]ـك في تلك الخطية على قدر ما كان بينهم والذي [تولى]
٨ كبر[ه يعني الذي ولي] تلك الخطية بنفسه فهو أعظم إثما عـ[ـند الله]
٩ [قال فإذا كانت خطية بين المسلمين فمن شهد وكره فهو]
١٠ [مثل الغائب ومن غاب] ورضي فهو مثل الشاهد ثم [وعـ]ـظ
١١ الذين خاضوا في أمر عائشة فقال لولا إذ سمعتموه يعني قذف
١٢ عايشة بصفوان هل كذبتم به ألا ظن المؤمنون والمؤمنات
١٣ [بـ]ـأ[نـ]ـفـ[ـسـ]ـهـ[ـم] لأ[ن] فيهم حمنة بنت [جحش خيرا يقـ]ـول ألا ظن بعضهم
١٤ قال يزنوا وهلا قالوا هذا إفك [مبين]
١٥ [يعني ألا قالوا هذا القذف كذب] بين لولا [يعنى] هلا جاؤا عل[ـيه يعني]
١٦ [على القذف بأربعة] شهداء فإذ لـ[ـم يأتو]ا بالشهداء فأ]ولـ[ـئك]
١٧ [عند الله هم الكاذبون في قولهم يعني الذين قذفوا عائشة ثم]
١٨ قال لولا فضل الله عليكم ورحمته لمسكم فـ| ١٩ |يما أفضتم فيه
١٩ يعني قلتم فيه من القذف عذاب عظيم بعد| ٢٠ |العقوبة في الدنيا
٢٠ والآخرة إذ تلقونه بألسنتكم وذلك يعني إذ [يرويه بعضكم عن بعض]
٢١ وتقولون بـ[ـأفـ]ـواهـ[ـكم يعنى بألسنتكم ما ليس لكم به علم يقول من غير]
٢٢ أ[ن تعلموا أن الذي قلتم من القذف حق وتحسبونه هينا يقول تحسنون]

٢٣ القذف ذنبا [هينا وهو عند] الله عظيم
٢٤ يعني عظيم في الوزر ثم وعظ الذين خاضوا في أمر عائشة فقال ولولا
٢٥ يعني هلا إذ سمعتموه يعني القذف قلتم يعني هلا قلتم ما يكون لنا
٢٦ أن نتكلم بهذا ولم تره أعيننا سبحانك يعـ[ـي] ألا قلتم [سبحانك]
٢٧ هذا بهتان عظيم يعني القذف بهتان عظيم [مثل ما قال سعد بن معاذ]
٢٨ الأنصاري ذلك أنه لما سمع من خاض في أمر عائـ[ـشة قال سبحانك] هذا
٢٩ بهتان عظيم والبهتان الذي لم يهبـ[ـت فيقول ما لم يكن من قذف أو غيره]

٣٠ [ثم و]عظ الذين خاضوا [في] أمر عائـ[ـشة فقال يعظكم الله أن تعودوا]
٣١ لمثله أبدا إن كنتم مؤمنين ويبين الله لكم الآيات والله عليم حكيم
٣٢ يعني الآيات ما ذكر من المواعظ ثم قال إن الذين يحبون يعني من
٣٣ قذف عائشة يحبون أن تشيع الفاحشة يعني أن تفشى
٣٤ ويظهر الزنا في نساء النبي من الذين آمنوا معه في [صفـ]ـوان وعا[ئشة]
٣٥ لهم عذاب أليم في الدنيا والأخرة فكان عذاب عند الله [بن أبي] في
٣٦ الدنيا الجلد وفي الآخرة عذاب النار والله يعلم وانتم لا تعلمو[ن]
٣٧ ولولا فضل الله عليكم ورحمته لعاقبكم بما قلتم لـ[ـعـ]ـا[ئشة ثم]
٣٨ قال وأن الله بكم لرؤف رحيم يعـ[ـني رفيق بكم]
٣٩ يعني حين عافا عنكم فيما قلتم من القذف [...]
٤٠ ....

P.Cair.Arab. inv. 1235 verso:
Dhū l-Rumma, *A-min Dimna*
(corresponding with Macartney, ed., no. 46)

١ [أَمِنْ دِمْنَةٍ بَيْنَ الْقِلَاةَ وَشَارِعٍ] تصابيتَ حتّى ظلَّتِ العينُ تدمعُ[○]
٢ [نعمْ عبرةً ظلَّتْ] إذا ما وزعتُها بحلمي أبتْ منها عواصٍ تترَّعُ ○
٣ [تصابيتَ واهتاجتْ لـ]ـها منكَ حاجةٌ خـ[...] أبتْ أقرانُها ألا تُقطَّعُ ○
٤ [إذَا حَا]نَ مِنْهَا دُونَ مَيّ تعرضٌ لنا حنَّ قلبٌ بالصَّبا[بةِ مولعُ ○]
٥ [وَمَا يَـ]ـرْجِـعُ الْوَجْـ[ـدُ] الزَّمَانَ الذِي مَضَا وهل للفتا في دمـ[ـنةِ الدارِ مجز]عُ ○

٦ [ألا ليتَ] أ[يـ]ـامَ القلاة وشارعٍ   رجعنَ لنا ثمَّ انقضا [العيشُ أجمعُ] ○

٧ [لَيَالِي لاَ مَيٌّ بعيدٌ مَزَارُهَـ]ـا   ولا قـ[ـلبهُ شتَّى الهوى متشيِّعُ ○]

٨ وَلاَ نَحْنُ مَـ[ـشْؤُ]ومٌ لَنَا ولا طَايرُ النَّوَا   ولا ذلَّ [بالبيـ]ـنِ [الفؤادُ المُرَوَّ]ع ○

٩ وَتَبْسِمُ عَنّ لنا كَأَنَّ غُرُوبَهُ   أقاح تردَّاها منَ الرَّملِ أجرعُ ○

١٠ جَرَا الإِسْحِلُ ا[لأَحْوَى بِطَفْلٍ مُطَرَّفٍ   على الزُّهرِ منْ أنيابِها فهي نصَّعُ [○]

١١ [...   ○]

١٢ وَأَسْحَمَ مَيَّالٍ كَأَنَّ قُرُونَهُ   أساودُ واراهنَّ ضالٌ وخروَعُ ○

١٣ [عشـ]ـيَّةَ ما لي حيلةٌ غيرَ أنَّني   بِـ[ـلَقْطِ الْحَصَا وَالخطِّ فِي التُّرْبِ مُولَعُ ○

١٤ [...   ○]

١٥ أَخُطُّ [و]أَمْحُو الخَطَّ ثُمَّ أُعِيدُ[هُ   بِكَفِّيَّ وَالْغِرْبَانُ فِي الدَّارِ وُقَّعُ ○

١٦ كأنَّ سنانًا فارسيًّا [أصابني   على كبدي بلْ لوعةُ الحبِّ أوجعُ [○]

١٧ أرى ناقتي عندَ الـ[ـمُحصَّبِ]| ١٨ | راعها   رواحُ اليماني والهديلُ المُرَجَّعُ ○

١٨ فقلتُ لها قِرّي فإنَّ ركا| ١٩ |بنا   وَرُكْبَانَهَا مِنَ حَيْثُ تَهْوِيْنَ نُزَّعُ ○

١٩ [...   ○]

٢٠ فَلَمَّا مَضَتْ بَعْدَ الْمُثَنَّيْنَ لَيْلَةٌ   وَزَادَتْ عَلَى عَشْرٍ مِنَ الـ]ـشَّهْرِ أَرْبَعُ ○

٢١ [سرتْ منْ منىً جنحَ ا]لظَّلا[مِ فأصبحتْ   ببسيانَ أيـ]ـديها معَ [الـ]ـفجرِ تملَعُ ○

٢٢ [...   ○]

٢٣ أَخِي قَفَراتٍ دَبَّبَت فِي [عِظَا]مِهَا   شُفَافَاتُ [أَعْجَا]زِ الْكَرَا [وَ]هوَ أَخْضَعُ ○

٢٤ إذا انجابتِ الظَّلماءُ أضحتْ رؤوسهم   عليهنَّ من طولِ الكرا فهيَ ظلَّعُ [○]

٢٥ يُقيمونها بالجهدِ حالًا وتنتحي   بهم نعسةُ [ا]لإدلاجِ أخرى فيركعُ [○]

٢٦ بِمُخْطَـ[ـفَةِ الأَرْجاءِ أَزْرَى بِنِيِّها   جذابُ السُّرا بالـ[ـقو]مِ و[الطَّيـ]ـرُ هُجَّعُ ○

٢٧ وَهَاجِـ[ـرَةٍ شَهْبَاءَ ذَ]اتِ وَدِيقَةٍ   يكادُ الحصا من حَميها يتصدَّعُ ○

٢٨ نصبتُ [لها وجهي وأطلا]لَ بعدما   أزى الظِّلُّ واكتنَّ اللَّياحُ المُوَلَّ[عُ] ○

٢٩ وَمَا قِلْنَ [إ]لاَّ سَاعَةً فِي [مُغَوَّ]رٍ   [وَمَا بِتْنَ إلاَّ تِلْكَ] وَالصُّبْحُ أَدْرَعُ ... ○

٣٠ وهامٍ تزلُّ الشَّمسُ عنْ أمَّهاتهِ   صِلاَبٍ وَأَلْحٍ فِي الْمَثَانِي تَقَعْقَعُ ○

٣١ إذا هَين قادتهن حرف كأنَّها   أحمُّ الشَّوا عارِ الظَّنابيبِ أقرعُ ○

٣٢ [قَلاَئِصُ مَا يُصْبِحْنَ إلاَّ] رَوَافِعًا   بِنَا [سِـ]ـيرةً أَعْنَاقُهُنَّ تَزَعْزَعُ ○

٣٣ إذَا أَبْطَأَتْ أَيْدِي امْرِئِ الْقَيْسِ بِالْقِرَا   عَنِ الرَّكْبِ جَاءَتْ حَاسِرًا لا تُقَنَّعُ ○

٣٤ من السُّودِ طلساءُ الثّيابِ يقودُها   إلى الرَّكْبِ في الظَّلما قلبٌ مشيَّعُ ○

٣٥ [أَبَـ]ـا اللّهُ إلاَّ أَنْ عَارَ بَنَاتِكُمْ   بِكُلِّ مَكَانٍ يَا امْرَأَ الْقَيْسِ أَشْنَعُ ○

٣٦ [كَأَنَّ مُنَاخَ الرَّاكِبِ] الْمُبْتَغِي [القِـ]ـرَا   إذَا لَمْ يَجِدْ إلاّ امْرَأَ الْقَيْسِ بَلْقَعُ ○

٣٧ [...]. الرمة واسمه غيلان   تمت بسمه تعـ(ـالى)

Dhū l-Rumma, *A-min Dimna* (Macartney, ed., no. 46)
Verses Found in Macartney Only

كَأَنَّ السُّلاَفَ الْمَحْضَ مِنْهُنَّ طَعْمُهُ   إذا جعلتْ أيدي الكواكبِ تضجعُ

على خصراتِ المستقى بعدَ هجعة   بِأَمْثَالِهَا تَرْوَى الصَّوَادِي فَتَنْقَعُ

وهنَّ لدى الأكوارِ يُعكسنَ بالبُرى   على غرضٍ منّا ومنهنَّ وُقَّعُ

إِذَا هَاجَ نَحْسٌ ذُو عَثَانِينَ وَالْتَقَتْ   سَبَارِيتُ أَشْبَاهٌ بِهَا الآلُ يَمْصَعُ

عسفتُ اعتسافَ الصَّدعِ كلَّ مهيبةٍ   تظلُّ بها الآجالُ عنّي تصوَّعُ

وَخَرْقٍ إِذَا الآلُ اسْتَحَارَتْ نِهَاؤُهُ   بِهِ لَمْ يَكَدْ فِي جَوْزِهِ السَّيْرُ يَنْجَعُ

قَطَعْتُ وَرَقْرَاقُ السَّرَابِ كَأَنَّهُ   سَبَائِبُ فِي أَرْجَائِهِ تَتَرَيَّعُ

وَقَدْ أَلْبَسَ الآلُ الأَيَادِيمَ وَارْتَقَى   على كلِّ نشزٍ منْ حوافيهِ مقنعُ

تَرَى كُلَّ مَغْلُوبٍ يَمِيدُ كَأَنَّهُ   بِحَبْلَيْنِ فِي مَشْطُونَةٍ يَتَبَوَّعُ

عَلَى مُسْلَهِمَّاتٍ شَغَامِيمَ شَفَّهَا   غريباتُ حاجاتٍ ويهماءُ بلقعُ

بَدَأْنَا بِهَا مِنْ أَهْلِنَا وَهْيَ بُدَّنٌ   فَقَدْ جَعَلَتْ فِي آخِرِ اللَّيْلِ تَضْرَعُ

تَرَامَتْ وَرَاقَ الطَّيْرَ فِي مُسْتَرَادِهَا   دمٌ في حوافيها وسخلٌ موضَّعُ

عَلَى مُسْتَوٍ نَازٍ إِذَا رَقَصَتْ بِهِ   دياميمُهُ طارَ النَّعيلُ المُرَقَّعُ

سمامٌ نجتْ منهُ المهارى وغُودرتْ   أَرَاحِيبُهَا وَالْمَاطِلِيُّ الْهَمَلَّعُ

جُمَالِيَّةٌ شَدْفَاءُ يَمْطُو جَدِيلَهَا   نهوضٌ إذا ما اجتابتِ الخرقَ أتلَعُ

عَلَى مِثْلِهَا يَدْنُو الْبَعِيدُ وَيَبْعُدُ الْـ   قريبُ ويُطوى النّازحُ المتنعنعُ

Bibliography

Dhū l-Rumma, Ghaylān b. ʿUqba. 1919. *The Dîwân of Ghailân Ibn ʿUqbah Known as Dhu ʾr-Rummah*. Edited by Carlile Henry Hayes Macartney. Cambridge: Cambridge University Press.

Dhū l-Rumma, Ghaylān b. ʿUqba. 1964. *Dīwān Dhī l-Rumma*. Edited by Muṭīʿ Bābilī. Beirut: al-Maktab al-Islāmī.

Grohmann, Adolf. 1934–1962. *Arabic Papyri in the Egyptian Library*. 6 vols. Cairo: Egyptian Library Press.

Ḥusayn, Ṭāhā. 1926. *al-Shiʿr al-jāhilī*. Cairo: Dār al-Kutub al-Miṣriyya.

Ḥusayn, Ṭāhā. 1345/1927. *Fī l-adab al-jāhilī*. 2 vols. Cairo: al-Iʿtimād.

Jayyusi, Salma K. 1983. "Umayyad Poetry." In *Arabic Literature to the End of the Umayyad Period*, edited by Alfred F.L. Beeston et al. The Cambridge History of Arabic Literature. Cambridge: Cambridge University Library, 387–432.

Mazrae, Elham, Mohammad Mohammadi Tabar, and Masoud Reisi. 2013. "Concept of Plagiarism in Arab Culture and Literature." In *Journal of American Science* 9: 91–95.

Montgomery, James E. 1998. "Dhū al-Rumma." In *Encyclopedia of Arabic Literature*, edited by Julie Scott Meisami and Paul Starkey. 2 vols. London and New York 2006, 1: 188–189.

Muehlhaeusler, Mark. 2014. "Fragments of Arabic Poetry on Papyrus: Questions of Textual Genesis, Attribution, and Representation." In *Journal of the American Oriental Society* 134: 673–687.

Muqātil b. Sulaymān. 1979–1989/2002. *Tafsīr Muqātil b. Sulaymān muʾassis al-taʾrīḥ al-ʿarabī*. Edited by ʿAbd Allāh Maḥmūd Shiḥāṭa. 5 vols. Cairo: Markaz Taḥqīq al-Turāṯ/Reprint Beirut: Muʾassasat al-Taʾrīkh al-ʿArabī.

al-Muttalibi, Abdu l-Jabbar Yusuf. 1960. *A Critical Study of the Poetry of Dhuʾl-Rumma*. PhD diss., University of London.

Papoutsakis, Nefeli. 2011. "Dhū l-Rumma." In *The Encyclopaedia of Islam Three*, edited by Kate Fleet et al. (last accessed February 22, 2021).

al-Rāfiʿī, Muṣṭafā Ṣādiq. 2000. *Taʾrīkh ādāb al-ʿArab*. Beirut: Dār al-Kutub al-ʿIlmiyya.

Sirry, Munʾim. 2012. "Muqātil b. Sulaymān and Anthropomorphism." In *Studia Islamica* 107: 38–64.

van Gelder, Geert Jan. 2005. "Dhū al-Rummah." In *Arabic Literary Culture, 500–925*, edited by Shawkat M. Toorawa and Michael Cooperson. Dictionary of Literary Biography 311. Detroit: Gale, 108–113.

Versteegh, Kees. 2012. "Muqātil b. Sulaymān and Anthropomorphism." In *Studia Islamica* 3: 51–82.

Figures

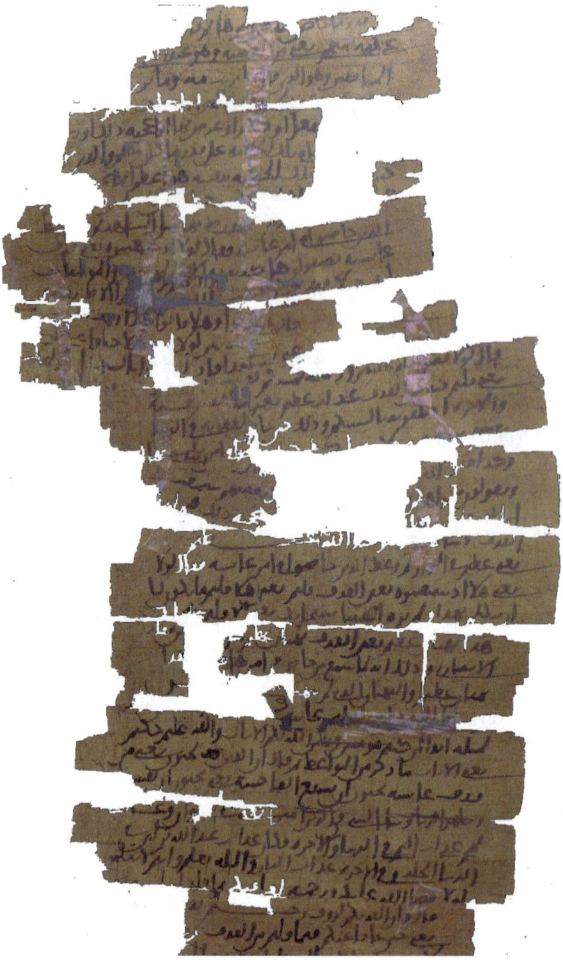

FIGURE 3.1 P.Cair.Arab. inv. 1235 recto: Dhū l-Rumma, *A-min Dimna* (Macartney, ed., poem no. 46)

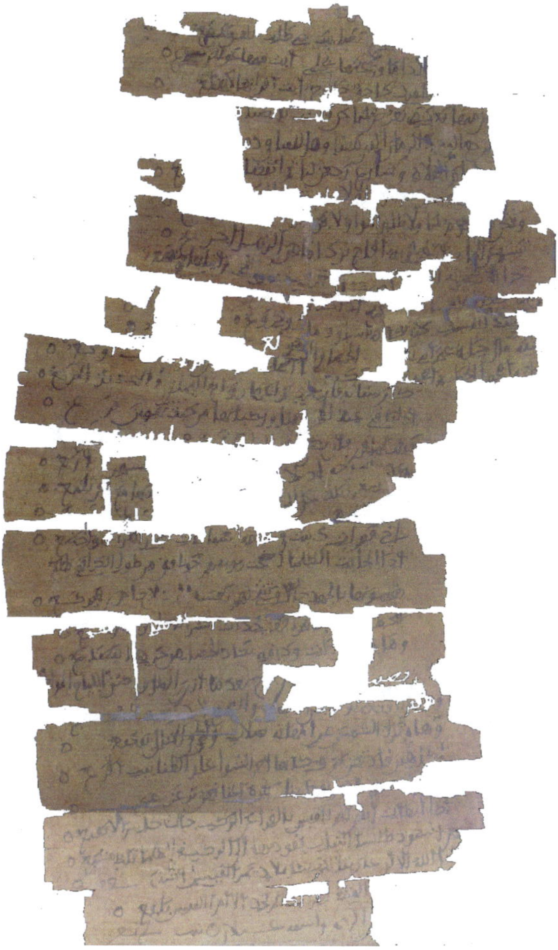

FIGURE 3.2 P.Cair.Arab. inv. 1235 verso: Muqātil b. Sulaymān, *Tafsīr* (Shiḥāṭa, ed., vol. 3: 189.7–192.2)

CHAPTER 4

A Prisoner's Fate in Fatimid Egypt: The Late Coptic Paitos Dossier

Vincent Walter

Abstract

The five texts published in this article constitute a part of the correspondence of a man called Paitos who lived in the Fayyum in the tenth–eleventh century CE. As they are chiefly concerned with his imprisonment and its consequences, they offer a new perspective on tax evasion in early Islamic Egypt. Their language exhibits many peculiarities typical for Late Coptic documentary texts and demonstrates the strong influence of Arabic epistolography on the Coptic letters of this period.

The dossier published in this article comprises five texts written by a single individual, a man named Paitos.[1] Remarkably, all five texts—four letters[2] and a piece of scrap paper with short notes (presumably for drafting a letter)[3]—seem to have been written over a relatively short span of time and deal with closely related matters. They all, in one way or another, are concerned with Paitos' incarceration, from the events leading up to it until his eventual release. Paitos uses these letters to plead his case and to delegate the handling of his affairs during the time of his imprisonment. The upcoming harvest of his fields is an important topic in the letters. Thus, this dossier offers a unique perspective on the very practical problems a prisoner faced in Fatimid Egypt.

The dossier can be dated to roughly the tenth or eleventh century by its writing material: paper. Paper was introduced to Egypt in the ninth century as a commodity imported from Syria, started to be produced locally soon after, and

1 I wish to express my sincerest gratitude to Anna Garnett (Petrie Museum, London), Jane Siegel (Rare Book and Manuscript Library, Columbia University, New York), and Daniel Bornemann (Bibliothèque Nationale et Universitaire, Strasbourg) for their kind help regarding the documents published in this article. I also would like to thank Anne Boud'hors, Jenny Cromwell, and Jelle Bruning for their comments and suggestions. Any remaining mistakes are entirely my own.

2 P.Lond.UniColl. inv. 71024; P.Stras. inv. Kopt. 332(D); P.Col. inv. 594; P.Col. inv. 597.

3 P.Lond.UniColl. inv. 71026.

DOI:10.1163/9789004527874_006

rapidly replaced papyrus as the main writing material during the course of the tenth century.[4] Therefore, it is reasonable to attribute any Coptic documentary text on paper to the tenth century or later.[5]

Nothing is known about the discovery of the texts or how they ended up in their respective collections in London, Strasbourg, and New York.[6] We therefore have to turn to internal evidence to gain insights about their provenance. The language of the texts clearly suggests a location in the Fayyum Oasis,[7] and the people mentioned in the dossier might more specifically point towards Naqlūn and its monastery. A certain Paitos is mentioned in a paper letter discovered in 1989 by the Polish mission in Naqlūn,[8] and a man named Palkait appears both in one of Paitos's letters[9] and in an unpublished paper account book from the monastery of Naqlūn.[10] While this is not conclusive proof, both names are rare enough to reasonably adopt a provenance in Naqlūn as a working hypothesis.

1 Paleography

Like most Late Coptic documentary texts, the four letters of the Paitos dossier are written in a style called sloping uncial—a bilinear script closely connected to the habits of copyists working in the scriptorium on literary manuscripts. In contemporary literary manuscripts, this style of writing was used for paratextual elements, such as colophons or the title of the work,[11] but it was

4 Bloom 2001: 74; Grob 2010: 11–13.

5 For a more in-depth study of the dating of Coptic paper documents, see Legendre 2014: 326–328.

6 There are no acquisition records regarding P.Lond.UniColl. inv. 71024 at the Petrie Museum, nor any regarding P.Stras. inv. Kopt. 332(D) at the BNU Strasbourg. The only information known about the acquisition of P.Col. inv. 594 and 597 is that they belong to a group of Coptic and Arabic papyri purchased on behalf of Columbia University's Semitics Department ca. 1932—most likely by Richard Gottheil, Columbia's professor for Rabbinic literature at that time (I am very grateful to Jane Siegel for this information). The Columbia texts' date of acquisition is further supported by the fact that Walter Ewing Crum quoted P.Col. inv. 594 (under its old inventory number PCol 2) in his dictionary, which was published in 1939.

7 See the section on the linguistic features of the dossier below.

8 SB Kopt. III 1277(B).5.

9 P.Lond.UniColl. inv. 71024.17.

10 BL Or. 13885 fol. 16^{b}.12; fol. 25^{b}.11–12. On the provenance of this important (yet still unpublished) manuscript, see van der Vliet 2015.

11 See Boud'hors 1997 on the use of the sloping uncial in literary manuscripts.

also used to write magical and scientific texts, as well as literary texts of a lower register.[12]

Paitos's hand exhibits a couple of distinctive traits that make it possible to securely identify texts written by him, even if his name is not preserved in the document. The letters ⲏ and ⲙ are written like an inverted ⲛ and are virtually indistinguishable from one another. ⲛ, on the other hand, is sometimes written in a way that a reader not accustomed to Paitos's style could mistake for ⲙ. The ⲃ is reminiscent of the cursive hands of the eighth century[13] and sometimes extends below the line. Several other letters, ⲓ, ⲗ, and ⲩ, can also extend below the line, and the second stroke of ⲭ always does. Also of note are ϭ, which always extends over the next letter in a straight horizontal line, and ⲟ, which occasionally is reduced to a single dot. The combination of ϩ and ⲁ (e.g., in the ubiquitous ⲁϩⲁ) is frequently ligatured.

The supralinear stroke of the nomen sacrum ⲡ̅ⲟ̅ⲥ̅ (for ⲡϫⲁⲉⲓⲥ, "the Lord") usually touches the three letters, creating an impression that it is a single unit rather than a combination of individual letters. This could well be intentional, as the supralinear stroke in the abbreviation ⲗ̅ⲡ̅ (for ⲗⲟⲓⲡⲟⲛ, "furthermore") never touches the letters below.

2 Linguistic Features

Linguistically, the texts exhibit a mixture of features from both the Sahidic and Fayyumic dialects—as documentary texts from this area often do—with a strong inclination towards the latter. Most of the distinctive features of Fayyumic can be observed,[14] as well as a number of linguistic habits that are common to all documentary texts from the wider Middle Egyptian region.[15] Furthermore, the texts exhibit some linguistic traits that are characteristic of texts from the tenth and eleventh centuries, as well as a couple of unique mannerisms hitherto unattested outside the Paitos dossier.

The Fayyumic vowel system is employed consequently, with only a few rare exceptions. Thus, we find ⲁ for ⲟ (e.g., ⲛϣⲁⲣⲡ, ⲉϣⲧⲉⲕⲁ, ⲉⲣⲁ⸗ⲕ),[16] ⲉ for ⲁ (e.g.,

12 See Richter 2018: 300–301.

13 A stylistic influence of the quadrilinear hands of the eighth century is often visible in the bilinear hands of the ninth century and beyond; see Delattre 2007: 128–129.

14 For a very brief overview, see Boud'hors and Calament 2015: 54–55.

15 From Memphis to Aphrodito, corresponding to Paul Kahle's regions A to D; see Kahle 1954: 51.

16 Note, however, ⲉⲣⲟ⸗ⲕ (P.Lond.UniColl. inv. 71024.3).

ⲥϩⲉⲓ, ϣⲉϫⲓ),[17] the atonic final vowel ⲓ (e.g., ϣⲏⲣⲓ, ϣⲓⲛⲓ, ⲡⲛⲟⲩϯ), and some variation between ⲟ (ϩⲟⲃ, ⲡⲟⲧ, ⲕⲁⲗⲟⲥ), ⲱ (ϩⲱⲃ), and sometimes ⲟⲩ (ⲭⲟⲩⲗⲏ, ⲡⲟⲩⲧⲏⲕ). The lexicon is thoroughly Fayyumic, as is most clear in the frequent use of ⲁϩⲁ and ϩⲉⲓ instead of the Sahidic ⲁⲩⲱ and ⲉⲓⲥ, but also, for example, in forms such as ⲃⲣⲉⲉⲓ, "seed," for the Sahidic ⲉⲃⲣⲁ. The ubiquitous use of the Greek loanword ⲕⲁⲗⲱⲥ, "fairly, beautifully," is typical for Fayyumic texts as well.

Yet, Fayyumic's most distinctive phonetic feature, lambdacism, is restricted to a few cases: the prenominal state of ⲉⲓⲣⲉ, "to do" (always (ⲉ)ⲗ- instead of ⲣ̄-), the prenominal state of the conjugation bases (ⲉⲗⲉ-, ⲛⲁⲗⲉ-), the verb ϣⲧⲁⲗⲧⲉⲗ (against Sahidic ϣⲧⲟⲣⲧⲣ), and the late Fayyumic form ⲙⲡⲁⲗ- rendering the Greek preposition παρά.

The following features are found in documentary texts throughout Middle Egypt:

– the suffix pronoun of the 3rd person singular masculine is regularly ⸗ⲃ not ⸗ϥ;[18]
– ⲉ- can replace ⲛ- as the genitive or attribute marker;
– the prepositions ⲙⲛ- and ϩⲛ- are regularly rendered as ⲙⲉ- und ϩⲉ-.

Additionally, Paitos sometimes reduplicates an ⲓ when it is written before a vowel, probably to indicate its syllabic usage.[19] This phenomenon is also attested in a few texts from Ashmunein and Bala'izah.[20]

Typical for the Late Coptic texts of the tenth century and beyond are the occasional omission of ⲉ- or ⲛ- as preposition,[21] genitive,[22] or adverb marker,[23] the appearance of Arabic loanwords,[24] the nomen sacrum ⲡⲟ̄ⲥ̄ for ⲡϫⲁⲉⲓⲥ, "the Lord," and the use of slide-in-blessings.[25] The Coptic terminology is decidedly late as well, with ϭⲱⲡⲉ, "to take, receive," being used instead of ϫⲓ or ⲃⲱϣ ⲉⲃⲟⲗ with its late legal meaning "to set someone free of debt."[26]

---

17 Note, however, ⲥϩⲁⲓ (P.Col. inv. 597.2) and ⲕⲁⲁ⸗ⲃ (P.Col. inv. 597.Add.).

18 The sole exception is ⲕⲉⲉ⸗ϥ in P.Stras. inv. Kopt. 332(D).Add.

19 He writes ⲓⲓⲱⲧ (P.Lond.UniColl. inv. 71024.4), ⲓⲓⲱϩⲓ (P.Col. inv. 594.5; P.Col. inv. 597.18; P.Stras. inv. Kopt. 332(D).11) and ⲁ⸗ⲓⲓ-ⲁϣⲥ (P.Stras. inv. Kopt. 332(D).3), but also ⲓⲱⲕⲓⲙ (P.Stras. inv. Kopt. 332(D).7) and ⲓⲁϩ (P.Col. inv. 597.6; P.Stras. inv. Kopt. 332(D).17).

20 BL Or. 6201 A 110(a); BL Or. 6201 B 52; BL Or. 6201 B 265; P.Bal. 155(?), P.Bal. 216; P.Lond.Copt. I 1124; see Kahle 1954: 80.

21 E.g., ⲧⲁⲟⲩⲁⲩ ø-ⲡⲁⲏⲓ (P.Col. inv. 594.8).

22 E.g., ϩⲉ ⲡⲟⲩⲱϣ ø-ⲡⲛⲟⲩϯ (P.Col. inv. 594.6).

23 E.g., ⲉⲃⲧⲁⲙⲁⲓ ⲡⲉⲛⲧⲉϩⲁ ø-ⲕⲉⲥⲁⲡ (P.Col. inv. 594.2–3).

24 Only a very few Arabic words were borrowed into Coptic before the tenth century. The most recent overview of the issue of Arabic loanwords in Coptic is Richter 2016a.

25 See the section on phraseology below.

26 See Richter 2008: 164 n. 683.

Within the Paitos dossier we find the following Arabic loanwords:

- ⲁⲗⲉⲥⲡⲉϩⲉⲛⲓ, "man from Isfahan, Persian" (from Arabic *al-iṣbahānī*): P.Stras. inv. Kopt. 332(D).7.
- ⲁⲗⲕⲁⲙ unknown meaning: P.Col. inv. 594.23; 25.
- ⲁⲗⲕⲁⲓⲧ, "commander" (from Arabic *al-qā'id*): P.Lond.UniColl. inv. 71024.17.
- ⲁⲗⲙⲟⲩϫⲕⲉⲧ unknown meaning: P.Col. inv. 594.7.
- ⲁⲗϩⲁⲣⲏⲥ, ⲁⲗϩⲁⲣⲉⲥ, "guard" (from Arabic *al-ḥāris*): P.Col. inv. 594.22; 24.
- ⲁⲗϭⲁⲟⲩ, "answer, reply" (from Arabic *al-jawāb*): P.Stras. inv. Kopt. 332(D).6.
- ⲁⲧⲟⲩⲟⲩⲉ, "to allege, claim; to bring an accusation" (from Arabic *iddaʿā* VIII): P.Stras. inv. Kopt. 332(D).8.

Another distinctly late phenomenon is the preposition ϩⲉⲗⲉ⸗, ϩⲓⲗⲉ⸗. In his dictionary, Walter Ewing Crum hesitantly listed some attestations under ϩⲓⲣⲛ-, ϩⲓⲣⲱ⸗,[27] and others under ϩⲁ-, ϩⲁⲣⲟ⸗,[28] but none of these is the correct lemma. Rather, ϩⲉⲗⲉ⸗, ϩⲓⲗⲉ⸗ has to be understood as a Late Fayyumic version of ⲛϩⲏⲧ⸗, since some of its attestations show a complementary distribution with instances of ϩⲛ-, ϩⲉ-, ϧⲉⲛ.[29]

The unusual form of the 2nd person plural suffix pronoun ⸗ⲛⲧⲉ—instead of regular ⸗ⲧⲛ—is hitherto only attested within this dossier,[30] as is the form ⲉⲗ⸗ as prepersonal state of ⲉⲓⲣⲉ.[31]

3 Punctuation

In all four letters of the dossier, Paitos frequently uses punctuation. He employs two different signs: the middle dot and the colon. The distribution of the two signs seems arbitrary, but the middle dot is used more frequently. The punctuation itself is systematic, but the system differs from text to text. Yet, one behavior is consistent across the entire dossier: Paitos never uses a dot at the end of the line.[32]

27 Crum 1939: 290[a].

28 Crum 1939: 634[b]. All attestations quoted by Crum are clearly late: P.Lond.Copt. I 582(A) includes a late blessing formula; P.Lond.Copt. I 643 and SB Kopt. II 884 can be dated to the tenth or eleventh century on paleographic grounds; P.Brux. inv. E 6346 and P.Lond.Copt. I 527 are written on paper.

29 ⲕⲉ ⲡⲉⲕϩⲁ ϩⲉⲗⲉⲛ (P.Lond.Copt. I 582.19–20), cf. ⲕⲉ ⲡⲉⲕϩⲁ ϩⲉ ⲛⲓⲕⲁⲛⲥⲁⲭⲁ (P.Stras. inv. Kopt. 332(D).10) and ⲕⲁⲓ ⲡⲉⲕϩⲁ ϩⲉ ⲡⲉⲛϩⲟⲃ ⲕⲁⲗⲟⲥ (P.Vindob. inv. K 55.10–11, ed. Garel 2016); ⲧⲉⲕⲥⲱ ϩⲉⲗⲉϥ ⲉϣⲁⲙⲧ ⲉϩⲁ[ⲁⲩ] (P.Lond.Copt. I 527.6), cf. ⲥⲱ ϧⲉⲛ, "drink of, from" (Crum 1939: 318[a]).

30 E.g., ⲡⲉ⸗ⲛⲧⲉ-ϣⲓⲛⲓ (P.Lond.UniColl. inv. 71024.20–21), ⲁ⸗ⲛⲧⲉ-ϫⲁ ⲛⲉ⸗ⲛⲧⲉ-ϣⲉϫⲓ (P.Stras. inv. Kopt. 332(D).7–8), ⲡⲉ⸗ⲛⲧⲉ-ϩⲁ (P.Col. inv. 594.2–3), ⲧⲉ⸗ⲛⲧⲉ-ⲁϩⲥ (P.Col. inv. 594.15).

31 P.Stras. inv. Kopt. 332(D).17; P.Col. inv. 594.24.

32 The only exception is at the end of line 12 in P.Col. inv. 594.

In P.Lond.UniColl. inv. 71024, punctuation is extremely frequent and is used consistently between prosodic units. However, there are no dots within the introductory formula in ll. 1–2: ⲥⲏⲛ ⲑ(ⲉ)ⲱ ⲛϣⲁⲣⲡ ⲛ|ϩⲱⲃ ⲛⲓⲙ (ϯϣⲓ|ⲛⲓ · ⲉⲣⲟⲕ). Apparently, this phrase was considered a single unit due to its formulaic nature. Only the omission of a dot before ϯϣⲓⲛⲓ does not fit the pattern.

In P.Col. inv. 594, the usage of punctuation is again relatively consistent, but the units are bigger. Instead of being between prosodic units, the dots are placed between larger semantic segments, sometimes comprising several sentences. In the first half of the text (until about l. 13), the punctuation is very consistent with almost no omitted dots, nor superfluous ones within discursive units. In the following part of the letter, the dots at the beginning of a new thought are occasionally omitted, several times before the discourse marker ⲁϩⲁ and once even before ⲗⲟⲓⲡⲟⲛ. In the final lines of the letter on recto (ll. 17–20), there are no dots at all, but Paitos obviously struggled with the amount of space remaining on the page when writing here. In a few instances, there are unexpected dots within sentences or discursive units. As in P.Lond.UniColl. inv. 71024, the formulaic first paragraph of the letter shows no punctuation. However, in P.Col. inv. 594, it includes the introductory formulae, the greeting, and the blessing.

In P.Stras. inv. Kopt. 332(D), the situation seems more chaotic, yet still systematic. Dots are consistently used before discourse markers such as ⲁϩⲁ, ϩⲉⲓ, ⲗⲟⲓⲡⲟⲛ, and ⲁⲗⲗⲁ, but they also occur before adverbs, prepositional or genitival phrases, and the conjunction ⲁϩⲁ. Dots even intrude in closely linked phrases: a dot is placed between the nominal subject and the infinitive once,[33] and once between the prenominal state of the verb and its direct object.[34] The invocation and greeting do not include any punctuation, but the following slide-in-blessing is separated by middle dots.

P.Col. inv. 597 is too fragmentary for a proper assessment of its system of punctuation. From what is preserved, it most closely resembles the habits of P.Stras. inv. Kopt. 332(D): there are dots before ⲁϩⲁ—both as discourse marker and as conjunction—and before prepositional phrases. As in the other texts, the first paragraph shows no punctuation. In P.Col. inv. 597, the initial paragraph comprises an introduction and greeting, there is no blessing.

Why Paitos used three different systems of punctuation in his letters is puzzling. On what models did he base his use of punctuation? The consistent omission of punctuation within the introductory paragraph, at least, is easily

33 ⲉⲗⲉⲡⲛⲟⲩϯ · ⲃⲁϣⲧ ⲉⲃⲁⲗ ⲕⲁⲗⲱⲥ (P.Stras. inv. Kopt. 332(D).13).

34 ⲛⲧⲁⲕϭⲙ · ϯⲗⲟⲩⲕⲥⲓ ⲛϫⲱⲙⲓ (P.Stras. inv. Kopt. 332(D).4). This is particularly strange; even P.Lond.UniColl. inv. 71024, with its frequent punctuation, does not place a dot there.

explained. This extremely formulaic part of the text was apparently understood as a single unit rather than a freely composed paragraph.

4 Phraseology

Coptic letters often pose problems regarding their contents, be it due to lacunae or the linguistic obscurity of certain passages. In this case, looking at the parts of the letter that are more functional in nature—namely, epistolary formulae and discourse markers—is often immensely helpful. Studying the formulae can help to reconstruct the text lost in a lacuna, often enabling the editor to estimate the number of signs until the end of a line, even if the margin is missing in the entire document. In turn, this can help reconstruct lacunae within the main body of the letter by reducing the number of possible options.

Analyzing discourse markers, on the other hand, can help the editor understand the structure of the writer's argument, even if the details remain elusive. At the very least, one can gain a broad picture of the letter as a whole and the number of different topics discussed.

Generally, a Coptic letter is composed of three parts: an introductory paragraph or prescript, the main body of the text, and a closing paragraph. In many cases, there is an external address, which is not necessarily to be understood as part of the letter as a text, but certainly as part of the letter as a document. The introductory paragraph usually contains an invocation, a greeting formula or internal address, and sometimes a blessing on behalf of the addressee.[35] The very end of the letter is often marked by the phrase ⲟⲩϫⲁⲓ ϩⲙ ⲡϫⲟⲉⲓⲥ, "Farewell in the Lord." Sometimes the closing paragraph also contains a plea for a prayer on the sender's behalf or greetings to be relayed to other parties. While the introductory paragraph is all but mandatory, the closing paragraph can occasionally be omitted. Naturally, the main body of the text is less predictable, but it can often be divided into different segments, with each new topic being introduced by a discourse marker, such as ⲗⲟⲓⲡⲟⲛ, "furthermore."

P.Col. inv. 594, P.Col. inv. 597, and P.Stras. Inv. Kopt. 332(D) all use ϩⲙ ⲡⲣⲁⲛ ⲡⲛⲟⲩⲧⲉ ⲛϣⲁⲣⲡ ⲛϩⲱⲃ ⲛⲓⲙ, "In the name of God. Before all things," as their

35 Biedenkopf-Ziehner (1983: 16) also analyzes some other formulae—for example, regarding the reception of a previous letter—as part of this introductory paragraph. I do not agree with this notion and prefer to analyze them as parts of the main body of the text. Their usual position at the very beginning of the main body is determined for pragmatic reasons.

invocation, while P.Lond.UniColl. inv. 71024 replaces ϩⲉⲙ ⲡⲣⲁⲛ ⲡⲛⲟⲩϯ with the shorter ⲥⲏⲛ ⲑ(ⲉ)ⲱ, "With God." In all four texts, the invocation is followed by the greeting ϯϣⲓⲛⲉ ⲉⲣⲁⲕ ⲕⲁⲗⲱⲥ, "I greet you warmly," with an additional personal address in P.Col. inv. 594 (ⲡⲁⲙⲉⲣⲓ ⲉⲥⲁⲛ, "my beloved brother") and P.Lond.UniColl. inv. 71024 (ⲡⲁϫⲁⲉⲓⲥ ⲛⲓⲱⲧ, "my fatherly lord"). In P.Col. inv. 597, the introductory paragraph ends with the greeting, while the other three texts each add a blessing: ⲡ̅ⲟ̅ⲥ̅ ϩⲁⲣⲉϩ ⲉⲡⲉⲕⲱⲛⲁϩ, "the Lord protect your life" (P.Lond.UniColl. inv. 71024.5–6), ⲡ̅ⲟ̅ⲥ̅ ⲕⲉⲉⲃ, "the Lord preserve him" (P.Stras. inv. Kopt. 332(D).2), and ⲡ̅ⲟ̅ⲥ̅ ⲕⲉⲉⲃ ⲉⲃⲧⲁⲙⲁⲓ ⲡⲉⲛⲧⲉϩⲁ ⲕⲉⲥⲁⲡ, "the Lord preserve him and show me your face one more time" (P.Col. inv. 594.2–3).

4.1 *Phraseology: Blessings*

Blessings, in general as well as in their specific usage in Paitos's letters, are worthy of further discussion. Blessings such as ⲡϫⲟⲉⲓⲥ ⲉϥⲉⲥⲙⲟⲩ ⲉⲣⲟⲕ, "may the Lord bless you," are regularly found in the introductory paragraphs of Coptic letters from the early seventh century onwards[36] until the very end of the use of Coptic as a productive language. Yet, over time these blessings changed, and in the Late Coptic letters of the tenth and eleventh centuries they are distinctly different from their earlier counterparts, in regard to their syntax, their pragmatic functions, and their phraseology.[37]

In the Late Coptic letters, there are two major innovations regarding the use of such blessings: the blessings start to be used on behalf of third parties, and they are no longer confined to the formulaic introductory and closing sections of the letter. Following the conventions of Arabic epistolography, they are also used in the main body of the text as so-called "slide-in-blessings."[38] In Arabic letters, slide-in-blessings are either used on behalf of the addressee—in the second position slot of a section or subsection—or on behalf of a third party—directly after the reference to that party.

Slide-in-blessings on behalf of third parties occur in all the external addresses of Paitos's letters and once in the main body of P.Lond.UniColl. inv. 71024, after a reference to a certain Abū l-Qāsim.[39] The only instance of a slide-

36 The early Coptic letters of the fourth and fifth centuries employ a different set of epistolary formulae than their later counterparts; see Choat 2007.

37 I am currently preparing an article that will offer a broader look at blessing formulae in Coptic documentary texts.

38 This term was introduced by Eva Mira Grob in her study of Arabic papyrus letters from Egypt; see Grob 2010: 33–38 on the usage of slide-in-blessings within Arabic epistolography.

39 ⲁⲡⲟⲩⲗⲕⲁⲥⲉⲙ ⲡ̅ⲟ̅ⲥ̅ · ⲕⲉⲉⲃ · ⲟⲩⲱϯ ⲛⲏⲓ, "Abū l-Qāsim—may the Lord preserve him—has written to me" (P.Lond.UniColl. inv. 71204.6–8).

in-blessing within the body of the text is in P.Lond.UniColl. inv. 71024, a letter characterized by its brevity. However, both the addressee of P.Lond.UniColl. inv. 71024 and Abū l-Qāsim appear to be Paitos's superiors. This relationship is made clear by the reference to the former as "my fatherly lord" and the tone towards Paitos in the quoted statement by the latter. Thus, a higher degree of politeness might have been necessary when communicating with them than when communicating with persons of equal or inferior standing.

The usage of slide-in-blessings referring to third parties can also help explain the unexpected and erroneous usage of 3rd person pronouns in the introductory blessings of P.Col. inv. 594 and P.Stras. inv. Kopt. 332(D). In P.Col. inv. 594.2, the blessing follows a direct address to the addressee, so the usage of a 3rd person pronoun in this place conforms to an internal logic, even if it is not the correct choice. In P.Str. inv. Kopt. 332(D).2, the 3rd person blessing directly follows the greeting, without a parenthetic element referring to the addressee in between. This can only be explained in light of the parallel in P.Col. inv. 594. Paitos's confusion about which pronoun to choose is further emphasized by the inconsistency within the string of blessings in P.Col. inv. 594.2–3. In the initial blessing, he refers to the addressee in the 3rd person, while he uses the 2nd person plural in the subsequent blessing. A range of possibilities may account for Paitos's confusion. Did he copy the blessing from a different text and fail to change all the pronouns? Are these lapses due to a lack in understanding of the Coptic language? Had his Coptic language skills started to fade since Arabic had become the main language in his daily life?

4.2 *Phraseology: Discourse Markers*

In the main body of the letters, Paitos uses a broad range of discourse markers to structure his arguments or introduce new topics. His most frequent discourse marker is ⲁϩⲁ, "and," which is used frequently in this function in P.Col. inv. 594 and 597, and twice in P.Stras. inv. Kopt. 332(D).[40] ⲁϩⲁ is also used as a coordinating conjunction linking nominal phrases, and it is not always easy (or even possible) to tell which function is intended. In addition to ⲁϩⲁ, we find ⲁⲗⲗⲁ, "but,"[41] ⲁϩⲁ ϩⲉⲓ, "and see,"[42] ⲗⲟⲓⲡⲟⲛ, "furthermore,"[43] ⲙⲁⲛ, "verily, for,"[44] ⲙⲁⲛ

40 P.Stras. inv. Kopt. 332(D).13,16.

41 Used with a clear discourse function in P.Stras. inv. Kopt. 332(D).8. In P.Stras. inv. Kopt. 332(D).6 and 17, it functions more like a conjunction, coordinating two clauses.

42 P.Col. inv. 594.13; 21.

43 Written with the abbreviation ⲗⲓ̅ⲡ̅: P.Col. inv. 594.3; 4; 23; P.Col. inv. 597.5; P.Stras. inv. Kopt. 332(D).9.

44 P.Col. inv. 594.9(?); 12.

ϩⲉⲓ, "for see,"[45] ϩⲉⲓ, "see,"[46] and ϫⲉ ϩⲉⲓ, "for see."[47] Only P.Col. inv. 594 uses a discourse marker, ⲗⲟⲓⲡⲟⲛ, to indicate the beginning of the main body of text. The other three texts switch from the introductory paragraph to the main text without any special marker. In P.Lond.UniColl. inv. 71024, Paitos does not use discourse markers at all, except in the two quotations—another indication of the stylistic brevity of the text.

The usual closing formula of Coptic letters, ⲟⲩϫⲁⲓ ϩⲙ ⲡϫⲟⲉⲓⲥ, "farewell in the Lord," occurs only in P.Stras. inv. Kopt. 332(D), following a greeting to a third party. In P.Col. inv 597.30–31, a greeting seems to conclude the letter;[48] the other two letters do not employ any closing formulae at all.

The external address is only preserved in its entirety in P.Col. inv. 594. In P.Col. inv. 597 and P.Stras. inv. Kopt. 332(D), important elements of each are lost to lacunae—only the slide-in-blessings on behalf of the addressee remain. The verso of P.Lond.UniColl. inv. 71024 is empty and shows no signs of an external address.[49]

The external address in P.Col. inv. 594 uses the Sahidic form ⲧⲁⲁ⸗ⲥ instead of an equally possible Fayyumic form, e.g., ⲧⲉⲉⲓ(ⲧ)⸗ⲥ. Considering Paitos's general tendency to use markedly Fayyumic forms, this is somewhat unexpected. However, the formulaic portions of Coptic letters often display a slightly more conservative use of language than the main body of text. This is also observed in the invocation ϩⲉⲙ ⲡⲣⲁⲛ ⲡⲛⲟⲩϯ at the beginning of the texts: everywhere else, ϩⲉ- has replaced ϩⲛ-, yet in the invocation the consonant ⲙ is retained. Additionally, ⲡⲣⲁⲛ follows the Sahidic vowel system, while the rest of the texts consistently use Fayyumic vocalization.

5 Editions

5.1 *No. 1: Letter to a Superior* (*P.Lond.UniColl. inv. 71024*)

17.5 cm high × 5.8 cm wide. 10th–11th centuries. Naqlūn?

A well-preserved strip of light brown paper. The lower right corner is torn off, but this must have happened before the text was written. There are some tiny holes in the document, but the 21 lines of the text are preserved in their entirety. The document lacks any obvious fold lines. Verso is empty.

---

45 P.Stras. inv. Kopt. 332(D).11; P.Lond.UniColl. inv. 71024.15.

46 P.Col. inv. 597.14; P.Stras. inv. Kopt. 332 (D).5; 9; P.Lond.UniColl. inv. 71024.18.

47 P.Col. inv. 597.8; 12.

48 Due to a lacuna, we cannot be entirely sure. But the preserved [...] ⲉⲣⲁⲃ ⲕⲁⲗⲱⲥ clearly points in this direction.

49 One has to wonder if P.Lond.UniColl. inv. 71024 was actually sent or if this document is just

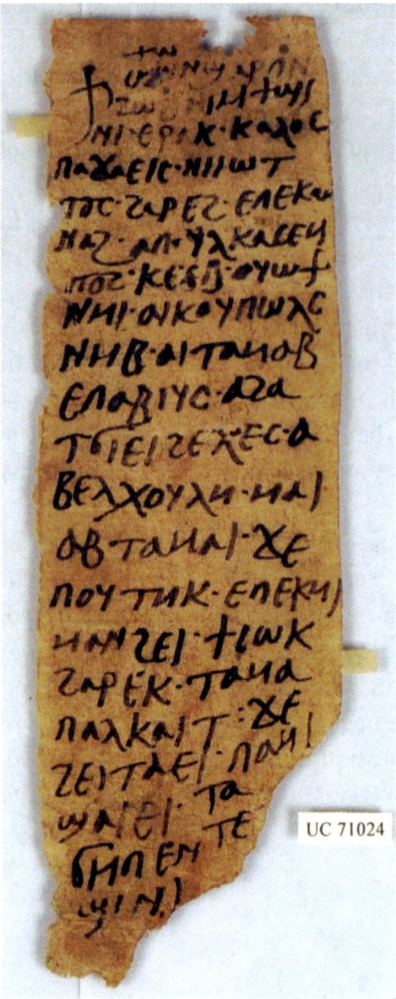

FIGURE 4.1
P.Lond.UniColl. inv. 71024 recto.

(1) ⳨ ⲥⲏⲛ `ⲑ(ⲉ)ⲱ´ ⲛϣⲁⲣⲡ ⲛ-
(2) ϩⲱⲃ ⲛⲓⲙ ϯϣⲓ-
(3) ⲛⲓ · ⲉⲣⲟⲕ · ⲕⲁⲗⲟⲥ
(4) ⲡⲁϫⲁⲉⲓⲥ · ⲛⲓⲓⲱⲧ
(5) ⲡ̅ⲟ̅ⲥ̅ · ϩⲁⲣⲉϩ · ⲉⲡⲉⲕⲱ-
(6) ⲛⲁϩ · ⲁⲡⲟⲩⲗⲕⲁⲥⲉⲙ
(7) ⲡ̅ⲟ̅ⲥ̅ · ⲕⲉⲉ̣ⲃ · ⲟⲩⲱϯ
(8) ⲛⲏⲓ · ⲁⲓⲕⲟⲩ ⲡⲱⲗⲥ
(9) ⲛⲏⲃ · ⲁⲓⲧⲁⲙⲁⲃ

---

the draft of a letter. The missing external address and the unusual format—in comparison with the other letters in the Paitos dossier—might indicate the latter.

(10) ⲉⲡⲁⲃⲓⲩⲥ · ⲁϩⲁ
(11) ⲧϭⲓ ⲉⲓϩⲉⲗⲉⲥ · ⲁ-
(12) ⲃⲉⲗ ⲭⲟⲩⲗⲏ · ⲙⲁⲓ
(13) ⲁⲃⲧⲁⲙⲁⲓ · ϫⲉ
(14) ⲡⲟⲩⲧⲏⲕ · ⲉⲡⲉⲕⲏⲓ
(15) ⲙⲁⲛ ϩⲉⲓ · ϯⲥⲱⲕ
(16) ϩⲁⲣⲉⲕ · ⲧⲁⲙⲁ
(17) ⲡⲁⲗⲕⲁⲓⲧ : ϫⲉ
(18) ϩⲉⲓ ⲧⲁ⟨ⲓ⟩ⲉⲓ · ⲡⲁⲏⲓ
(19) ϣⲁⲓⲉⲓ · ⲧⲁ-
(20) ϭⲙ ⲡⲉⲛⲧⲉ-
(21) ϣⲓⲛⲓ

(1) With God (σὺν θεῷ)! Before (2) all things I greet you warmly (καλῶς), (3) my fatherly lord—(5) may the Lord protect your (6) life. Abū l-Qāsim—(7) may the Lord preserve him—has written (8) to me.

I have provided the harvest (9) for him. I told him (10) about my life (βίος) and (11) the situation I am in. (12) He was angry with me. (13) He told me: (14), "Go to your house! (15) For, see, I am liable (16) for you(r debts). Tell (17) Palkait (*al-qā'id*): (18) 'See, I have come to my house.'"

(19) I will come and (20–21) visit you.

6–8 ⲁⲡⲟⲩⲗⲕⲁⲥⲉⲙ | ⲡⲟ̅ⲥ̅ ⲕⲉⲉⲃ ⲟⲩⲱϯ | ⲛⲏⲓ: The initial ⲁ is to be understood as both the perfect base ⲁ and the beginning of the name Abū.[50] A man named Abū l-Qāsim is mentioned in P.Ryl.Copt. 464.5, a tax receipt dated to the year 397/1006–1007. The slide-in-blessing separating subject and verb is noteworthy, but not without parallel; see, for example, ⲛⲧⲉⲁⲡⲟⲩ ⲓⲁⲕⲱⲃ ⲡⲉϥⲣⲱⲙⲓ | ⲡⲟ̅ⲥ̅ ⲭⲁϥ ⲃⲱⲣⲡ ⲛⲏⲓ (P.Lond.Copt. I 545(A).6–7).

10 ⲡⲁⲃⲓⲩⲥ: The ⲩ in ⲃⲓⲩⲥ for Greek βίος is highly unusual. Hans Förster lists no similar spelling in his dictionary of Greek loanwords in Coptic documentary texts,[51] and Paul Kahle mentions no instance of ⲩ replacing ⲟ in his analysis of dialectical variations in Sahidic nonliterary texts.[52] Ypsilon is regularly attested as an alternative spelling for ⲏ or ⲓ, and

50 The name "Abū" could be rendered in Coptic both with or without an initial ⲁ; see Legendre 2014: 403–407.

51 Förster 2002: 136.

52 Kahle 1954: 48–192.

sometimes even ⲉ, but there is no phonetic reason why ⲩ should be able to replace ⲟ. A possible explanation could lie in the contemporary pronunciation of βίος in the Fayyum. If the ⲟ was pronounced like a shwa, ⲩ would be as good a choice as any other vowel to render it.

11 ⲧϭⲓ ⲉⲓϩⲉⲗⲉⲥ: ϭⲓ seems to be a reanalysis of the nominalizing prefix ϭⲓⲛ-, "act of, manner of."[53] It is used in a very similar fashion in another text in this dossier: ⲁⲓⲉⲓⲙⲓ ⲧϭⲓ ⲛ̣ⲧ̣ⲁⲕ|ⲥϩⲉⲓ ⲛⲏⲓ ϩⲓⲗⲉⲥ (P.Col. inv. 594.3–4).

14 ⲡⲟⲩⲧⲏⲕ · ⲉⲡⲉⲕⲏⲓ: I read ⲡⲟⲩⲧⲏⲕ as a variant for ⲡⲱⲧ ⲛⲏⲕ, "go." The meaning is gleaned from the context, while the analysis as ⲡⲟⲩⲧⲏ⸗ⲕ with a reflexive pronoun is supported by a parallel in a contemporary Fayyumic text: ⲗ ⲡⲉϥⲙⲉⲉⲩⲉ ⲧⲉϥⲡⲟⲩⲧⲏϥ (P.Brux. inv. E. 6346.19). Note, though, that Paitos writes ⲡⲟⲧ ⲛⲏⲃ in P.Col. inv. 594.23–24.

15–16 ϯⲥⲱⲕ | ϩⲁⲣⲉⲕ: ⲥⲱⲕ ϩⲁ-, "to be liable for something" is a Coptic legal term used primarily in deeds of surety, particularly from the region of Ashmunein. Usually, the syntax of ⲥⲱⲕ is slightly different, specifying after ϩⲁ- the kind of payment owed rather than the debtor.[54] This passage shows that Abū l-Qāsim acted as a guarantor on Paitos's behalf. Guarantors played a vital role in the collection of taxes from rural Egypt. In the first centuries after the conquest, Christian notables were the ones guaranteeing the full payment of the taxes, but in the middle of the eighth century, Muslim officials increasingly assumed this role.[55]

16–18 ⲧⲁⲙⲁ ⲡⲁⲗⲕⲁⲓⲧ : ϫⲉ ϩⲉⲓ ⲧⲁ⟨ⲓ⟩ⲉⲓ · ⲡⲁⲏⲓ: It is not clear if this sentence is part of the quote from Abū l-Qāsim's earlier letter or an instruction for the addressee of P.Lond.UniColl. inv. 71024. ⲡⲁⲗⲕⲁⲓⲧ renders the Arabic *al-qāʾid*, "the commander."[56] In Arabic documents from the Fatimid period, the term *qāʾid* could either refer to a military commander or the governor of a city or province, or be used as a honorific title.[57] The title is used both in connection with tax collection[58] and the arrest of a man.[59] A ⲡⲁⲗⲕⲁⲓⲧ is attested as the sender of the Fayyumic letter CPR XXXIV 73, mentioned twice in the unpublished Fayyumic account book BL Or. 13885 from Naqlūn,[60] and twice in the letter P.Lond.Copt. I 1119 from Ashmunein. It is not possible in any of these

53 Crum 1939: 819ᵃ.
54 For examples of ⲥⲱⲕ ϩⲁ- in Coptic legal documents, see Richter 2008: 258.
55 Sijpesteijn 2014: 159–160.
56 For attestations of *qāʾid* in Arabic letters from Egypt, see Diem 2017: 408.
57 Diem 1997: 294.
58 P.Berl.Arab. II 33.
59 P.Vind.Arab. II 36.
60 This text has most recently been discussed in van der Vliet 2015.

attestations to decide conclusively if the term is used as an official title or as a personal name.[61]

5.2 *No. 2: Letter concerning Various Issues* (*P.Stras.inv.Kopt.332*(*D*)*recto*)

13.0 cm high × 13.0 cm wide. 10th–11th centuries. Naqlūn?

A well-preserved sheet of light brown paper with 19 lines of text. All the edges are preserved, but the upper right corner has been torn off. Otherwise, the text is complete. On the verso, parts of the external address are preserved in two lines, the rest of the page is empty. Four horizontal folding lines are visible.

Recto

(1) ⳨ ϩⲉⲙ ⲡⲣⲁⲛ ⲡⲛⲟⲩϯ ⲛϣⲁⲣⲡ ⲛϩⲟ̣[ⲃ ⲛⲓⲙ ϯϣⲓⲛⲓ]
(2) ⲉⲣⲁⲕ ⲕⲁⲗⲟⲥ · ⲡ̅ⲟ̅ⲥ̅ ⲕⲉⲉⲃ · ⲁⲧⲉⲕ[ⲥϩⲉⲓ ⲉⲓ ⲛⲏⲓ]
(3) ⲁⲓⲓⲁϣⲥ ⲁ⟨ⲓ⟩ⲉⲓⲙⲓ ⲧϭⲓ ⲛⲧⲁⲕⲥϩⲉⲓ ϩⲉ̣ⲗⲉ[ⲥ 5–6]
(4) ⲣⲓ ⲙⲁⲕ : ⲛⲧⲁⲕϭⲏ · ϯⲗⲟⲩⲕⲥⲓ ⲛϫⲱⲙⲓ ⲁ[ⲕ 2–3]
(5) ⲛⲏⲓ : ϩⲓⲗⲉⲥ · ϩⲉⲓ ⲡⲣⲱϣⲓ ⲛⲥϩⲉⲓ ⲁⲓⲥϩⲉⲧⲟⲩ ⲛⲏⲕ̣
(6) ⲙⲡⲉⲕⲥⲧⲁ ⲟⲩⲁⲗϭⲁⲟⲩ ⲉⲣⲁⲓ · ⲁⲗⲗ̣ⲁ ⲁⲕϫⲓ ⲡϣⲉ-
(7) ϫⲓ · ⲡⲁⲗⲉⲥⲡⲉϩⲉⲛⲓ ⲁϩⲁ ⲓⲱⲕⲓⲙ : ⲁⲛⲧⲉϫⲁ ⲛⲉⲛⲧⲉ-
(8) ϣⲉϫⲓ · ⲁⲗⲗⲁ ⲡⲉⲧϣⲁⲕⲁⲧⲟⲩⲟⲩⲉ ϫⲁⲁⲃ · ϣⲁⲃⲟⲗ
(9) ⲙⲉ ⲡⲛⲟⲩϯ · ϩⲉⲓ ⲕⲥⲁⲟⲩⲛ · ⲉⲡⲉⲧϩⲓ ⲡⲁϩⲏⲧ : ⲗⲓ̅ⲡ̅ ⲡⲁ⟨ⲥⲁⲛ⟩
(10) ⲕⲉ ⲡⲉⲕϩⲁ · ϩⲉ ⲛⲓⲕⲁⲛⲥⲁⲭⲁ : ⲁϩⲁ ⲛⲁⲥⲛⲏⲩ · ⲁϩⲁ ⲕⲉ
(11) ⲡⲉⲕϩⲁ : ϩⲉ ⲛⲓⲓⲱϩⲓ ϣⲁⲛⲧⲟⲩⲁϩⲥⲟⲩ : ⲙⲁⲛ ϩⲉⲓ
(12) ⲕⲥⲁⲟⲩⲛ · ⲉⲡⲁⲃⲓⲩⲥ · ⲁϩ̣ⲁ̣ ⲡⲁⲉϣⲧⲉⲕⲁ ⲉⲓϩⲉⲗⲉⲃ
(13) ⲉⲗⲉⲡⲛⲟⲩϯ · ⲃⲁϣⲧ ⲉⲃⲁⲗ ⲕⲁⲗⲱⲥ · ⲁϩⲁ ϯ ⲡⲁϣⲓ-
(14) ⲛⲓ ⲛⲥⲧⲁⲩⲣⲱⲥ · ⲕⲁⲗⲱⲥ · ⲧⲁⲙⲁⲃ · ϫⲉ ⲥⲁⲙⲉ ⲛⲉⲕ-
(15) ⲥⲛⲏⲩ : ⲁϩⲁ ⲥⲁⲙⲉ ⲧⲁϣⲱϣⲓ ϣⲁⲛⲧⲉⲡⲛⲟⲩϯ
(16) ⲃⲁϣⲧ ⲉⲃⲁⲗ : ϩⲉ ⲡⲓⲉϣⲧⲉⲕⲁ · ⲁϩⲁ ⲧⲁⲙⲁⲃ · ϫ(ⲉ) ⲁⲕ-
(17) ⲓⲁϩ ⲡⲉⲧⲁⲡⲉⲕⲥⲁⲛ ⲉⲗⲃ ⲉⲣⲁⲛ : ⲁⲗⲗⲁ ⲡⲉⲃϩⲉ-
(18) ⲙⲁⲧ ϣⲉⲡ : ϯϣⲓⲛⲓ ⲥⲁⲙⲟⲩⲏⲗ ⲡⲉⲕϣⲏⲣⲓ
(19) ⲟⲩϫⲁⲓ ⲡ̅ⲟ̅ⲥ̅

Verso: Address

(1) [ⲧⲁⲁⲥ ⲉ- 4–5]ⲥ ⲡ̅ⲟ̅ⲥ̅ ⲕⲉⲉϥ
(2) [ϩⲓⲧⲉⲛ ⲡⲁⲓⲧ]ⲟⲥ

(1) In the name of God. Before [all] things. [I greet] (2) you warmly (καλῶς)—may the Lord preserve him (i.e., you). Your [letter] has [reached me]. (3) I have

61 Coptic names based on occupations or titles are not uncommon; see Heuser 1929: 69–70.

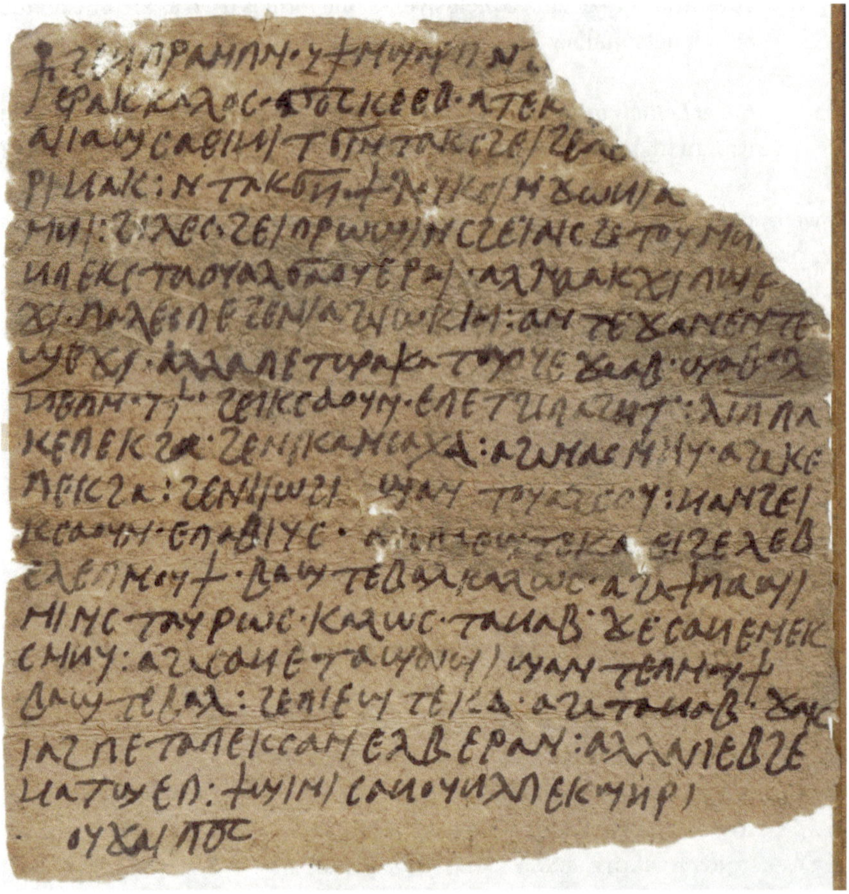

FIGURE 4.2 P.Stras. inv. Kopt. 332(D) recto.

read it. I understood what you wanted to tell me. […] (4) … you. You have received the … -book. [You] have […] (5) for me in it.

See, many letters have I written to [you], (6) (yet) you did not return a (single) reply to me. Rather (ἀλλά), you believed the statement (7) by al-Iṣbahānī and Jôkim. You (2nd plur.) said your (8) words. But (ἀλλά) what you will claim (*iddaʿā*), say it finally (9) with God. See, you know what is on my mind.

Furthermore: My ⟨brother⟩, (10) take care of the *kansacha* and my brethren. And take (11) care of the fields until they have been harvested. For see, (12) you know about my life (βίος) and the (lit.: my) prison I am in—(13) may God properly set me free.

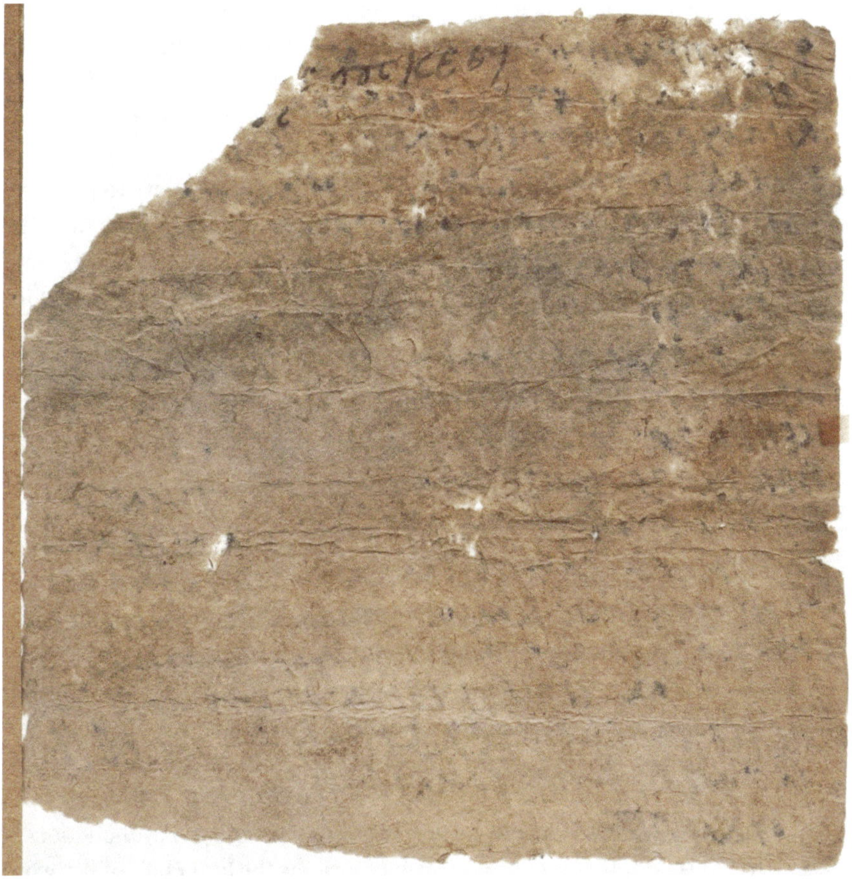

FIGURE 4.3 P.Stras. inv. Kopt. 332(D) verso.

And give my greetings (14) to Stauros warmly (καλῶς). Tell him: "Provide for your (15) brethren and pay for my field until God (16) releases me from this prison." And tell him: "You have (17) seen what your brother has done for us." But (ἀλλά) thanks be to him.

(18) I greet Samuel, your son. (19) Farewell in the Lord.

2 ⲡ̅ⲟ̅ⲥ̅ ⲕⲉⲉⲃ: The 3rd person pronoun in ⲕⲉⲉⲃ is a scribal error.[62]

62 See also the section on phraseology above.

3 ⲁ⟨ⲓ⟩ⲉⲓⲙⲓ ⲧϭⲓ ⲛⲧⲁⲕⲥϩⲉⲓ ϩⲉ̣ⲗⲉ[ⲥ]: Literally: “I understood the way you have written in [it].” ϭⲓ is a reanalysis of the nominal base ϭⲓⲛ-, which forms nouns of action with the meaning “act of, manner of.”[63] The phrase is a reflection of the confirmation section found in many contemporary Arabic letters.[64]

4 ⲛⲧⲁⲕϭⲏ ϯⲗⲟⲩⲕⲥⲓ ⲛϫⲱⲙⲓ ⲁ[ⲕ 2–3] | ⲛⲏⲓ : ϩⲓⲗⲉⲥ: ϭⲏ- for ϭⲛ-, the prenominal state of ϭⲓⲛⲉ, is attested in a small number of Fayyumic letters.[65] There might be some semantic confusion with ϫⲓ.[66]

The identification of ⲗⲟⲩⲕⲥⲓ is difficult. Its morphology points towards a Greek origin and is reminiscent of the Fayyumic renderings of Greek ὁλοκόττινος, “solidus” (referring to the Arabic *dīnār*) as ⲗⲟⲩⲕⲟⲧⲥⲓ, ⲗⲟⲩⲕⲱⲥⲓ, or similar. ὁλοκόττινος, a masculine noun in Greek and most Coptic texts, is sometimes used as a female noun in Fayyumic documentary texts.[67] If we read ⲗⲟⲩⲕⲥⲓ as ὁλοκόττινος, ϫⲱⲙⲓ should signify “papyrus (sheets)” rather than “book.” The entire passage would then read “you have received (lit.: found) a dinar’s worth of papyrus.” However, considering what is preserved of the following sentence, an actual book seems more likely—maybe a ledger or account book. Another possibility is to read ⲗⲟⲩⲕⲥⲓ as a (hitherto unknown) rendering of Greek λόγος, which in this context would refer to an account or list.[68] This understanding does not, though, remove the problem concerning gender, as λόγος is a masculine noun as well.

6 ⲟⲩⲁⲗϭⲁⲟⲩ: ⲁⲗϭⲁⲟⲩ is to be read as a loanword from Arabic *al-jawāb*, “the answer, the reply,” a term frequently attested in Arabic letters.[69] Yet, its Coptic orthography is problematic, as the latter half of the word seems to be missing. One would expect ⲁ or ⲉ for ā and ⲡ for b.[70] The usage of an Arabic loanword instead of the well-established and widely used Graeco-Coptic term ⲁⲡⲟⲕⲣⲓⲥⲓⲥ, “reply,” demonstrates the extent of the cultural and linguistic exchange between Egyptians and Arabs by the tenth century.

63 Crum 1939: 819[a].
64 See Grob 2010: 48–52.
65 P.Fay.Copt. 16.11; P.Fay.Copt. 22.4; 5; 14; P.Lond.Copt. I 583.7; P.Vindob. inv. K 163 (see Krall 1892: 47); P.Vindob. inv. K 1132 recto (see Krall 1892: 49).
66 Pointed out by Crum in his comments on P.Fay.Copt. 16.
67 E.g., P.Lond.Copt. I 583.8; CPR IV 37.4; CPR IV 86.5.
68 I am indebted to Anne Boud’hors for this suggestion.
69 See Diem 2017: 95–96.
70 See Richter 2016a for an overview of Arabic loanwords in Coptic.

There is an interesting structural parallel in another unpublished letter: ⲁⲧⲉⲕⲁⲣⲣⲟⲩⲕⲁⲁⲩ ⲉⲓ ⲛⲁⲓ, "your letter has reached me" (P.Stras. inv. Kopt. 409.4) uses the Arabic *al-ruqʿa*, "the letter,"[71] instead of the Coptic ⲥϩⲁⲓ in a very common epistolary phrase.

7 ⲡⲁⲗⲉⲥⲡⲉϩⲉⲛⲓ: ⲁⲗⲉⲥⲡⲉϩⲉⲛⲓ renders the Arabic nisba *al-iṣbahānī*, "the man from Iṣfahān." The same term is borrowed as an attributive adjective in the Late Coptic medical papyrus P.Louvre AF 12530.ro. 79: ϫⲱϩⲣ̄ ⲁⲥⲡⲓϩⲉⲛⲓ, Arabic *kuhl iṣbahānī* "Iṣbahānī antimony."[72]

8 ⲁⲗⲗⲁ ⲡⲉⲧϣⲁⲕⲁⲧⲟⲩⲟⲩⲉ ϫⲁⲁⲃ · ϣⲁⲃⲟⲗ: The nominalized relative clause lacks a resumptive element. The verb ⲁⲧⲟⲩⲟⲩⲉ appears to be of Arabic origin. I propose reading it as *iddaʿā* VIII, "to allege, claim; to bring an accusation."[73]

9 ⲡⲁ⟨ⲥⲁⲛ⟩: ⲡⲁ⟨ⲉⲓⲱⲧ⟩ would be plausible as well. There is no clear indication of the hierarchical relationship between Paitos and the addressee within this letter.

10 ⲕⲉ ⲡⲉⲕϩⲁ · ϩⲉ ⲛⲓⲕⲁⲛⲥⲁⲭⲁ: The phrase ⲕⲱ ⲡⲉ⸗pron-ϩⲟ usually means "to take care of, to pay attention to."[74] *Kansacha* are also attested in P.Lond.Copt. I 609(A);[75] P.Lond.Copt. I 1135;[76] and SB Kopt. I 280.[77] The first element, ⲕⲁⲛ-, is a construct form of ⲕⲟⲩⲓ, "small, little." The second element ⲥⲁⲭⲁ literally means, "great scribe," an official title that is still poorly understood, and so ⲕⲁⲛⲥⲁⲭⲁ could be understood either as "deputy ⲥⲁⲭⲟ" or "apprentice ⲥⲁⲭⲟ."[78] Their exact function remains obscure.

13 ⲉⲗⲉⲡⲛⲟⲩϯ · ⲃⲁϣⲧ ⲉⲃⲁⲗ ⲕⲁⲗⲱⲥ: The structural differences between this prayer and the dossier's frequent slide-in-blessings[79] are striking. In this prayer, the full form of the optative (ⲉⲗⲉ-) is used, while

71 Diem 2017: 206–207.

72 For P.Louvre AF 12530, see Richter 2014: 165–183.

73 Diem 2017: 171.

74 See Garel 2016: 52.

75 The text is only partially edited; the term (spelled ⲕⲁⲛⲍⲁⲭⲁ) is written in the last line of the text and no context is provided.

76 ϭⲛ | ⲡϣⲓⲛⲉ ⲛⲓⲕⲟⲩⲓ ⲍⲁⲭⲟ ϩⲁⲣⲟⲓ, "visit the koui(n)saxo on my behalf" (P.Lond.Copt. I 1135.14–15).

77 ⲁⲡⲕⲁⲛ|ⲥⲁⲭⲁ ⲧⲁⲙⲁⲓ, "the *kansacha* told me" (SB Kopt I 280.3–4, a reedition of this text is being prepared by Esther Garel).

78 For this interpretation, see ⲛⲉⲕⲟⲩⲛⲧⲉⲭⲛⲓⲧⲓⲥ ⲛⲧⲁⲩⲧⲉⲓⲧⲟⲩ ⲛⲉⲥⲉϩ ϫⲉ ⲧⲥⲁⲙⲁⲩ ⲛⲉⲧⲉⲭⲛⲓ, "the apprentice-craftsmen who had been given to the teacher (with the words): 'teach them the crafts'" (CPR IV 1.12).

79 P.Col. inv. 594.2; address; P.Stras. inv. Kopt. 332(D).2; address; P.Lond.UniColl. inv. 71024.5; 7.

the slide-in-blessings employ an unmarked form.[80] Additionally, the prayer invokes ⲡ-ⲛⲟⲩϯ, “God,” while the slide-in-blessings use the abbreviation ⲡ̅ⲟ̅ⲥ̅, “the Lord,” which is restricted to formulaic uses within this dossier. ⲃⲱϣ ⲉⲃⲟⲗ, “to set (someone) free of debt” is a legal term only attested in Late Coptic texts;[81] see also P.Col. inv. 594.5; 17.

14–15 ⲥⲁⲙⲉ ⲛⲉⲕ|ⲥⲛⲏⲩ ⲁϩⲁ ⲥⲁⲙⲉ ⲧⲁϣⲱϣⲓ: ⲥⲁⲙⲉ is a hitherto unknown Coptic verb. I suggest reading it as a construct form of ⲥⲙⲓⲛⲉ (which is usually ⲥⲙⲛ- or ⲥⲙⲉⲛ-) with the meaning “to provide, pay for” as it is used in the colophons.[82] In the colophons, it is only used regarding books, but this is due to the restricted content of this text type. Since most of the known Coptic colophons are decidedly late texts, they constitute a good point of comparison.

17 ⲡⲉⲧⲁⲡⲉⲕⲥⲁⲛ ⲉⲗⲃ ⲉⲣⲁⲛ: The prenominal state of ⲉⲓⲣⲉ, “to do,” ⲉⲗ-, is used with a suffix pronoun instead of the grammatically correct prepersonal state ⲉⲓ(ⲧ)⸗. I am not aware of any parallels outside this dossier, raising the possibility that this might be an innovation by Paitos.

Address: The arrangement of the external address with the recipient’s name in the upper line and the sender’s name in the line below is slightly unusual. Normally, the recipient’s name is written on the left and the sender’s name on the right, with some space left empty between the names for the placement of a seal.

5.3 *No. 3: Letter concerning the Harvest* (*P.Col. inv. 594*)

13.5 cm high × 15.6 cm wide. 10th–11th centuries. Naqlūn?

A dark brown sheet of paper, reasonably well-preserved. The upper left corner has been torn off and there are a few small lacunae within the text. All edges are preserved. The lower edge is not a straight line, but the writer adjusted his text accordingly. Recto contains 20 lines of Coptic text, verso another 11. The external address is written over two lines at the lower edge of verso, at 180° to the main text. The last three lines of Coptic text on verso are obscured by the remnants of three lines of an earlier Arabic text. Six horizontal fold marks are visible, as well as a vertical one.

80 The phenomenon is noteworthy in its own right. This unmarked optative form, which is only attested in slide-in-blessings (a distinct form of blessing based on Arabic phraseology), has to be explained by its derivation from the Arabic imperfect, which can be used as an optative. I plan to discuss this issue in more detail in a forthcoming article about blessing formulae in Coptic documentary texts.

81 Richter 2008: 190.

82 Crum 1939: 338a.

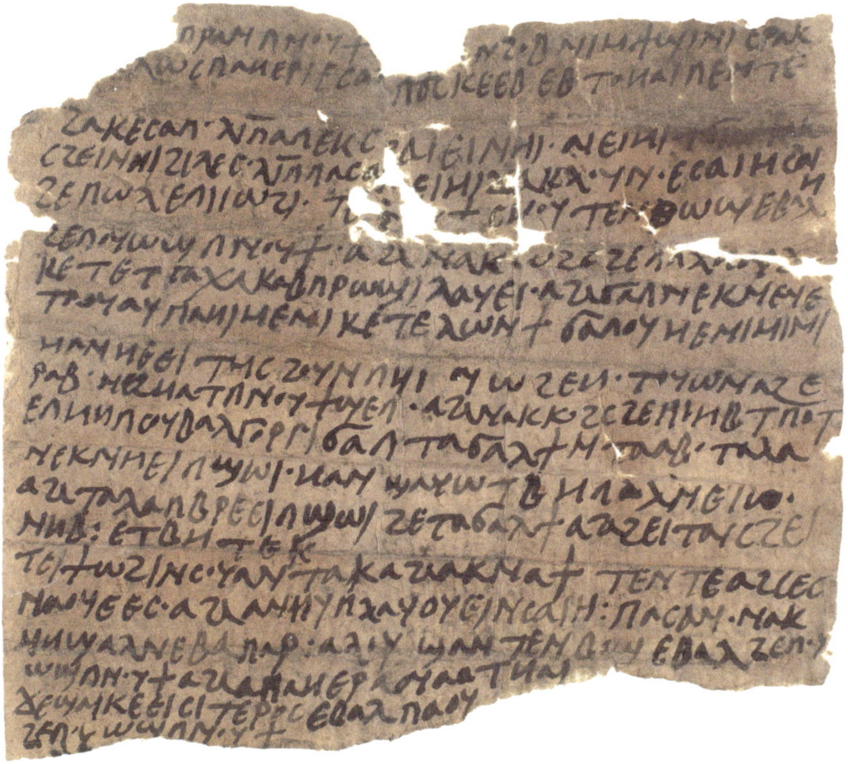

FIGURE 4.4 P.Col. inv. 594 recto.

Recto

(1) [⳨ ϩⲉⲙ] ⲡⲣⲁⲛ ⲡⲛⲟⲩϯ [ⲛϣⲁⲣⲡ] ⲛϩⲟⲃ ⲛⲓⲙ ϯϣⲓⲛⲓ ⲉⲣⲁⲕ
(2) [ⲕⲁ]ⲗⲱⲥ ⲡⲁⲙⲉⲣⲓ ⲉⲥⲁⲛ̣ ⲡ̅ⲟ̅ⲥ̅ ⲕⲉⲉⲃ ⲉⲃⲧⲁⲙⲁⲓ ⲡⲉⲛⲧⲉ-
(3) ϩⲁ ⲕⲉⲥⲁⲡ · ⲗⲓ̅ⲡ̅ ⲁⲡⲉⲕⲥϩⲁⲓ ⲉⲓ ⲛⲏⲓ · ⲁⲓⲉⲓⲙⲓ ⲧϭⲓ ⲛ̣ⲧⲁⲕ-
(4) ⲥϩⲉⲓ ⲛⲏⲓ ϩⲓⲗⲉⲥ · ⲗⲓ̅ⲡ̅ ⲡⲁⲥⲁ[ⲛ] ⲉⲓⲙⲓ ϫ(ⲉ) ⲁⲕⲗ ⲟⲩⲛ · ⲉⲥⲁⲓⲏⲥⲁⲓ´ⲏ`
(5) ϩⲉ ⲡⲱⲗ ⲉⲡⲓⲓⲱϩⲓ · ⲧⲉ̣ . [.] . ϯ ⲥⲙⲟⲩ ⲧⲉⲛⲃⲱϣ ⲉⲃⲁⲗ
(6) ϩⲉ ⲡⲟⲩⲱϣ ⲡⲛⲟⲩϯ · ⲁϩⲁ ⲛⲁⲕⲱϩⲥ ϩⲉ ⲡⲁ̣ⲗⲙ̣ⲟⲩϫ-
(7) ⲕⲉⲧ ⲉⲧⲥⲁⲭⲁ ⲕⲁⲃ ⲡⲣⲱϣⲓ ⲗⲁⲩⲉⲓ · ⲁϩⲁ ϭⲁⲡ ⲛⲉⲕⲛⲉⲩⲉ
(8) ⲧⲁⲟⲩⲁⲩ ⲡⲁⲏⲓ ⲙⲉ ⲛⲓⲕⲉⲧⲉⲗⲱⲛϯ ϭⲁⲡⲟⲩ ⲙⲉ ⲛⲓⲙⲓⲛⲓ
(9) ⲙⲁⲛ ⲙⲉⲉⲓⲧⲏⲥ ϩⲟⲩⲛ ⲡⲏⲓ ⲟⲩⲱϩⲉⲙ · ⲧⲟⲩⲱⲛⲁϩ ⲉ-
(10) ⲣⲁⲃ · ⲛⲉϩⲙⲁⲧ ⲡⲛⲟⲩϯ ϣⲉⲡ · ⲁϩⲁ ⲛⲁⲕⲕⲟϩⲥ ϩⲉ ⲡⲓⲏⲃⲧ ⲡⲟⲧ
(11) ⲉⲡⲙⲏ ⲡⲥⲟⲩⲃⲁⲗ ⲅⲟⲣⲅⲓ ϭⲁⲡ ⲧⲁϭⲁⲗϯ ⲛⲧⲁⲁⲃ · ⲧⲁⲗⲁ
(12) ⲛⲉⲕⲛⲏⲉⲓ ⲡϣⲱⲓ · ⲙⲁⲛ ϣⲁⲩⲱⲧⲃ ⲙⲡⲁⲗ ⲛⲉⲓϣ̣ ·
(13) ⲁϩⲁ ⲧⲁⲗⲁ ⲡⲃⲣⲉⲉⲓ ⲡϣⲱⲓ ϩⲉ ⲧⲁϭⲁⲗϯ ⲁϩⲁ ϩⲉⲓ ⲧⲁⲓⲥϩⲉⲓ
(14) ⲛⲏⲃ : ⲉⲧⲃⲏⲧⲉⲕ

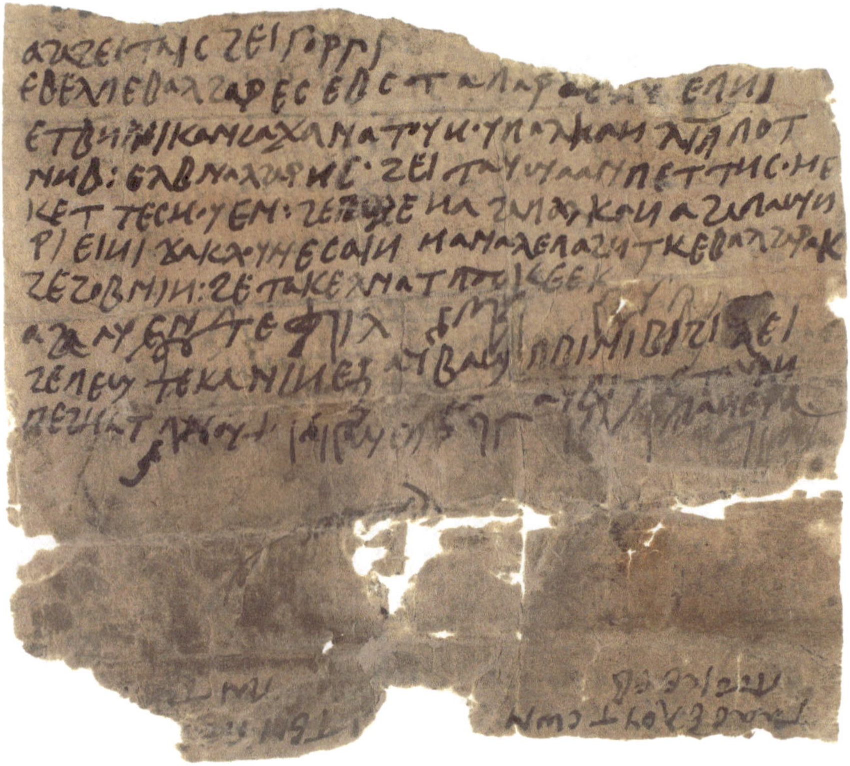

FIGURE 4.5 P.Col. inv. 594 verso.

(15) ⲧⲥⲓϯⲱϩⲓ ⲛⲥⲟⲩⲁ ⲛⲧⲁⲕ ⲁϩⲁ ⲁⲕⲛⲁϯ ⲧⲉⲛⲧⲉⲁϩⲥ ⲉⲥ-
(16) ⲛⲁϣ̣ⲉⲉⲥ · ⲁϩⲁ ⲁⲛⲏⲩ ⲡⲗⲁⲩⲟⲩⲉⲓ ⲛⲥⲁⲓⲏ : ⲡⲁⲥⲁⲛ · ⲛⲁⲕ-
(17) ⲛⲏϣⲁⲗ ⲛⲉⲃⲁⲡⲁⲣ : ⲁⲗⲟⲩ ϣⲁⲛⲧⲉⲛⲃ̣ⲁϣ̣ ⲉⲃⲁⲗ ϩⲉ ⲡⲟⲩ-
(18) ⲱϣ̣ ⲡⲛⲟⲩϯ ⲁϩⲁ ⲁⲡⲁⲙⲉⲣⲁ ⲟⲩⲁⲁⲧ ⲙⲁⲓ
(19) ϫ̣ⲉ ϣⲁⲓⲕⲉ ⲉⲓⲥⲓⲧⲉⲣⲟⲥ ⲉⲃⲁⲗ ⲡⲁⲟⲩ
(20) ϩⲉ ⲡⲟⲩⲱϣ̣ ⲡⲛⲟⲩϯ

Verso

(21) ⲁϩⲁ ϩⲉⲓ ⲧⲁⲓⲥϩⲁⲓ ⲅⲟⲣⲅⲓ
(22) ⲉⲃⲉⲗ ⲡⲉⲃⲁⲗϩⲁⲣⲉⲥ ⲉⲃⲥⲧⲁ ⲡⲁⲣⲁⲥⲏ̣ⲩ̣ ⲉⲡⲏⲓ
(23) ⲉⲧⲃⲏ ⲛⲓⲕⲁⲛⲥⲁⲭⲁ ⲛⲁⲧⲟⲩⲙⲟⲩ ⲡⲁⲗⲕⲁⲙ ⲗⲓ̅ⲡ̅ ⲡⲟⲧ
(24) ⲛⲏⲃ : ⲉⲗⲃ ⲛⲁⲗϩⲁⲣⲏⲥ · ϩⲉⲓ ⲧⲁⲩϣ̣ⲁⲁⲛ ⲡⲉⲧⲧⲏⲥ · ⲙⲉ
(25) ⲕⲉⲧⲧⲉ ⲥⲙⲟⲩⲉⲛ : ϩⲉ ⲡϣ̣ⲉⲙ ⲁϩⲁ ⲡⲁⲗⲕⲁⲙ ⲁϩⲁ ⲡⲁϣ̣ⲏ-
(26) ⲣⲓ ⲉⲓⲙⲓ ϫ̣(ⲉ) ⲁⲕⲗ ⲟⲩⲛ ⲉⲥⲁⲓⲏ ⲙⲁⲛ ⲁⲗⲉⲡⲁϩⲏⲧ ⲕⲉ ⲃⲁⲗ ϩⲁⲣⲁⲕ

(27) ϩⲉ ϩⲟⲃ ⲛⲓⲙ : ϩⲉ⟨ⲓ⟩ ⲧⲁⲕⲉⲗ ⲛⲁⲧ ⲡ̅ⲟ̅ⲥ̅ ⲕⲉⲉⲕ
(28) ⲁϩⲁ ⲁⲩⲉⲛⲧⲉ . ⲓⲗ
(29) ϩⲉ ⲡⲉϣⲧⲉⲕⲁ ⲛⲓⲙⲉⲓ ⲁⲩⲃⲁϣ ⲡⲃⲓⲛⲓⲃⲓ ϩⲓⲗⲉⲓ
(30) ⲡⲉϩⲙⲁⲧ ⲡⲛⲟⲩϯ ϣⲉⲡ ⲁⲩⲃⲓ ⲧⲉⲧⲁ̣ⲩⲗⲏ
(31) ⲡⲁⲏⲉ . ⲁ

Verso: address, at 180°
(1) ⲧⲁⲁⲥ ⲉⲗⲟⲩⲧⲥⲱⲛ [locum sigilli ϩ]ⲓⲧⲉⲛ ⲡⲉ̣ⲃ̣[ⲥⲁⲛ]
(2) ⲡ̅ⲟ̅ⲥ̅ ⲕⲉⲉⲃ ⲡⲁⲓⲧⲟ̣[ⲥ]

(1) [In] the name of God. [Before] all things. I greet you (2) warmly (καλῶς), my beloved brother—may the Lord preserve him (i.e., you) and show me your (2nd plur.) (3) face one more time.

Furthermore (λοιπόν): Your letter reached me. I understood what you (4) wanted to tell me in it. Furthermore (λοιπόν): My brother, (you have to) know very well what you do (5) during the harvest of the field. […] pray (lit.: give blessing) that we may be set free—(6) God willing.

And when you reap in the … (7) of Tsacha, … the sufficient (quantity) of straw. And take the sheaves. (8) Send them to my house—and the duties (τελώντιον), too. Take them and the … (9) Indeed, give it (fem.) back into the house again, that they may live on it (masc.). (10) Thank God. And when you reap in the east, go (11) to Gorgi's … . Take the cart from him. Load (12) up the sheaves. Verily, it will amount to more than one assload. (13) And load up the grain unto the cart.

And see, I have written (14) to him on your behalf. (15) The (plot measuring one) *aroura* (for the cultivation) of wheat is yours. And you will give your (plur.) plentiful harvest. (16) And bring the good-quality straw. My brother, if you (17) can gather the …, gather them until we are released—(18) God willing.

And: The *amīr* (ἀμιρᾶ) has written to me: (19), "I will release Isidoros today"—(20) God willing. And see, I have written to Gorgi, (22) who acted as his guard (and) returned Parasêw to the house (23) because of the *kansacha* … . Furthermore: Go (24) (and) make him guard. See, they have … (25) … in/by/with … and ….

And: My son, (26) (you have to) know well what you do. For because of you my heart is at ease (27) in all matters. See, you were compassionate—may the Lord preserve you. (28) And: They ... (29) in the prison with me. They removed the shackles from me—thank God ... (29) ...

Address:
Give it to Loutsôn—may the Lord preserve him—from his [brother] Paitos.

2–3 ⲡⲁⲙⲉⲣⲓ ⲉⲥⲁⲛ ⲡ̅ⲟ̅ⲥ̅ ⲕⲉⲉⲃ ⲉⲃⲧⲁⲙⲁⲓ ⲡⲉⲛⲧⲉ|ϩⲁ ⲕⲉⲥⲁⲡ: After the name of the recipient in the greeting section, one would expect a 2nd person pronoun in the blessing, but there are similar attestations of blessings with a 3rd person singular pronoun in this slot, e.g., ϯϣⲓⲛⲉ ⲉⲡⲁⲙⲉⲣⲓⲧ ⲛϣⲓⲣⲉ ⲉⲣⲉⲡ|ⲟ̅ⲥ̅ ⲕⲁϥ ⲁⲩⲱ ϥⲥⲙⲟⲩ ⲉⲣⲟϥ (P.Lond.Copt. I 545(B).2–3). The circumstantial present ⲉ⸗ⲃ- is one of several strategies to connect further blessings. The switch from a 3rd person singular pronoun in the initial blessing to a 2nd person pronoun in the subsequent blessing is a scribal error. This, too, is not without precedent, e.g., ⲡ̅ⲟ̅ⲥ̅ ⲕⲁⲁϥ : ⲉϥϯ ⲭⲁⲣⲓ`ⲥ´ | ⲛⲁⲕ ϩⲓ ⲡⲁⲣϩⲉⲥⲓⲁ (P.Fay.Copt. 14.4–5). However, the use of the plural is confusing—could it be intended as a particularly polite form? Or, did he copy the formula from another text and forgot to adapt the pronoun?

4 ⲡⲁⲥⲁ[ⲛ] ⲉⲓⲙⲓ ϫ(ⲉ) ⲁⲕⲗ ⲟⲩⲛ · ⲉⲥⲁⲓⲏⲥⲁⲓ´ⲏ`: Crum quoted this passage under its old inventory number PCol 2 and translated, "be very sure thou knowest what thou doest."[83] ⲟⲩⲛ is the Fayyumic form of the interrogative ⲟⲩ, "what, who." There is a Sahidic parallel: ⲉⲓⲙⲉ̣ [ϫ]ⲉⲕⲣⲟⲩ (P.Lond. 1639.7).

5 ⲧⲉ̣ . [.] . ϯ ⲥⲙⲟⲩ ⲧⲉⲛⲃⲱϣ ⲉⲃⲁⲗ: The traces at the beginning of this sentence are somewhat difficult to interpret. The small fragment in the lacuna may be placed incorrectly. The shape of the preserved letter does not fit the paleography of this dossier. Rotated 90° degrees to the right, it could be read as ⲛ, which would fit the context. Given the space of the lacuna and what is to be expected syntactically, this passage likely has to be read ⲧⲉ̣ⲛ̣[ⲧ]ⲉ̣ϯ ⲥⲙⲟⲩ—a conjunctive with Paitos's unusual form of the 2nd person plural suffix. Even if this reconstruction is correct, the translation of this passage remains problematic. It is not clear who the 2nd person plural pronoun would refer to and how this sentence should be connected to the preceding one.

6–7 ⲛⲁⲕⲱϩⲥ ϩⲉ ⲡⲁ̣ⲗⲙ̣ ⲟⲩϫ|ⲕⲉⲧ ⲉⲧⲥⲁⲭⲁ ⲕⲁⲃ ⲡⲣⲱϣⲓ ⲗⲁⲩⲉⲓ: Reading the conjugation base ⲛⲁ⸗ as the usual preterit is semantically implausible.

83 Crum 1939: 315b.

In this text, ⲛⲁ⸗ appears to be used in conditional clauses—just like the conditional prefix ⲙⲁ⸗ that Crum identified in a couple of Fayyumic texts.[84] ⲡⲁⲗⲙⲟⲩϫⲕⲉⲧ is certainly an Arabic loanword, most likely a participle, but I have not been able to identify it. The context suggests an interpretation as a specific kind of field or garden. The following imperative ⲕⲁⲃ is problematic as well. There is no known Coptic verb ⲕⲁⲃ, and its morphology does not fit that of Arabic verbs borrowed into Coptic.[85] Perhaps one could read it ⲕⲁⲃ as an alternative spelling of ϭⲁⲡ, but ⲃ for ⲡ is phonetically unlikely. ⲗⲁⲩⲉⲓ stands for the Sahidic ⲣⲟⲟⲩⲉ (for the translation "straw," see O.Brit.Mus. I pl. XC 1).

For ⲧⲥⲁϫⲁ as a personal name, cf. ⲧⲥⲁϫⲟ/ⲧⲥⲁϫⲱ in O.CrumST 153; O.CrumST 357; O.Brit.Mus. I pl. LXXIII 2.

8 ⲛⲓⲕⲉⲧⲉⲗⲱⲛϯ: ⲧⲉⲗⲱⲛϯ has to be read as *τελώντιον, a hitherto unknown variant of the Greek τελώνιον, "custom, duty."[86] The Greek ending -ιον is frequently rendered as -ⲓ in Fayyumic texts.[87]

8 ⲛⲓⲙⲓⲛⲓ: Reading ⲙⲓⲛⲓ as ⲙⲓⲛⲉ, "sort, quality, manner," does not fit the context. I cannot offer any other suggestions for its identification.

9 ⲙⲉⲉⲓⲧⲏⲥ: The reference to the 3rd person singular feminine pronoun is unclear.

9–10 ⲧⲟⲩⲱⲛⲁϩ ⲉⲣⲁⲃ: There are two ways to analyze this phrase: either as a 3rd person plural conjunctive ⲧⲟⲩ-ⲱⲛⲁϩ ⲉⲣⲁⲃ, "that they may live on it," or as a relative clause (ⲉ)ⲧ⸗ⲟⲩ-ⲱⲛⲁϩ, "which they live on." What the 3rd person masculine suffix pronoun refers to is unclear. While the preceding ⲡ-ⲏⲓ would fit grammatically, it does not fit semantically—as ⲱⲛϩ ⲉ- means "to live on, by." Thus, the former interpretation is more plausible.

11 ⲡⲥⲟⲩⲃⲁⲗ: This must refer to another kind of agricultural plot or some kind of storage space or workshop for agricultural produce.

11 ⲛⲧⲁⲁⲃ: ⲛⲧⲁⲁ⸗ is regularly used for Sahidic ⲛⲧⲟⲟⲧ⸗ in Fayyumic documentary texts.[88]

12 ⲛⲉⲕⲛⲏⲉⲓ: ⲕⲛⲏⲉⲓ seems to be an alternative spelling for ⲕⲛⲉⲩ, "sheaf" (cf. ⲕⲛⲉⲩⲉ in P.Col. inv. 594.7), even though this is phonetically problematic. The word is also used in P.Col. inv. 597.27.

12 ϣⲁⲩⲱⲧⲃ ⲙⲡⲁⲗ ⲛⲉⲓⲱ: Read ϣⲁ⸗ⲩ-ⲟⲩⲟⲧⲃ. ⲙⲡⲁⲗ is a late Fayyumic

84 Crum 1930.

85 See Richter 2015: 230–231.

86 Sophocles 1900: 1074[a].

87 Boud'hors 2017: 430–431.

88 See Garel 2016: 50.

spelling for the Greek preposition παρά.[89] For ⲟⲩⲟⲧⲃ ⲡⲁⲣⲁ, “surpassing …,” see Crum 1939: 496[a].

13–14 ⲧⲁⲓⲥϩⲉⲓ | ⲛⲏⲃ : ⲉⲧⲃⲏⲧⲉⲕ: Who the 3rd person pronoun refers to is unclear; is it possible that it refers to Gorgi?
Line 14 is surprisingly short. Apparently, the fold was already present when Paitos was writing the letter, causing problems with the ink flow. This is clearly visible in the letters ⲧⲉⲕ at the end of the line, as well as in the upper part of the ϯ from the following line. This feature likely caused Paitos to abandon this line and start a new one below.

15–16 ⲁⲕⲛⲁϯ ⲧⲉⲛⲧⲉⲁϩⲥ ⲉⲥ|ⲛⲁϣⲉⲉⲥ: Yet again, the 2nd person plural pronoun is puzzling. Is it referring to the addressee and the person mentioned in l. 13? And to whom is the addressee supposed to give the harvest?

16 ⲗⲁⲩⲟⲩⲉⲓ: ⲗⲁⲩⲟⲩⲉⲓ for Sahidic ⲣⲟⲟⲩⲉ (cf. ⲗⲁⲩⲉⲓ in P.Col. inv. 594.7).

16–17 ⲛⲁⲕ|ⲛⲏϣⲁⲗ ⲛⲉⲃⲁⲡⲁⲣ : ⲁⲗⲟⲩ: ⲁⲗ is used both as prenominal and prepersonal state of ϣⲗ (cf. ⲉⲗ⸗ as the prepersonal state of ⲉⲓⲣⲉ in P.Col. inv. 594.24; P.Stras. inv. 332(D).17). ⲉⲃⲁⲡⲁⲣ most likely specifies a crop or another kind of agricultural produce.

17 ϣⲁⲛⲧⲉⲛⲃⲁ̣ϣ ⲉⲃⲁⲗ: Why a 1st person plural pronoun? Who else is imprisoned with Paitos?

19 ⲁⲙⲉⲣⲁ: The term *amīr* is used to refer to Arab officials, often—but not always—the *pagarch*. Contrary to other Arabic loanwords, ⲁⲙⲉⲣⲁ does not include the Arabic article al-, because it was borrowed by way of the Greek ἀμιρᾶς.[90]

22 ⲉⲃⲉⲗ ⲡⲉⲃⲁⲗϩⲁⲣⲉⲥ: ⲁⲗϩⲁⲣⲉⲥ is likely to be the Arabic word *al-ḥāris*, “the guard.”[91] To whom the possessive pronoun refers is unclear.

22–23 ⲉⲃⲥⲧⲁ ⲡⲁⲣⲁⲥⲏⲩ ⲉⲡⲏⲓ | ⲉⲧⲃⲏ ⲛ̣ⲓⲕⲁⲛⲥⲁⲭⲁ: A person named Parasêw is also mentioned in P.Col. inv. 597.7. The name Parasêw is hitherto unattested, but it could be a woman’s name—in analogy to names like Anastahêw.[92] The context in P.Col. inv. 597 supports this interpretation with two suffix pronouns of the 3rd person singular feminine in the following lines (l. 8: ϩⲁⲣⲁⲥ; l. 9: ⲁⲥⲉⲗ ϣⲉⲙⲁ). Was Parasêw a relative of Paitos, who had to flee, too, due to his debts and was later returned to her house—and thus, her administrative district? Cf. ⲡⲟⲩⲧⲏⲕ · ⲉⲡⲉⲕⲏⲓ,

---

89 This form is also attested in the work contract P.Heid. inv. Kopt. 451 (see Richter and Schmelz 2010: 195) and the account book P.Gascou 60 (see Richter 2016b: 60–61).

90 This is one of very few Arabic words borrowed into Coptic before the ninth century, see Richter 2004: 107–109.

91 Diem 2017: 106.

92 I am grateful to Anne Boud’hors for pointing out this possibility.

"go to your house" (P.Lond.UniColl. inv. 71024.14) and ⲁⲥⲉⲗ ϣⲉⲙⲁ ⲉⲧⲃⲏ ⲛⲓ[ⲕⲁⲛ]|ⲥⲁⲭⲁ, "she was a fugitive because of the *kansacha*" (P.Col. inv. 597.9–10). A woman being arrested due to her husband's debt is, for example, attested in P.Apoll. 46.

23 ⲛⲁⲧⲟⲩⲙⲟⲩ ⲡⲁⲗⲕⲁⲙ: I do not know how to understand ⲛⲁⲧⲟⲩⲙⲟⲩ. ⲁⲗⲕⲁⲙ looks like an Arabic loanword. The word appears again in l. 25, but the context is equally obscure.

24 ⲉⲗⲃ ⲛⲁⲗϩⲁⲣⲏⲥ: ⲉⲗ⸗ is an unusual form of the prepersonal state of ⲉⲓⲣⲉ; see also P.Stras. inv. 332(D).17.

24–25 ϩⲉⲓ ⲧⲁⲩϣⲁⲁⲛ ⲡⲉⲧⲧⲏⲥ · ⲙⲉ | ⲕⲉⲧⲧⲉ ⲥⲙⲟⲩⲉⲛ : ϩⲉ ⲡϣⲉⲙ ⲁϩⲁ ⲡⲁⲗⲕⲁⲙ: This entire passage is obscure.

25–26 ⲁϩⲁ ⲡⲁϣⲏ|ⲣⲓ ⲉⲓⲙⲓ ϫ(ⲉ) ⲁⲕⲗ ⲟⲩⲛ ⲉⲥⲁⲓⲏ: Why is the recipient addressed as "my son" if he is called "my brother" in the parallel passage in l. 4?

26 ⲙⲁⲛ ⲁⲗⲉⲡⲁϩⲏⲧ ⲕⲉ ⲃⲁⲗ ϩⲁⲣⲁⲕ: This passage is quoted by Crum under a sublemma, "be, exist," for the qualitative of ⲕⲱ ⲉⲃⲟⲗ.[93] With ϩⲏⲧ as subject, a translation of "to be at ease" seems more plausible in this context.

27 ϩⲉ⟨ⲓ⟩ ⲧⲁⲕⲉⲗ ⲛⲁⲧ: ϩⲉⲓ is consistently spelled with a final ⲓ in the dossier, so this must be a scribal error. ⲛⲁⲧ stands for ⲛⲁⲏⲧ, "pitiful of heart, compassionate."[94]

28 ⲁϩⲁ ⲁⲩⲉⲛⲧ̣ⲉ . ⲓ ⲗ: The few letters of this line are obscured by the earlier Arabic text below, which appears to be the reason why Paitos switched to the next line before even reaching the middle of the document.

29 ⲁⲩⲃⲓ ⲧⲉⲧⲁ̣ⲩⲗⲏ | ⲡⲁⲏⲉ . ⲁ: Written over earlier Arabic text and partly worn away.

Address: ⲗⲟⲩⲧⲥⲱⲛ is a variation of the Greek name Λούτζων. The only other Coptic attestation of this name occurs as ⲗⲟⲧⲥⲱⲛ in CPR XII 31.11, a list of names, likely from the Fayyum. This name is also attested in various spellings in four Greek texts from the Fayyum (BGU 2 368; P.Mich. 12 642; P.Ross.Georg 5 66; SB 20 14576).

5.4 *No. 4: Letter concerning Various Issues (P.Col. inv. 597)*

6.6 + 4.0 cm high × 9.8 cm wide. 10th–11th centuries. Naqlūn?

Two large fragments of a light brown sheet of paper. Top and left edge of the document are preserved, little is missing at the right edge. Judging by the text on verso, the lower edge is preserved as well, albeit with only traces of the last line on recto. It is impossible to tell how much space is missing between the

93 Crum 1939: 97b.
94 Crum 1939: 217b.

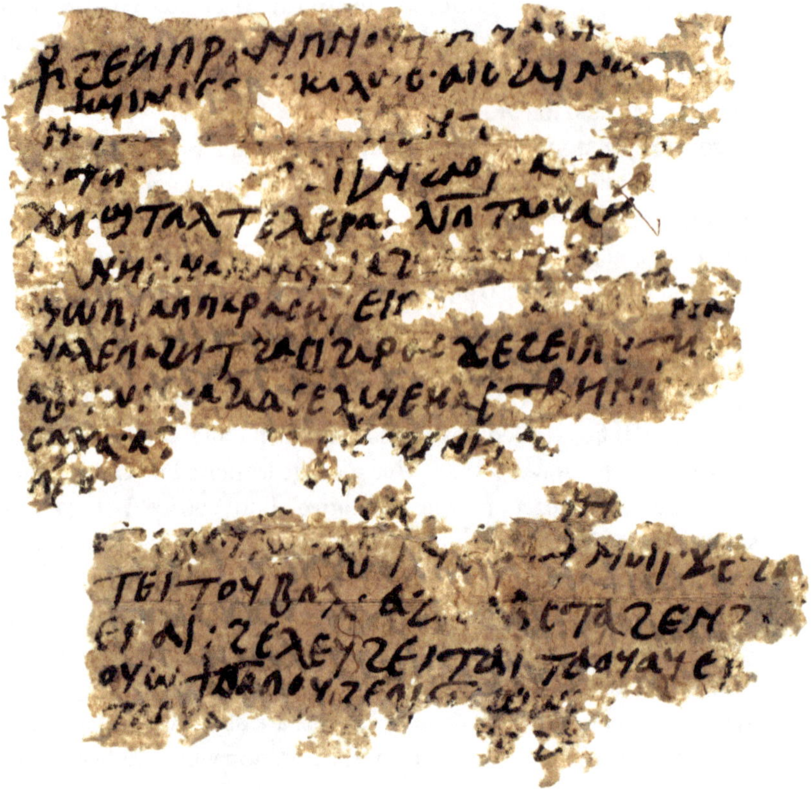

FIGURE 4.6 P.Col. inv. 597 recto.

two fragments. Yet, in light of the (more or less) square format of P.Col. inv. 594 and P.Stras. inv. Kopt. 332(D), it might be reasonable to assume a similar format for this document. Both fragments are plagued by lacunae and portions of the text where the ink has disappeared. In total, the remains of 16 lines on recto and 15 lines on verso are preserved. The external address on verso is written in two lines, at 180° to the main text.

Fragment 1, recto
(1) ⳨ ϩⲉⲙ ⲡⲣⲁⲛ ⲡⲛⲟⲩϯ ⲛ̣ϣ̣ⲁ̣ⲣ̣ⲡ̣ [ⲛϩⲟⲃ ⲛⲓⲙ]
(2) ϯϣⲓⲛⲓ ⲉ̣ⲣ̣[ⲁ]ⲕ̣ ⲕⲁⲗⲱⲥ · ⲁⲓⲥϩⲁⲓ ⲛⲏ̣[ⲕ 3–4]
(3) ⲛ̣ . . . [.] . [.] . . . . ⲛ̣ⲧ̣[8–10]
(4) . ⲧ̣ⲏ̣ . [3–4] . . . ⲓ̣ . . ϩ̣ⲁⲟ . . . . [ⲁⲧⲁⲯⲩ-]
(5) ⲭⲏ ϣⲧⲁⲗⲧⲉⲗ ⲉⲣⲁⲓ̣ ⲗⲓ̅ⲡ̅ ⲧⲁⲟⲩⲁ ⲙ̣[4–5]
(6) . . ⲛⲏⲓ · ⲛⲁ . . . ⲧ̣ ⲓⲁϩ . . . . ⲧ. [. .] . [3–4]

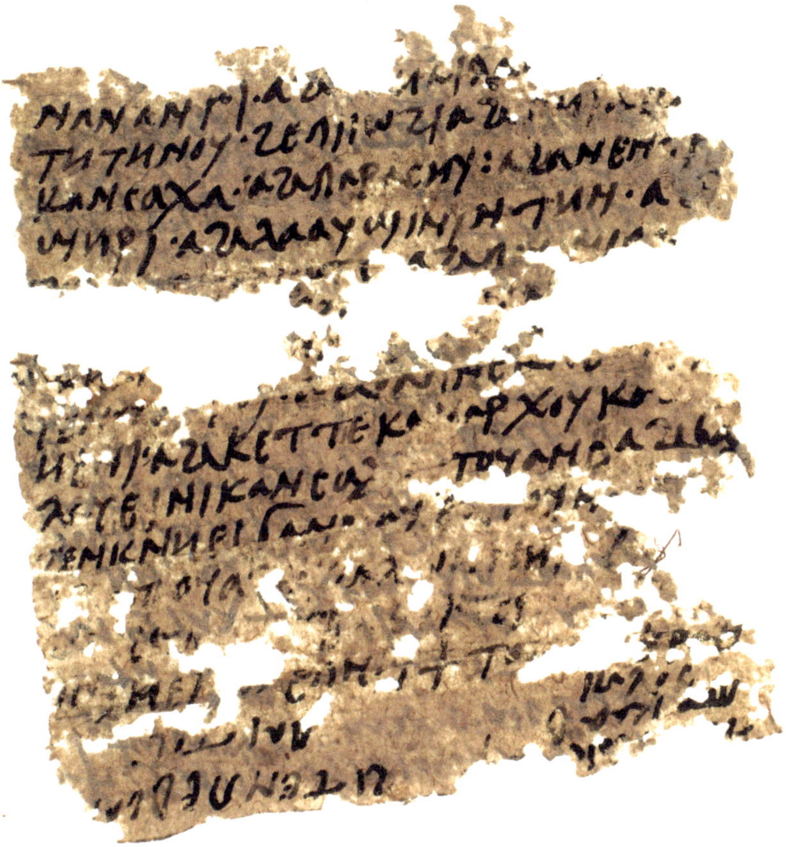

FIGURE 4.7 P.Col. inv. 597 verso.

(7) ϣⲱⲡⲓ̣ ⲁⲡⲡⲁⲣⲁⲥⲏⲩ̣ ⲉⲓ . [.] . . [.] . . . . ⲛ̣ⲁ[. .]
(8) ⲛⲁⲗⲉⲡⲁϩⲏⲧ ϩⲁⲥⲓ ϩⲁⲣⲁⲥ ϫⲉ ϩⲉⲓ ⲡⲉⲧⲙ[2–3]
(9) ⲁ̣ⲃ . ⲕ̣ . . . ⲁϩⲁ ⲁⲥⲥⲗ ϣⲥⲓⲛⲁ ϭⲧⲃⲏ ⲛⲓ[ⲕⲁⲛ-]
(10) ⲥⲁⲭⲁ · ⲁϩ[. . .] . . . . . ϩⲉ ⲛⲓⲧ̣ . [7–8]

Fragment 2, recto

(11) ⲡ . . [.] . [. .] . . [. . .] . . [4–5]ϯⲛ[5–6]
(12) . . . . ⲁⲩ . . . ⲡ̣ⲁⲃⲓ̣ⲩⲥ̣ . . . ϯ ⲛⲏⲓ ϫⲉ̣ ϩ[ⲉⲓ]
(13) ⲧⲉⲓⲧⲟⲩ ⲃⲁⲗ · ⲁϩ[ⲁ] ⲁ̣ⲃⲥⲧⲁ ϩⲉⲛϩ . [. .]
(14) ⲉⲓ ⲁⲓ : ϩⲉⲗⲉⲩ ϩⲉⲓ ⲧⲁⲓⲧⲁⲟⲩⲁⲩ ⲉⲣ̣[ⲁ 2–3]
(15) ⲟⲩⲱϯ ϭⲁⲡⲟⲩ ϩⲉ ⲡⲓϭ . . ⲱ . . . [7–9]
(16) ⲧⲁⲥ . .[5–6] . [.] . ϩ . [8–10]

Fragment 2, verso

(17) ⲛⲁⲛⲁⲛⲅⲓ · ⲁϩⲁ [2–3]ⲙ . ⲓ ⲗⲁ̣[7–8]
(18) ⲧⲏ ⲧⲏⲛⲟⲩ · ϩⲉ ⲡⲓⲓⲱϩⲓ ⲁϩⲁ ⲡ̣ⲏⲓ ⲁϩ̣ⲁ̣[ⲛⲓ]-
(19) ⲕⲁⲛⲥⲁⲭⲁ : ⲁϩⲁ ⲡⲁⲣⲁⲥⲏⲩ : ⲁϩⲁ ⲛⲉⲛⲧ̣ⲉ̣-
(20) ϣⲏⲣⲓ · ⲁϩⲁ ⲗⲁⲁⲩ ϣⲓⲛⲓ ⲛⲧⲏⲛ · ⲁϩ̣[ⲁ]
(21) . . . [. . .] . . . . . .ⲧ̣ . [.] ⲁϩⲁ ⲡ . [.] . ⲓⲁ̣. [±2]
(22) [only a few traces left]

Fragment 1, verso

(23) [only a few traces left]
(24) ϩ̣ⲉ̣ . . . [.] . . . · ⲁϩ̣ⲁ . ⲛⲓⲛⲉ̣ . . . . . [±3]
(25) ⲙⲉⲛ̣ⲓ · ⲁϩⲁ ⲕⲉⲧ ⲧⲉⲕⲁ . ⲁⲣⲭⲟⲩ ⲕⲁ[2–3]
(26) ⲗⲁ̣ⲩⲉⲓ ⲛⲓⲕⲁⲛⲥⲁⲭ[ⲁ] ⲧⲟⲩ ⲁⲛⲃⲁ ϩⲁϭⲁ[ⲣ̣]
(27) ⲧ̣ⲉⲛⲕⲛⲏⲉⲓ ϭⲁⲛ . ⲁⲩ . . [.]ⲣ̣ⲟⲩ ⲛ̣ . . [± 3]
(28) . . . ⲡ̣ⲟⲩⲁ[3–4] . ⲗ . . . ⲛ̣ⲏⲓ[.] . [4–5]
(29) [only a few traces left]
(30) . . ⲙⲉⲓ[.] . ⲉⲡⲛⲟⲩϯ ⲧ . [±5] ⲉ̣ⲣ̣ⲁ̣ⲃ̣
(31) ⲕⲁⲗⲟⲥ

Fragment 1, verso: address, at 180°

ⲧ[ⲁⲁⲥ] ⲉ̣ . ⲕ̣[ ] locum sigilli ϩⲓⲧⲉⲛ ⲡⲉⲃⲥⲁ[ⲛ]
ⲡ̅ⲟ̣̅ⲥ̣̅ ⲕⲁⲁⲃ ⲡⲁⲓⲧⲟⲥ

(1) In the name of God. Before [all things]. (2) I greet you warmly (καλῶς). I have written to [you ... (3) ... (4) ... My] (5) soul (ψυχή) was troubled. Furthermore (λοιπόν): Send [the ...] (6) to me ... . [...] (7) happen.

Parasêw came [to ...] (8) My heart was suffering because of her, for see ... (9) ... And she was a fugitive because of the [*kan*]*sacha*. (10) And [... (11) ...] (12) ... my life (βίος) ... to me. For [...] (13) sell them.

And he returned ... (14) ... in (?) them. See, I have sent them to [you?]. (15) Write (and) take them in/at ... [... (16) ...] (17) immediately (ανάγκη).

And [...] (18) ... you (plur.) in/at (?) the field and the house and [the] (19) *kansacha* and Parasêw and your (20) children and anyone/anything (else). Greet (them?) from us. And (21) [...] and [... (22–23) ...] (24) ... [...] (25) ... And ... (26) at all. The *kansacha* ... Anba Hagar (27) ... [...] (28) ... [... (29) ...] (30) ... God [...] him (31) well.

Address:
G[ive it] to [...]—may the Lord preserve him—from his brother, Paitos.

4–5 [ⲁⲧⲁⲯⲩ]|ⲭⲏ ϣⲧⲁⲗⲧⲉⲗ ⲉⲣⲁ̣ⲓ̣: Literally: "My soul troubled me." My reconstruction and translation of this sentence is based on a literary parallel from a Bohairic sermon by Zacharias, bishop of Shôou: ⲟⲩ ⲡⲉ ⲉ̄ⲧⲁϥⲑⲣⲉⲧⲉⲕⲯⲩⲭⲏ ϣⲑⲟⲣⲧⲉⲣ ⲉⲣⲟⲕ, "what is it that troubles your soul?"[95]

9 ⲁⲥⲉⲗ ϣⲉⲙⲁ, "stranger," is the usual term for (tax) fugitives in Coptic documentary texts. The Coptic ϣⲙⲙⲟ is used in this way in P.Ryl.Copt. 277, while the texts from Aphrodito prefer the equivalent Greek loanword φυγάδες (e.g., in P.Lond. 1565).

17 ⲛⲁⲛⲁⲛⲅⲓ: For the interpretation of ⲛ-ⲁⲛⲁⲛⲅⲓ as "urgently," see Boud'hors 2017: 428.

20 ϣⲓⲛⲓ ⲛⲧⲏⲛ: ⲛⲧⲏⲛ probably has to be understood as an equivalent of the Sahidic ⲛⲧⲟⲟⲧⲛ, "from us." The prepersonal state of ⲛⲧⲛ- is frequently rendered as (ⲛ)ⲧⲁ(ⲁ)⸗ in Fayyumic texts.[96] The ⲏ remains puzzling, as we find ⲛⲧⲁⲁⲃ in P.Col. inv. 594.11. The phrase as a whole is difficult to interpret, as it lacks an object for ϣⲓⲛⲓ. It is possible that the preceding list of people is meant.

25 ⲁϩⲁ ⲕⲉⲧ ⲧⲉⲕⲁ . ⲁⲣⲭⲟⲩ ⲕⲁ[2–3]: The entire line is problematic, and I cannot propose any solutions. ⲕⲉⲧ could be interpreted as the prenominal state of either ⲕⲱⲧ, "to build, form," or ⲕⲱⲧⲉ, "to turn"—though both should be ⲕⲁⲧ- in Fayyumic. The object ⲧⲉⲕ-ⲁ . ⲁⲣⲭⲟⲩ does not appear to be a native Coptic noun; the initial ⲁ suggests an Arabic loanword.

26 ⲗⲁⲩⲉⲓ ⲛⲓⲕⲁⲛⲥⲁⲭ[ⲁ] ⲧⲟⲩ ⲁⲛⲃⲁ ϩⲁϭⲁ[ⲣ]: The entire line is obscure. Anba Hagar was possibly a monk: in Byzantine times, the title ⲁⲃⲃⲁ (or ⲁⲛⲃⲁ) was used exclusively to refer to monks or bishops.[97]

30–31 ⲧ . [±5] ⲉ̣ⲣ̣ⲁ̣ⲃ̣ | ⲕⲁⲗⲟⲥ: Probably to be reconstructed as ⲧⲉ̣[ⲛϣⲓⲛⲉ] ⲉ̣ⲣ̣ⲁ̣ⲃ̣ ⲕⲁⲗⲟⲥ, "we greet him warmly."

5.5 *No. 5: Notes for Drafting a Letter (P.Lond.UniColl. inv. 71026)*

15.3 cm high × 5.6 cm wide. 10th–11th centuries. Naqlūn?

Strip of light brown paper. The original edges are not preserved; it is impossible to determine how much text is missing. On recto, there are traces of 19 lines preserved, though most of it has worn away. On verso, the remains of an earlier

95 De Vis 1922: 50.
96 Garel 2016: 50.
97 Derda and Wipszycka 1994: 44.

FIGURE 4.8
P.Lond.UniColl. inv. 71026 recto.
© UNIVERSITY COLLEGE LONDON, PETRIE MUSEUM OF EGYPTIAN ARCHAEOLOGY

Arabic text are preserved. There are 12 lines of Coptic written between the lines of the Arabic text. The text on recto is too fragmentary to interpret; the text on verso seems to be made up of short notes intended for writing practice or the drafting of a letter. Several words and phrases from the other texts of the dossier occur in this text. Due to the fragmentary nature of the document, no translation is given.

Recto

(1) [ ]ⲙⲡ . [ ]
(2) [ ]ⲁ̣ⲕ ⲕⲁⲗⲱⲥ̣ [ ]
(3) [ ]ⲉ̣ⲃ ⲉϭⲉⲛ ⲧⲁ[ ]
(4) [ ] . ⲉⲓ . . [ ]
(5) [ ]ⲏ̣ⲃ traces [ ]
(6) [ ] traces [ ]

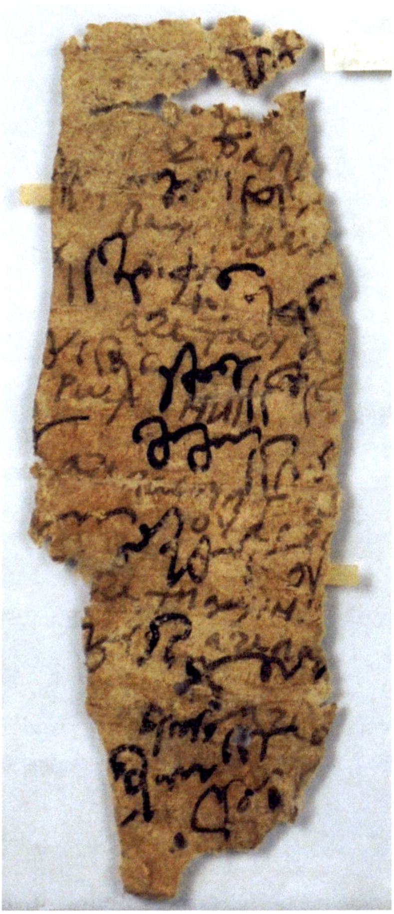

FIGURE 4.9
P.Lond.UniColl. inv. 71026 verso.

(7) [ ] traces [ ]
(8) [ ] traces [ ]
(9) [ ] ⲥⲧ[. . .] ⲥ̣ϩ[. . . .] . [ ]
(10) [ ] traces [ ]
(11) [ ] traces [ ]
(12) [ ] ⲕⲉⲧ ⲧ . ⲱ [. .] . [ ]
(13) [ ] ⲓⲏ ⲏ traces [ ]
(14) [ ] . ⲡ . traces [ ]
(15) [ ] ⲓϣ traces [ ]
(16) [ ] . ⲡϣⲓⲛ̣ⲓ̣ . . [ ]
(17) [ ] . ⲁ̣ϩⲏⲧ . . [ ]
(18) [ ] ⲉ̣ⲧⲃⲏ[ⲧ]ⲉⲥ [ ]
(19) [ ] . ⲗ . . ⲉ ⲧ . [ ]

Verso

(1) [ ] . [ ]
(2) [ ] traces [ ]
(3) [ ] . ⲭ̣ ϭⲁⲡ . [ ]
(4) [ ] ⲃⲁϣ . ⲉⲃⲁⲗ̣ [ ]
(5) [ ] ⲁϩⲁ ⲧⲁⲟⲩⲁ [ ]
(6) [ⲃ]ⲩⲓⲥ [ ]
(7) [ ]ⲣⲱϯ ⲛⲏⲓ [ ]
(8) [ ]ⲁϩⲁ̣ ⲡ . . . ⲡ ⲧ . . [ ]
(9) [ ] ⲟⲩⲁ . . . [ ]
(10) [ ]ⲁ̣ϩⲁ ⲧⲡⲁϣ̣ⲓⲛⲓ̣ [ ]
(11) [ ] ⲁϩⲁ ⲡⲁ . [ ]
(12) [ ] ⲁϩⲁ ⲉ̣[ ]

Bibliography

Greek and Coptic documents are quoted according to the Checklist of Editions,[98] Arabic documents according to the ISAP Checklist of Arabic Documents.[99]

Biedenkopf-Ziehner, Anneliese. 1983. *Untersuchungen zum koptischen Briefformular unter Berücksichtigung ägyptischer und griechischer Parallelen.* Koptische Studien 1. Würzburg: Zauzich.

Bloom, Jonathan M. 2001. *Paper Before Print: The History and Impact of Paper in the Islamic World.* New Haven: Yale University Press.

Boud'hors, Anne. 1997. "L'onciale penchée en copte et sa survie jusqu'au XVe siècle en Haute-Égypte." In *Scribes et manuscrits du Moyen-Orient,* edited by Francois Deroche and Francis Richard. Etudes et recherches. Paris: Bibliothèque nationale de France, 117–133.

Boud'hors, Anne. 2017. "Greek Loanwords in Fayyumic Documentary Texts." In *Greek Influence on Egyptian-Coptic: Contact-Induced Change in an Ancient African Language,* edited by Eitan Grossman et al. Lingua Aegyptia, Studia Monographica 17. DDGLC Working Papers 1. Hamburg: Widmaier, 423–439.

Boud'hors, Anne, and Florence Calament. 2015. "Pour une étude des archives coptes de Medinet el-Fayoum (P.Louvre inv. E 10253, E 6893, E 6867 et E 7395)." In *From Bāwīṭ to Marw: Documents from the Medieval Muslim World,* edited by Andreas Kaplony, Daniel Potthast, and Cornelia Römer. Islamic History and Civilization 112. Leiden: Brill, 23–58.

98 An up-to-date version can be found at http://papyri.info/docs/checklist.

99 An up-to-date version can be found at https://www.naher-osten.lmu.de/isapchecklist.

Choat, Malcolm. 2007. "Epistolary Formulae in Early Coptic Letters." In *Actes du huitième Congrès international d'études coptes: Paris, 28 juin–3 juillet 2004*, edited by Nathalie Bosson and Anne Boud'hors. Orientalia Lovaniensia Analecta 163. Leuven: Peeters, 667–678.

Crum, W[alter] E[wing]. 1930. "Ein neues Verbalpräfix im Koptischen." In *Zeitschrift für ägyptische Sprache und Altertumskunde* 65: 124–127.

Crum, W[alter] E[wing]. 1939. *A Coptic Dictionary*. Oxford: Clarendon Press.

de Vis, Henri. 1922. *Homélies coptes de la Vaticane*. Vol. 2. Edited and translated by Henri de Vis. Coptica 5. Copenhagen: Gyldendal.

Delattre, Alain. 2007. *Papyrus coptes et grecs du monastère d'Apa Apollō de Baouīt conservés aux Musées royaux d'art et d'histoire de Bruxelles*. Mémoires de l'Académie royale de Belgique, Classe des Lettres 3, 43. Brussels: Académie royale de Belgique.

Derda, Tomasz, and Ewa Wipszycka. 1994. "L'emploi de titres 'abba', 'apa' et 'papas' dans l'Egypte byzantine." In *Journal of Juristic Papyrology* 24: 23–56.

Diem, Werner. 1997. *Arabische Briefe des 7. bis 13. Jahrhunderts aus den Staatlichen Museen Berlin*. Documenta Arabica Antiqua 4. Ägyptische Urkunden aus den Staatlichen Museen Berlin, Arabische Urkunden. 2 vols. Wiesbaden: Harrasowitz.

Diem, Werner. 2017. *Glossar zur arabischen Epistolographie nach ägyptischen Originaldokumenten des 7.–16. Jahrhunderts*. Mitteilungen aus der Papyrussammlung der Österreichischen Nationalbibliothek. Neue Serie 43. Berlin: De Gruyter.

Förster, Hans. 2002. *Wörterbuch der griechischen Wörter in den koptischen dokumentarischen Texten*. Texte und Untersuchungen zur Geschichte der altchristlichen Literatur 148. Berlin: De Gruyter.

Garel, Esther. 2016. "Lettre concernant l'envoi d'un papyrus iatro-magique et une réquisition de laine de mouton (P.Vindob. inv. K 55)." In *Journal of Coptic Studies* 18: 45–55.

Grob, Eva Mira. 2010. *Documentary Arabic Private and Business Letters on Papyrus: Form and Function, Content and Context*. Archiv für Papyrusforschung und verwandte Gebiete, Beiheft 29. Berlin: De Gruyter.

Heuser, Gustav. 1929. *Die Personennamen der Kopten: Untersuchungen*. Studien zur Epigraphik und Papyruskunde 1–2. Leipzig: Dieterich.

Kahle, Paul Eric. 1954. *Bala'izah: Coptic Texts from Deir El-Bala'izah in Upper Egypt*. London: Oxford University Press.

Krall, Jakob. 1892. "Koptische Briefe." In *Mittheilungen aus der Sammlung der Papyrus Erzherzog Rainer* 5: 21–58.

Legendre, Marie. 2014. "Perméabilité linguistique et anthroponymique entre copte et arabe: l'exemple de comptes en caractères coptes du Fayoum Fatimide." In *Coptica Argentoratensia: Textes et documents de la Troisième université d'été de papyrologie copte (Strasbourg, 19–25 Juillet 2010)*, edited by Anne Boud'hors et al. Cahiers de la Bibliothèque copte 19. Études d'archéologie et d'histoire ancienne. Paris: Éditions de Boccard, 323–440.

Richter, Tonio Sebastian. 2004. "O.Crum Ad. 15 and the Emergence of Arabic Words in Coptic Legal Documents." In *Papyrology and the History of Early Islamic Egypt*, edited by Petra Sijpesteijn and Lennart Sundelin. Islamic History and Civilization 55. Leiden: Brill, 97–114.

Richter, Tonio Sebastian. 2008. *Rechtssemantik und forensische Rhetorik: Untersuchungen zu Wortschatz, Stil und Grammatik der Sprache koptischer Rechtsurkunden*. Philippika 20. 2nd ed. Wiesbaden: Harrassowitz.

Richter, Tonio Sebastian. 2014. "Neue koptische medizinische Rezepte." In *Zeitschrift für ägyptische Sprache und Altertumskunde* 141: 154–194.

Richter, Tonio Sebastian. 2015. "On the Fringes of Egyptian Language and Linguistics. Verb Borrowing from Arabic into Coptic." In *Fuzzy Boundaries: Festschrift für Antonio Loprieno*, edited by Hans Amstutz et al. Hamburg: Widmaier, 227–242.

Richter, Tonio Sebastian. 2016a. "Arabische Lehnwörter in koptischen Texten: Ein Überblick." In *Zwischen Philologie und Lexikographie des Ägyptisch-Koptischen: Akten der Leipziger Abschlusstagung des Akademieprojekts "Altägyptisches Wörterbuch,"* edited by Peter Dils and Lutz Popko. Abhandlungen der Sächsischen Akademie der Wissenschaften zu Leipzig, Philologisch-Historische Klasse 84, 3. Stuttgart: Sächsische Akademie der Wissenschaften zu Leipzig, 137–163.

Richter, Tonio Sebastian. 2016b. "Ein fatimidenzeitliches koptisches Rechnungsheft aus den Papieren Noël Girons." In *Mélanges Jean Gascou: textes et études papyrologiques (P.Gascou)*, edited by Jean-Luc Fournet and Arietta Papaconstantinou. Travaux et mémoires 20, 1. Paris: Association des Amis du Centre d'histoire et civilisation de Byzance, 381–402.

Richter, Tonio Sebastian. 2018. "A Scribe, His Bag of Tricks, What It Was for, and Where He Got It: Scribal Registers and Techniques in Bodl.Mss.Copt.(P) a.2 & 3." In *Scribal Repertoires in Egypt from the New Kingdom to the Early Islamic Period*, edited by Jennifer Cromwell and Eitan Grossman. Oxford Studies in Ancient Documents. Oxford: Oxford University Press, 296–313.

Richter, Tonio Sebastian, and Georg Schmelz. 2010. "Der spätkoptische Arbeitsvertrag P.Heid. inv. kopt. 541 [sic, should be 451]." In *Journal of Juristic Papyrology* 40: 185–203.

Sijpesteijn, Petra M. 2014. *Shaping a Muslim State: The World of a Mid-Eighth-Century Egyptian Official*. Oxford Studies in Byzantium. Oxford: Oxford University Press.

Sophocles, E.A. 1900. *Greek Lexicon of the Roman and Byzantine Periods (From B.C. 146 to A.D. 1100)*. New York: Scribner.

van der Vliet, Jacques. 2015. "Nekloni (al-Naqlūn) and the Coptic Account Book British Library Or. 13885." In *From Bāwīṭ to Marw: Documents from the Medieval Muslim World*, edited by Andreas Kaplony, Daniel Potthast, and Cornelia Römer. Islamic History and Civilization 112. Leiden: Brill, 155–169.

CHAPTER 5

The *Book of Twitches of Shem, Son of Noah*, and Other Manuals of Palmomancy from the Cairo Genizah and al-Quṣayr

Gideon Bohak

Abstract

Twitch divination (palmomancy) entails observing the involuntary twitches of a person's body to predict his or her future. It is a practice attested already in the Assyro-Babylonian world and it circulated widely in late antiquity and in the Middle Ages. It is well attested in the Cairo Genizah, which shows its great popularity among the Jews of medieval Cairo. The present paper provides an edition and translation of the extant Genizah fragments of *Kitāb al-Ikhtilāj*, "The Book of Twitches," attributed to Shem, son of Noah. This is followed by a detailed survey of all the palmomantic fragments from the Cairo Genizah in Aramaic, Judeo-Arabic, and Hebrew. Finally, I offer a reedition of a palmomantic fragment from al-Quṣayr, which has previously been misidentified as an amulet. Together, all these fragments attest to the vitality of the palmomantic tradition in medieval Egypt.

1 Introduction

Twitch divination, also known under its Greek name, palmomancy, is the art of predicting a person's fortunes from the involuntary twitches of different parts of his or her body.[1] It is attested already in the Assyro-Babylonian world and seems to be of a Mesopotamian origin.[2] It was further developed in the Hellenistic world, where palmomantic manuals circulated in several different Greek versions, the most famous of which was attributed to the Greek seer

1 The research for the present paper was funded by the Israel Science Foundation (Grant No. 986/14). I am grateful to Edna Engel for the paleographic analysis of the fragments in Hebrew script, to Aviam Ben-Naim for his assistance in deciphering the Arabic and Judeo-Arabic texts, and to Simon Hopkins for many helpful comments on an earlier draft of this paper. All remaining errors are, of course, my own.

2 For the Assyro-Babylonian texts, see Furlani 1949; Böck 2000: 63, 66; Geller 2001–2002: 70–71.

 | DOI:10.1163/9789004527874_007

Melampus.[3] But it also circulated widely in other languages in late antiquity, including Syriac, and became extremely popular in the Arabic-speaking world as well.[4] It is one of the most common modes of divination from the human body and is attested in numerous languages all over the world.[5]

Palmomantic manuals tend to be quite repetitive and to consist of long lists of protaseis and apodoseis, the former listing a specific limb ("If a limb x twitches"), the latter providing a short prediction for the person whose limb twitched. The limbs are arranged from head to toe, and for all symmetrical limbs, the right one always comes before the left one. Yet the number of limbs changes from one text to another, with some texts covering only the major external organs of the human body and others providing predictions for each tiny organ or even parts thereof. Moreover, in some texts, further distinctions are introduced in the protaseis, in line with the person's social position, such as, e.g., "If a limb x twitches, if the person is a slave it foretells X, if a virgin woman, it foretells Y, if a widow, it foretells Z." In some texts, in some of the apodoseis, advice is given as to which god to pray to. And in some texts, more than one prediction is given, and the predictions are arranged according to their postulated sources, such as, e.g., "If a body-part x twitches, Alexander the Great says it foretells X, Daniel says it foretells Y, the Persians say it foretells Z," and so on. These textual variations—which are paralleled in other genres of divination, such as oneiromancy—reflect two different processes: first, the awareness of the users and composers of such texts that in the realm of personal divination, personal circumstances must be taken into account. And second, their awareness of the existence of many different lists, and their constant composition, copying, editing, translation, and adaptation of these lists over many centuries. The end result of both processes is a bewildering array of palmomantic texts, in many different languages, all sharing the same basic structure and the same predictions, but mostly differing from each other in the correspondence between specific limbs and specific predictions.

In the Jewish world, the use of this divination technique is amply attested in the Middle Ages (including, for example, among the Jews of medieval Ashkenaz) but clearly began much earlier.[6] Evidence of its early entry into the Jew-

3 For the Greek texts, see Diels 1908–1909: 1: 20–42; and especially Costanza 2009. For broad surveys of this material, see Dasen 2008; Wilgaux and Dasen 2013; Mowat 2016; Costanza 2018.

4 The Syriac palmomantic texts were studied by Furlani 1917; Furlani 1918. For the Arabic palmomantic tradition, see Diels 1908–1909: 2: 51–91; Furlani 1946; Fahd 1966: 392–402, 418–429; Ullmann 1972: 195, 320, 340, 381; Sezgin 1979: 64; Mavroudi 2009: 225, 326.

5 And cf. Shakespeare, *Macbeth* IV.i.44–45: "By the pricking of my thumbs, / Something wicked this way comes."

6 Unfortunately, no good study of Jewish palmomancy has been attempted since Moritz Stein-

ish world is provided by an Aramaic palmomantic text from the Cairo Genizah that probably reflects the use of such texts by Jews in pre-Islamic times. As we shall note below, this text was translated into Hebrew, and the Hebrew version circulated widely in the Jewish world from the Middle Ages onwards and is still available in print today. The same applies to another Hebrew palmomantic text, which was popular in the Middle Ages and is still in print today, and a thorough survey of Hebrew manuscripts in search of palmomantic texts is likely to come up with more such texts.[7] Moreover, such texts circulated among the Jews in other languages as well, including Judeo-Persian.[8]

In the Cairo Genizah, manuals of divination are found in great abundance, which demonstrates the appeal of numerous divinatory techniques to the Jews of medieval Cairo, and to the Islamicate world as a whole.[9] Among these, *goralot* (lot-casting, sortes), oneiromancy (dream interpretation), and geomancy (literally, "sand divination," but usually carried out with randomly scribbled dots whose patterns are then analyzed) are the most popular, but palmomancy is well-documented as well, as we shall see below.[10] Its appeal is also attested by the fact that at least one Genizah booklist mentions such a book.[11] Moreover, this appeal was in no way limited to Jews in medieval Cairo, and we may note: (a) that some of the Genizah palmomantic fragments are written in the Arabic script, and probably were written by Muslim or Christian scribes; (b) that some of the Judeo-Arabic manuals probably were transliterated from Arabic originals, copied and owned by non-Jews; and (c) that the fragment of an Arabic palmomantic manual from the thirteenth century was found in al-Quṣayr, a trading port on the shores of the Red Sea. We shall return to all these points below.

The present study is divided in two main parts. In the first, I offer an edition and translation of the extant fragments of one such text, the so-called *Book of Shem*. In the second, I offer a brief survey of all the Genizah palmomantic

---

schneider's brief note in Steinschneider 1893/1956: 893–894 (§ 539), which conflates two different Hebrew versions and is unaware of the Aramaic and the Judeo-Arabic versions; see also below no. 8. For the medieval Ashkenazi use of twitch- and itch-divination, see Ta-Shma 1994: 136; with Trachtenberg 1939/2004: 210–211; Shyovitz 2017: 94–95.

7 For the time being, see Leicht 2006: 405 s.v. *Sefer Refafot*; Muchowski 2012.

8 For a printed palmomantic manual in Judeo-Persian, see Steinschneider 1938: 140.

9 These texts have yet to receive the attention they deserve. For the time being, see Shaked 2000; Bohak 2010; Swartz 2012: 69–72; Bohak 2016.

10 For the geomantic fragments from the Cairo Genizah, see Villuendas Sabaté 2015; for the oneirocritical fragments, see Villuendas Sabaté 2020.

11 For this booklist, see Allony 2006: 85 (no. 22, ll. 54–55): *Kitāb al-ikhtilāj*; as Miriam Frenkel notes in her comments *ad locum*, it was written no later than the thirteenth century.

fragments currently known to me. Finally, I add a short discussion of the palmomantic fragment from al-Quṣayr, which has previously been misidentified and mispublished.

2 *Kitāb al-Ikhtilāj*, "The Book of Twitches," Attributed to Shem, Son of Noah

Kitāb al-Ikhtilāj, "The Book of Twitches," attributed to Shem, son of Noah, is a palmomantic manual in Judeo-Arabic that is attested in the Cairo Genizah in two different manuscripts and—to the best of my knowledge—is thus far unattested anywhere else.[12] Of the first manuscript, only the first folio survives, and it has already been edited by Simon Hopkins, whose text and translation I reproduce here, with some modifications. The second copy is a small format ("pocketbook") manuscript of which I have thus far identified four fragments, which make up three bifolia, as explained in greater detail below. Together, they cover the text from its very beginning to the twitches of the lower lip and—after a long hiatus that is due to missing folios—from the twitches of the thighs to the end of the text. To facilitate the examination of both copies, I adduce them synoptically and divide the text into its constituent units of protasis and apodosis.

2.1 *Edition*

Kitāb al-Ikhtilāj, copy 1 Cambridge, CUL T-S A 45.21, edited and translated Hopkins 1978: 67–71	*Kitāb al-Ikhtilāj*, copy 2[13] Oxford, Bodleian Heb. g 8.52–53 (whose pages are listed in my transcription as A1–4); Cambridge, T-S Ar. 45.11 (B1–4); Cambridge T-S AS 157.179 (C1–2) + T-S AS 173.423 (C3–4) (for a fuller codicological description, see below)

12 This text is not to be confused with the *Treatise of Shem*, an astrological text (known in Arabic as *Kitāb Qansar*), for which see Charlesworth 1983–1985; Leicht 2006: 45–55. The tenth-century Karaite polemicist Salmon ben Yeruḥim also mentions a *Book of Shem, Son of Noah*, whose contents seem to deal with magical practices for various aims; see Davidson 1934: 111–113. And the medical *Book of Asaf*, which probably was written before the rise of Islam, claims to have been copied from a *Book of Shem, Son of Noah*; see Scharbach 2010: 114–117. Another text, dealing with predictions from lunar risings and eclipses, is attributed to Shem, son of Noah, in the Genizah fragment Cambridge, T-S Ar. 10.15.

13 In my transcription, [ ] stands for a lacuna in the text and ⟨ ⟩ for an interlinear insertion; a small circle above a letter means that its reading is uncertain.

(A2)[14] בשמ׳ רחמ׳:

– הדא כתאב אלאכתלאג׳ תאליף שם בן נח על׳ השל׳:

– קאל: מן אכתלג׳ת עינה אלימין פאנה בשארה חסנה תג׳יה ורזק חסן ירזק (B1) ופרח קלב ותג׳ד[16] עיש:

– ומן אכתלג׳ת עינה אלשמאל פאנה סוף יחמל הם וגם ויסמע שי יגם קלבה ויתאדא מנה ג׳סמה:

– ומן אכתלג׳ חאג׳בה אלימין יג׳יה עִז וירזק ג׳אה (B2) לם יכון קט פי אמלה:

– ומן [אכ]תלג׳ חאג׳בה אליסאר יצ׳יע מן ידה שי כאן קד דכרה לוקת שדה:

– ומן אכתלג ג׳פנה אלימין יוקצ׳א עליה ספר בעיד

– ומן אכתלג גפנה אליסאר יוקצ׳א (C1) [עליה ספר קריב:

– ומן אכתלג כדה אלימין] אן כאן [לה חאמל יגיה ולד דכ]ר ואן כאן ליס [ל]ה ח[אמל פיגי]ה שי יסר קלבה:

– מן [אכתלג כדה] אליסאר אן כאן לה חאמ[ל תגיה] אנתא ואן לם יכון ל[ה חאמל (C2) פיגם קלבה בשי:

– מן אכתלג ר]אס אנפה [יוקצא עליה מראר מ]ע בעץ׳ אהלה:

(recto) בשמ״ה נע׳ ונצליח

– הדא כתאב אלאכתלאגאת תאליף שם בן נח עליה אלסלאם ותנאקלוה בני אסראיל גיל בעד גיל אלי זמאן שלימאן שלמא[15] בן דויד עליה אלסלאם ואכדוה אליונאניה מן כזאנה שלמא בן דויד ואקאם מעהם יעמלון בה אלי זמאן בוסתאני הנשיא בן דויד ולמא דכל אלי דיארהם אסתכלצה מן ידהם לאנה כאן מכתוב בלשון הקדש בכט שם בן נח וחצל פי יד בני אסראיל ותנאקלוה ותוארתוה מן בעד דלך בני אסראיל והו מגרב צחיח ויגב אלאסתחפאץ בה לאנה חסן אלטריקה.

– קאל שם בן נח מן אכתלגת עינה אלימין פאנה בשארה חסנה תגיה ורזק חסן ירזק ופרח קלב ורגד עיש:

– (verso) ומן אכתלגת עינה אלשמאל פאנה סוף יחמל הם וגם ויסמע שי יגם קלבה ויתאדא מנה נפסה:

– ומן אכת׳ חאגבה אלימין יגיה עז וירזק גאה לם יכן קט פי אמלה:

– ומן אכת׳ חאגבה אליסאר יציע מן ידה שי יכון קד אכרה לוקת שדה:

– ומן אכת׳ גפנה אל ימין יוקצא עליה ספר בעיד:

– ומן אכת׳ גפנה אליסאר יוקצא עליה ספר קריב:

– מן אכת׳ כדה אלימין פסוף אן כאן לה חאמל יגיה ולד דכר ואן כאן ליס לה חאמל פיגיה שי יסר קלבה:

– ומן אכת׳ כדה אליסאר אן כאן לה חאמל תגיה אנתא ואן כאן ליס לה חאמל פיגם קלבה רשי:

– מן אכת׳ ראס אנפה יוקצא עליה מראר מע בעץ אהלה:

---

14 A1 is blank.

15 The scribe clearly tried to write the name Solomon in both Judeo-Arabic and in Hebrew, but in both cases his spelling is quite wobbly.

16 Lege ורגד.

– מן [אכתלגת שפתה אל]פוקא ימלך
ממלוכה או מ[מלוד ואן כ]אן ליס הו אהל
לדלך פ[ימלך ב]הימה:
– מן אכתלגת ש[פתה] ...[17]
– (C3) [מן אכתלגת] סאקה אלימ[י]ן֯
[י]קע פי שדה֯ [מן?] ק֯ריבה אלמ֯אכר:
– מן אכת[לגת סאקה] אליסאר ימרץ׳
מ[ר]צ֯׳א֯ שדידא:
– מן אכתלגת רכבת֯[ה אלי]מין ינג׳ו מן
סלטאן ו֯ר֯י֯י֯ס֯[18]
– (C4) ו֯[מ]ן אכתלגת ר[כב]תה
אלשמ[אל] [ינ]גו מן פם וחש או מן
ד֯א.[...]
– מן אכתלג כעבה אלימן[19] ירז֯ק֯ [......]
א֯ל֯בית מכיוף מתיוב מן בית֯[...] תע⟨א⟩לי:
– מן אכתלג כעבה אלי[סאר] (B3) ימרץ
במרץ שדיד פי רגליה:
– [ומן] אכתלג משט רגלה אלימ⟨י⟩ן יבטל
מ֯ן מעישתה וקת:
– מן אכתלג משט רגלה אליסאר סוף
יתכ֯תר עליה רזקה:
– מן אכתלגת אחדא אצאבע רגלה אלימין
ירזק יסאר טאיל ויקבל֯ אקבל[20] עט׳ים:
– מן אכתלגת אח[ד]י אצא⟨ב⟩ע רגלה
אליסאר פאנה יכסר כסרה וסית..[21]
– (B4) ומן אכלגת עליה אחדי ערוק גסמה
פירזק ע֯ן קרב דכר וסמעה חסנה.
– והדא מא רואה שם בן נח ע׳ אלס׳
ואללה אלעאלם אלחכים עאלם אלגיוב
ואלצ׳מאיר אלחמד ללה כתירא וחסבנא
אללה וחדה ושלום[22]

– מן אכת׳ שפתה אלפוקא ימלך ממלוכה או
ממלוד ואן כאן ליס הו אהלא לדלך פימלך
בהימה:

17 Several pages are missing here, covering the body parts from the lower lip to the thighs.

18 Another possible reading is ו֯ר֯א֯ס֯.

19 Lege אלאימן or אלימין.

20 Lege אקבאל.

21 I cannot decipher the last two letters.

22 The next page, A3, has a calendrical text, and A4 is blank.

2.2 *Translation*

In the following translation, I have marked in italics the section that is found only in copy 1 and have added in italics, and within parentheses, sections where the text of copy 1 differs from that of copy 2.

In the Name of the Merciful One (*In God's name we shall do and succeed*)

- This is the book of twitching (*twitches*) composed by Shem, son of Noah, peace be upon him, *and handed down by the Children of Israel generation after generation down to the time of Solomon, son of David, peace be upon him. And it was taken by the Greeks from the treasury of Solomon, son of David, and remained in use among them until the time of Būstānī the Nasi, the son of David. And when he entered their territory, he retrieved it from them, for it was written in the sacred tongue*[23] *in the handwriting of Shem, son of Noah. And so it arrived to the Children of Israel, and from then on the Children of Israel handed it down and passed it on as an inheritance. It is tested and true, and must be preserved, for it is a fine method.*
- He (*Shem, son of Noah*) said: If anyone's right eye twitches, good news will come to him, and he will be blessed with a good earning and happiness of the heart and a comfortable life.
- And if anyone's left eye twitches, he will suffer sorrow and distress, and will hear something that will distress his heart, and his body (*soul*) will be troubled by it.
- And if anyone's right eyebrow twitches, honor will come to him, and he will be blessed with a standing that he had never even hoped for.
- And if anyone's left eyebrow twitches, he will lose from his possession something that he had been storing (*keeping back*) for a time of hardship.
- And if anyone's right eyelid twitches, a long journey will be destined for him.
- And if anyone's left eyelid twitches, a short journey will be destined for him.
- And if anyone's right cheek twitches—if he has a pregnant wife, he will have a son, and if he does not have a pregnant wife, something will come to him that will please his heart.
- And if anyone's left cheek twitches—if he has a pregnant wife, he will have a daughter, and if he does not have a pregnant wife, his heart will be distressed by something.
- If anyone's tip of the nose twitches, there will be destined for him sour relations with some of his family.

23 I.e., Hebrew.

- And if anyone's upper lip twitches, he will come into possession of a female slave or a male slave. But if he is not worthy of this, he will only come into possession of an animal.[24]
- If anyone's [lower] l[ip] twitches ...[25]
- [And if anyone's] right thigh [twitches], he will find himself in trouble [because of] his deceitful relative.
- And if anyone's left [thigh tw]itches, he will fall into a serious illness.
- And if anyone's rig[ht k]nee twitches, he will be saved from a king and a leader (?).
- And [if] anyone's left kn[ee] twitches, he will be saved from the jaws of a wild beast or from a [ ].
- And if anyone's right ankle[26] twitches, he will be blessed with [ ] ...[27]
- And if anyone's le[ft] ankle twitches, he will fall into a serious illness of his legs.
- [If anyone's] inner arch of the right foot twitches, he will be deprived of his livelihood for a while.
- If anyone's inner arch of the left foot twitches, his earning will be great for him.
- If one of anyone's toes of the right foot twitch, he will be blessed with great wealth and will gain a great success.
- If one of anyone's toes of the left foot twitch, he will suffer a loss and will ...
- And if one of anyone's veins of the body twitch, he will soon be blessed with a reputation and good news.
- And this is what Shem, son of Noah, peace be upon him, narrated, and God, the knowing, the wise, is the one who knows the secrets and the inner thoughts. Much praise be to Allah, and Allah alone is sufficient for us. And peace.[28]

24 Copy 1 breaks off here.
25 Several pages are missing here from copy 2.
26 Or, heel.
27 I do not know how to translate the last part of this sentence.
28 The text ends here, and the next textual unit is a short calendrical text. See also below the description of this manuscript.

3 A Brief Survey of the Palmomantic Texts from the Cairo Genizah

As noted above, the Cairo Genizah preserves numerous fragments of palmomancy, and the following list covers all the fragments currently known to me. It is arranged according to the language and writing system in which the text is written, and in each case in which several fragments may be joined together in a single manuscript I have grouped them together. Given the great variety of palmomantic texts in many different languages, and the absence of critical editions of the relevant Arabic texts, I did not try to identify the texts below by systematically comparing them with the non-Jewish texts, but I did try to compare them with each other whenever they overlap. Moreover, whenever a fragment preserves more than a single text, I note the other texts copied in it in order to show the "manuscript contexts" of the palmomantic texts in the Cairo Genizah. For each fragment, I note its size (width × height), and the likely date, based on the paleographical analyses of the Hebrew scripts by Dr. Edna Engel.

3.1 *Aramaic*

(1) Oxford, Bodleian Heb. g 8.47–48 (20.2×7.9 cm) + Heb. g 8.49 (10.9×7.6 cm).[29] Parchment; one bifolium and one folio, each written by a different hand, the bifolium dating from the eleventh or twelfth century, the folio from the early tenth. As the text continues seamlessly from the bifolium to the folio, it seems as if in an older manuscript some pages had been missing, or been worn out, so a new copy of the missing sections was affixed to the well-preserved folio from the older manuscript. The bifolium preserves the end of a midrashic text, followed by a short magical recipe for erotic purposes and the beginning of the palmomantic text, which then continues into the folio. The palmomantic text is preserved in its entirety, including the title "the twitches of a person" (*RPPYH DBR NŠʾ*) and the body parts from the top of the head to the bottom of the feet. The text is quite short and covers only the main parts of the body; it provides no differentiation of the protaseis according to social status and no alternative predictions in the apodoseis. It is written in Palestinian (rather than Babylonian) Jewish Aramaic, a language that presumably was no longer in daily use by the time these fragments were copied. This text is paralleled by a Hebrew version that was clearly translated from the Aramaic and is found in numerous manuscripts—including many Ashkenazi and Italian prayer books—dating from the thirteenth century onwards. The Hebrew version has been printed several times (e.g., in *Midrash Talpiyyot*), and it is still in print today and readily

29 I plan to publish this text elsewhere.

available in some bookshops in Israel.[30] A German translation of this version was published by Diels (1908–1909) in his "Beiträge zur Zuckungsliteratur," and it is by far the best known Jewish palmomantic text.[31] However, this Hebrew version is not yet attested in the Cairo Genizah itself, and as far as I can see, none of the Judeo-Arabic texts mentioned below is based on this Aramaic text or on its Hebrew translation.

3.2 *Early Judeo-Arabic in Phonetic Spelling*[32]

(2) Jerusalem, National Library of Israel, Heb. 4^0 577.5.18 (33.8×15.7 cm).[33] Parchment; a bifolium, probably written in the tenth or eleventh centuries. The text begins with a title, *hādhā kitāb al-*[*ikhtilājā*]*t li-l-rajul wa-l-mara*, "This is the book of [twitche]s of man and woman." The most important word is missing in a lacuna, and the text itself begins with *in qāma shaʿr ra*[*sak*], "if the hair of [your he]ad stands"; later, the protaseis only use the formula *wa-in kāna*, "and if it is" + limb x, without using a more specific verb. Thus, the identification of this text as a manual of palmomancy is not entirely certain, and other types of physiognomy may also be considered, but palmomancy seems to be the most likely genre. The extant text, found on the first folio of this bifolium, covers the body parts from the hair to the arteries of the neck, with the rest of the text continuing in the next bifolium, which has not been preserved. From the extant section, it seems that the text covered quite a few limbs of the human body and would have been quite long. Most of the protaseis do not consider social distinctions, but in one case we find such a distinction, when we learn that (a twitch of) the back of the neck (*al-qafā*) foretells pain and suffering, and that if the person is fighting in a war (*wa-in kāna fī ḥarb*) his neck will be cut off, and if he is in prison (*wa-in kāna fī ḥabs*), he will be flogged with a whip. The apodoseis offer no alternative predictions.

The second folio of this bifolium has the end of another text, whose nature is not entirely clear, followed by a short medical text, supposedly written by ancient physicians at the behest of Alexander the Great (*Dhū l-qarnayn*), perhaps indicating that the copyist of this text was a physician himself.

30 For some of the relevant manuscripts, see Leicht 2006: 113, 114, 118, 120, 122, 125, 127, 131, 134, 157, 161, 167. Many more such manuscripts can be found through the catalogue of the Institute of Microfilmed Hebrew Manuscripts in Jerusalem.

31 Diels 1908–1909: 2: 96–100.

32 For the characteristics of this manner of writing Arabic in the Hebrew alphabet, see Blau and Hopkins 1984; Blau and Hopkins 2017.

33 I have prepared this text for publication in Blau and Hopkins forthcoming.

3.3 *"Standard" Judeo-Arabic*

(3) Cambridge, T-S A 45.21 (14.4 × 21.1 cm).[34] Paper; a single folio, probably dating from the twelfth century. The text begins with a title, *hādhā kitāb al-ikhtilājāt ta'līf shēm ben noaḥ 'alayhi l-salām*, "This is the Book of Twitches, composed by Shem, son of Noah, peace be upon him," which is followed by an introductory explanation of how the ancient Israelites transmitted it continuously up to the time of King Solomon, from whose treasury the Greeks took it (presumably in the days of Alexander the Great, or slightly later) and used it until the time of the Nasi al-Būstānī, son of David (who lived in Babylonia in the seventh century CE!). He found it in the Greeks' possession, still written in Hebrew and in the handwriting of Shem, son of Noah (!), and brought it back into the Jewish world, where it has remained ever since. This introductory formula is not found in the second copy of our text and probably was added to a text that originally was transliterated from an Arabic manuscript in order to enhance its legitimacy in Jewish eyes.[35] The text itself begins with the right eye and reaches the upper lip, where the text clearly continued in more folios, which are no longer extant. For text and translation, see above, and for a more detailed assessment of the text's features, see the next set of fragments.

(4) Oxford, Bodleian Heb. g 8.52–53 (16.8 × 6.1 cm); Cambridge, T-S Ar. 45.11 (18.3 × 6.6 cm); Cambridge, T-S AS 157.179 (6.6 × 4.9 cm) + T-S AS 173.423 (8.3 × 5.3 cm).[36] Parchment, probably written in the twelfth century; three bifolia, which consist of the three outermost bifolia of a "pocketbook" quire, with one—or, more likely, two—bifolia still missing in the middle of the quire (and covering the body parts from the lower lip to the thighs).[37] The booklet may have been written by two different scribes, but this is not certain. After a blank cover page, the booklet opens with a title, *hādhā kitāb al-ikhtilāj ta'līf shēm ben noaḥ 'al(av) ha-sh(alōm)*, "This is the Book of Twitching, composed by Shem, son of Noah, peace be upon him," and the text begins with the right eye and continues to the lower lip, after which several folios are missing. The text resumes

34 Published by Hopkins 1978: 67–71; see also above, copy 1.

35 For the wider theme of the Greek appropriation of Jewish wisdom, and its use as an inner Jewish justification for the appropriation of Greek wisdom, see Roth 1978; Melamed 2010, esp. 94–177.

36 The great discrepancy in the size of the folios of this booklet is in part due to the poor state of preservation of some folios, but the original booklet must also have been quite irregular in shape, made up of bifolia of different sizes.

37 The use of a miniature codex for a palmomantic manual is paralleled in the Greek-speaking world of late antiquity; see the detailed discussion by Mowat 2016: 418–419.

with the thighs and the knees and runs to the bottom of the feet, and to one more general prediction about the twitching of all the veins of the body. This is followed by an ending formula, explaining that all this was told by Shem, son of Noah, and concluding with praises to God. Finally, in the next folio, we find a short calendrical note and a colophon identifying the scribe—or one of them—as "Menashe birabbi Isaac the cantor, may he rest in peace," who is known from other Genizah documents of the mid-twelfth century.[38] The last page of the original booklet is again blank, serving as a back cover page. The small format of this booklet, and the irregular size of the folios, probably reflect the production of this booklet as a handy *vademecum* to be carried around and used for predicting the future of whoever might experience an involuntary twitch and be troubled by its potential significance.

The palmomantic text found here is identical with that of the previous item, except for the long introduction, which is not found in this copy. The text provides predictions for the twitching of many parts of the body but is not as detailed as some of the other texts (for example, it does not provide a prediction for each toe of the two feet). In the extant fragments of this text, the protaseis usually do not refer to the person's social position, but in two cases a distinction is made, "If he has a pregnant wife ... and if he does not have a pregnant wife" (*in kāna lahu ḥāmil ... wa-in lam yakūn lahu ḥāmil*), and one prediction says that he will acquire a slave, but if he is not in a social position to do so (*wa-in kāna laysa huwa ahl li-dhālika*), he will acquire an animal. Throughout the text, only one prediction is provided in each apodosis. For the text and its translation, see the previous section of the present paper.

(5) T-S AS 157.50 (5 × 13.5 cm): Paper; a single folio; torn, holed, and badly effaced; probably dating from the twelfth century. Only a part of each line survives, and the extant text covers the body parts from the male organ (*dhakar*) to the hip joint (*mawḍiʿ ḥaqq al-wark*). The text is the same as that of T-S NS 288.186, which is much better preserved (see the next item). The hand in which this fragment was written was identified by Esther-Miriam Wagner as that of the scribe Ḥalfon ben Menashe, who was active in al-Fusṭāṭ (Old Cairo) in the first half of the twelfth century, and this identification was independently confirmed to me by Mordechai Akiva Friedman.[39]

38 For example, as a signatory witness in Cambridge, T-S 13 J 3.9, dated 1151 CE.

39 For an online publication, by Wagner and myself, see http://www.lib.cam.ac.uk/Taylor-Schechter/fotm/april-2008/. See also Wagner 2017: 125–126. For some astrological texts copied by Ḥalfon ben Menashe, see Goitein 1967–1993: 5: 625, n. 28.

(6) T-S NS 33.130 (13.5×15 cm) + T-S NS 288.186 (14.2×18.6 cm): Paper; two folios that join to make a single bifolium; torn and effaced. Probably dating from the twelfth or thirteenth centuries. Four consecutive pages, covering most of the body, from the back of the neck (*qafā*) to the toes, where the text probably ended (but this section is badly damaged). The text is the same as that of T-S AS 157.50 (see the previous item). The text covers numerous small parts of the body, but there are no distinctions according to social status, and no alternative predictions.

(7) T-S Ar. 48.38 (14×12.6 cm): Paper; a single folio; torn, and partly effaced. Probably dating from the twelfth or thirteenth centuries but perhaps dating from a later period. The recto has the end of an onomantic text used to predict from two persons' names whether they will marry or not.[40] The verso has the beginning of a book of twitches titled "The Book of Twitching, to be used as a guide for the twitching that occurs to a man in his entire body" (*kitāb al-ikhtilāj mā yustadall bihi ʿalā l-ikhtilāj alladhī yuʿāriḍ al-insān fī jamīʿ badanihi*). The extant text covers different parts of the head, from the fontanelle (*yāfūkh*) to the side of the head (*shiqq raʾsihi*), where the text breaks off, and clearly continued for several more pages, which are no longer extant. One of the protaseis allows for differentiation according to the person's social position, "If he is a rich person … and if he is a poor person …" (*in kāna ghanī … wa-in kāna faqīr*). Several apodoseis offer alternative predictions, preceded by "perhaps" (*rubba-mā* and *la-ʿalla*). Some of the predictions in this text parallel those found in the palmomantic text usually attributed to Jaʿfar al-Ṣādiq, which is widely available on the internet, but it is not the same text.

3.4 *Arabic (in the Arabic Alphabet)*

(8) T-S AS 181.130 (11×8.5 cm). Paper; torn and partly effaced. The extant section begins with the right eyelid (*jafn ʿaynihi al-yumnā*) and reaches as far as the nose (*anf*). There are no distinctions in the protaseis, but in each apodosis a prediction is given, followed by "and the Persians say" (*wa-qālat al-Furs*) and an alternative prediction. This probably is the same text—but definitely not the same hand—as the next item, but as there is no overlap between the two texts, their identity cannot be demonstrated. The text has some affinities, but is not identical, with a palmomantic text, which is widely available on the internet, that is usually attributed to Jalāl al-Dīn al-Suyūṭī.

---

40 Such texts are extremely common in Jewish manuscripts; see, e.g., Bohak 2014: 1: 158.

(9) T-S AS 177.21 + T-S AS 177.56 (12.2×13.5 cm). Paper; the two fragments join to make a single folio that is torn and holed. The extant text covers the feet, from the ankle (*kaʿb*) to the toes (*aṣābiʿ al-qadam*) and the entire foot (*al-qadam kulluhā*). There are no distinctions in the protaseis, but in each apodosis a prediction is given, followed by "and the Persians say" (*wa-qālat al-Furs*) and an alternative prediction. This probably is the same text as the previous item.

3.5 *Hebrew*

(10) Oxford, Bodleian Heb. f. 106.60–61 (22.2×15.5 cm).[41] Paper; a bifolium, slightly torn on the margins. Unlike all the Aramaic and Judeo-Arabic fragments that were listed above, which are written in Oriental hands, this fragment is written in a Spanish hand, and probably dates from the fifteenth century. It consists of two nonconsecutive folios, which contain a florilegium of Hebrew texts. The first folio contains rabbinic maxims, a magical recipe for protection against robbers, and riddles based on biblical passages. The folio ends at the beginning of the fourth riddle, and—after a gap of several folios—the second folio of our bifolium contains a palmomantic text. The extant section covers the regions from the shoulders to the knees, and the text covers mainly the larger limbs and offers no differentiation of the protaseis according to social status and no alternative predictions in the apodoseis. This palmomantic text clearly was translated from Spanish, as may be deduced from the presence of Spanish, or Judeo-Spanish, words, such as שובאקו *sobaco*, "armpit," or פיג'ו *pecho*, "chest." The booklet in which this text was copied looks very much like a Renaissance hodgepodge of educational, magical, divinatory, and playful texts. It probably was produced in Spain and reached Cairo after the expulsion of the Jews from Spain in 1492.

(11) Cambridge, T-S Misc. 17.8. Paper; two dozen pages (each measuring 11.7×18.8 cm) from a printed book, including the title-page, *Refuʾot ha-Talmud im Sefer Refafot*, "The Medicines found in the Talmud, with the Book of Twitches," printed by Gershom Soncino in Cairo in 1562.[42] However, the extant

41 I did not measure the fragment, and the photos on the Friedberg website (fjms.genizah .org) and the Bodleian's website (genizah.bodleian.ox.ac.uk) have no ruler. The size given here is based on Cowley's handwritten catalogue, available on the Friedberg website.

42 T-S Misc. 17.5 and 17.6 contain fragments from another book, with oneiromancy and lots (*goralot*), printed by the same press a few years earlier, but the fragments of the two books are dispersed between these three shelf marks. The importance of these Genizah frag-

pages do not include the palmomantic manual, and no other copies of this printed edition are currently known to me.

Looking at the above list, we may safely conclude that palmomantic texts were borrowed by Jews from many different places. The earliest text clearly is the Aramaic text, which probably was borrowed from Greek (or Syriac?) sources in late antiquity. It was subsequently translated into Hebrew, but its Hebrew version is absent from the Cairo Genizah, at least as far as we can tell at this stage. But the Jews of medieval Cairo had many Arabic palmomantic texts to choose from, texts which they read both in Arabic letters and in Judeo-Arabic. The earliest of these texts is still written in the phonetic spelling of Judeo-Arabic and probably dates from the last two or three centuries of the first millennium CE. But the phonetic system eventually was discarded in favor of the "standard" form of writing Arabic in Hebrew letters, and in this form we have the fragmentary remains of three different palmomantic texts, including one that is attributed to Shem, the son of Noah. We also have fragments of yet another palmomantic manual, written in Arabic and in the Arabic script and presumably borrowed by the Jews of Cairo from their non-Jewish neighbors. And there is also a Hebrew palmomantic text, dating from a later period and clearly translated from Spanish, and we even learn that one of the texts printed in the first, and short-lived, Hebrew printing house in Cairo was a palmomantic manual. In other words, the Cairo Genizah bears ample testimony to the continuous Jewish interest in palmomancy from late antiquity to the sixteenth century, thus complementing the extensive evidence found in non-Genizah manuscripts, which has yet to receive the attention it deserves. And, as we shall soon see, the interest in palmomancy in medieval Egypt is well attested outside the Cairo Genizah as well.

4 A Palmomantic Manual from al-Quṣayr (P.Cair.IslArt inv. Quseir82 1016 b)

The last palmomantic fragment to be examined here is contemporaneous with some of the Genizah fragments we have already examined but comes from a very different source. It was found in the trading port of al-Quṣayr on the Red Sea, along with many other documents dating from the thirteenth cen-

ments for the study of the history of Jewish printing in Cairo was first noted by Cowley 1935; for a recent survey, and further bibliography, see Heller 2014: 145.

tury and belonging to a local merchant. In the editio princeps, it was classified as an "amulet," and the readings and translations offered there make it look like a set of recipes and instructions, divided into sections devoted to different parts of the head.[43] However, the recurrent noun that was read by its editor as اصلاح *iṣlāḥ*, "maintenance, treatment," should in fact be read as اختلاج *ikhtilāj*, "twitching," and the verbs which he read as اصلح *aṣlaḥa* should in fact be read as اختلج *ikhtalaja*. Moreover, as all the palmomantic texts are arranged from head to toe, it is clear that the editor's order of recto and verso should be reversed. Unfortunately, I have not been able to examine the fragment itself, which is now in Cairo, nor have I been able to obtain good photos of the recto and verso.[44] Thus, the following reedition is based on what I could make out from a low-quality black-and-white image of the recto, which is the only image at my disposal. My tentative reedition will therefore have to be improved upon by others, who may have access to the original or to better photographs, but for the time being I offer the following reading and translation:

P.Cair.IslArt inv. Quseir82 1016 b   7 cm high × 9 cm wide   13th century
al-Quṣayr al-Qadīm

Recto

١ [...] ربه (؟) صحيح ... و[جـ]سم ...
٢ باب أختلاج الصّدغين
٣ من أختلج صدغه الأيمن سعا (؟) إليه (؟) أقرب (؟) الناس إليه
٤ ومن أختلج صدغه الأيسر صحّ جسمه وقرّت عينه
٥ باب أختلاج الأذنين
٦ من أختلج أذنه اليمين فرح وسرور وأجر(؟) ا ...
٧ واليسار ... أملاك (؟) سو[..]ـه [...]

43 Guo 2004: 309–311 no. 81. In the Arabic Papyrological Database (https://www.apd.gwi.uni-muenchen.de/apd/project.jsp; accessed May 15, 2019), P.QuseirArab. I 81 is still listed as an "Amulet" and described as "An amulet, providing prevention of, and cures for, certain physical ailments; Hand-written amulet," and the text provided is that of the editio princeps.

44 I am grateful to Li Guo for sending me the photographs available to him, and to Donald Whitcomb for supplying further information on the current whereabouts of the Quṣayr fragments.

(1) ... will be healthy in ... and body ...
(2) The section on the twitching of the temples:
(3) If anyone's right temple twitches, to him the people closest to him will draw
(4) and if anyone's left temple twitches, his body will be healthy and he will be at his ease.
(5) The section on the twitching of the ears:
(6) If anyone's right ear twitches, gladness and rejoicing and a reward (?) ...
(7) And the left one ... possessions ...

FIGURE 5.1 P.Cair.IslArt inv. Quseir82 1016 b recto; the palmomantic text is in the middle of the bottom row
IMAGE COURTESY OF LI GUO

Verso

١ ... من أختلج [منخاره] الأيمن ...
٢ ومن أختلج منخاره (؟) الأيسر أدل على غائب يذكره
٣ باب اُختلاج ذقن :
٤ من أختلج ذقنه ....
٥ ...
٦ .... الأيسر يستفيد كلامه
٧ ... ظلّت (؟) تطيل (؟) ...

(1) If anyone's right [nostril (?)] twitches …
(2) and if his left nostril (?) twitches, it means that someone who is absent will mention him.
(3) The section on the twitching of a chin:
(4) If anyone's chin twitches …
(5)
(6) … and if his left [twitches], his speech will benefit.
(7) … …

FIGURE 5.2 P.Cair.IslArt inv. Quseir82 1016 b verso; the palmomantic text is in the middle of the bottom row
IMAGE COURTESY OF LI GUO

Looking at the extant text, we see that it covers the body parts from the temples to the chin and that this text probably offered no distinctions according to social position, and no alternative options for each apodosis. We also see that it is very similar to the Genizah palmomantic fragments, and this resemblance fits within a much larger set of similarities between the Cairo Genizah fragments and those from al-Quṣayr and is yet another demonstration of how a familiarity with the Genizah documents can help our reading and understanding of the Quṣayr fragments.[45] Moreover, it also serves to highlight how

45 This point was forcefully demonstrated by Friedman 2006; Kaplony 2014. For other magical texts from al-Quṣayr, see also Cohen 2006: 303–304.

common such texts were in medieval Egypt, among Muslims and Jews (and presumably Christians) alike. Merchants—always unsure about the success and failure of their business ventures—clearly found them very useful, but so did everyone else.

5 Conclusion

Palmomancy is one of many divinatory techniques that were extremely popular in antiquity and the Middle Ages but were demoted in our own world to the realms of nonsense and superstition. But as a historian of Jewish culture, my task is to look at all the texts produced by ancient and medieval Jews, not just those that suit our modern sensibilities. And it is in the Cairo Genizah, more than in any other cache of Hebrew manuscripts and documents, that we can find the common beliefs and practices of ordinary people. We may snub our noses at their superstitions, but if they could watch us, they would probably tell us that Shem, the son of Noah, had written long ago that if the tip of our nose twitches, it must mean that we will have sour relations with a member of our family—or, in this case, with our distant ancestors.

Bibliography

Allony, Nehemiah. 2006. *Ha-Sifriyya ha-yehudit bi-yeme ha-benayim: reshimot sefarim mi-genizat Qahir* [The Jewish Library in the Middle Ages: Book Lists From the Cairo Genizah]. Edited by Miriam Frenkel and Haggai Ben-Shammai. Jerusalem: Ben-Zvi.

The Arabic Papyrological Database. www.naher-osten.lmu.de/apd (accessed May 15, 2019).

Blau, Joshua, and Simon Hopkins. 1984. "On Early Judaeo-Arabic Orthography." In *Zeitschrift für Arabische Linguistik* 12: 9–27.

Blau, Joshua, and Simon Hopkins. 2017. *Ha-ʿAravit-ha-Yehudit ha-qedumah bi-ketiv foneṭi: ṭeqsṭim mi-shalhe ha-elef ha-rishon* [Early Judaeo-Arabic in Phonetic Spelling: Texts From the End of the First Millennium]. Vol. 1. Jerusalem: Ben-Zvi.

Blau, Joshua, and Simon Hopkins. Forthcoming. *Ha-ʿAravit-ha-Yehudit ha-qedumah bi-ketiv foneṭi: ṭeqsṭim mi-shalhe ha-elef ha-rishon* [Early Judaeo-Arabic in Phonetic Spelling: Texts from the End of the First Millennium]. Vol. 2. Jerusalem: Ben-Zvi.

Böck, Barbara. 2000. *Die babylonisch-assyrische Morphoskopie*. Archiv für Orientforschung, Beiheft 27. Vienna: Institut für Orientalistik.

Bohak, Gideon. 2010. "Towards a Catalogue of the Magical, Astrological, Divinatory, and Alchemical Fragments from the Cambridge Genizah Collections." In *"From a Sacred*

Source": Genizah Studies in Honour of Professor Stefan C. Reif, edited by Ben Outhwaite and Siam Bhayro. Études sur le judaïsme médiéval 42. Cambridge Genizah Studies Series 1. Leiden: Brill, 53–79.

Bohak, Gideon. 2014. *Sefer keshafim Yehudi me-ha-me'ah ha-15: ketav yad New York, ha-Sifriyah ha-Tsiburit 190 (leshe'avar Sassoon 56): mavo, mahadurah mevo'eret ṿe-tsilum ketav ha-yad* [A Fifteenth-Century Manuscript of Jewish Magic: MS New York Public Library, Heb. 190 (Formerly Sassoon 56): Introduction, Annotated Edition and Facsimile]. Sources and Studies in the Literature of Jewish Mysticism 44. 2 vols. Los Angeles: Cherub Press.

Bohak, Gideon. 2016. "Manuals of Mantic Wisdom: From the Dead Sea Scrolls to the Cairo Genizah." In *Tracing Sapiential Traditions in Ancient Judaism*, edited by Hindy Najman, Jean-Sébastien Rey, and Eibert J.C. Tigchelaar. Supplements of the Journal for the Study of Judaism 174. Leiden: Brill, 191–216.

Charlesworth, James H. 1983–1985. "Treatise of Shem." In *The Old Testament Pseudepigrapha*, edited by James H. Charlesworth. 2 vols. Garden City, NY: Doubleday, 1: 473–486.

Cohen, Mark R. 2006. "Goitein, Magic, and the Geniza." In *Jewish Studies Quarterly* 13: 294–304.

Costanza, Salvatore. 2009. *Corpus Palmomanticum Graecum*. Papyrologica Florentina 39. Florence: Gonnelli.

Costanza, Salvatore. 2018. "Fateful Spasms: Palmomancy and Late Antique Lot Divination." In *"My Lots are in Thy Hands": Sortilege and Its Practitioners in Late Antiquity*, edited by AnneMarie Luijendijk and William E. Klingshirn. Religions in the Graeco-Roman World 188. Leiden: Brill, 78–100.

Cowley, Arthur Ernest. 1935. "Ein Soncino-Druck aus Kairo, 1566." In *Festschrift für Aron Freimann*, edited by Alexander Marx and Herrmann Meyer. Berlin: Soncino-Gesellschaft, 89–90.

Dasen, Véronique. 2008. "Le langage divinatoire du corps." In *Langages et métaphores du corps*, edited by Véronique Dasen and Jérôme Wilgaux. Cahiers d'histoire du corps antique 3. Rennes: Presses Universitaires de Rennes, 223–242.

Davidson, Israel. 1934. *Salmon ben Yeruḥim, The Book of the Wars of the Lord: Containing the Polemics of the Karaite Salmon ben Yeruhim Against Saadia Gaon. Sēfer milḥāmōt: kôlel taanôt ha-Qaraî Salmôn ben Yerûhîm neged Rav Saadya Gaôn*. New York: Jewish Theological Seminary of America.

Diels, Hermann Alexander. 1908–1909. "Beiträge zur Zuckungsliteratur des Okzidents und Orients." In *Abhandlungen der Preussischen Akademie der Wissenschaften, Philosophisch-historische Klasse, 1907–1908*. 2 vols. Berlin: Königliche Akademie der Wissenschaften.

Fahd, Toufic. 1966. *La divination arabe: études religieuses, sociologiques et folkloriques sur le milieu natif de l'Islam*. Leiden: Brill.

The Friedberg Jewish Manuscript Society (fjms.genizah.org).

Friedman, Mordechai A. 2006. "Qusayr and Geniza Documents on the Indian Ocean Trade." In *Journal of the American Oriental Society* 126: 401–409.

Furlani, Giuseppe. 1917. "Due trattati palmomantici in siriaco." In *Rendiconti della Reale Accademia Nazionale dei Lincei, Classe di scienze morali, storiche e filologiche*. Series 5, vol. 26: 719–732.

Furlani, Giuseppe. 1918. "Ancora un trattato palmomantico in lingua siriaca." In *Rendiconti della Reale Accademia Nazionale dei Lincei, Classe di scienze morali, storiche e filologiche*. Series 5, vol. 27: 316–328.

Furlani, Giuseppe. 1946. "Un trattato palmomantico in garsciunico." In *Rivista degli Studi Orientali* 21: 183–187.

Furlani, Giuseppe. 1949. "Sur la palmomantique chez les Babyloniens et les Assyriens." In *Archiv Orientální* 17: 255–269.

Geller, Markham J. 2001–2002. "West Meets East: Early Greek and Babylonian Diagnosis." In *Archiv für Orientforschung* 48–49: 50–75.

Genizah Fragments at the Bodleian Libraries (genizah.bodleian.ox.ac.uk).

Goitein, Shlomo Dov. 1967–1993. *A Mediterranean Society: The Jewish Communities of the Arab World as Portrayed in the Documents of the Cairo Geniza*. 6 vols. Berkeley: University of California Press.

Guo, Li. 2004. *Commerce, Culture, and Community in a Red Sea Port in the Thirteenth Century: The Arabic Documents from Quseir*. Islamic History and Civilization 52. Leiden: Brill.

Heller, Marvin J. 2014. "Unicums, Fragments, and Other Hebrew Book Rarities." In *Judaica Librarianship* 18: 130–153.

Hopkins, Simon. 1978. *A Miscellany of Literary Pieces from the Cambridge Genizah Collections: A Catalogue and Selection of Texts in the Taylor-Schechter Collection, Old Series, Box A45*. Genizah Series 3. Cambridge: Cambridge University Library.

Kaplony, Andreas. 2014. *Fünfundzwanzig arabische Dokumente aus dem Rotmeer-Hafen al-Quṣayr al-Qadīm (7./13. Jahrhundert) [P.QuseirArab. II]: Edition, Übersetzung und Kommentar*. Islamic History and Civilization 109. Leiden: Brill.

Leicht, Reimund. 2006. *Astrologumena Judaica: Untersuchungen zur Geschichte der Astrologischen Literatur der Juden*. Texts and Studies in Medieval and Early Modern Judaism 21. Tübingen: Mohr Siebeck.

Mavroudi, Maria. 2009. "Islamic Divination in the Context of Its 'Eastern' and 'Western' Counterparts." In *Falnama: The Book of Omens*, edited by Massumeh Farhad and Serpil Bağci. Washington, DC: Smithsonian Institution, 221–229; 324–329.

Melamed, Abraham. 2010. *Raqaḥot ve-ṭabaḥot: ha-mitos ʿal meqor ha-ḥokhmot* [The Myth of the Jewish Origins of Science and Philosophy]. Haifa and Jerusalem: Haifa University Press and Magnes Press.

Mowat, Chris. 2016. "A Study on Spontaneity: Some Notes on the Divinatory Handbook P.Ryl. 28." In *Religion in the Roman Empire* 2: 415–440

Muchowski, Piotr. 2012. "Notes on Two Karaite Texts Edited by Ananiasz Zajączkowski." In *Folia Orientalia* 49 (= Studia Andreae Zaborski Dedicata): 327–337.

Roth, Norman. 1978. "The 'Theft of Philosophy' by the Greeks from the Jews." In *Classical Folia* 32: 53–67.

Scharbach, Rebecca. 2010. "The Rebirth of a Book: Noachic Writing in Medieval and Renaissance Europe." In *Noah and His Book(s)*, edited by Michael E. Stone, Aryeh Amihay, and Vered Hillel. Early Judaism and Its Literature 28. Atlanta: Society of Biblical Literature, 113–133.

Sezgin, Fuat. 1979. *Geschichte des arabischen Schrifttums bis ca. 430 H.* Volume 7: *Astrologie: Meteorologie und Verwandtes*. Leiden: Brill.

Shaked, Shaul. 2000. "Medieval Jewish Magic in Relation to Islam: Theoretical Attitudes and Genres." In *Judaism and Islam: Boundaries, Communication and Interaction. Essays in Honor of William M. Brinner*, edited by Benjamin H. Hary, John R. Hayes, and Fred Astern. Brill's Series in Jewish Studies 27. Leiden: Brill, 97–109.

Shyovitz, David I. 2017. *A Remembrance of His Wonders: Nature and the Supernatural in Medieval Ashkenaz*. Jewish Culture and Contexts. Philadelphia: University of Pennsylvania Press.

Steinschneider, Moritz. 1893/1956. *Die hebräischen Übersetzungen des Mittelalters und die Juden als Dolmetscher: ein Beitrag zur Literaturgeschichte des Mittelalters, meist nach handschriftlichen Quellen*. Berlin: Bibliographisches Bureau/Reprint Graz: Akademische Druck- und Verlagsanstalt.

Steinschneider, Moritz. 1938. *Allgemeine Einleitung in die jüdische Literatur des Mittelalters: Vorlesungen*. Jerusalem: Bamberger und Wahrmann. (First published in *Jewish Quarterly Review* 15–17, 1903–1905).

Swartz, Michael D. 2012. *The Signifying Creator: Nontextual Systems of Meaning in Ancient Judaism*. New York and London: New York University Press.

Ta-Shma, Israel. 1994. "Zekher Aasah le-Nifleotav" [He made a remembrance of his wonders]. In *Qovetz al-Yad* 22: 121–146.

Trachtenberg, Joshua. 1939/2004. *Jewish Magic and Superstition: A Study in Folk Religion*. New York: Behrman's Jewish Book House/Reprint Philadelphia: University of Pennsylvania Press.

Ullmann, Manfred. 1972. *Die Natur- und Geheimwissenschaften im Islam*. Handbuch der Orientalistik. Abteilung 1: Der Nahe und Mittlere Osten, Ergänzungsband 6,2. Leiden: Brill.

Villuendas Sabaté, Blanca. 2015. *La geomancia en los manuscritos judeo-árabes de la Gueniza de El Cairo*. Judaeo-Islamica 2. Cordoba: Universidad de Cordoba.

Villuendas Sabaté, Blanca. 2020. *Onirocrítica islámica, judía y cristiana en la Gueniza de El Cairo: edición y estudio de los manuales judeo-árabes de interpretación de sueños*. Estudios árabes e islámicos 23. Madrid: Consejo Superior de Investigaciones Científicas.

Wagner, Esther-Miriam. 2017. "A Matter of Script?: Arabic and Judaeo-Arabic in the Genizah Collections." In *Jewish-Muslim Relations in Past and Present: A Kaleidoscopic View*, edited by Josef W. Meri. Studies on the Children of Abraham 5. Leiden: Brill.

Wilgaux, Jérôme, and Véronique Dasen. 2013. "De la palmomantique à l'éternuement, lectures divinatoires des mouvements du corps." In *Kernos* 26: 111–122.

CHAPTER 6

Scientific Textbooks and Their Application in Practice: Interdependencies of Literary and Documentary Evidence of Scientific Activities

Johannes Thomann

Abstract

The purpose of the present article is to show how scientific activities appear in documentary evidence and in what way this agrees with evidence from scientific handbooks. This cannot be presented in a systematic way, since the research in the field of Arabic documents related to the sciences is only at its beginning and greatly varies across disciplines. Historians of the scientific disciplines in the Islamic world have based their accounts almost exclusively on literary works, and documents have played no significant role. This contrasts with the situation in research on the sciences in classical antiquity, in which both literary and documentary sources inform scholarly consensus/opinion.

The aim of this article is to give documentary examples of scientific activities and to explain how they are a significant contribution to our understanding of scientific practice. In most cases, scientific textbooks give little information about their social context and their *Sitz im Leben*. Often it remains an open question if their relevance goes beyond the restricted areas of school and education. As in many other domains of civilization, documents shed more light on practices in everyday life. This is also true for the domain of the sciences. The following examples for medicine, pharmacy, alchemy, magic, geomancy, cryptography, astronomy, and astrology will provide positive evidence for their practice outside the great cities. Naturally, the materials presented here are all from Middle or Upper Egypt. On the one hand, this limits the results based on them. On the other hand, they shed new light on a region for which no other source for scientific activities is available. At the end, the question of the continuity of astronomy from late antiquity to Islamic times will be discussed. It turns out that it returned to Egypt, after a break of 300 years, which is where it had been created more than a thousand years ago.

 | DOI:10.1163/9789004527874_008

1 Medicine and Pharmacy[1]

The most comprehensive study on "pharmaceutical documents" is Albert Dietrich's (1954) monograph on a papyrus order for drugs preserved in the Heidelberg Collection (P.DietrichDrogenkunde). Starting from Greek, Coptic, and Arabic textbooks on pharmacy, Dietrich was able to identify 14 out of the 17 drugs mentioned in the document. This indicates a close relationship between theory and practice.

But there are many open questions concerning the organization of healthcare in the premodern Islamic world. The fact that many textbooks on pharmacy, either as independent works or as parts of medical works, have been preserved points to the fact that pharmaceutical knowledge formed part of a physician's education.[2] It has been thought that a druggist's competence was restricted to the judgment of the quality of drugs and how to store them.[3] However, Arabic documents show that the practice in Egypt was different. According to Dietrich, patients went to contact druggists without consulting a physician.[4]

A good example is a letter to a druggist, in which a patient orders two mixtures, that is preserved with the druggist's package inserts (P.Grohmann-Wirtsch. 1; 3rd/9th c.).[5] At the end the patient adds "explain the quality and how I make it and how I drink it" (*bayyin mā l-ṣifa wa-kayfa aʿmaluhu wa-kayfa ashrabuhu*): he obviously regarded the druggist as competent in this respect and sees no need to consult a physician.

2 Alchemy

A discipline related to pharmacy but different in its goal is alchemy. It has been argued that alchemy was an entirely academic discipline—or, possibly, a purely spiritual occupation—without any practical significance in everyday life.[6] But there are documents that point to the contrary and show that short notes with alchemical receipts were produced, obviously as aide-mémoire for practical

1 In the call for papers for the conference where this paper was presented, it was mentioned as an achievement in recent years that "scholars working on the Islamic world up to the 16th century counterbalance literary tradition with documentary evidence."
2 Bürgel 2016: 99–215.
3 Schwarz 1976: 33–39.
4 Dietrich 1954: 5.
5 Grohmann 1935: 439–440.
6 Căian 2010; Schwartz-Salant 1998.

activities, since they lack any allusion to spirituality. A parcel of Arabic documents was found by Monneret in a ruin on the west bank of the Nile opposite Aswan and published by Margoliouth and Holmyard in 1931. Among them are several alchemical texts (P.MargoliouthMonneret 1–4), yet there are no reproductions, and the whereabouts of the original documents are unknown. Margoliouth and Holmyard remark that their content has some similarities with Syriac texts on alchemy without giving a precise reference.[7] In a prescription on how to transform tin or silver to gold (P.MargoliouthMonneret 1), the word *zirnīkh* is used, which means "orpiment" or "arsenic sulfide," a toxic substance that in nature, occurs in crystalline form.[8] It is rarely found in Arabic alchemical texts, yet *zarniḵo*, "orpiment," is mentioned in similar prescriptions in Syriac alchemical texts.[9] Orpiment has a golden color, so it makes perfect sense that it would figure in efforts to produce gold from other minerals. As it seems, alchemy was a multicultural phenomenon. A Coptic alchemical document, to be edited by Sebastian Richter, shows a close relationship with both Greek and Arabic alchemical texts.[10]

3 Magic

Documentary evidence does not always corroborate the impression gained from literary sources. The *Ghāyat al-ḥakīm* (fourth/tenth century), the first encyclopaedic work in Arabic on magic, mentions a number of magical operations and objects. But on the one hand, examples of only a small number of these are found in documents, and on the other hand, many types of magical documents have no correspondence to things mentioned in the *Ghāyat al-ḥakīm*. A common type of talisman consists of passages from the Quran written on paper, the preferred Suras being Q 1, 112, 113, and 114. The practice with such amulets is described in a story in al-Tanūkhī's *al-Faraj ba'd al-shidda* (fourth/tenth century): a servant (*mamlūk*) who lost his master's favor asks a scribe for help; the scribe then produces a talisman with passages from Q 2, 3, 8, 30, 59, 113, and 114 and instructs the servant to wear the paper on his right upper arm.[11] A similar extant example of an amulet with Q 1, 112, 113, and 114 is

7 Margoliouth and Holmyard 1931: 249.
8 Margoliouth and Holmyard 1931: 250 no. 1 B, line 3.
9 Berthelot 1893: 28,44, 76, 129, 144, 160.
10 Richter 2015: 162, 171.
11 Al-Tanūkhī 1955/1999: 55; al-Tanūkhī 1979: 18–20.

preserved in the Heidelberg Papyrus Collection (P.Bad. V 143).[12] In the *Ghāyat al-ḥakīm*, one finds a few quotations from the Quran, but they serve always to underline a point in an argument and are never recommended for magical use. In the instructions on how to produce talismans, the astrological conditions for the time of production appear as the crucial element. The so-called *Brillenbuchstaben* or *charakteres* said to represent star constellations,[13] and other symbols are drawn on the talismans, but no texts. *Brillenbuchstaben* also occur on magical documents but actually show only occasional resemblance to those in the *Ghāyat al-ḥakīm*.

4 Geomancy

A much closer relationship between textbooks and documents is found in the field of geomancy.[14] Geomantic figures are frequently found on documents and prove the popularity of this discipline. In two cases, the different phases of the standard geomantic procedure are found on a single page, exactly as they are described in textbooks. One example is an unpublished paper document preserved in the Vienna Papyrus Collection (P.Vind. inv. A.Ch. 8516).[15]

5 Cryptography

A problematic case is cryptography. There is an early treatise by al-Kindī on how to encrypt texts by a cipher, and how to decipher them.[16] A cryptographic papyrus (P.Vind. inv. A.P. 11016) from the epoch of al-Kindī has been preserved. It is definitively not fake but encryptions of human language, since it follows Zipf's law, which characterizes the letter frequencies of natural languages. George Kingsley Zipf (1902–1950) found this law in the 1930s, long after the papyrus had come into the Vienna collection. It has been deciphered by Gideon Bohak and will soon be published.

---

12 Grohmann 1934: 416–418.

13 Winkler 1930: 163; Ritter and Plessner 1962: 80, 81, 104, 105, 307–309; de Groot 1967: 6.2: 1043, 1073; Rachmati 1937: 12–14 no. 3, plate 4.

14 Examples in the Cairo Genizah: Villuendas Sabaté 2017.

15 Thomann 2018.

16 Mrāyātī, ʿAlam, and al-Ṭayyān 1988–1997: 1: 204–259; al-Kindī 2003.

6 Astronomy and Astrology

Let me now turn to the main topic of my paper. Extensive literature on astrology was produced in the Islamic world from the third/ninth to the thirteenth/nineteenth century. Most of the texts are manuals describing the discipline or parts of the discipline on a theoretical level.[17] They do not contain much information on how astrological consultation took place in practice or how astrological judgments were presented to customers. Documents with astrological content are rare, but they are all the more important for our understanding of what astrological practice looked like.

6.1 *Horoscopes*

There are three main types of astrological documents: horoscopes, almanacs, and ephemerides (sing. ephemeris). Horoscopes seem at first to correspond to birth astrology, the part on which most astrological manuals were produced. However, most of the early Arabic horoscopes say nothing about the occasion for which they were cast. In one case, in a horoscope for 398/1007 (?), it becomes clear that the occasion for which it was cast was most probably an anniversary, since it contains data for two different dates.[18] Among the horoscopes from the Cairo Genizah, this was the most frequent type.[19] They first contain the horoscope of the anniversary, typically the date and time at which the sun has the same position in the Zodiac as it had at the birth of the person. These data are written inside the diagram. Second, they contain the birth horoscope of the person. These data are written outside the diagram. The 12 fields at the border of the diagram correspond to the 12 astrological houses and contain the names of the planets at the position they were in at the moment for which the horoscope was cast.

The particular square form of the diagrams, used in Arabic horoscopes, had no archetype in ancient Greek horoscopes, which had circular diagrams, if they had diagrams at all. The square design is of eastern origin. Its archetype is most probably a Chinese cosmological diagram.[20] The first Arabic example of this square-type diagram is found in an unpublished papyrus horoscope for the year 255/869 (P.Vind.Inv. A.P. 4732). Another papyrus horoscope for the year 894 contains only text.[21] There is a literary source from the same epoch that

17 Sezgin 1979; Rosenfeld and İhsanoglu 2003.
18 Thomann 2015c.
19 Goldstein and Pingree 1977.
20 Thomann 2016.
21 Thomann 2012.

mentions the square form of horoscope diagrams: in a work on anniversary astrology, Abū Maʿshar gives instructions on how to draw an anniversary horoscope.[22] He gives the options of a circular or a square diagram. Obviously, both the Greek and the eastern traditions were alive in his time, but only the latter survived in practice.

I continue with the content of the diagrams. The central field is used for information on *rabb al-sāʿa*, "the lord of the hour," and *rabb al-yawm*, "the lord of the day." These are concepts connected with the doctrine of the planetary week, which came into fashion in the Roman Empire, probably in the first century CE, and today survives in the names of the weekdays in Romance and Germanic languages. According to this doctrine, every hour of the day is thought to be ruled by one of the seven planets. It starts with the outmost planet, Saturn, followed by Jupiter, and so on down to the lowest planet, the Moon, and then they follow again in the same order beginning with Saturn. The lord of the first hour of the day (sunrise) is also the lord of the day, i.e., the day and the night following that day. After seven days, the pattern of the system is repeated. This simple doctrine became extremely popular but played only a marginal role in Ancient Greek, Indian, and Arabic astrological literature. In the handbooks of Abū Maʿshar and al-Qabīṣī the system of the planetary week is briefly described, but no hint is given on how to use it.[23] However, in practice, its lords must have played a significant role in life, since they were written so prominently in the center of a horoscope diagram.[24]

6.2 *Almanacs and Ephemerides*

Besides horoscopes, almanacs and ephemerides are the most common types of astrological documents. Almanacs are lists with daily information on the position of the Moon, its astrological aspects to the other planets, together with astrological judgments and calendrical data for every individual period of time. The earliest example is a fragment of an almanac for the Hijra year 297 (910–911 CE) (P.ThomannAlmanac) in the Berlin collection.[25] For this type of document, no antecedent exists in classical antiquity. A second example is a fragment of an almanac for the Hijra year 320 (932–933 CE).[26] It has a similar

22 For the Arabic text and English translation, see Thomann 2008: 109–110; for the Byzantine Greek translation, see Abū Maʿshar 1968: 13.

23 Thomann 2016: 1093; Abū Maʿshar 1994: 66–69; Abū Maʿshar 1995: 3: 417–418; Abū Maʿshar 2019: 1: 710–713; al-Qabīṣī 2004: 88–89.

24 Thomann 2016; Thomann 2019b: 103.

25 Thomann 2017a; Thomann forthcoming.

26 Thomann 2019a: 319.

layout, but the order of the columns has been changed. No later examples exist. However, during the same epoch there was another type of document with daily astronomical positions, the ephemerides. The oldest Arabic example was compiled for the Persian year 300 (931–932 CE) (P.ThomannEphemeris931).[27] Further ephemerides for the Persian years 323 (954–955 CE) (P.ThomannEphemeris954), 363 (994–995 CE), 371 (1002–1003 CE), 395 (1026–1027 CE) (P.ThomannEphemeris1026), and 413 (1044–1045 CE) and the Hijra year 544 (1149–1150 CE) (P.ThomannEphemeris1149) all show a layout of the same type.[28] Ultimately, its arrangement and layout come from ancient Greek ephemerides, which are known from Egyptian papyri. Al-Bīrūnī (362–after 442/973–after 1050) exactly describes the type of ephemeris to which the early Arabic examples from Egypt belong.[29] He says that it is *al-mustaʿmal fī bilādinā*, "the one in use in our country," most probably referring to his native city Khwārazm. Al-Bīrūnī mentions another type of yearbook, which gives the positions less accurately. He calls it by a Sanskrit name, *tithi-patra*, literally "book of lunar day." Today, *tithi-patra* is the common Hindi word for calendar. Further, he says that such books were written on birch bark and that they were shown to him in Kashmir. It is very likely that the archetype of the Arabic almanac for 297/910 was such a *tithi-patra* in northwestern India. Common to both is the dominant role of the Moon at the expense of the other planets.

The first literary record in an Arabic source referring to astronomical yearbooks containing planetary positions is found in a letter from Thābit b. Qurra (d. 288/901) to al-Qāsim b. ʿUbayd Allāh (d. 291/904 CE). Thābit refers to the yearbook as *daftar al-sana*, "the book of the year."[30] It is noteworthy that a scholar with a Syriac background and working in Baghdad uses the Persian word *daftar* to refer to it. In Pahlevi, *daftar* had the meaning of "register" or "account book." This points to an eastern origin of such yearbooks and confirms al-Birūnī's account, who uses the same name, *daftar al-sana*, for them.

The layout and structure of the Arabic ephemerides in the fourth/tenth century had a long and stable tradition, but in the fifth/eleventh century, they underwent a significant change. From then onwards, they were always combined with the astrological information that hitherto was only found in alman-

27 Thomann 2015a.

28 Thomann 2013; Thomann 2014; Thomann 2015b; Thomann 2015d; Thomann 2015e; Thomann 2015f.; Thomann 2019a.

29 Al-Bīrūnī 1934: 186; al-Bīrūnī 1983: 272.

30 Caussin de Perceval 1803: 114–115; Hofelich 1998: 146 refers to page 98, which does not correspond to the pagination of the first edition in the *Notices et extraits* but to the separate print, Caussin de Perceval (1804) having a different pagination.

acs. The double-page layout, with astronomical positions on the right side and the astrological aspects on the left side, became the standard form of ephemerides. However, almanacs of the traditional form without planetary positions were still produced. Ephemerides, the more technical type of yearbooks, were made for people practicing astrology, while the almanacs could easily be used by laymen.

The astrological content in both the later ephemerides and the almanacs was titled, in the heading of the tables, *al-ikhtiyārāt*, “the choices,” referring to the procedure of choosing good times for a particular action, or avoiding bad times for it. The *ikhtiyārāt* were one part of the discipline of astrology, and many handbooks deal with their theory. In the handbooks, the methods described are always based on the customer's birth horoscope, which was compared to the actual positions of the planets. In the almanacs and ephemerides, however, the predictions were based only on the actual planetary positions. Therefore, they were the same for all people, whatever birth horoscopes they had. It was a much simpler method than the one in the handbooks. There is only one little treatise in which this method is described.[31] It is ascribed to the philosopher al-Kindī (d. between 243 and 252 / 857 and 866), who had a wide interest in every scientific field in the Greek tradition. And indeed, there is a Greek text with similar content, which is found in manuscripts of the works of Theon of Alexandria (d. 405 CE).[32] In that text, these kinds of predictions were called *katarchai katholai*, “general [predictions] for the beginnings [of actions].” In al-Kindī's text, they are called *ikhtiyārāt al-ayyām*, “the choices of the days.”

Astrological documents show in what form astrology was presented to the customers, but they give us no idea about how it was received by the public. One can imagine that the relationships between astrologers and their clients were not always free of conflict. Indeed, there is a statement in a letter (P.Vind.Arab. I 41) in which the sender informs the addressee, who seems to be a business partner, about his encounter with a third person, an astrologer.[33] It was a case of question astrology, in which the astrologer informs the client that his elderly wife would soon become severely ill. The client became angry, paid, and cursed the astrologer, who fled in fear. After that he tried to comfort his wife and promised her, if she was afraid of the horoscope, to buy a new dress for her. In another letter (P.Heid.Arab. III 11), the sender, who seems to have been either a professional astrologer or an expert in astrology, refers to a former letter by the

---

31 MS Leiden UP Or. 199; German translations: Wiedemann 1912; Thomann 2019a: 322.

32 MS Paris BnF gr.2425; Delambre 1817: 635–637; Halma 1825: 3: 38–42; Curtis and Robbins 1934: 83; Tihon 1978: 359; Thomann 2019a: 322.

33 Diem 1995: 218, 221.

addressee, who seems to have been a person of a higher rank, describing a problematic situation and the astrological constellation related to it.[34] The sender now repeats the planetary positions—which allow for assigning a precise date to the event, Rajab 26, 410/November 27, 1019—and finally gives a positive interpretation of the horoscope. We can only guess that the addressee was relieved and grateful. The fact that the addressee had included the planetary positions in his former letter could mean that he had consulted an astrologer before and then wrote a letter to get a second opinion.

6.3 *The Path of Transmission of Astrology and Mathematical Astronomy*

Let me finish with some more general considerations about the path of transmission of astrology and its prerequisite, mathematical astronomy. We have seen that Greek-style ephemerides and non-Greek-style almanacs appeared in Egypt in the fourth/tenth century. We have argued in the previous section that they correspond to the two types of yearbooks described by al-Bīrūnī and said to have been used in Central Asia and in Kashmir, respectively. But does this fit into the general context of the transmission of astronomy and astrology?

I will address this question through quantitative analysis. Let us look at the literary activities represented by textbook manuscripts. In figure 6.1, the circles represent the number of authors who were active during a period of 35 years and who were known to have written such textbooks.[35] The count is based on the lists in Keyser and Irby Massy (2012). You can see that the number of Greek authors peaks in the second century, the age of Ptolemy (d. ca. 170 CE). After 500 CE the numbers drop continuously, reaching zero around 700 CE. Arabic literary activities in astronomy and astrology started in the second half of the second/eighth century, grew rapidly, had a short decline towards the end of the third/ninth century, and then in the fourth/tenth century a second revival took place. The counts are based on Rosenfeld and İhsanoğlu (2003). In figure 6.2 the circles represent the number of authors active in a 35-year period.[36]

But is the gap between late Greek and early Islamic scientific activities significant or not? The biases of biographical sources concerning the authors they mention, and the selective character of manuscript transmission in later generations, might have distorted the pattern. For this reason, it is fortunate that we have another source that is free from these dangers. Ephemerides, almanacs, and horoscopes from Egypt were ephemeral products that were not copied by

34 Diem 2013: 31–33.
35 For further explanations, see Thomann 2017b: 913.
36 Thomann 2017b: 915.

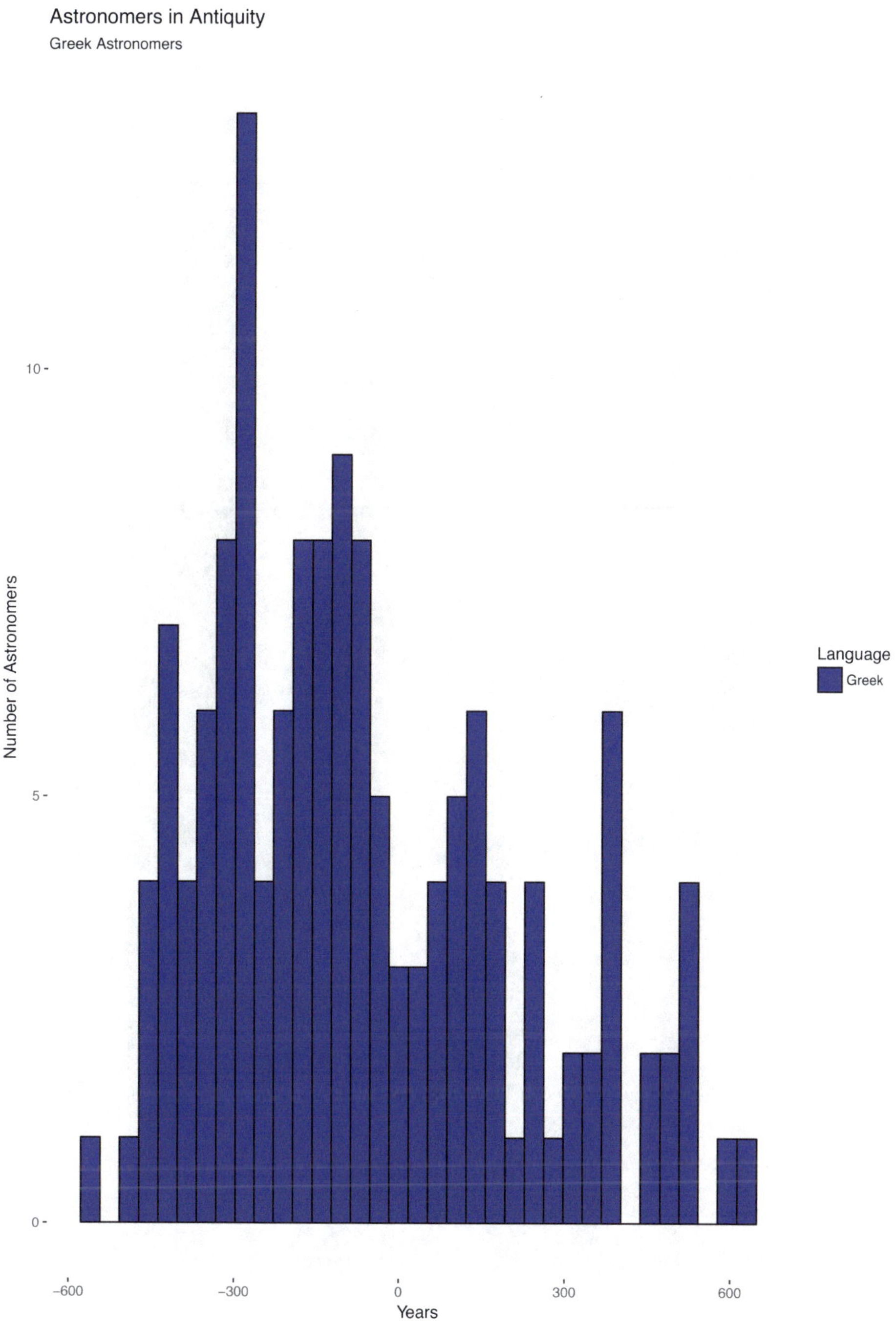

FIGURE 6.1 Number of Greek authors on astronomy and astrology (per 35 years)

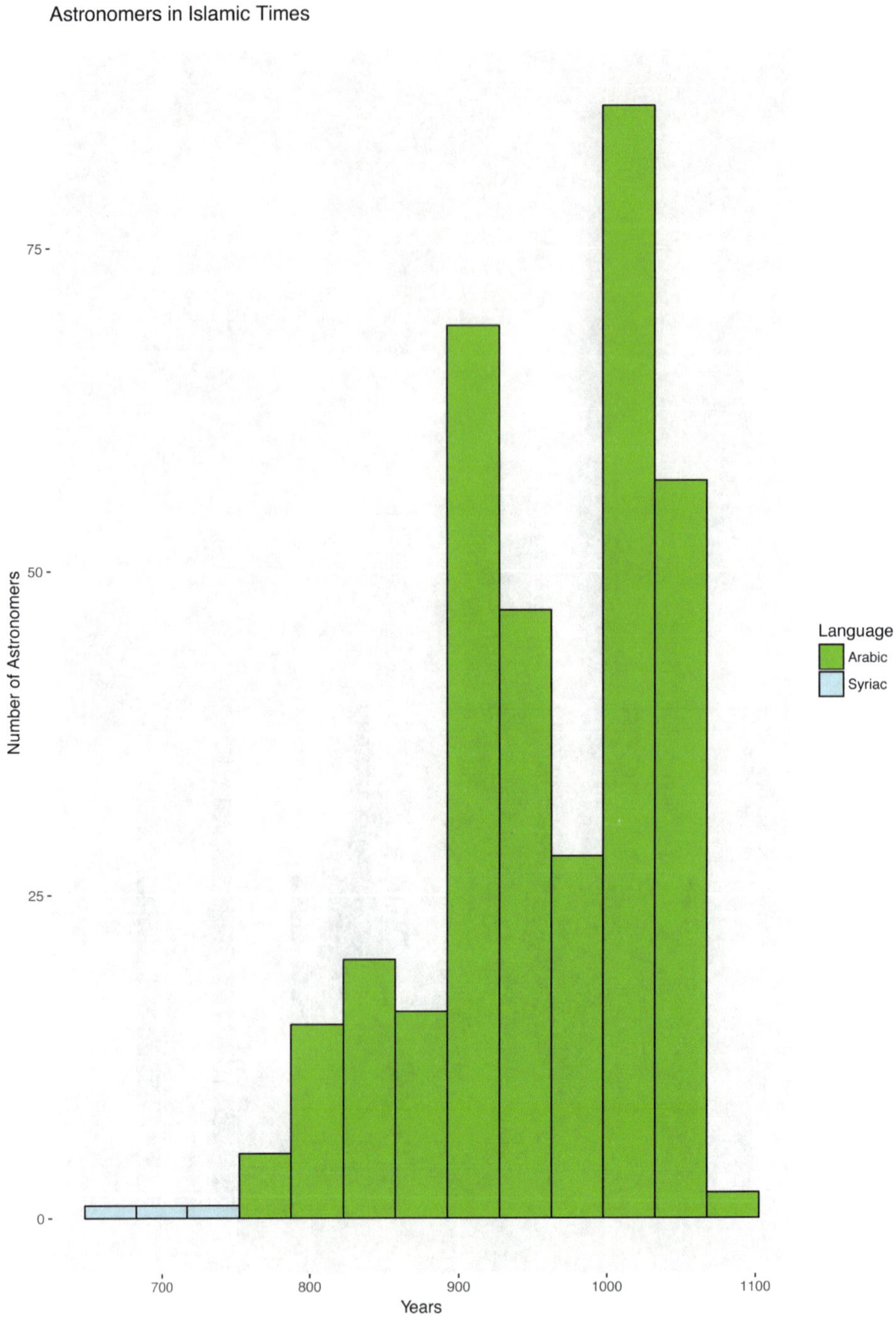

FIGURE 6.2 Number of Arabic authors on astronomy and astrology (per 35 years)

later generations and are datable by the astronomical information they contain. In this case, the gap between Greek and Arabic activities is much larger.

We have many surviving documents from the seventh century. If people were doing astrology in the seventh century, there should be some ephemerides, etc. from that time, but there are none, so astrology must have died out.

But if the Greek scientific tradition died out before its revival in early Abbasid times, what was the path of transmission? The solution becomes evident if we include Sanskrit literature in the timeline (fig. 6.3).[37] The many (anonymous) works are counted by title instead of author. They are taken from Pingree (1970–1994). Now we get a pattern of an uninterrupted chain of activities. The former gap is now filled by Indian scholars, together with a few Syriac writers. What is not included in the picture is the Buddhist literature from Central Asia, which might have played a major role but was later excluded from manuscript tradition. This becomes evident when the geographical origins of early authors of Arabic text books are considered.[38] They came from the Farghāna Valley, Khwārazm, Marw, Balkh, and other places in Central Asia and Khurasan. These were the places with a lively scientific tradition of Greek mathematical astronomy. The entire process of transmission started in ancient Alexandria. From there scholars, reached central India, where, in the capital of Ujjain, a school was founded and many of the existing Sanskrit works were produced. From there scholars brought their knowledge to China in the east and to Kashmir in the west. In early Abbasid times, scholars of the Hellenistic tradition were also present in Central Asia, and scholars from both central India and Central Asia came to Baghdad and had their works translated. Finally, mathematical astronomy returned to Egypt, where it had been created more than a thousand years ago.

37 Thomann 2017b: 915.
38 Thomann 2017b: 916–918.

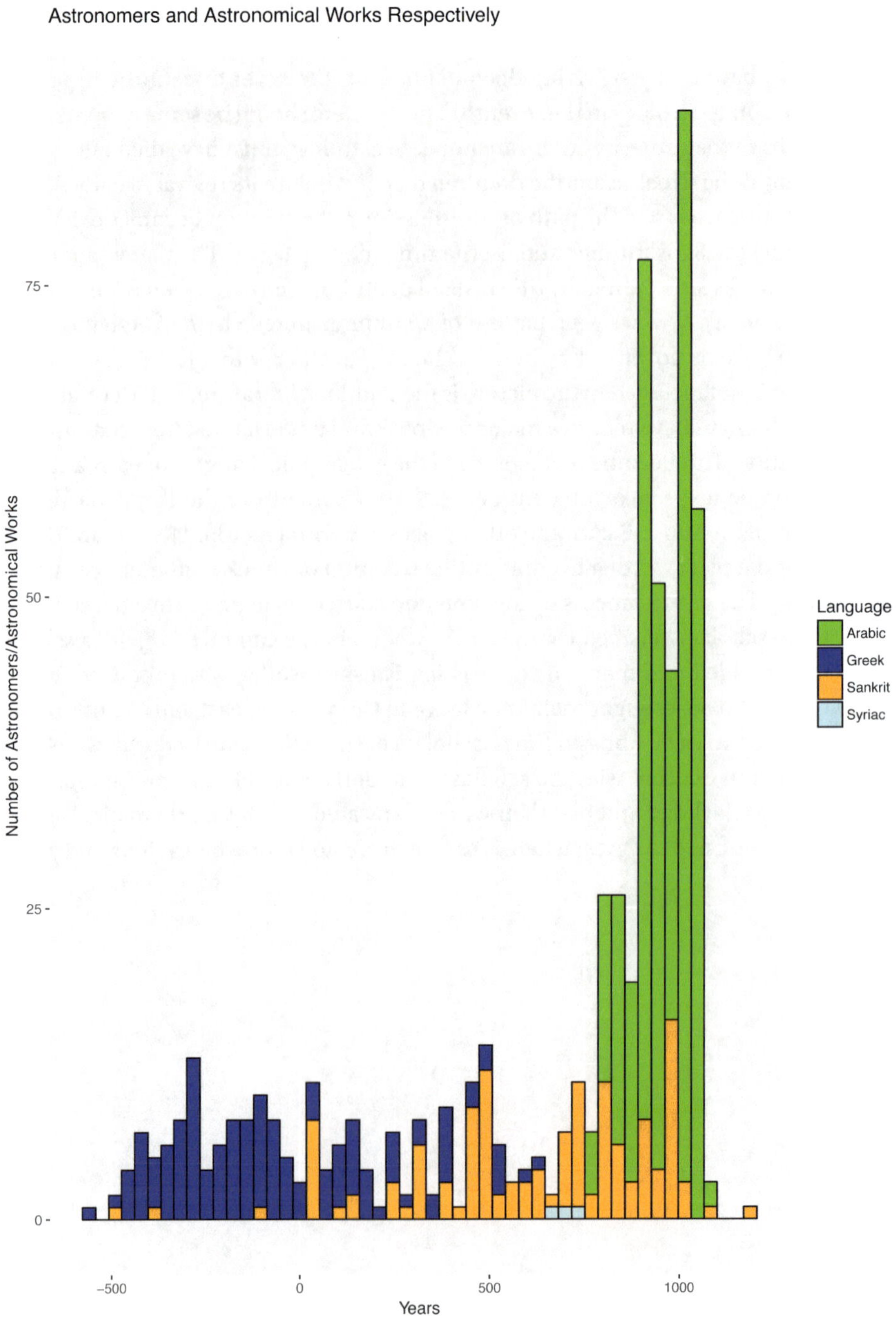

FIGURE 6.3 Number of Sanskrit works on astronomy and astrology (per 50 years)

Appendix: A Geomantic Tableau (P.Vind. inv. A.Ch. 8516)

At the top, (1) a series of uncounted dots are written in two columns and eight lines (fig. 6.4) and pairs of dots are connected by a line. This way it becomes clear if the number of the dots in a series is odd or even without counting them. (2) Below this, eight geomantic figures corresponding to the odd and even series of dots above are written. An odd series is represented by one dot and an even by two dots in the figure. (3) Further below, four figures are written that represent the combination of a pair of figures above by comparing corresponding lines in the figures. This process is repeated with (4) two figures left and right until (5) one figure in the center remains at the end. (6) This figure is combined with the right figure of the second row, and the resulting figure serves as the base for the interpretation.[39] In the present document, this resulting figure is placed to the left on the bottom line. It is usually called *inkīs*, an unusual form derived from the root n-k-s, meaning "to turn something upside down."[40] It is an unfortunate omen, called *bayt al-humūm wa-l-ghumūm wa-l-mukhāṣama*, "the house of anxieties, sorrows, and quarrels."[41]

Below the geomantic figures follows an exercise of a text encrypted by isolated letters, together with the clear text, followed by a repetition of the exercise with isolated letters. This method of encryption is found in magical documents.[42] There seems to be no relation to the geomantic figures above.

A schematic reconstruction of the geomantic part of the document with the lines of strokes and dots and the pyramid of geomantic figures appears below in Figure 6.5.

The document is a proof that the procedure of geomancy was carried out in practice exactly as described in the theoretical manuals.[43]

39 Savage-Smith and Smith 1980: 12.
40 Savage-Smith and Smith 1980: 25.
41 Al-Zanātī 1341/[1922]: 17.
42 Thomann 2018: 227.
43 A precise description of the procedure is given by Ibn Khaldūn 1958: 1: 226–233.

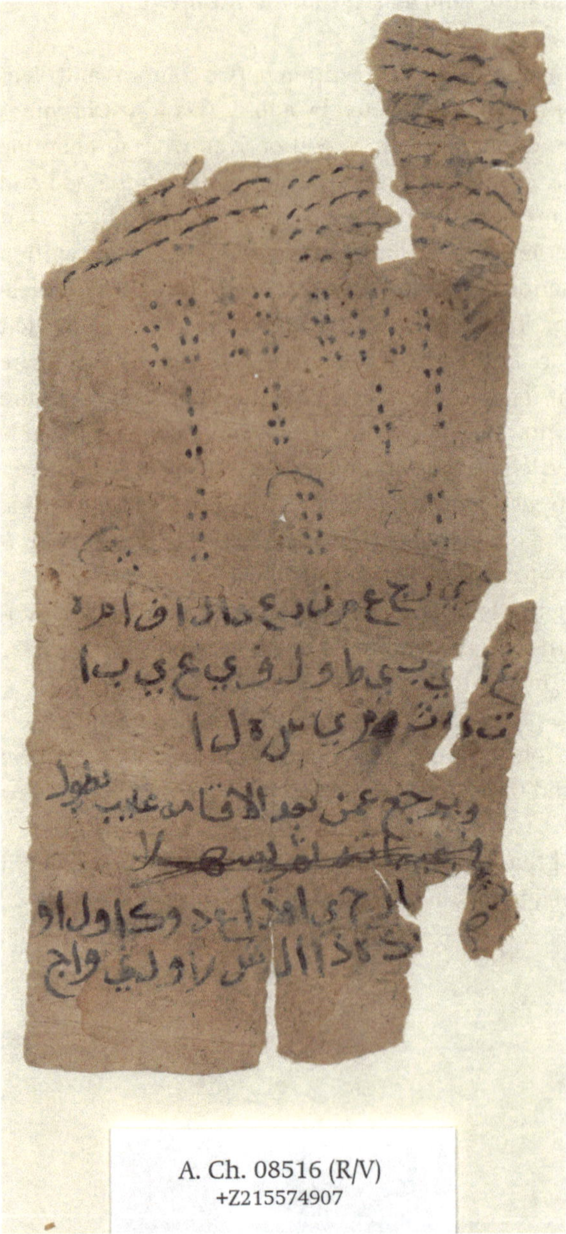

FIGURE 6.4 A Geomantic Tableau (P.Vind. inv. A.Ch. 8516). 18.0 cm high × 8.6 cm wide. Twelfth–thirteenth centuries. Egypt

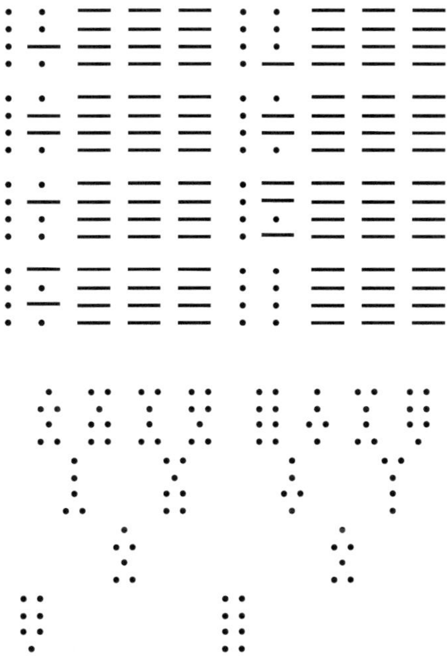

FIGURE 6.5
Reconstruction of the geomantic part of P.Vind. inv. A.Ch. 8516

Bibliography

Abū Maʿshar, Jaʿfar b. Muḥammad. 1968. *Albumasaris De revolutionibus nativitatum*. Edited by David Pingree. Bibliotheca Scriptorum Graecorum et Romanorum Teubneria. Leipzig: Teubner.

Abū Maʿshar, Jaʿfar b. Muḥammad. 1994. *The Abbreviation of the Introduction to Astrology: Together with the Medieval Latin Translation of Adelard of Bath*. Edited and translated by Charles Burnett, Keiji Yamamamoto, and Michio Yano. Islamic Philosophy, Theology and Science 15. Leiden: Brill.

Abū Maʿshar, Jaʿfar b. Muḥammad. 1995. *Liber introductorii maioris ad scientiam judiciorum astrorum*. Edited by Richard Lemay. 8 vols. Napoli: Istituto Universitario Orientale.

Abū Maʿshar, Jaʿfar b. Muḥammad. 2019. *The* Great Introduction to Astrology *by Abu Maʿshar*. Edited and translated by Keiji Yamamoto and Charles Burnett. Islamic Philosophy, Theology and Science 106. 2 vols. Leiden: Brill.

Berthelot, Marcellin 1893. *La chimie au moyen âge*. Volume 2: *L'alchimie syriaque*. Histoire des sciences. Paris: Imprimerie Nationale.

al-Bīrūnī, Abū Rayḥān Muḥammad b. Aḥmad. 1934. *The Book of Instruction in the Elements of the Art of Astrology. Kitāb al-tafhīm li-awāʾil ṣināʿat al-tanjīm*. Edited by Robert Ramsay Wright. London: Luzac.

al-Bīrūnī, Abū Rayḥān Muḥammad b. Aḥmad. 1983. *Kitāb al-tafhīm li-awā'il ṣinā'at al-tanjīm*. Edited by Jalāl al-Dīn Humā'ī. Tehran: Bābak.

Bürgel, Johann Christoph. 2016. *Ärztliches Leben und Denken im arabischen Mittelalter*. Islamic History and Civilization 135. Leiden: Brill.

Căian, Florin George. 2010. "Alkimia Operativa and Alkimia Speculativa: Some Modern Controversies on the Historiography of Alchemy." In *Annual of Medieval Studies at CEU* 16: 166–190.

Caussin de Perceval, Armand-Pierre. 1803. "Kitāb al-zīj al-kabīr al-ḥākimī raṣd al-shaykh ... Ibn Ḥayyān. Le livre de la grande table Hakémite observée par le sheikh ... ebn Hiyan." In *Notices et extraits des manuscrits de la Bibliothčque Nationale et autres bibliothčques* 7: 16–240.

Caussin de Perceval, Armand-Pierre. 1804. *Kitāb al-zīj al-kabīr al-ḥākimī raṣd al-shaykh ... Ibn Ḥayyān. Le livre de la grande table Hakémite observée par le sheikh ... ebn Hiyan*. Paris: Imprimerie de la République.

Curtis, Heber D., and Frank E. Robbins. 1935. "An Ephemeris of 467 A.D." In *Publications of the Observatory of the University of Michigan* 6: 77–100.

Delambre, Jean-Babtiste Joseph. 1817. *Histoire de l'astronomie ancienne*. 2 vols. Paris: Courcier.

Diem, Werner. 1995. *Arabische Geschäftsbriefe des 10. bis 14. Jahrhunderts aus der Österreichischen Nationalbibliothek in Wien*. Documenta Arabica antiqua 1. Wiesbaden: Harrassowitz.

Diem, Werner. 2013. *Arabische Briefe auf Papier aus der Heidelberger Papyrus-Sammlung*. Veröffentlichungen aus der Heidelberger Papyrus-Sammlung 13. Heidelberg: Winter.

Dietrich, Albert. 1954. *Zum Drogenhandel im islamischen Aegypten: eine Studie über die arabische Handschrift Nr. 912 der Heidelberger Papyrus-Sammlung*. Veröffentlichungen aus der Heidelberger Papyrus-Sammlung 1. Heidelberg: Winter.

Goldstein, Bernard R., and David Pingree. 1977. "Horoscopes from the Cairo Geniza." In *JNES* 36: 113–144.

Grohmann, Adolf. 1934. "Islamische Zaubertexte." In *Griechische, koptische und arabische Texte zur Religion und religiösen Literatur in Ägyptens Spätzeit*, edited by Friedrich Bilabel and Adolf Grohmann. Veröffentlichungen aus den badischen Papyrussammlungen 5. 2 vols. Heidelberg: n.p., 1: 415–447; 2: pls. 1–12.

Grohmann, Adolf. 1935. "Texte zur Wirtschaftsgeschichte Ägyptens in arabischer Zeit." In *Archív Orientální* 7: 437–472; pls. LII–LVII.

de Groot, Jan Jakob Maria. 1967. *The Religious System of China: Its Ancient Forms, Evolution, History and Present Aspect. Manners, Customs and Social Institutions Connected Therewith*. 6 vols. Taipei, Taiwan: Ch'eng-wen.

Halma, Nicolas B. 1825. *Ptolemaiou kai Theōnos procheiroi kanones*. 3 vols. Paris: Merlin.

Hofelich, Michael. 1998. "Taḳwīm. 1 Its Use in Astronomy." In *Encyclopaedia of Islam: Second Edition*, edited by Clifford Edmund Bosworth et al. 10: 145–146.

Ibn Khaldūn, ʿAbd al-Raḥmān b. Muḥammad. 1958. *The Muqaddimah: An Introduction to History*. Translated by Franz Rosenthal. Bollingen Series 43. 3 vols. New York: Pantheon.

Keyser, Paul T., and Georgia L. Irby Massy, 2012. *The Encyclopedia of Ancient Natural Scientists: The Greek Tradition and Its Many Heirs*. London: Routledge.

al-Kindī, Yaʿqūb. 2003. *al-Kindī's Treatise on Cryptanalysis*. Series on Arabic Origins of Cryptology 1. Riyadh: King Faysal Center for Research and Islamic Studies.

Margoliouth, David Samuel, and Eric John Holmyard. 1931. "Arabic Documents from the Monneret Collection." In *Islamica* 4: 249–271.

Mrāyātī, Muḥammad, Yaḥyā Mīr ʿAlam, and Ḥasan al-Ṭayyān. 1988–1997. *ʿIlm al-taʿmiyya wa-stikhrāj al-muʿammā ʿinda l-ʿArab: dirāsa wa-taḥqīq li-rasāʾil al-Kindī wa-Ibn-ʿAdlān wa-Ibn-Durayhim. Origins of Arab Cryptography and Cryptanalysis*. 2 vols. Damascus: Arab Academy of Damascus.

Pingree, David. 1970–1994. *Census of Exact Science in Sanskrit*. 5 vols. Philadelphia: American Philosophical Society.

al-Qabīṣī, ʿAbd al-ʿAzīz b. ʿUthmān. 2004. *The Introduction to Astrology: Editions of the Arabic and Latin Texts and an English Translation*. Edited and translated by Charles Burnett, Keiji Yamamamoto, and Michio Yano. Warburg Institute Studies and Texts 2. London: Warburg Institute.

Rachmati, Gabdul Rashid. 1937. *Türkische Turfantexte*. Vol. 7. Abhandlungen der Preussischen Akademie der Wissenschaften. Philosophisch-historische Klasse 1936, 12. Berlin: Akademie der Wissenschaften.

Richter, Tonio Sebastian. 2015. "The Master Spoke: 'Take One of the "Sun" and One Unit of Almulgam': Hitherto Unnoticed Coptic Papyrological Evidence for Early Arabic Alchemy." In *Documents and the History of the Early Islamic World*, edited by Alexander T. Schubert and Petra M. Sijpestijn. Islamic History and Civilization 111. Leiden: Brill, 194–233.

Ritter, Hellmut, and Martin Plessner. 1962. *Picatrix: das Ziel des Weisen von Pseudo-Maǧrīṭī*. Studies of the Warburg Institute 27. London: Warburg Institute.

Rosenfeld, Boris A., and Ekmeleddin İhsanoğlu. 2003. *Mathematicians, Astronomers and Other Scholars of Islamic Culture and Their Works (7th–19th C.)*. İlim tarihi kaynakları ve araştırmaları serisi 11. Istanbul: Research Center for Islamic History, Art and Culture.

Savage-Smith, Emily, and Marion B. Smith. 1980. *Islamic Geomancy and a Thirteenth-Century Divinatory Device*. Studies in Near Eastern Culture and Society. Malibu: Undena.

Schwartz-Salant, Nathan. 1998. *The Mystery of Human Relationship: Alchemy and the Transformation of the Self*. London: Routledge.

Schwarz, Gunnar Werner. 1976. *Zur Entwicklung des Apothekerberufs und der Ausbildung des Apothekers vom Mittelalter bis zur Gegenwart: eine Studie zur Geschichte des Apothekerberufs von den Anfängen im Islam bis zur allgemeinen Verbreitung in Europa im 15. Jh. und zur fachlichen Ausbildung des europäischen Apothekers, unter besonderer Berücksichtigung des deutschsprachigen Raums*. PhD diss., Universität Frankfurt am Main.

Sezgin, Fuat. 1979. *Geschichte des arabischen Schrifttums*. Volume 7: *Astrologie: Meteorologie und Verwandtes*. Leiden: Brill.

al-Tanūkhī, al-Muḥassin b. ʿAlī. 1955/1999. *al-Faraj baʿd al-shidda*. Cairo: al-Khanjī.

al-Tanūkhī, al-Muḥassin b. ʿAlī. 1979. *Ende gut, alles gut: das Buch der Erleichterung nach der Bedrängnis*. Translated by Arnold Hottinger. Manesse Bibliothek der Weltliteratur. Zurich: Manesse.

Thomann, Johannes. 2008. "Square Horoscope Diagrams in Middle Eastern Astrology and Chinese Cosmological Diagrams: Were These Designs Transmitted Through the Silk Road?" In *The Journey of Maps and Images on the Silk Road*, edited by Philippe Forêt and Andreas Kaplony. Brill's Inner Asian Library 21. Leiden: Brill, 97–117; pl. 5.9.

Thomann, Johannes. 2012. "P.Stras. Ar. Inv. 266: le dernier horoscope sur papyrus—le premier horoscope en arabe." In *Actes du 26e Congrès international de papyrologie: Genève, 16–21 aout 2010*, edited by Paul Schubert. Recherches et rencontres: Publications de la Faculté des Lettres de l'Université de Genève 30. Geneva: Droz, 747–750.

Thomann, Johannes. 2013. "An Arabic Ephemeris for the Year 954/955 CE and the Geographical Latitude of al-Bahnasā/ Oxyrhynchus (P.Stras. Inv. Ar. 446)." In *Chronique d'Egypte* 88: 385–396.

Thomann, Johannes. 2014. "An Arabic Ephemeris for the Year 1026/1027 CE. in the Vienna Papyrus Collection." In *Scientific Cosmopolitanism and Local Cultures: Religions, Ideologies, Societies: Proceedings of the 5th International Conference of the European Society for the History of Science*, edited by Gianna Katsiampoura. Athens: National Hellenic Research Foundation/Institute of Historical Research, Section of Neohellenic Research, 54–60.

Thomann, Johannes. 2015a. "An Arabic Ephemeris for the year 931–932 CE." In *From Bāwīṭ to Marw: Documents From the Medieval Muslim World*, edited by Andreas Kaplony, Daniel Potthast, and Cornelia Römer. Islamic History and Civilization 112. Leiden: Brill, 115–153.

Thomann, Johannes. 2015b. "The Arabic Ephemeris for the Year 1149/1150 CE (P.Cambridge UL Inv. Michael. Chartae D 58) and the Arabic *Baḫnīṭas*, Greek Παχνίτης and Coptic ⲡⲁϣⲟⲛⲥ." In *Chronique d'Egypte* 90: 207–224.

Thomann, Johannes. 2015c. "Arabisches Horoskop für 1007 n. Chr. (?) ACh 189." In *Orakelsprüche, Magie und Horoskope: wie Ägypten in die Zukunft sah*, edited by Angelika Zdiarsky. Nilus 22. Vienna: Phoibos, 122–123.

Thomann, Johannes. 2015d. "Ephemeride für das persische Jahr 363 (994/995 n. Chr.)" In *Orakelsprüche, Magie und Horoskope: wie Ägypten in die Zukunft sah*, edited by Angelika Zdiarsky. Nilus 22. Vienna: Phoibos, 136–137.

Thomann, Johannes. 2015e. "Ephemeride für das persische Jahr 371 (1002/1003 n. Chr.)" In *Orakelsprüche, Magie und Horoskope: wie Ägypten in die Zukunft sah*, edited by Angelika Zdiarsky. Nilus 22. Vienna: Phoibos, 136–137.

Thomann, Johannes. 2015f. "Ephemeride für das persische Jahr 413 (1044/1045 n. Chr.)" In *Orakelsprüche, Magie und Horoskope: wie Ägypten in die Zukunft sah*, edited by Angelika Zdiarsky. Nilus 22. Vienna: Phoibos-Verlag, 138–140.

Thomann, Johannes. 2016. "An Arabic Horoscope on Parchment With a Square Diagram for AD 1002 (P.Vind. inv. A.Perg. 236)." In *Proceedings of the 27th International Congress of Papyrology, Warsaw, 29 July–3 August 2013*, edited by Tomasz Derda, Adam Łajtar, and Jakub Urbanik. The Journal of Juristic Papyrology Supplements 28. Warsaw: University of Warsaw, Faculty of Law and Administration, Chair of Roman and Antique Law, 1085–1089.

Thomann, Johannes. 2017a. "A Fragment of an Unusual Arabic Almanac for 297 AH/910 CE (P.Berl.inv. 12793)." In *New Frontiers of Arabic Papyrology: Arabic and Multilingual Texts from Early Islam*, edited by Sobhi Bouderbala, Sylvie Denoix, and Matt Malczycki. Islamic History and Civilization 144. Leiden: Brill, 179–196.

Thomann, Johannes. 2017b. "The Second Revival of Astronomy in the Tenth Century and the Establishment of Astronomy as an Element of Encyclopedic Education." In *Putting the House of Wisdom in Order: The Fourth Islamic Century and the Impulse to Classify, Arrange and Inventory*, edited by James Weaver, Letizia Osti, and Ulrich Rudolph. Special Issue, *Asiatische Studien* 71, no. 3: 907–957.

Thomann, Johannes. 2018. "Arabische magische Dokumente: Typen, visuelle Gestaltung und Traditionslinien." In *Die Geheimnisse der oberen und der unteren Welt: Magie im Islam zwischen Glaube und Wissenschaft*, edited by Sebastian Günther and Dorothee Pielow. Islamic History and Civilization 158. Leiden: Brill, 223–243.

Thomann, Johannes. 2019a. "From *katarchai* to *ikhtiyārāt*: The Emergence of a New Arabic Document Type Combining Ephemerides and Almanacs." In *Proceedings of the 28th International Congress of Papyrology, Barcelona 2016*, edited by Amalia Zomeño Rodríguez et al. Barcelona: Universitat Pompeu Fabra, 317–329.

Thomann, Johannes. 2019b. "Tools of Time: Devices for Organizing Public and Private Life in the Premodern Islamic World." In *Re-defining a Space of Encounter: Islam and Mediterranean: Identity, Alterity and Interactions: Proceedings of the 28th Congress of the Union Européenne des Arabisants et Islamisants, Palermo 2016*, edited by A. Pellitteri and N. Elsakaan, Orientalia Lovaniensia Analecta 283. Leuven: Peeters, 97–105.

Thomann, Johannes. Forthcoming. *Arabische Ephemeriden, Almanache und Horoskope*. Corpus Papyrorum Raineri. Vienna.

Tihon, Anne. 1978. *Le "Petit Commentaire" de Théon d'Alexandrie aux Tables faciles de Ptolemée: histoire du texte, édition critique, traduction*. Studi e testi 282. Rome: Biblioteca Apostolica Vaticana.

Villuendas Sabaté, Blanca 2017. "Arabic Geomancy in Jewish Hands: Specimens from the Cairo Genizah." In *Geomancy and Other Forms of Divination*, edited by Alessandro Palazzo and Irene Zavattero. Micrologus' Library 87. Florence: SISMEL—Edizioni del Galluzzo, 271–288.

Wiedemann, Eilhard. 1912. "Über einen astrologischen Traktat von al-Kindi." In *Archiv für Geschichte der Naturwissenschaften und der Technik* 3: 224–226.

Winkler, Hans Alexander. 1930. *Siegel und Charaktere in der muhammedanischen Zauberei*. Studien zur Geschichte und Kultur des islamischen Orients 7. Berlin: de Gruyter.

al-Zanātī, Muḥammad. 1341/[1922]. *Kitāb al-Faṣl fī uṣūl ʿilm al-raml*. Miṣr: Muḥammad Faḥmī Ḥusayn al-Zuhayrī.

CHAPTER 7

Christian and Islamic Documents in Arabic: The Concept of *Sunna* (Appendix: On the Sale of a Mosque)

Rocio Daga Portillo

> The legal rules and procedures which were applied in the various legal orders of the West in the period prior to the late eleventh and early twelfth centuries were largely undifferentiated from social custom and from political and religious institutions … Very little of the law was in writing … Law was not consciously systematised.
>
> BERMAN 1983: 50

Abstract

After the conquest of Toledo in 1085 the Christians, Muslims, and Jews of Toledo continued writing their legal documents in Arabic for a period of 250 years, following the pattern of Muslim administrative handbooks, such as those of Ibn al-Mughīth and Ibn al-ʿAṭṭār. The Toledo collection of legal documents has been preserved in the Cathedral of Toledo and in 1930 was partially edited by A. Gonzalez Palencia. However, it is an exceptional collection that deserves a complete edition, since this is the only known existing collection in the world of Arabic legal documents written by non-Muslims who were living under Christian rule. It is also a pristine portrait of the process of change in Toledo's society—the economy, the balance of power, and the process of conversion and assimilation of Muslims and Jews—from the eleven to the fourteenth century. Moreover, with over a thousand documents, this is one of the biggest collections of Arabic documents existing in Spain, most of the documents being written on parchment, some on paper.

The similarities in between Christian documents from Toledo and Islamic documents are great, the differences few. One of the main differences is the introduction of "Christian law" (*sunnat al-naṣārā*). However, the law applied in Toledo, in spite of some differences detected in the document, reflects commonalities. I will argue that

 | DOI:10.1163/9789004527874_009

Arabic *sunna* and Spanish *fueros* had an element of orality that allowed the share of customary law anchored in the life of the communities across religious borders. The term *sharīʿa*, with the meaning of law, is not found at all in al-Andalus, with exception of some late documents from fifteenth-century Granada. In the east, the term is not found prior to the thirteenth century. Indeed, the change from *sunna* to *sharīʿa*, to refer to law, reveals a process of the institutionalization and professionalization of legal activity and a more predominant written legal culture.

1 Introduction[1]

After the conquest of Toledo in 1085 the Christians, Muslims, and Jews of Toledo preserved their Arabic legal culture. They continued writing their legal documents in Arabic for about 250 years, one of the reasons being the absence of a highly developed technical legal language in Latin or Castilian. Indeed, Visigothic legal documents lacked precision[2] compared to the refined technicality of the legal formulas of Arabic documents. Thus, Arabic as a legal language and elements of the Islamic legal system were adopted by the Christian conquerors for a period of more than two centuries. Toledo documents prove the influence of Islamic legal thought on Christian law and the legal system. Moreover, they reflect a sociolinguistic reality: Arabic continued to be spoken and used as a written language, which points to the presence of the Arab-speaking population and the vitality of Arab culture in the city of Toledo until the middle of the fourteenth century.

In the Archivos de la Catedral de Toledo and the Archivos de los conventos de San Clemente, Santo Domingo de Silos has preserved a large number of Arabic legal documents written by Christian notaries. Another 16 documents were found in the Archivos de la Iglesia de San Nicolas and another nine in the Archivo Municipal de Toledo.[3] At present, the collection is preserved in the Archivo Histórico Nacional de Madrid and contains 1,175 documents (dated

1 This research is based on the documents of the Arabic Papyrology Database (www.naher-osten.lmu.de/apd), a project led by Andreas Kaplony, Chair of Arabic and Islamic Studies, LMU Munich, Germany. It does not intend to be a definitive statement on the topic. The limits given by the sources used and the complexity of the subject make it clear that further research is needed. However, this paper intends to open the discussion on the concept of "law" in the period and region studied here.

2 González Palencia 1930: 4: 361.

3 González Palencia 1930: 4: 9–10.

1083–1391), the bulk of them being contracts of sales. With over 1,000 documents, this is the largest collection of Arabic legal documents in Spain[4] and the only collection of documents from Toledo known of from the eleventh up to the fourteenth century.

Moreover, the Toledo documents are unique insofar as they are the only known collection of Arabic legal documents written by non-Muslims living under Christian rule. In fact, Muslim notaries in Aragon and Sicily living under Christian rule wrote Arabic documents in almost the same period; however, the Toledo documents were written by Christian notaries, and the documents involved Christian parties in the majority of cases. They were contracts written by Christians for Christians.

Most of the Toledo documents are written on parchment. Only four documents from the twelfth century are on paper: after the *Breviarium goticum sive mozarabicum* of Silos (eleventh century), the Toledan documents are the oldest paper documents from Christian Spain that have been preserved (P.Mozarab. 80; 1166; P.Mozarab. 87; 1168; P.Mozarab. 1096; 1167; P.Mozarab. 467; 1222)[5] before paper became extensively used in the thirteenth century.[6]

Seals and ornaments are rare in the Toledo documents. Use of seals, such as that of Abad of Husillos, bishop of Cuenca and *al-qāʾid* of Madrid (P.Mozarab. 274; 1197; P.Mozarab. 628; 1266), are exceptions.[7] In the same way, ornamental script is rare, only one Latin-Arabic list of a dowry (P.Mozarab. 1175; 1285) possesses an ornamental Latin script.[8]

In this article we will compare Christian and Islamic documents by focusing especially—but not only—on their "law formula." The documents of this collection use the law formula *ʿalā sunnat al-naṣārā*, "according to the legal custom ('law') of the Christians." An exception is the first document of the collection (P.Mozarab. 1; 1083), an Islamic document written *ʿalā sunnat al-muslimīn*,

4 Other Arabic collections of documents preserved in Spain: 167 Arabic documents (fourteenth–fifteenth centuries) are kept in the Archivos de la Biblioteca de la Universidad de Granada, Hospital Real, 16 Arabic documents (1117–1501) in the Archivos de la Catedral de Nuestra Señora del Pilar, Zaragoza (Aragon), 12 Arabic documents (1145–1269) in the Archivos de la Catedral of Huesca (Aragon), and about 200 documents (twelfth–thirteenth centuries) in the Archivos de Veruela-Tudela (Navarra); see Carro Martin and Zomeño 2017: 111; Garcia de Linares 1904; Bosch Vilá 1957; García-Velasco Bernal 2017: 237. The number of Arabic documents preserved in the Islamic world is scarce; see Vidal Castro 2012: 38–39; Potthast 2017: 447.

5 González Palencia 1930: 1: 57–58, 62; 2: 69; 3: 515.

6 González Palencia 1930: 4: 44.

7 González Palencia 1930: 1: 214–215; 2: 229–230.

8 González Palencia 1930: 4: 44.

"according to the legal custom ('law') of the Muslims." This document is a contract of sale between a woman, Jamīla, and a rabbi, Abū Isḥāq b. Nehemīsh, and is the only document of the collection that has a roll format. The Christian documents of the collection, on the contrary, are flat pages, which indicates a break with the previous archival and documental tradition.

The first Arabic documents written in the first 30 years after the conquest (ca. 1085–1114) are all contracts of sale. After 1114, the transactions are of different kinds, donations, pleas, emancipations, legacies, testaments, etc., but the number of documents in total is very scarce: 50 documents until the middle of the twelfth century, which may indicate that there was still no organized notarial class of Christian Mozarabs,[9] that many transactions had an oral character, or that many documents did not survive. The majority of documents are dated from the middle of the twelfth century to the middle of the thirteenth century. Towards the middle of the thirteenth century the number of Latin and Romance documents would increase gradually, and the writing of legal documents in Arabic reached an end in the early fourteenth century. The last Arabic document in the Toledo collection dates from 1315 and is a payment for the relief of an enslaved Muslim husband (P.Mozarab. 1140). The last Judeo-Arabic documents in the Toledo collection (P.Mozarab. 1140; 1391) come from a later date, 1391, and show the attachment of the Jewish community to the Arabic language; this last document is a contract of sale and makes us guess that the Jewish seller was about to leave the country due to the pogrom that had occurred the same year.

Indeed, the whole collection, and especially the last documents from the fourteenth century, witness crucial events in society and illustrate the process of social upheaval and the changing balance of power, as well as the nascent structural foundations of a unified nation or country that led to the expulsion of members of the Jewish and Muslims communities.

2 A Social Portrait as Rendered by the Toledo Documents

Angel Gonzáles Palencia entitled the partial edition of the Toledo documents "Los mozárabes de Toledo en los siglos XII y XIII" and called the scribes of the Toledo documents and the parties involved in the transactions "Mozarabs." The scribes were attached to the cathedral, as clerics carrying the function of notaries in the absence of an established notarial class. The cathedral and the

9 Olstein 2006a: 33.

convents would have functioned as archives, especially since the majority of transactions were related to officials and clerics affiliated with the cathedral and convents.

But who were the Mozarabs?

Present historiography has shed new light on the subject. The term "Mozarab" is not found in Islamic sources, but in Latin sources—the first time in 1024—it is used to refer to a group with specific rights. The Latin sources do not define them according to religion or language.[10] Similar to the *dhimmīs*, the "protected subjects" of Islamic societies defined by their legal status, the Mozarabs were first defined by the Christian king according to their specific legal status. Olstein emphasizes that "current historiography presents the Mozarab minority as 'worthy bearers of Islamic culture,'"[11] as the transmitters of the achievements of Islamic culture into the Christian kingdoms, by means of translations or expertise. A group of them were also bearers of Visigothic culture.

In Toledo, three kinds of Mozarabs can be distinguished:

(1) The original small group of Christians in Toledo who were bearers of their own Visigothic culture. Rubiera Mata questioned their existence, arguing that the Mozarabs had disappeared in Toledo in the tenth century,[12] a thesis rejected by Olstein.[13]

(2) Neo-Mozarabs, i.e., Muslims who took up the religion of the Christian conquerors, in Arabic sources called *mutanaṣṣir*, "Christianized."[14] The massive conversion of Muslims was a logical consequence of the conquest.

(3) Christians who had emigrated from al-Andalus and al-Maghrib fleeing from the Almoravids and Almohads. The *Cronica Adefonsi Imperatoris* mentions that some of the exiled Mozarabs who fled from al-Andalus to Marrakesh under the Almoravids arrived in Toledo after the fall of the city of Marrakesh to the Almohads: *Quo tempore, multa milia militum et peditum christianorum, cum suo episcopo et cum magna parte clericorum, qui fuerant de domo regis Ali et fili eius Texufini, transierunt mare et venerunt Toletum*, "At that time, many thousands of the Christian knights and foot soldiers serving in the military under ʿAli and his son Tashufīn, together

10 Maser 2011: 15.

11 Olstein 2006b: 434.

12 Epalza and Rubiera 1986: 129–134.

13 Olstein 2006a: 34.

14 Olstein 2011: iv, 161.

with their bishop and a big part of their clerics, crossed the sea and came to Toledo."[15]

In addition, the society of Toledo was composed of Franks—many of French origin—, Galicians, and Castilians, the military and ruling class after the conquest.

Jews carried the function of representing the Convent of St. Clement and the archbishop of Toledo in many transactions in our Toledo documents.[16] The titles[17] employed to address them were as honorific as those employed to address the archbishop. However, fortune changed in the second part of the thirteenth century, and in 1391 a pogrom obliged them to leave the city.

A few Muslims kept practicing their religion in small mosques and had their own jurists and *qāḍīs*. Muslims lived among Christians, as documented in this collection (P.Mozarab. 160; P.Mozarab. 417). The main mosque was expropriated and converted in a cathedral; however, Muslims kept praying in the mosque located in the quarter of the Franks (P.Mozarab. 317).[18] Other mosques became private property, as the annexed documents (P.Mozarab. 82; P.Mozarab. 92) witness.

By the middle of the thirteenth century, there was a gradual inversion of demographic and cultural hegemony from the Mozarabs to the Castilians. As many Castilians came from the north, they surpassed the Mozarab population that had blended with Castilians. By the beginning of the fourteenth century, the Mozarab element had lost its preponderance and Arabic ceased to be written. The Castilian period (1300–1500) replaced the Mozarab one (1085–1300).[19]

The documents in this collection portray the diversity of cultures and languages that existed in Toledo from the eleventh to the fourteenth centuries. The majority of documents are written in Arabic, but there are also Latin and Romance documents, bilingual Latin-Arabic and Romance-Arabic documents, and Judeo-Arabic documents.[20] Arabic and Latin were languages used for different purposes by the native habitants of Toledo and by the ruling Christian class coming from outside. Arabic was mostly used in private documents of an economic character until 1260, and occasionally until 1315. Royal and ecclesiastical documents of a political-legal character were written in Latin from the

15 *Cronica Adefonsi Imperatoris*: 162. Also in Molenat 1994: 479.

16 González Palencia 1930: 4: 142–144.

17 *Al-wazīr al-akmal*; *al-musharraf*; *al-aʿazz al-afḍal*; see González Palencia 1930: 4: 143.

18 Gonzalez Palencia 1930: 4: 152.

19 Olstein 2006a: 147.

20 González Palencia 1930: 4: 10.

beginning until 1243.[21] The parallel use of monolingual Arabic and Latin documents shows that each language had a function in the economic-political and property system in Toledo. After 1180 there was an increase of Arabic documents because the Church and nobility were more involved in the local market, especially by buying the property of small owners from among the Mozarabs.[22]

Indeed, the Toledo collection reflects the hierarchical transfer of property after the conquest, the repopulation, the legal and commercial activity of the Church, nobility, and small owners in the city of Toledo, the interaction among religious communities, and the microhistory of entire Toledan families from generation to generation.

Moreover, they portray the process of conversion and assimilation of the Jewish and Muslim population into the Castilian society, as well as the decrease of first the Muslim and then the Jewish population. The transition from Arabic to Romance is well-documented, a process in which Mozarabs played an important role until the fourteenth century, when Romance replaced Latin and Arabic as the official language.[23]

Remarkable indeed is the portrait of women in the Toledo documents. The documents depict women (e.g., P.Mozarab. 79; 1166),[24] many from the nobility, as agents in their own transactions and present a great number of women selling and buying property without being represented by men—contrary to what it was the case in Toledo society before the conquest.[25] Some Christian women acted from a position of responsibility, e.g., they were abbesses or nuns, others were married women who acted without their husbands being present and without any ratification by them. Granted, some documents do have the ratification of the husband but other documents show wives ratifying the transactions of their husbands (e.g., P.Mozarab. 156; 1181).[26]

A possible reason to explain the high presence of women taking part in transactions in the Toledo documents may be that men were engaged in the military and were most of the time absent or had passed away. Another reason might have been the legal status of Christian women, who had the right to own property, and the fact that married women had a regime of accrued gains—different from what Islamic law stipulates for Muslim women. The *Fuero Juzgo*,

21 Olstein 2006b: 438.

22 Olstein 2011: 169–171.

23 Olstein, 2006b: 438.

24 González Palencia 1930: 1: 57.

25 This portrait differs from the one in the Islamic documents from Huesca, where women are represented (*wakāla*) in court by their husbands, as it is customary in Maliki law, the law applied in Toledo before the conquest; Bosch Vilá 1957.

26 González Palencia 1930: 1: 114–115.

a codex of Castilian law of Visigothic origin states that in marriage, *toda cosa que el marido e la muger ganaren o compraren de consouno, ayanlo amos por medio*, "a regime of community of accrued gains exists."[27] For that reason, women's names appear in the Toledo documents along with those of men when a man buys property.

Regarding representation in court, *Fuero Real* of Alfonso X of 1255 states that *ninguna muger no rezone pleito ageno; mas su pleito propio puedalo razonar*, "Women can appear in court to represent her own affairs, although she cannot represent another person."[28] However, her being legally represented by a man was allowed, probably due to the inclusion and influence of Islamic law: *todo marido pueda demander e responder por su mugger, e todo pariente*, "A husband or close relative can represent the woman in court."[29]

Another social aspect reflected in the Toledo documents is the rapid change of religious and cultural identity after the conquest, as reflected in name changes. The names of individuals change gradually from the Arabic structure with the second name introduced by *ibn* to a double name without *ibn*. In the fourteenth century, Arabic names follow the general Castilian pattern of forename plus family name. A register of multiple transactions by members of the same family shows this very clearly (P.Mozarab. 3; 30; 118; 728). In the first transaction, the parties bear Arabic names, but this seems to be a Jewish family due to some of their names: Khayr b. Zakarī buys a house from Yaḥyā b. ʿAbd al-Salām in the year 1093, less than a decade after the conquest. In the second transaction, dated 1142, the son of Khayr bears a Christian name, Shaṭurnīn b. Khayr, and Shaṭurnīn buys a *qurrāl*, "corral," from Ḥassān b. ʿAbd al-Malik, who still has a full traditional Arabic name. In the third transaction, dated 1152, Khayr b. Zakarī's grandson bears the title *dūn*, "don" or "lord," before his Christian name Ṭomā b. Shaṭurnīn: *dūn* Ṭomā buys a share of the house belonging to his sister Amīra. A testimony of both his sisters, Shushāna, a Jewish name, and Amīra is given in favor of their brother Ṭomā in 1175. Onomastics are, of course, problematic, and they are not the most accurate indicator of social changes such as religious conversion. Some people—especially converts—had double names, one of them in Arabic and another in Romance.[30] Nevertheless, names reveal much about cultural changes, e.g., the process of the Christian Castilian culture overtaking Jewish and Muslim culture in Toledo.

27 *Opúsculos legales* 1836: 69, 70.
28 *Opúsculos legales* 1836: 25.
29 *Opúsculos legales* 1836: 25.
30 Aguilar 1994: 363; Olstein 2006a: 33.

Monetary systems are another element portraying the balance of power between Toledo and al-Andalus. Almoravid coins were used from 1112 to 1150 and then replaced by the strong gold coin, *mithqāl al-bayāsī wa-saʿdī*, from Baeza, a city that fell in the hands of the Christian ruler of Toledo, from 1152 to 1172. When Christian rule over Toledo was well established in 1173, Alfonsi coins became the official monetary system in Toledo.

By the beginning of the fourteenth century, Castilla felt strong enough to embark on a program of unifying territory, religion, and language. The conditions for the formation of a unified nation or country in the Peninsula had gained ground, and our documents also give testimony to this historical process. The process of the assimilation of the Mozarabs and the exclusion of Muslims and Jews culminated in the pogrom of the Jews at the end of the fourteenth century, and the final expulsion of both communities at the beginning of the seventeenth century.

3 Toledo Documents: Continuity and Discontinuity

After the conquest of Toledo, there was a continuity in the society and institutions as well as in the legal system.

This continuity is clear foremost in the use of the Arabic language. Language, social norms, and institutions remained alive among a newly re-Christianized Neo-Mozarab majority that had converted from Islam en masse when it pledged allegiance to the Christian King Alfonso VI.[31] Religious conversion was a logical result of the conquest because religion was associated with allegiance to a ruler, especially among the masses. (In contrast, the elite had already started abandoning the city well before the conquest.)

Arabic remained the language of the majority of the population. Through dialectal expressions and grammar, the Toledo documents show that Arabic continued to be a spoken language until the fourteenth century.[32] However, by the middle of the thirteenth century, Alfonso X (1221–1284) promoted the spoken language of the Castilians, Romance, as a written language at the expenses of written Arabic and Latin. Indeed, the gradual disappearance of Arabic is first been documented in 1169, when P.Mozarab. 1098 states: *quriʾa l-kitāb ʿalā l-mubtāʾīn* [...] *wa-fussira maʿānīhi ilayhim bi-lisān fahimūhu fa-ʿtarafū bi-dhālika*, “the document was read to the parties [...] and its meanings

31 Vallvé Bermejo 1999: 265.

32 Molenat: 1994: 485.

were translated in a language that they understand, and they declared that they had understood it." The same formula is found in P.Mozarab. 1100 (dated 1193) and becomes frequent in the thirteenth century.[33] Judeo-Arabic documents witness the understanding of Arabic until 1391 (P.Mozarab. 1140).

Continuity is also expressed in the use of Arabic standard legal documents for another 250 years. After the conquest, Arabic documents continued to be written, as they are described in the notarial treatises *Kitāb al-wathāʾiq wa-l-sijillāt* by Muḥammad b. Aḥmad b. al-ʿAṭṭār al-Umawī (d. ca. 399/1009) and *al-Muqniʿ fī ʿilm al-shurūṭ* by Aḥmad b. Muḥammad b. al-Mughīth of Toledo (d. 459/1067). The Toledo documents are, indeed, replicas of the templates given by Ibn al-Mugīth and Ibn al-ʿAṭṭār. There are not many differences between the Christian Arabic documents from Toledo and Islamic Arabic documents. An account of these differences is provided in the following section.[34]

Discontinuity is introduced with the promulgation of the *Lex Visigothorum*, i.e., the *Liber Iudicorum* or *Fuero Juzgo* (see below) in Toledo. The *Fuero* possibly had been enacted and existent prior to the Christian conquest, as copies have been preserved from the tenth to the thirteenth centuries.[35] However, the *Fuero Juzgo* was sanctioned in Toledo in 1101, a few years after the conquest. In parallel, the king recognized the law of the Mozarabs and the right of preserving their status quo.[36] Nonetheless, there was a new hierarchy of courts and the gradual introduction of new "laws," *fueros*, within a hierarchical system of laws and courts. The Islamic legal system lost its distinguished rank and ceased to be the leading official legal system in the city.

Accordingly, in our documents all transactions—with the exception of pre-conquest P.Mozarab. 1 (dated 1083)—were done *ʿalā sunnat an-naṣārā*, "according to the legal custom ('law') of the Christians." The law of the now diminished Muslim community continued to coexist and to be applied as autonomous customary law, following the pattern of the Islamic system of law, but was subordinated to the Christian system of law. In case of legal actions between a Muslim and a Christian, Christian courts were in charge and judged according to the *sunna* (legal custom, "law," or *fuero*) of the Christians.

33 González Palencia 1930: 3: 517, 520; 4: 129.

34 Continuity of legal culture is nothing new. Grohmann has shown that Arabic notaries borrowed from Greco-Egyptian legal documents; Grohmann 1934–1962: 1: 143, 152–153.

35 Díaz y Díaz 1976: 163–224.

36 Olstein 2011: 164. As in the Islamic system, the Mozarabs were first identified according to their specific laws and legal status but not according to their language or ethnicity, and not primarily according to their religion.

In Castilian Toledo, all documents—with the one exception mentioned—were signed according to the "law" of the Christians, and this was also the case if the parties belonged to different religious communities. The *Fuero Juzgo* states that the Christian court is responsible for all lawsuits where a Christian is involved.[37] Yet in Aragonese Huesca,[38] Christian parties involved in transactions with Muslims were signing legal contracts *ʿalā sunnat al-muslimīn*, "according to the legal custom ('law') of the Muslims" (e.g., P.BoschHuesca 2; 6; 7)[39] and *ʿalā bayʿ al-islām*, "according to Islamic selling" (P.BoschHuesca 3; 8; 9; 10; 12),[40] which may point to the absence or scarcity of Christian courts in some regions. Christian Aragon, as far as it is known, witnessed a wider cultural and legal interaction among communities than Castile. For instance, in P.BoschHuesca 12, in 1269 CE, a Christian couple buys a garden from a Muslim lady *ʿalā bayʿ al-islām wa-sharṭihi*, "according to Islamic selling and its condition"; the documents prove the intermingling of cultures by saying that the taxes to be paid by the Christians are to be paid on the first day of *ramāḍān al-naṣārā al-kabīr*, "the Great Ramadan of the Christians," meaning the first day of Lent.[41]

In spite of the hierarchical order and predominance of the *Fueros* in Castilla, these *Fueros* were a framework where customary law had its place. It is difficult to succinctly define the term *fuero* for it had multiple meanings that changed over time, place, and context. *Fueros* included royal decrees and privileges given to a town or community, customary laws, as well as ecclesiastical laws and (then nascent) Canon Law, including decretals and letters from the pope. In the book of *Siete Partidas*, Alfonso X explains: *Se llama costumbre al derecho o fuero no escrito, el cual ha usado los hombres largo tiempo. Fuero es cosa en que se encierran el uso y costumbre y se vuelve ley*, "Use is what is born of what man says or does and that continues in time. Custom is called the unwritten law or *fuero*, which have been in use (in a society) for a long time. *Fuero* is something in which use and custom are enclosed and it becomes law."[42]

In any case, "law" was not territorial but personal or communitarian. Different people living in the same city had the right to apply their own law, which had the character of customary law anyway.

37 Camino y Velasco 1740: 38–39; González Palencia 1930: 4: 122.

38 Aragon was one of the kingdoms of Christian Spain that favored its Muslim population more. The numerous Muslim populations of Aragon produced legal documents witnessing Christians signing a contract under the Muslim *sunna*, contrary to what happened in Castilia. These documents have been edited by Jacinto Bosch Vilá (1957).

39 Bosch Vilá 1957: 19, 30–32.

40 Bosch Vilá 1957: 22, 36–43, 46–47.

41 Bosch Vilá 1957: 47.

42 *Las Siete Partidas* 2011: 11–13; Strong 1893: 318.

The *Fueros* given to the city of Toledo were:

(1) The *Fueros* or privileges given in 1101 to the Mozarabs by King Alfonso VI have been preserved in an original copy from the thirteenth century in the Archivo secreto del Ayuntamiento de Toledo. Today, only a copy from 1740 is preserved.[43] This document englobes prescriptions regulating the use and distribution of land, taxes, and the military. Moreover, the *Liber Iudicorum* or *Lex Visigothorum*—a compendium of Visigothic, Roman, and Church law, rewritten once again—was supposed to be the legal foundation in all lawsuits. In the case of murder, Jews, Muslims, and Christians would be judged by the same law. A council of 12 noble and wise men, together with the judge of the city, were in charge of imparting justice.[44]

(2) The *Fuero* of Alfonso VII of 1118 was expressly addressed *ad omnes cives Toledanos, Castellanos, Mozarabes atque Francos*, "to all Toledo citizens, Castilians, Mozarabs and Franks," i.e., to all Christians living in the city, sometimes also to Galicians.[45]

(3) The *Fuero Juzgo*, a Romance version of the *Liber Iudicorum*, with its 500 laws, was in 1241 implemented by King Fernando III, and in 1255 by his son King Alfonso X, in an effort to unify and centralize the governance of his territory. Moreover, it was the law that the royal court used in order to answer the appeals from lower tribunals.[46]

(4) The *Siete Partidas* or the *Libro de las Leyes* by King Alfonso X (ruled 1252–1284) were an attempt to fuse the new achievements in civil and canon law—fusing St. Raymundo Penafort's commentaries of the *Corpus Iuris* at Bologna with previous laws and royal decrees such as the *Fuero Juzgo* and the *Fuero Real*—with customary law. The king's intention was to establish the *Siete Partidas* as the law of his kingdom, but he did not succeed in replacing the law existing in Castilla. The *Siete Partidas* did not become the official law of Castilla until 1348, when Alfonso X's grandson Alfonso XI promulgated them throughout his kingdom, yet only as a supplementary source of law within a hierarchy of sources of law.[47]

---

43 Camino y Velazsco 1740: 38–39; Muñoz y Romero 1847: 360.

44 *Opúsculos legales* 1836: 2: 18.

45 González Palencia 1930: 4: 121.

46 Watkin 1999: 104.

47 Watkin 1999: 104.

In the eleventh century, the Digest of Justinian's *Corpus Iuris* was discovered in Italy, and this became the basis for studying law at the nascent Europeans universities. The earliest collection of Canon Law had been written in the eleventh century, but only in 1140, with the *Decretum Gratianum*, was there a systematic and comprehensive display of the system of Canon Law. In 1234, Pope Gregory IX (d. 1241) urged the Spanish canonist St. Raymond of Penafort (d. 1275) to compose an official addition to the *Decretum Gratianum*.[48] But, as we have seen regarding the *Siete Partidas*, the theory written in books and taught in schools was only later put into daily legal practice.

Therefore, the question as to how much discontinuity resulted from the introduction of the *Fueros* in Toledo in 1101 and 1118 is legitimate: oral law and custom had always been a channel for shaping the written law, and had been a source of law. Even if officially the king was said to be the origin of the law, in reality jurists were legislators, bishops, and legal counselors. But most importantly, custom was the major material source of law. In this sense, legal continuity existed.

Maria Luz Alonso affirms, referring to *sunnat al-naṣārā* of the Toledo documents, "The 'Law' could be interpreted sometimes as customary unwritten law, but a law known by everyone." Alonso quotes Vreña who states that during the Middle Ages, Jewish and Islamic law had influenced the law of Christian Spain.[49] Olstein tried to answer the puzzle of the coexistence of the *Liber* and the notarial documents of Toledo, with their origin in Maliki law, by recognizing some compatibility between both systems.[50] But, in my opinion, he falls short by not specifying the origin of this compatibility and where the compatibility is rooted. Indeed, a large component of Maliki law as well as the law of the *fueros* was oral practice and custom that made the "law" not be perceived as a "law" or legal system by the other and rejected as a whole. Indeed, as Maria Luz Alonso states, this notion of law is different from the modern one *because it includes and it fuses with custom*. The "law," the legal principles regulating social life, had the form of written and unwritten legal customs anchored in the living and customary legal practice of a community—not on a formal code of written laws. At times, oral legal customs found written expression with the passing of time. Therefore, we need to acknowledge that local custom, including Islamic local custom, shaped the

48 Watkin 1999: 88–89.

49 Alonso 1978: 339, "La 'Ley' se confunde a veces con un derecho consuetudinario no escrito, pero que todos conocen"; 337.

50 Olstein 2011: 164.

fueros that included and recognized local custom as long as it did not contradict religious principles—in the same way that Islamic law does. Thus, even though the specificities of the laws and customs of each community prevailed—especially those determined by religious norms, legal authorities, and even by additional customary laws—there was an existing common legal ground that allowed a shared social life, and vice versa, a shared life that allowed a common legal ground.

Thus, the notion of law rendered by *fuero* is similar to the idea of *sunna* in Islamic law. The legal is the religious norm and the customary. This legal notion of law is also anchored in the oral character of the law—at least in part—and the role of customs. The Maliki law ruling in al-Andalus relied greatly on customary law and considered it part of the legal system. In fact, customary law was accepted within the system as long as it did not contradict the religious norms.

In Granada in 1474, Maliki jurists defined the legal as the *jārī*, "usual," and the *jāʾiz*, "permitted." Thus, *jārī* refers to community consensus and common practice, while *jāʾiz* refers to the religious precepts and jurisprudence of one specific community.[51] All of the different norms, uses, and prescriptions of a community constitute the legal framework of the community or the *sunna*, which can be translated as *fuero*.

Hence, I argue that until the thirteenth century, both *sunna* and *fuero*[52] had an element of orality that makes it easy to assume a common shared legal ground regarding *muʿāmalāt*, "transactions," in Toledo. In this way, blurred legal boundaries facilitated the relations and transactions between communities and provided a certain continuity in the legal system.[53]

51 Hoenerbach 1965: 272.

52 Local *Fueros* were based on customary law. The term changed its meaning with the development from oral into written law and a legal system based on written documents. This process took over gradually from the eleventh century onwards and was finished by the end of the thirteenth century. Today some regions in Spain follow written *Fueros* that preserve the customs and privileges of the region.

53 Due to the difficulty of research on an oral or semi-oral tradition, the issue needs to be studied in more detail and following a proper methodology.

4 Comparing Arabic Christian and Arabic Islamic Documents

TABLE 7.1 Characteristic features of Christian and Islamic documents

Toledo. Christian Arabic documents	Islamic documents from Iberian Peninsula	Islamic eastern documents
No certification, no *ʿalāma*	Certification (occasionally)	Certification with *thabata* or validation with *ṣaḥḥa*; *ʿalāma* (from 10th century)
Basmala-Ḥamdala or *Basmala-Tawakkul* (11th–14th c.)	*Basmala-Tawakkul* or *Basmala-Taṣliya* (Huesca 12th–13th c.) *Basmala-Taṣliya* (Granada 14th–15th c.)	*Basmala* only *Basmala-Taṣliya* (from 9th or 10th c.)
Nonmonumental introduction by *ishtarā* or *bāʿa*, rarely by *ibtāʿa*	Nonmonumental introduction by *ishtarā* or *bāʿa* or *ibtāʿa*	Monumental introduction by *hādhā mā ishtarā … ishtarā minhu* (until 14th c.) Nonmonumental introduction by *ishtarā* (after 14th c.)
Order of boundaries: *Sharq-Gharb-Qibla-Jawf*	Order of boundaries: *Qibla-Jawf-Sharq-Gharb*	Order of boundaries: *Qibla-Baḥr/Shām-Sharq-Gharb*
Nonperformative	Performative: *qabaḍa al-mabīʿ*	*safqan wāḥidan*
No *Wakāla*, "representation," of women	*Wakāla*, "representation," of women	*Wakāla*, "representation," of women
Qāḍī calls for witness: *Ishhād* *Qāḍī* does not call for witness,	No *ishhād*	*Qāḍī* calls for witness: *Ishhād* (after 11th c.)

TABLE 7.1 Characteristic features of Christian and Islamic documents (*cont.*)

Toledo. Christian Arabic documents	**Islamic documents from Iberian Peninsula**	**Islamic eastern documents**
Date: Ṣufr	⟨Christian month⟩ *al-muwāfiq li-*⟨Muslim month⟩, hijra year (Aragon 13th c.)	Date: Hijra
Bilingual Signatures: Latin, Hebrew, Arabic	Arabic Signatures:	Arabic Signatures:
Individualized signatures	No individualized signatures (Aragon)	Not written by own hand, part of main text in earlier documents
	Signatures of notaries (Granada 14th–15th c.)	Increase of signatures written by own hand. Individualized signatures. Referential date added (later on)

Christian documents are clearly rooted in the tradition of the *wathāʾiq*, "notarial formularies," described in the books of Ibn al-Mugīth of Toledo and Ibn al-ʿAṭṭār of Cordoba. They dispose, however, of a number of peculiarities.

(1) Christian documents have no *taṣliya* or praise of Muḥammad. This is replaced by the ecumenical *ḥamdala, al-ḥamdu li-llāh waḥdahu,* "Praise to God alone," which is not an exclusive formula of Christian documents but also well-known in Islamic ones.[54] In the Toledo documents, the *taṣliya* might also be replaced by a formula of *tawakkul,* relying on God's help; this is frequently also the case in the Islamic documents from Huesca. In Granada, on the contrary, the *taṣliya* is often used as a formula of identity for the Muslim community. In the east, the *taṣliya* was introduced in the ninth century by order of Harūn al-Rashīd.[55]

54 Grohmann and Khoury 1995: 8; Richards 2013: 5, 13.

55 Grohmann 1934–1962: 1: 215–216.

(2) The Toledo documents have neither *ʿalāma* nor certification by *thabata*, "it is firm," and no validation by *ṣaḥḥa*, "it is sound," above the *basmala*. This may indicate a difference of function between Christian and Islamic documents, since the latter had to be certified (*ʿalāma* or *thabata*) by the judge and the witnesses (*bayyina*) in order to constitute a proof. From the thirteenth century on, Christian documents were considered as proof that needed no further certification, as the *Fuero Real* in 1255 states: *Todas cartas que fueren fechas de compras* [...] *por escribanos públicos* [...], *faganse con tres testigos almenos sin escribano, valan. Et si moriesen los testigos o notario, no dexen devaler la carta, se prueba la escritura*, "All documents (*cartas*) that are contracts of sale [...] have to be written by public notaries [...] or at least witnessed by three witnesses without a notary, to be valid. If the witnesses or notary die, the document does not lose it validity and the writing will be checked."[56]

On their part, Islamic documents were validated by a *ṣaḥḥa* formula by the *qāḍī* in order to be used as *ḥujja*, "proof," in certain litigious cases at court after oral witness had been given. Maliki law recognizes a document as proof under restricted circumstances and after the witnessing of *ʿudūl*, "qualified witnesses."[57] Yet, in the east, validation by *ṣaḥḥa* (FahmiTaaqud 8; 951) and certification by *thabata* (P.FahmiTaaqud 10 = P.Vente 8; 979) is found as early as the tenth century and became usual from the eleventh century onwards.[58]

The *ʿalāma*, the judge's authentication, usually a stylized signature, is not found in the Toledo documents. *ʿAlāma* as a religious sentence, e.g., *al-ḥamdu li-llāhi wa-l-shukru li-llāh*, "Praise to God and thanks to God," located above the *basmala*, is a characteristic part of late Islamic documents in the east. Each judge had his own *ʿalāma*.[59]

(3) Christian and Islamic documents from the Iberian Peninsula have no monumental introduction with *hādhā mā ishtarā*, "the following is what has bought." This introduction is characteristic of eastern documents until the end of the fourteenth century;[60] after that date, eastern documents also use the nonmonumental introduction *ishtarā*.

---

56 *Opúsculos legales* 1836: 50.

57 Al-Ṭaḥāwī says that in the case of a sale paid on spot in cash, God does not ask for documents, only in the case of delated payment. Moreover, documents were only instruments of proof together with a proper *bayyina*, "proof," i.e., oral witness; al-Ṭaḥāwī 1972: 9, 29. See also Müller 2013: 23–24.

58 Grohmann 1934–1962: 1: 210.

59 Grohmann 1934–1962: 1: 150.

60 Cf. the *Arabic Papyrology Database* (www.naher-osten.lmu.de/apd). The database currently contains the full text of over 4,000 documents.

(4) Where describing boundaries, Christian documents follow the Roman and Byzantine order starting *ab oriente*, "from the East," as Frontinus (ca. 40–103, Roman governor of Britain), in *De agri mensura*, says: "our ancestors [...] first drew out two limits, one stretching from east to west, which they called the *decumanus*, the other from south to north that they called *cardo*."[61] In Islamic documents, following the old Egyptian orientation, boundaries were defined starting from *al-qibla*, "the South" (not "the East"), as first attested in ninth-century Arabic papyrus documents from Egypt. The order is that of south, north, east, and west in Arabic papyri, as well as in Demotic, Greek, and Coptic papyri.[62] North is referred to as *al-baḥr* in Egypt, *al-shām* in Jerusalem, and *al-jawf* in the Iberian Peninsula.

(5) Christian documents do not make use of archaic performative features of transaction, which reflect the oral origin and character of these transactions. Thus, Christian documents do not have the formula of physically taking over the possession, *qabaḍa*,[63] nor the formula of closing the deal, *ṣafqan wāḥidan*, "by a single handshake."

(6) A feature in Christian documents is the lack of compulsory *wakāla*, "representation," of women by men. Women, present all over the Toledo documents, carry on the transactions in their own names. Sometimes their husbands were present and ratified the transaction, yet women also ratified the transactions of their husbands. However, the *Fuero Real* of Alfonso X (1255) declared *Ninguna muger non razone pleito ageno nin pueda seer personera de otre; mas su pleito propio puedalo razonar, si quiere*, "Woman cannot represent another person and cannot be represented by another person, but she can appear in court to represent her own affairs, if she wishes so." and *Todo marido pueda demandar e responder por su muger*, "A husband can represent his wife in court."[64]

(7) Christian documents from Toledo are dated using the era of Ṣufr.[65] Islamic documents from Aragon, written under Christian rule (twelfth–thirteenth centuries), use the Hijra era but incorporate the Christian month.

61 Metcalfe 2012: 37, 40; Müller 2013: 354–357.
62 Metcalfe 2012: 46–47.
63 Grohmann 1934–1962: 1: 143–144; Córcoles Olaitz 2008: 327.
64 *Opúsculos legales* 1836: 25.
65 Fischer 1918: 266–267.

(8) The formula of *ishhād*, the *qāḍī*'s call for witnessing the act of transaction, is present in Toledo, but not in Aragon. In the east, the formula is unknown until the tenth century; however, it became a well-used formula from the eleventh century on.

(9) The Toledo documents reflect a plural society by rendering signatures in Latin, Hebrew, and Arabic. The system is quite sophisticated and appears as columns of signatures, sometimes artistic ones. The Aragon documents[66] do not show this characteristic; they have no column of individualized signatures written by their own hands, but these are part of the main text and frequently not written by the witness himself. The Granada documents,[67] written in the fourteenth and fifteenth centuries, have professional signatures of two notaries whose names are unreadable because the two signatures almost take the form of a monogram.[68]

5 The Law Formula

Christian Müller has written[69] on the term *sharīʿa*, "law," and has established a new benchmark in studies on Islamic law and its terminology. He states that *sharīʿa*—and I would specify, *sharīʿa* with the connotation of "law"—does not appear in legal documents before the twelfth–thirteenth centuries in regular cases. This claim is confirmed by consulting the *Arabic Papyrology Database*. However, *sharīʿa* with the meaning of "ritual law" starts appearing in the eleventh century in certificates of pilgrimages (P.SourdelMekka 1; 1084; P.SourdelMekka 14; 1089–1096) in *ʿalā mā yūjibuhu ḥukm al-sharīʿa*, "according to what ritual law prescribes." The word *sharīʿa* with the additional meaning of "law" regularly appears only after the thirteenth century.

Departing from Müller's insightful contribution, I realized that in legal documents, the word used before *sharīʿa* has been *sunna*, in addition to other law formulae. Expressions like *ʿalā sunnat al-muslimīn*, "according to the law of the

66 These documents are named P.BoschHuesca, Huesca being the city in the kingdom of Aragon were the documents have been preserved. The documents have been studied and edited by Jacinto Bosch Vilá (1957).

67 Granada has a large collection of documents kept in different archives, such as Archive of the Biblioteca de la Universidad de Granada, Archive Provincial de Granada, Archivo de la Catedral de Granada, etc. The majority of them are from the fourteenth–fifteenth centuries; see Alvarez de Morales 2010.

68 Carro Martin and Zomeño 2017: 1113–1114.

69 Müller 2018: 60–62.

Muslims," and *ʿalā sharṭ bayʿ al-islām*, "according to the condition of sale in Islam," were common in the east, in al-Andalus, and in Christian Spain.

However, in al-Andalus and Christian Spain, in contrast to the East, the word *sharīʿa* was not an option in law formulae and only *sunna* was used until the end of the Naṣrid Kingdom of Granada (P.Moriscos 27; 1476; P.Granada 25; 1470; P.Granada 40[a]; 1484).[70] In Granada, the adjective *sharʿī*, "legal," is found in documents, together with the law formula *ʿalā l-sunna*, "according to the law" (P.Moriscos 27; 1476). In Granada, the law formula did not specify which *sunna*, while Christian Spain differentiated between *sunnat al-muslimīn*, "the law of the Muslims," and *sunnat al-naṣārā*, "the law of the Christians."

The following is an overview of the law formulae from al-Andalus and Christian Spain:

TABLE 7.2 Law formulae from al-Andalus and Christian Spain

Documents	Formula	Date and place
P.Mozarab. 1	*ʿalā sunnat al-muslimīn fī ṭayyib buyūʿihim wa-marǧiʿ al-darak*	1083 Toledo
P.Mozarab. 21	*ʿalā sunnat al-naṣārā fī buyūʿihim wa-ashriyatihim wa-marǧiʿ al-darak fī mā baynahum*	1134 Toledo
P.Mozarab. 23		1135 Toledo
P.Mozarab. 30		1142 Toledo
P.Mozarab. 39; 40		1150 Toledo
P.Mozarab. 63		1160 Toledo
P.Mozarab. 72		1163 Toledo
P.Mozarab. 82		1167 Toledo
P.Mozarab. 92		1170 Toledo
P.BoschHuesca 2	*alā sunnat al-muslimīn fī ṭayyib buyūʿihim wa-marǧiʿ idrākīhim*	1154 Huesca
P.BoschHuesca 6		1202 Huesca
P.GarciaPilar 1		1117 Zaragoza
P.BoschHuesca 3	*ʿalā bayʿ al-islām wa-sharṭihi wa-marǧiʿ al-darak fīhi bayna ʾahlihi*	1155 Huesca
P.BoschHuesca 8–9		1215–1216 Huesca
P.BoschHuesca 10		1229 Huesca
P.BoschHuesca 12		1269 Huesca

70 Seco de Lucena Paredes 1961: 51–52, 74.

TABLE 7.2 Law formulae from al-Andalus and Christian Spain (*cont.*)

Documents	Formula	Date and place
P.GarciaArenal 3; 5; 6	*ʿalā fuwayr ṭuṭīla*, "according to the *fuero*	1174 Tudela
P.GarciaArenal 8	of Tudela"	1177 Tudela
P.GarciaArenal 11	*ʿalā sunnat al-muslimīn fī ṣaḥīḥ buyūʿihim al-jāʾiza baynahum wa-marǧiʿ al-darak*	
	1391 Tudela	
P.Marques 8b; 8c	*ʿalā l-sunna*	1473 Granada
P.Marques 10d		1476 Granada

The usual formula in al-Andalus and Christian Spain was *ʿalā sunnat al-muslimīn* or *ʿalā sunnat al-naṣārā*.

The expression *ʿalā bayʿ al-islām wa-sharṭihi*, "according to Islamic selling and its condition," is also found in al-Andalus. In the east, the most common law formula is *ʿalā bayʿ al-islām wa-ʿuhdatihi*, "according to Islamic selling and its usage" (P.FahmiTaaqud 1; 852; P.FahmiTaaqud2; 861; P.FahmiTaaqud 3; 879; P.FahmiTaaqud 5; 879), and there were also are other expressions without *sunna*,[71] such as *bayʿ al-muslim min al-muslim*, "as the Muslim buys from the Muslim" (P.Vente 7; 966; Chrest.Khoury I 53 = P.Vente 9; 983). In the east, we only once found the expression *ʿalā sunnat al-muslimīn wa-ʿalā shurūṭihim*, "according to the law of the Muslims and according to their conditions" (P.Fay.Monast. 1; 946).

The term *sharīʿa* is rarely mentioned in the law formulae of al-Andalus or Christian Spain. In the east, *sharīʿa* is found in pilgrimage certificates from Damascus[72] and in marriage contracts (P.MariageSeparation 7A; 1100–1154; P.MariageSeparation 30; 1130–1179), especially as *fī sharīʿat sayyidinā Muḥammad*, "in the *sunna* of our Lord Muḥammad." The use of the term in pilgrim certificates and marriage contracts reflects the need for introducing a strong religious element in these documents. Marriage contracts call upon God's and Muḥammad's blessings and appeal to obeying God in dealing with one another. Therefore, the term *sharīʿa* in this context was possibly considered more appropriate than *sunna*, "law." However, until the eleventh cen-

71 In tenth-century Egypt, the Fatimids did not use *sunna* because the source of the law was supposed to be the imam.

72 For the use of *sharīʿa*, "ritual law," in pilgrimage certificates from eleventh-century Damascus, see above.

tury *sunna* was the common term in marriage contracts in the east: *ka-mā amara llāh wa-sunnat Muḥammad*, "as God and the *sunna* of Muḥammad dispose" (P.Cair.Arab. 38; 873; P.Cair.Arab. 39; 878; P.Cair.Arab. 41; 892; P.Cair.Arab. 42; 801–900; P.Cair.Arab. 44; 928; P.Cair.Arab. 45; 1069).

Interestingly enough, *sharīʿa* is also found in a Mozarab document from Toledo, also a marriage contract: *ka-lladhī tūjibuhu al-sharīʿa al-qatūliqiyya*, "as the Catholic law makes necessary," referring to the rules of the Church or Canon Law—yet the law formula still speaks of the *sunna*. We even find the expression *zawja sunniyya*, "legal wife" (P.Mozarab. 1010; 1185).[73]

In al-Andalus *sunna* continued to be used in marriage contracts *ʿalā sunnat nabiyyihi al-muṣṭafā Muḥammad*, "according to the law of His chosen Prophet Muḥammad" (P.Moriscos 4; 1297). After the conquest, the expression *ʿalā ḥukm al-sharʿ al-ʿazīz wa-muqtaḍāhu*, "according to the rule of the noble law and its requirement," is found in sixteenth-century Valencia (P.LabartaContratosMatrimoniales 2).

Sharīʿa started gradually replacing *sunna* in the east after the eleventh century, as can be seen in the Arabic translation of Socrates' philosophical treatise *On Law and Philosophy*, where the copyist wrote *sharīʿa* in the margin to replace *sunna*.[74] Indeed, the term *sharīʿa* became common after the thirteenth century. However, from the eleventh to the fourteenth centuries al-Andalus and Christian Spain provide almost no examples of the term *sharīʿa* for reasons that we will try to elucidate later in this article.

TABLE 7.3 Examples of law and validity formulas in the east

Before the 13th century		
ʿalā bayʿ al-Islām wa-ʿuhdat al-Islām	P.Cair.Arab. 56 = P.Cair.Archives 866	Edfu 854
ʿalā sunnat buyūʿ al-muslimīn wa-ʿalā shurūṭihi	P.Fay.Monast. 1	Naqlūn 946
ʿalā shurūṭ bayʿ al-Islām wa ʿuhdatihi	P.FahmiTaaqud 8	Buljusūq 951
After the 13th century		
shirāʾan ṣaḥīḥan sharʿiyyan or *baʿda al-muʿāqada al-sharʿiyya baynahumā*	P.Vente 12	Bahnasā 1284
shirāʾan ṣaḥīḥan sharʿiyyan or *ḥaythu yajibu sharʿan*	P.BaudenAchat 1	Alexandria 1409

73 I am preparing a reedition of the document.

74 Berman and Alon 1980: 265.

6 The Concept of *Sunna*, "Law"

The use of the word *sunna* or similar expressions, such as *ʿalā bayʿ al-Islām*, reflects a concept of law anchored in use, custom, and tradition, including religious tradition.[75]

Sunna, as used in the Toledo documents, was a legal framework mostly based on the praxis of the community, that which was customary, came from their ancestors—including religious prescriptions—and was improved upon, all of this complemented by the work of the experts in law, i.e., the jurists. The works of the jurists and the decrees of the king were part of this *sunna*. *Sunna*, as well as *fuero*—a similar notion of law that sometimes has been used to translate *sunnat al-muslimīn*[76]—were, in the first place, a framework where the work of jurists, customary law—and royal decrees, in the case of the *fueros*—came together to form layers of laws in a legal structure shaped into a hierarchy of laws, at times mirrored by a hierarchy of courts (as in Christian Spain and the Islamic legal system).

In parallel to fixed rules and written norms given by jurists and kings, there were unwritten laws anchored in tradition that took shape as customs, and mores. These norms represented the common understanding of what was good and bad and sometimes materialized in law and ethics. Thus, concrete laws sometimes originated in customs, laws, which were those that had been approved by the common consent by the passing of time and, at some point, sanctioned by the jurists. Alonso similarly states that "*Εϑη* και *νομοι* became in Hellenistic and Roman times a commonplace to refer to the law in its entirety, or, more often, to the whole social order. The Latin equivalent, *mores et leges*, was to describe the legal order in the city."[77]

This complex notion of law was also different from modern customary law, as opposed to positive law. Customary law today has the connotation of "popular customs bearing a secondary value as laws." Medieval customary law, however, included religious understandings and living religious tradition and were not just customs. Finally, law as equated with legislation is a product of modern positivism, and it would be anachronistic to think in these terms when dealing with medieval law and the medieval system of law.[78]

---

75 In this article, I use *sunnat al-muslimīn* as a shorthand when referring to similar law formulas used in east, such as *ʿalā bayʿ al-Islām* or *ʿalā sharṭ bayʿ al-Islām*, "according to the legal custom/conditions of sale in Islam."

76 García-Velasco Bernal 2017: 255.

77 Alonso 2013: 366.

78 Alonso 2013: 390–391.

The concepts of *sunna* and *sharīʿa* were embedded in an ancient and medieval debate on written and unwritten law.

Plato[79] defined *hoi agraphoi nomoi*, "the unwritten laws," as the valid and binding practice of the community. The Arabic term *sunna* was used to translate the Greek *nomos*[80] and thus had both a divine as well as a practical and concrete dimension. In that sense, the practical and concrete dimension of *sunna* was the tradition or customs that had been passed down from generation to generation, the consensus of the community on concrete norms, and the binding force of the community, in its origin mostly in the form of unwritten law. Unwritten laws should not be named "law," but as they have to be named, they were, says Plato. They form the ties or bonds between the written laws and laws still to be created. These unwritten "archaic laws" inherited from the ancestors are the moral environment without which the legal system, left to itself, would collapse.[81]

The Romans also distinguished between laws as *ius scriptum* and natural law as *ius non scriptum*.[82] In the Aristotelian tradition, Ibn Rushd speaks of *sunna ʿāmma*, "common or general law," and *sunna khāṣṣa*, "particular law." *Sunna ʿāmma* is the unwritten law that every human being recognizes as law: being respectful towards parents, thankful to benefactors, and pious towards God. *Sunna khāṣṣa* is the particular law of each people, as well as each community, that takes the concrete form of the practice of the community. In the case of the Arabs, this particular law would be the *sharīʿa*, says Ibn Rushd.[83] Al-Fārābī defines *dīn*, "religion" as consisting of *ārāʾ*, "creeds," and *afʿāl muqaddara*, "estimated actions," the latter being called *sunna* or *sharīʿa*, both being synonymous.[84]

Sunna also meant the tradition and norms of the ancestors. *Sharīʿa* was not used with the strict meaning of "law" before the tenth century and acquired this meaning gradually from the eleventh to the thirteenth century.[85]

The "Sharīʿatic turn," as Christian Müller called it, i.e., the change of the term *sharīʿa* from the twelfth–thirteenth centuries onwards, was linked to specific developments in *fiqh*, "Islamic jurisprudence," and *uṣūl al-fiqh*, "the fundaments of jurisprudence."[86] Complementary and external factors also may have

79 Platon 1977: 17.793a–d.
80 Daga Portillo 2020.
81 Platon 1977: 17.793a–d.
82 Watkin 1999: 3.
83 Ibn Rushd 2002: 3: 327.
84 Al-Fārābī 1991: 43, 46.
85 This process is described in the excellent article by Christian Müller; Müller 2018: 72–81.
86 Müller 2018: 64–68.

influenced the Sharīʿatic turn. The use of the term *sunna* versus *sharīʿa* seems to be linked to the oral character of culture and the transformation of culture into a primordially written cultural system after the eleventh century, and especially from the thirteenth century onwards. This transformation was possible due to the extensive use of paper that, in most Islamic countries, spread after the eleventh century, and this is what fostered written culture and was a precondition for the institutionalization of the legal profession. In the East, paper had been used since the eighth–ninth centuries, but the use of paper became widespread in the eleventh century.[87] In al-Andalus, paper is attested from the eleventh century onwards; some documents were written on paper in the twelfth century, and the use of paper became common in the thirteenth century.[88] The change in terminology from *sunna* to *sharīʿa*, in the East, might also have had to do with the institutionalization and professionalization of legal activity in the thirteenth century. This professionalization of the legal activity started in Iraq with Niẓām al-Mulk (1018–1092) and the foundation of the madrasa, and the creation of a network of madrasas promoted writing culture and the professionalization of the legal activity. In Egypt, this took place under the Mamluks in the thirteenth century, with the growth in influence of the four legal schools and the development of educational institutions. The madrasa, however, arrived in the Kingdom of Granada only in the fourteenth century.

I therefore argue that the reason why, in al-Andalus, *sunna* was never replaced by *sharīʿa* in the law formulae is that the professionalization of the legal activity and the development of a written legal culture, linked to the use of paper, did not take place in al-Andalus to such a high degree as it had taken place in the east.

Finally, the use of *sunna* in al-Andalus could be understood by the fact that customary law, i.e., the law of the community, was peculiar for Maliki law, a law that greatly relied on the custom and the consensus of the community of Medina. The Maliki emphasis on *al-jārī*, "the current and customary," would help to preserve, in al-Andalus and Christian Spain—by osmosis—the notion of law as *sunna*, as a framework where orality, living tradition, and customs played an important role.

In the legal documents of the East, in the thirteenth century *sharīʿa* had replaced *sunna*, as the professionalization of the legal activity, within a writ-

87 Schatzmiller 2018: 462–463, 474–475.

88 González Palencia 1930: 4: 44.

ten legal culture, had reached its peak. Yet al-Andalus (as we see from the documents) and Christian Spain continued to use *sunna* until the fourteenth–fifteenth centuries.

7 Conclusion

Christians, Jews, and Muslims continued writing their legal documents in Arabic for a period of about 250 years after the conquest of Toledo. Mozarabs and Neo-Mozarabs continued writing Arabic legal documents as Muslim jurists had before the conquest. By putting their expertise in the service of the newcomers, they became transmitters of the Islamic legal practice to the Castilian conquerors.

The legal documents of Toledo show the continuity and discontinuity of Islamic legal praxis. The expressions *sunnat al-muslimīn* and *sunnat al-naṣārā* betray continuity and discontinuity regarding the practice of legal customs ("law"). Nonetheless, *sunna* was understood as the accepted practice of the community, i.e., the framework that included jurists' law, royal decrees (in the case of Christian law), and customary law (including religious tradition). It was embedded in the living traditions and local customs of the community, and peculiar to the community's religious norms and legal tradition.

The oral character of the law and the conception of law as being—at least in part—the practice of the community were the factors that were shared and that facilitated communication among religious groups and allowed for the coexistence of different law systems. In addition, in the field of *muʿāmalāt*, "transactions," the common legal ground and written legal culture—as documented by the Toledo documents—facilitated interaction among the communities.

In al-Andalus and Christian Spain no law formula containing the word *sharīʿa* was used. In the East of the eleventh century, the rise of madrasas and the wide spread of paper led to the institutionalization of a written legal culture. This never occurred on the Iberian Peninsula. When the madrasa reached the shores of Iberia in the fourteenth century, the Arabic language had come to an end on most of it, and the remaining small Kingdom of Granada was too isolated to follow the legal and sociopolitical changes in the east.

Sunna remained the term used to refer to the "law" in Granada, very much in conjunction with the legal practice of the Maliki school of law that incorporated legal custom within the legal system. As part of the wider development, *sharīʿa*, originally meaning the path given by revelation, had acquired the additional meaning of "law" and started replacing the word *sunna*, but the concept of law expressed by the word *sharīʿa* was, in some aspects, different from the one expressed by the term *sunna*.

In Christian Spain the gradual replacement of Arabic by the Romance language took place in the thirteenth–fourteenth centuries. The legal activity that had started in the eleventh century was developed, especially in the thirteenth century, in the newly created universities, and by the fourteenth century, it focused on the formation of its own legal system and an emphasis on territoriality. There were specific requirements: the need of one language, religion, and legal system as defining factors for the nascent unified country or nation.

Appendix: Two Documents on the Sale of a Mosque

No. 1: First Document on Buying a Mosque (Reedition of P.Mozarab. 82)

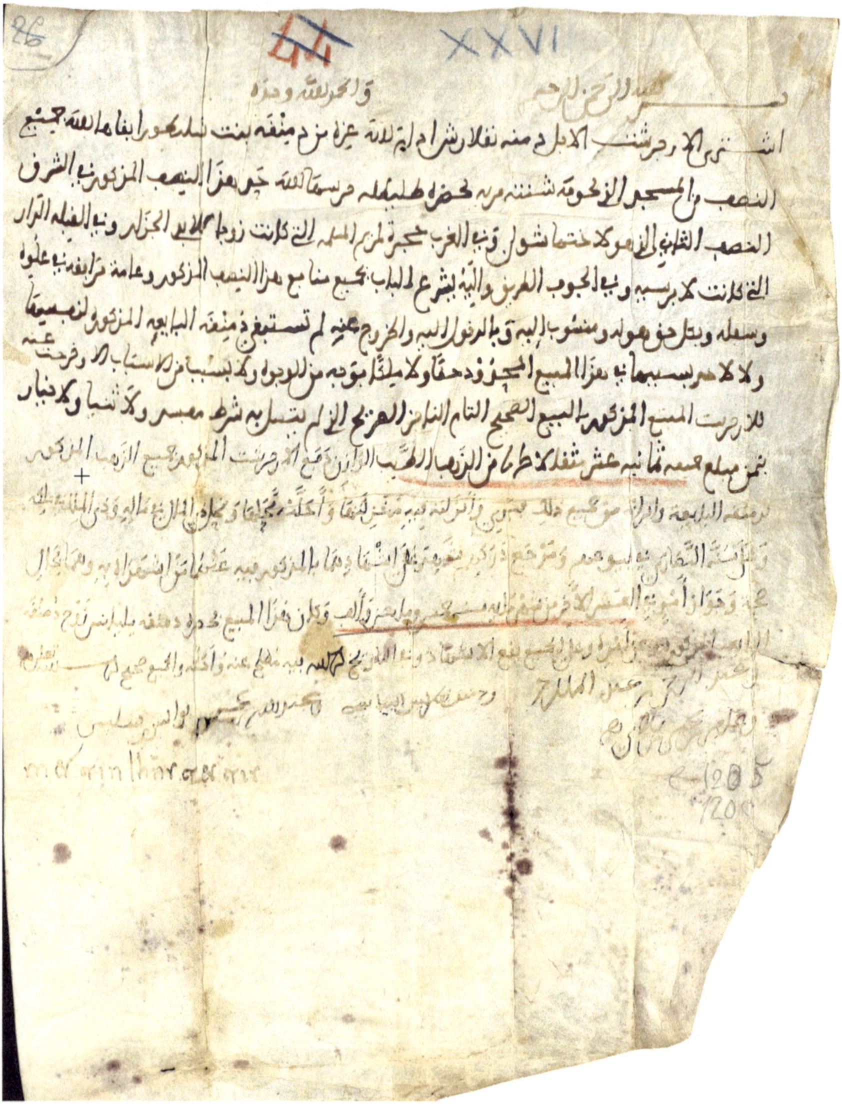

FIGURE 7.1 First document on buying a mosque (P.Arch.Hist.Nac.inv. Clero-Secular_Regular, Car. 3036, N.15_1 recto = P.Mozarab. 82; 1205).

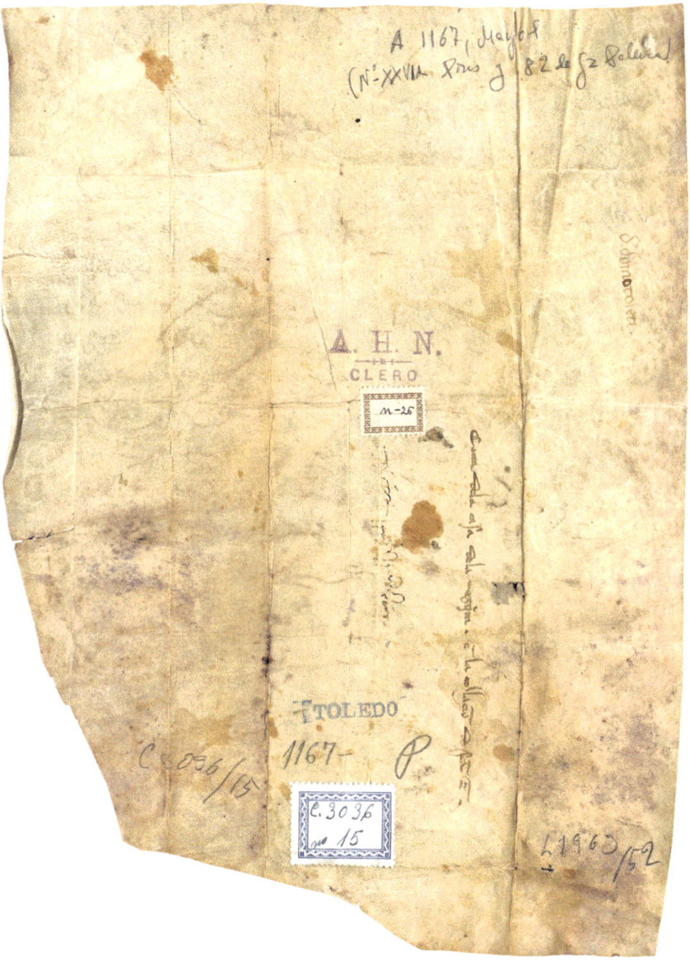

FIGURE 7.2 First document on buying a mosque (P.Arch.Hist.Nac.inv. Clero-Secular_Regular, Car. 3036, N.15_1 verso = P.Mozarab. 82; 1205)

Pergament in good condition. Side stains do not prevent the reading of the text. On recto, three different inks are used: one for the *basmala* and the header, a second for part of the main text, and a much faded third one, similar to the first one, for the rest of the main text. Maghribi-style writing with a dot below the *fāʾ* (*al-niṣf* 3) and one dot above the *qāf*. There are occasional *ihmāl* signs under *ḥāʾ* (*ḥadd* 3) and *ʿayn* (*ʿanhu* 6, *al-bāyiʿa* 6; *al-maḥdūd* 7; *wa-maḥallahā 10*). The final *yāʾ* of the relative pronoun goes back to the right. Vowels signs are used to mark long vowels and to emphasize words. Extensive use of *tamdīd* to emphasize key words and text parts.

Recto

١ بسم الله الرّحمن الرحيم وَالحمد للّٰه وحدَه

٢ اشترى الارجبرشت الاجل دمنه نقلاوش ادامَ اللَه عِزه من دمِنْقَه بنت شلبطور ابقاها اللّٰه جمْيع

٣ النصف من المسجد الذي بحومَة شنته مرية بحضرة طليطلة حرسهَا اللَه حَد هذَا النِصف المذكور في الشرق

٤ النصف الثانِي الذي هو لاختها شولي وَفي الغرب حجرة لمريم المسلمة التي كانت زوجا للابدى الجزَار وفي القِبلة الدَار

٥ التى كانت لابرسيه وفي الجوف الطريق وإلَيهُ يشرع الباب بجميع منافع هذا النِصف المذكور وعامة مرَافقه في علوَه

٦ وسفله وبكل حق هو له ومنسُوب اِليه وَبالدخول اليه والخروج عنه لم تستبقي دُمِنْقَه البايعة المذكورة لنفسِهَا

٧ ولا لاحد بسببها في هذَا المبيع المحدُوْد حقًا ولا مِلكًا بوَجه من الوجوه ولا بسبب من الاسبَاب الا وخرجت عنه

٨ للارجبرشت المبتع المذكور بالبيع الصحيح التام الناجز الصريح الذي لم يتصل به شرط مفسد ولَا ثنيا ولا خيار

٩ بثمن مبلغ جميعه ثمانية عشر مثقالا طريا من الذَهب الطيِّب الوَازن دَفَع الارجبرشت المذكور جميع الذَهب المذكور

١٠ لدمنقه البايعة وابراته من جميع ذلِك فبَرِي وَاَنزَلته فِيهِ مَنْزِلَتَهَا وَأَحَلَّتْه محَلَهَا وَمحل ذي المال في مَالِه وَذي الملِك في مِلكه

١١ وَعَلَى سُنَّة النَّصَارَي في بيوعهم وَمَرْجَع دَرَكهم شَهِدَ عَلَي اشْهَادِهمَا بالمذكور فيه عَنْهُما مَن اشهَدَاه بِهِ وهمَا بحَالِ

١٢ صحة وجَوَاز أَمرٍ في العَشر الأَخر من شهْر مَايه سنة خمس ومايتين وَأَلف وَكان هذَا المبيع بحضرة دمنقه يليانس زَوْج دُمنْقَة

١٣ البايعة المذكورة وعن امْرِه وعلي الجميع يقع الاشهاد وفي التاريخ (الذي كتبه) فيه مُصلح عنه وَأخته والجميع صحيح ان شاء الله تعلى (انتـ)ـهى

١٤ وعبد الرحمن بن عبد الملك . ودمنقه بيطرس البياسي وعبد الله بن عمر يوانش بن سليمن

١٥ وعامر بن يحيي بن بلاي (انتـ)ـهى martin i(o)h(a)n(ni)s testis

Verso

١ حجة نِصْف المسجِد المبتع من دمِنقَه

٢ Carta firmada casa de la mosqea e la ... de parte ...[89]

Recto

(1) In the Name of God the Clement, the Merciful Thanks be to God Alone.

(2) The Most Honorable Archpriest (*al-arjibrisht al-ajall*) domino Nicolaus (*Niqulāwush*)—may God let His glory endure—has bought from Dominga bt. Salvador (*Dominqah bint Shalbaṭūr*)—may God give her long life—the whole

(3) half of the mosque (located) in the quarter of Santa Maria in the city of Toledo—may God preserve it. The limits of this mentioned half (of the mosque) are: in the east,

(4) the second part (of the mosque) which belongs to her sister Soli (*Shūlī*); in the west, a room that belongs to Maryam the Muslim who has been a wife of Abdī the Butcher (*al-jazzār*); in the south, the house

(5) that has belonged to Aparicio (*Abarisiyuh*); and in the north the way, towards which the door has its exit. (The sale was done) with all the uses of this half (of the mosque) and all its benefits, above

(6) and below and with all the rights attached to it and related to it, as well as the right of path. Dominga, the mentioned seller, did not retain any right or property in any form, be it for herself or

(7) for someone else, for any reason whatsoever, regarding the delimited object that has been sold not until she released (her rights and property)

(8) to the Archpriest, the mentioned buyer, in a valid, perfect, accomplished, unambiguous way, with no idle condition attached, neither prevention nor option (to return the sale)

(9) for a price of which was the whole 18 *mithqāl* freshly minted good gold of good weight. The Archpriest paid the complete mentioned (amount) of gold

(10) to Dominga, the seller. She exonerated him of all of this (payment), and he was exonerated. She placed him concerning it in her place and position as owner and proprietor

89 Uncertain reading.

(11) and according to the law of the Christians (*ʿalā sunnat al-naṣārā*) regarding their sale and purchases and warranty. Those whom they both called to testify testified on their two being called to testified on what is mentioned in it, both with full

(12) legal capability, in the last decade of the month of May, year 1205. This sale was done in the presence of Domingo Julianus (*Yulyānus*), husband of Dominga

(13) the mentioned seller and by his order and accord. The call for testimony was made for all of this and on the date that has been mentioned. It has been corrected from him and his sister (*ʿanhu wa-ukhtihi*). (Now) everything is correct, with God's—the Most High—will. (End)

(14) ʿAbd al-Raḥmān b. ʿAbd al-Malik . al-Bayāsī and ʿAbd Allāh b. ʿUmar   Domingo Petrus (*Duminquh Bīṭrus*) Ioannis (*Yuwānish*) b. Sulaymān

(15) ʿĀmir b. Yaḥyà b. Balāy (End)   (Latin:) Martin Johannis, witness

Verso

(1) Title of deed of half of a mosque bought from Dominga.

(2) (Romance:) Title of a signed deed of the house-mosque and the … of part …

1 *li-llāhi* is written with three *lāms*.

3 *masjid … bi-ḥaḍrat ṭulayṭula*: The object of the agreement and the capital city of Toledo are emphasized by thick pen and a bigger size.

3 *bi-ḥūmat …*: Vowels signs (*fatḥa* over the *mīm* of *bi-ḥūmat*) are used to emphasize the word, in this case the place or location of the property.

3 *ḥadd*: The limit is emphasized by thick pen and *tamdīd*.

4 *zawjan l-lʾbd*: Wife of al-Abadī, al-ʿAbadī, al-Abī?

6 *lam tastabqā*: Should be iussiv *lam tastabqa*.

8 *al-mbt*: *al-mubtāʿ*.

9 *bi-thaman*: Emphasized by the bigger size of the *nūn*.

No. 2: Second Document on Buying a Mosque (Reedition of P.Mozarab. 92)

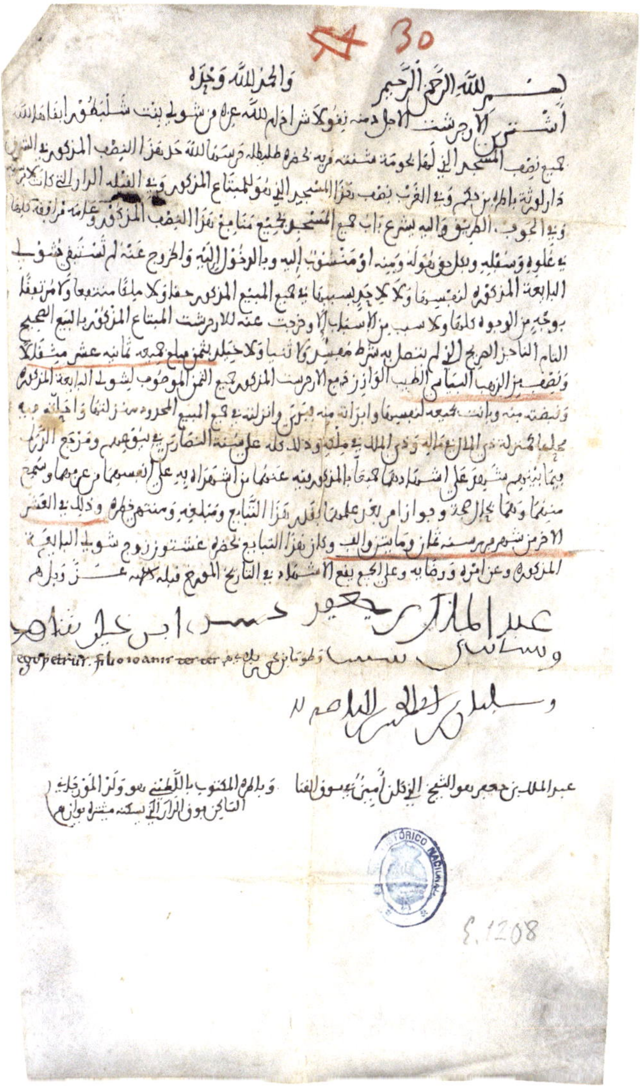
بسم الله الرحمن الرحيم والحمد لله وحده

FIGURE 7.3 Second document on buying a mosque (P.Arch.Hist.Nac.inv. Clero-Secular_Regular, Car. 3037, N. 4_1 recto = P.Mozarab. 92; 1208).

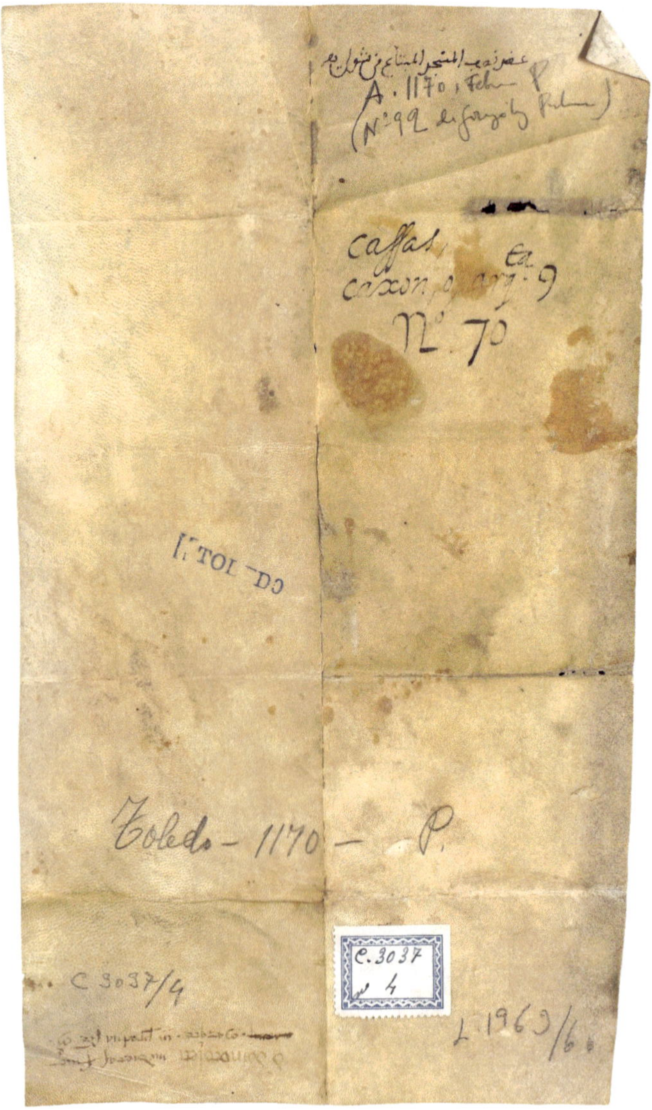

FIGURE 7.4 Second document on buying a mosque (P.Arch.Hist.Nac.inv. Clero-Secular_Regular, Car. 3037, N. 4_1 recto = P.Mozarab. 92; 1208).
© ARCHIVO HISTÓRICO NACIONAL DE MADRID

Parchment is in very good condition. Text is in small letters, except for the heading and the first introductory phrase. Signatures are extreme big, except one Arabic and the only Latin signature. *Tamdīd* of final *yāʾ* towards right. Maghribi-style writing with a dot below the *fāʾ* (*niṣf* r3; v1; *al-niṣf* r3) and one dot above the *qāf*. There are occasional *ihmāl* signs under *ḥā*ʾ (*li-aḥad* r7; *waa-ḥallathu* r11; *maḥallahā* r12; *bi-ḥāl* r14). Extensive use of *sukūn*, which implies the influence of how Latin and Romance is vocalized if written in Arabic characters. Vowels signs are used to emphasize long vowels and words. Below the signatures, there are remarks to identify the parties mentioned in the contract.

Recto

١ بِسْمِ اللَّهِ الرَّحمن ٱلرَّحِيم وَالحمدُ للّه وَحْدَه

٢ أَشْترِي الارجبرشت الاجل دمنه نِقُولَاش ادَام اللّه عِزه من شولي بِنْت شَلْبَطُورْ ابقَاهَا اللّه

٣ جميع نِصْف المسجد الذي لَهَا بحومَة شنتة مَرية بحضرة طليطلة حَرَسَهَا اللّه حَد هَذَا النِصْف المذكور في الشرق

٤ دَار لورثة باطره بن حكم وَفي الغَرْب نِصْف هَذَا المسْجِدِ الذي هُوَ للمبتَاع المذكور وَفِي القبْلة الدار التي كانَت لابرسيه

٥ وَفِي الجوْفْ الطرِيْق وَاليه يشرع بَابُ جميع المَسْجِد بجَمِيْع مَنَافِعْ هَذَا النِصْف المذكُور وعَامَة مرافقه كلِه

٦ فِي عُلوِهِ وسُفْلِهِ وبكل حق هُوَ لَهُ وَمِنه اوْ مَنْسُوبٌ اِلَيه وبالدخُوْل إِلَيْه وَالخروج عَنْهُ لم تَسْتَبقي شُوْلِي

٧ البايعة المذكُورة لنفْسِهَا وَلَا لِاحَدٍ بسببهَا فِي جميع المبيْع المذكور حقا وَلا مِلكًا منتفعا ولا مُرتفقًا

٨ بوجْهِ من الوجوه كلهَا ولا سببٍ مِن الاسبَاب إِلَا وخرجت عنه للارجـ⟨ـبـ⟩ـرشت المبتاع المذْكُوْر بالبَيع الصحِيح

٩ التام الناجز الصرِيح الذي لم يتصل به شرط مُفسِد وَلا ثنيا وَلا خِيَار بثمن مبلغ جمِيعه ثمانية عشر مثقَالًا

١٠ وَنِصْف مِن الذَهب البيَاسي الطيب الوَازِن دَفع الارجبرشت المذكور جميع الثمن الموصُوف لِشولى البايعة المذكورة

١١ وَقبضته مِنه وبانت بجمبعه لنفسِهَا وابرَاته مِنه فرَيَ وانزلته فِي جميع المبيع المحدود منزلتهَا وَاحَلّته فيه

١٢ محلها كمنزلة ذي المال في مَالِه وَذي الملك فِي مِلْكِه وذلك كله علي سُنة النصَارَي فِي بيُوْعِهم ومَرْجَع الدّرَك

١٣ فِيمَا بينِهِم شَهِدَ عَلي اشهَادهمَا جميعًا بالمذكور فيْه عَنهُما من اشهَدَاه بِهِ علي انفسِهِمَا من عرفهما وسَمِعَ

١٤ مِنهُمَا وَهُما بحال صحة وجواز امر بعد علمهمَا بقَدر هَذَا التَّبايع ومَبْلغِهِ وَمنتهي خطره وذِلك في العَشر

١٥ الاخر من شهر فبرير سنة ثمان ومَايتـ⟨يـ⟩ـن والف وكان هذَا التبايع بحضرة غشتون زوج شولي البايعَة

١٦ المذكورة وعن امْره وَرضَايه وعلي الجميع يقع الاشهَاد في التاريخ المورخ قبله (ان شا الله) عَزَّ وَجل (انتـ)ـهى

١٧ عبد الملك بن جعفر حسن ابن خلف شاهد

١٨ وبسانت بن شبيب وَطومَا بن يحيي بن بلاي (انتـ)ـهى ego petrus, filio Ioanis testes

١٩ ويليان بن ابي الحسن بن الباصه (انتـ)ـهي

٢٠ عبد الملك بن جعفر هو الشيخ الذي كان أَمِينٌ في السُوق القنا وَ باطره المكتوبِ بِاللَّطيْني هو وَلَدْ الحوْن حاني

٢١ السَاكِن فوق الدَارَ الَتي يسكنه ميشثره يوان (انتـ)ـهى

Verso

١ عقد نصف المسجد المبتاع من شولى (انتـ)ـهى

٢ (Unreadable Latin text)

Recto

(1) In the name of God, the Clement, the Merciful Praise be to God Alone

(2) The Most Honorable Archpriest (*al-arjibrisht al-ajall*) domino Nicolaus (*Niqulāwush*)—May God let His glory endure—has bought from Soli bt. Salvator (*Shūlī bint Shalbaṭūr*)—may God give her long life—

(3) the whole half of the mosque that belongs to her (located) in the quarter of Santa Maria in the city of Toledo—God preserve it. The limits of this mentioned half (of the mosque) are: in the east, a house belonging to the

(4) heirs of Pedro (*Bāṭruh*) b. Ḥakam; in the west, half of this mosque, which belongs to the mentioned buyer; in the south, the house, which has belonged to Aparicio (*Abarisiyuh*);

(5) and in the north, the way towards which the door of the mosque as a whole has its exit. (The sale was done) with all the uses of this half (of the mosque) and all its benefits,
(6) above and below and with all the rights attached to it, for and from it, as well as the right of path. Soli,
(7) the mentioned seller, did not retain any right or property in any form, be it for herself or for somebody else, for any reason whatsoever, regarding the whole object sold, neither right nor property, neither use nor benefit
(8) in any form or for any reason, not until she released (her rights and property) to the Archpriest (*al-arji⟨b⟩risht*), the mentioned buyer, in a valid sale,
(9) perfect, accomplished, unambiguous way, with no idle condition attached, neither prevention nor option (to return the sale) for the price, which was the whole 18 *mithqāl*
(10) and a half, of gold of Baeza, good gold and of good weight. The mentioned Archpriest paid the whole price as it is described to Soli, the mentioned seller.
(11) She took possession of it (the payment) that became the whole of it for herself. She exonerated him of all of this (payment), and he was exonerated.
(12) She placed him concerning the defined object sold in her place and position as owner and proprietor, and all of this according the law of the Christians (*ʿalā sunnat al-naṣārā*) in their sales and warranties as it is usual
(13) among them. Those whom they both called to testify testified on their two being called to testify on what is mentioned in it, who knew them and heard
(14) them (during the act of transaction), both with full legal capability and being lawful witnesses, after they both were informed of the amount and quantity of this transaction and the end of the contractual negotiations, in the last decade
(15) of the month of February, year 1208. This transaction was done in the presence of Gastón (*Gashtūn*), husband of Soli,
(16) the mentioned seller, and by his order and accord. The call to testimony concerns all of this on the date written above, with God's will—Praise and Glory to Him. (End)

(17) ʿAbd al-Malik b. Jaʿfar Ḥasan b. Khalaf witness (*shāhid*)
(18) Vicente (*Bizānt*) b. Shabīb Ṭūmā ibn Yaḥyā b. Belayo (*Bilāy*) (Latin:) I, Petrus son of Ioannis, witness

(19) and Julián (*Yulyān*) b. Abī l-Ḥasan b. al-Baza. (End)

(20) ʿAbd al-Malik b. Jaʿfar is the shaykh who had been the *amīn* in the Market al-Qannā. Pedro (*Bāṭruh*) written in Latin is the son of al-Juan Jani
(21) who lives on top of the house where Mister Juan (*mīshtar Yuwān*) lives. (End)

Verso
(1) Agreement on half the mosque, which has been bought from Soli (*Shūlī*). (End)
(2) (Unreadable Latin text)

r1 *li-llāhi* is written with three *lāms*.
r3 *masjid* is emphasized by thick pen and *tamdīd*.
r6 *lam tastabqā*: should be iussiv *lam tastabqa*.
r20 *alladhī kāna amīnun*: should be *alladhī kāna amīnan*.

Bibliography

Abbott, Nabia. 1937. *The Monasteries of the Fayyūm*. Studies in Ancient Oriental Civilization 16. Chicago: University of Chicago Press.

Aguilar Sebastián, Victoria. 1994. "Onomástica de origen árabe en el Reino de León (siglo X)." In *Al-Qanṭara* 15: 351–364.

Aillet, Cyrille. 2010. *Les Mozarabes: christianisme, islamisation et arabisation en péninsule Ibèrique (IX–XII siècle)*. Madrid: Casa de Velázquez.

Alonso, José Luis. 2013. "The Status of Peregrine Law in Roman Egypt: Customary Law and Legal Pluralism in the Roman Empire." In *Journal of Juristic Papyrology* 43: 351–404.

Alonso, Maria Luz. 1978. "La dote en los documentos toledanos de los siglos XII–XV." In *Anuario de historia del derecho español* 48: 379–456.

Alvarez de Morales, Camilo. 2010. "La geografía documental arabigogranadina." In *Documentos y manuscritos árabes del Occidente musulmán medieval*, edited by Nuria Martinez de Castilla, Maria Jesús Viguera, and Pascal Buresi. Colección Ductus 2. Madrid: Consejo Superior de Investigaciones Científicas, 205–223.

Berman, Lawrence V., and Ilai Alon. 1980. "Socrates on Law and Philosophy." In *Jerusalem Studies in Arabic and Islam* 2: 263–279.

Berman, Harold J. 1983. *Law and Revolution: The Formation of the Western Legal Tradition*. Cambridge, MA: Harvard University Press.

Bosch Vilá, Jacinto. 1957. "Los documentos árabes del Archivo Catedral de Huesca."

In *Revista del Instituto de Estudios Islámicos en Madrid* 5: 1–48; 12 plates. [P.Bosch-Huesca]

Camino y Velasco, Pedro. 1740. *Noticia históricocronológico de los privilegios de las nobles familias de Mozarabes dela imperial ciudad de Toledo*. Toledo: n. p.

Carro Martin, Sergio, and Amalia Zomeño. 2017. "Identifying the *ʿudūl* in Fifteenth-Century Granada." In *Legal Documents as Sources for the History of Muslim Societies: Studies in Honour of Rudolph Peters*, edited by Maaike van Berkel, Léon Buskens, and Petra M. Sijpesteijn. Studies in Islamic Law and Society 42. Leiden: Brill, 109–128.

Cronica Adefonsi Imperatoris. 1950. Edited by Luis Sánchez Belda. Textos 14. Madrid: Diana.

Córcoles Olaitz, Edorta. 2008. "El contrato de compraventa a la luz de las formulas Visigodas." In *Revista Internacional de Derecho Romano* 1: 309–330.

Daga Portillo, Rocio. 2020. "Abū Qurra (ca.750–720) and His Concept of Sunna: A Debate on the Tradition of the Church in the Context of the Formation of Islamic Law, fiqh." In *Aram* 32: 1–23.

Díaz y Díaz, Manuel Cecilio. 1976. "La Lex Visigothorum y sus manuscritos: un ensayo de reinterpretacion." In *Anuario de Historia del Derecho Espanol* 46: 163–224.

Diem, Werner. 1991. *Arabische Briefe auf Papyrus und Papier aus der Heidelberger Papyrus-Sammlung*. [Veröffentlichungen der] Heidelberger Akademie der Wissenschaften, Philosophisch-historische Klasse, Kommission für Papyrus-Editionen. 2 vols. Wiesbaden: Harrassowitz.

Donner, Fred McGraw. 1998. *Narratives of Islamic Origins: The Beginnings of Islamic Historical Writing*. Studies in Late Antiquity and Early Islam 14. Pennington: Darwin.

Epalza, Michel, and María Jesús Rubiera. 1986. "Los christianos toledanos bajo dominación musulmana." In *Simposio Toledo Hispanoarabe: colegio universitario 6–8 may 1982*. Collectión Toledo Universitario. Toledo: n.p., 129–134.

Fahmī, Muḥammad ʿAbd al-Raḥmān [Fahmy, Abdel Rahman]. 1972–1973. "Wathāʾiq li-l-taʿāqud min fajr al-islām [Early Islamic Contracts from Egypt]." In *Majallat al-Majmaʿ al-ʿĀlī al-Miṣrī* [Bulletin de l'Institut d'Egypte] 54: 1–58; pls. 1–10.

al-Fārābī, Abū Naṣr Muḥammad 1991. *Kitāb al-Milla wa-nuṣūṣ ukhrā* [al-Farabi's Book on Religion and Related Texts]. Edited by Muḥsin Mahdī. 2nd ed. Beirut: Dār al-Mashriq.

Fischer, August. 1918. "Der taʾrīkh al-ṣufr (die 'spanische Ära')." In *Zeitschrift der Deutschen Morgenländischen Gesellschaft* 3–4: 263–267.

Fuero Juzgo. 1815. *Fuero Juzgo en latin y castellano cotejado con los mas antigos y preciosos códices*. Madrid: Real Academia Española.

Fuero Juzgo. 1910. *The Visigothic Code* (*Forum Judicum*). Translated by S[amuel] P[arsons] Scott. Boston: Boston Book.

Garcia de Linares, R[amon]. 1904. "Escrituras árabes pertenecientes al Archivo de Ntra.

Sra. del Pilar de Zaragoza." In *Homenaje á … Francisco Codera en su jubílación del profesorado: estudios de erudición oriental*, edited by Eduardo de Saavedra. Zaragoza: Mariano, 171–197.

García-Velasco Bernal, Rodrigo. 2017. "ʿAlā für Tuṭīla: Jews and Muslims in the Administrative Culture of Post-Conquest Tudela, c. 1118–1220." In *Al-Masāq* 29: 235–257.

González Palencia, Angel. 1930. *Los Mozárabes de Toledo en los siglos XII y XIII*. 4 vols. Madrid: Maestre.

Grohmann, Adolf. 1934–1962. *Arabic Papyri in the Egyptian Library*. 6 vols. Cairo: Egyptian Library Press.

Grohmann, Adolf, and Raif Georges Khoury. 1993. *Chrestomatie de papyrologie arabe: documents relatifs à la vie privée, sociale et administrative dans les premiers siècles islamiques*. Handbuch der Orientalistik. 1: Der Nahe und Mittlere Osten. Ergänzungsband 2,2. Leiden: Brill.

Grohmann, Adolf, and Raif Georges Khoury. 1995. *Papyrologische Studien: zum privaten und gesellschaftlichen Leben in den ersten islamischen Jahrhunderten*. Codices Arabici Antiqui 5. Wiesbaden: Steiner.

Hoenerbach, Wilhelm. 1965. *Spanisch-islamische Urkunden aus der Zeit der Naṣriden und Moriscos*. University of California Publications, Near Eastern Studies 3. Berkeley: University of California Press.

Ibn al-Mughīth al-Ṭulayṭulī, Aḥmad b. Muḥammad. 1994. *al-Mugniʿ fī ʿilm al-shurūṭ*. (= *Formulario notarial*). Edited by Francisco Javier Aguirre Sádaba. Fuentes Arábico-Hispanas 5. Madrid: Instituto de cooperación con el mundo árabe.

Ibn Rushd, Muḥammad b. Aḥmad. 2002. *Commentaire moyen à la Rhétorique d'Aristote*. Edited by Maroun Aouad. 3 vols. Paris: Vrin.

Ibn al-ʿAṭṭār, Muḥammad b. Aḥmad. 1983. *Kitāb al-Wathāʾiq wa-l-sijillāt: formulario notarial hispano-árabe*. Edited by P[edro] Chalmeta and F[ederico] Corriente. Madrid: Instituto Hispano-Árabe de Cultura.

Labarta, Ana. 1983. "Contratos matrimoniales entre moriscos valencianos." In *Al-Qanṭara* 4: 57–88. [P.LabartaContratosMatrimoniales]

Maser, Matthias. 2011. "Die Mozaraber: ein undefinierbares Phänomen?" In *Die Mozaraber: Definitionen und Perspektiven der Forschung*, edited by Matthias Maser and Klaus Herbers. Geschichte und Kultur der Iberischen Welt 7. Münster: LIT-Verlag, 11–35.

Metcalfe, Alex. 2012. "Orientation in Three Spheres: Medieval Mediterranean Boundary Clauses in Latin, Greek and Arabic." In *Transactions of the Royal Historical Society* 22: 37–55.

Molenat, Jean Pierre. 1994. "L'arabe à Tolede, du XII au XVI siècle." In *Al-Qanṭara* 15: 473–496.

Mouton, Jean-Michel, Dominique Sourdel, and Janine Sourdel-Thomine. 2013. *Mariage et séparation à Damas au moyen âge: un corpus de 62 documents juridiques inéd-*

its entre 337/948 et 698/1299. Documents relatifs à l'histoire des croisades 21. Paris: Académie des inscriptions et belles-lettres.

Die Mozaraber: Definitionen und Perspektiven der Forschung. 2011. Edited by Matthias Maser and Klaus Herbers. Geschichte und Kultur der Iberischen Welt 7. Münster: LIT-Verlag.

Müller, Christian. 2013. *Der Kadi und seine Zeugen: Studie der mamlukischen Ḥaram-Dokumente aus Jerusalem*. Abhandlungen für die Kunde des Morgenlandes 85. Wiesbaden: Harrassowitz.

Müller, Christian. 2018. "Islamische Jurisprudenz als Gottesrecht: die schariatische Wende des 12. Jahrhunderts." In *Islamische und westliche Jurisprudenz des Mittelalters im Vergleich*, edited by Christian R. Lange, Wolfgang P. Müller, and Christoph K. Neumann. Tübingen: Mohr Siebeck, 57–83.

Muñoz y Romero, Tomás. 1847. *Coleccion de fueros municipales y cartas pueblas de los reinos de Castilla, Leon, Corona de Aragon y Navarra*. Madrid: Alonso.

Olstein, Diego Adrián. 2006a. *La era mozárabe: los mozárabes de Toledo (siglos XII y XIII) en la historiografía, las fuentes, y la historia*. Acta Salmanticensia: estudios históricos y geográficos 135. Salamanca: Universidad de Salamanca.

Olstein, Diego [Adrián]. 2006b. "The Arabic Origins of Romance Private Documents." In *Islam and Christian-Muslim Relations* 17: 433–443.

Olstein, Diego [Adrián]. 2011. "The Mozarabs of Toledo (12th–13th Centuries) in Historiography, Sources, and History." In *Die Mozaraber: Definitionen und Perspektiven der Forschung*, edited by Matthias Maser and Klaus Herbers. Geschichte und Kultur der Iberischen Welt 7. Münster: LIT-Verlag, 151–186.

Opúsculos legales del Rey Don Alfonso el Sabio publicados y cotejados con varios códices antiguos. 1836. Vol. 2. Madrid: Real Academia de la Historia.

Platon. 1977. *Nomōn = Gesetze, Teil 2: Buch VII–XII. Minōs*. Edited by Auguste Diès. Translated by Joseph Souilhé, Klaus Schöpsdau, and Hieronymus Müller. Platon, Werke in acht Bänden griechisch und deutsch 8,2. Darmstadt: Wissenschaftliche Buchgesellschaft.

Potthast, Daniel. 2017. "Diplomatischer Austausch zwischen Muslimen und Christen: religiöses Formular in mittelalterlichen Briefen arabischer Herrscher." In *Medien der Aussenbeziehungen von der Antike bis zur Gegenwart*, edited by Peter Hoeres and Anuschka Tischer. Köln: Böhlau, 445–467.

Rāġib, Yūsuf. 2002–2006. *Actes de vente d'esclaves et d'animaux d'Egypte médiévale*. Publications de l'Institut français d'archéologie orientale 893; 955. Cahiers des Annales Islamologiques 23; 28. 2 vols. Cairo: Institut français d'archéologie orientale.

Richards, Donald S. 2013. "Three (Twelfth-Century?) Guarantees Issued for the Monks of St Catherine's Monastery in Sinai." In *Les non-dits du nom: onomastique et documents en terres d'Islam*, edited by Christian Müller and Muriel Roiland-Rouabah. Beirut: Institut français du Proche-Orient, 15–27.

Schatzmiller, Maya. 2018. “The Adoption of Paper in the Middle East, 700–1300 AD.” In *Journal of the Economic and Social History of the Orient* 61: 461–490.

Seco de Lucena Paredes, Luis. 1943. “Documentos granadinos 1: Documentos de Colegio de niños nobles.” In *Al-Andalus* 8: 415–429.

Seco de Lucena Paredes, Luis. 1961. *Documentos arábigo-granadinos*. Madrid: Publicaciones del Instituto de Estudios Islámicos (Manšūrāt Maʿhad ad-dirāsāt al-islāmiyya).

Las Siete Partidas de Alfonso X: edición de 1555, glosada por Gregorio López. 2011. Textos Históricos. Madrid: Boletín Oficial del Estado.

Simonet. Francisco Javier. 1897–1903. *Historia de los mozárabes en España: deducida de sus mejores y más auténticos testimonios de los escritores cristianos y árabes*. 3 vols. Madrid: Tello.

Strong, W.T. 1893. “The Fueros of Northern Spain.” In *Political Science Quarterly* 8: 317–334.

al-Ṭaḥāwī, Aḥmad b. Muḥammad. 1972. *The Function of Documents in Islamic Law: The Chapters on Sales From Ṭahāwī's* Kitāb al-Shurūṭ al-kabīr, edited by Jeanette A. Wakin. Albany: State University of New York Press.

Thung, Michael H. 1996. “Written Obligations from the 2nd/8th to the 4th/10th Century.” In *Islamic Law and Society* 3: 1–12.

Vallvé Bermejo, Joaquín. 1999. *Al-Andalus: sociedad e instituciones*. Clave historial 20. Madrid: Real Academia de la Historia.

Vidal Castro, Francisco. 2012. “Un tipo de manuscrito ‘documental.’ Las escrituras árabes notariales en al-Andalus nasrí (s. XIII–XVI).” In *Manuscritos, papel, técnicas y dimensión cultural: IV Primavera del manuscrito andalusí*, edited by Mostafa Ammadi. Casablanca: Universidad Hasan II, 23–57.

Watkin, Thomas Glyn. 1999. *An Historical Introduction to Modern Civil Law*. Laws of the Nations Series. Aldershot: Dartmouth.

Quoted Editions

Berk 187	Weber, Dieter. 2014. "Arabic Activities Reflected in the Documents of the 'Pahlavi Archive' (Late 7th and Early 8th Centuries)." In *Res Orientales* 22: 179–189.
Cambridge, CUL T-S A 45.21	Hopkins, Simon. 1978. *A Miscellany of Literary Pieces from the Cambridge Genizah Collections: A Catalogue and Selection of Texts in the Taylor-Schechter Collection, Old Series, Box A45*. Genizah Series, vol. 3. Cambridge: Cambridge University Library: 76–71.
Chrest.Khoury I	Grohmann, Adolf and Raif Georges Khoury. 1993. *Chrestomatie de papyrologie arabe: documents relatifs à la vie privée, sociale et administrative dans les premiers siècles islamiques*. Handbuch der Orientalistik. 1: Der Nahe und Mittlere Osten. Ergänzungsband 2,2. Leiden: Brill.
Chrest.Khoury II	Grohmann, Adolf and Raif Georges Khoury. 1995. *Papyrologische Studien zum privaten und gesellschaftlichen Leben in den ersten islamischen Jahrhunderten*. Codices Arabici Antiqui, vol. 5. Wiesbaden: Steiner.
CPR XXII	Hasitzka, Monika R.M. 1987. *Koptische Texte*. 2 vols. Vienna: Holinek.
CPR XXXIV	Hasitzka, Monika R.M. 2018. *Koptische dokumentarische Texte aus der Papyrussammlung der Österreichischen Nationalbibliothek*. Berlin: De Gruyter.
Mount Mugh Document I	Livshits, Vladimir A. 2015. *Sogdian Epigraphy of Central Asia and Semirech'e*. Translated by Tom Stableford. Edited by Nicholas Sims-Williams. Corpus Inscriptionum Iranicarum, part 2, vol. 3. London: School of Oriental and African Studies: 88–92.
O.Brit.Mus.Copt. I	Hall, Harry Reginald. 1905. *Coptic and Greek Texts of the Christian Period from Ostraka, Stelae, etc. in the British Museum*. London: British Museum Press.

 | DOI:10.1163/9789004527874_010

O.CrumST — Crum, Walter Ewing. 1921. *Short Texts from Coptic Ostraca and Papyri.* London: Oxford University Press.

P.Bad. V — Bilabel, Friedrich and Adolf Grohmann. 1934. *Griechische, koptische und arabische Texte zur Religion und religiösen Literatur in Ägyptens Spätzeit.* Veröffentlichungen aus den badischen Papyrus-Sammlungen, vol. 5. Heidelberg: Verlag der Universitätsbibliothek.

P.BaudenAchat I — Bauden, Frédéric. 2005. "L'achat d'esclaves et la rédemption des captifs d'Alexandrie d'après deux documents arabes d'époque mamelouke conservés aux Archives de l'Etat à Venise (ASVe)." In *Regards croisés sur le Moyen Âge arabe: mélanges à la mémoire de Louis Pouzet s.j.* (1928–2002), ed. Anne-Marie Eddé and Emma Gannagé. Mélanges de l'Université St. Joseph, vol. 58. Beirut: Université St. Joseph, 269–325.

P.BoschHuesca — Bosch Vilá, Jacinto. 1957. "Los documentos árabes del Archivo Catedral de Huesca." In *Revista del Instituto de Estudios Islámicos en Madrid* 5: 1–48.

P.Cair.Arab. I — Grohmann, Adolf. 1934. *Arabic Papyri in the Egyptian Library.* Vol. 1. Cairo: Egyptian Library Press.

P.Cair.Masp. I–II — Maspero, Jean. 1911–1913. *Papyrus grecs d'époque byzantine: catalogue général des antiquités égyptiennes du Musée du Caire.* Vols. 1–2. Cairo: Institut français d'archéologie orientale.

P.DietrichDrogenkunde — Dietrich, Albert. 1954. *Zum Drogenhandel im islamischen Ägypten: eine Studie über die arabische Handschrift Nr. 912 der Heidelberger Papyrus-Sammlung.* Veröffentlichungen aus der Heidelberger Papyrussammlung. Neue Folge, vol. 1. Heidelberg: Winter.

P.DonnerFragments — Donner, Fred. 2016. "Fragments of Three Umayyad Official Documents." In *The Heritage of Arabo-Islamic Learning: Studies Presented to Wadad Kadi*, ed. Maurice A. Pomerantz and Aram A. Shahin. Islamic History and Civilization, vol. 122. 30–47. Leiden: Brill.

P.FahmiTaaqud	Fahmy Muhammad, A. 1972–1973. “Wathāʾiq li-l-taʿāqud min fadjr al-Islām fī Miṣr.” In *Bulletin de l'Institut d'Egypte* 54: 1–58.
P.GarciaArenal 11	García-Arenal, Mercedes. 1984 “Un nuevo documento arabe de Tudela, año de 1509.” In *Al-Qantara* 5: 455–462.
P.Granada	Seco de Lucerna Paredes, Luis. 1961. *Documentos arábigo-granadinos. Edición critica del texto árabe y traduccíon al español con introduccíon, notas, glosarios e indices.* Madrid: Imprenta del Estudios islámicos.
P.Grohmann-Wirtsch.	Grohmann, Adolf. 1935. “Texte zur Wirtschaftsgeschichte Aegyptens in arabischer Zeit”, In *Archív Orientální* 7: 437–472.
P.Fay.Copt.	Crum, Walter Ewing. 1893. *Coptic Manuscripts Brought from the Fayyum by W.M. Flinders Petrie, Esq., D.C.L., Together with a Papyrus in the Bodeian Library*. London: D. Nutt.
P.Fay.Monast	Abbott, Nabia. 1937. *The Monasteries of the Fayyūm*. Studies in Ancient Oriental Civilization, vol. 16. Chicago: University of Chicago Press.
P.Gascou	Fournet, Jean-Luc and Arietta Papaconstantinou. 2016. *Mélanges Jean Gascou. Textes et études papyrologiques* (*P.Gascou*). Travaux et Mémoires, vol. 20/1. Paris: Association des Amis du Centre d'Histoire et Civilisation de Byzance.
P.Heid.Arab. I	Becker, Carl H. 1906. *Papyri Schott-Reinhardt I*. Veröffentlichungen aus der Heidelberger Papyrussammlung, vol. 3. Heidelberg: Winter.
P.Heid.Arab. II	Diem, Werner. 1991. *Arabische Briefe auf Papyrus und Papier aus der Heidelberger Papyrus-Sammlung*. 2 vols. Veroffentlichungen der Heidelberger Akademie der Wissenschaften, Philosophisch-historische Klasse, Kommission fur Papyrus-Editionen. Wiesbaden: Harrassowitz.
P.Heid.Arab. III	Diem, Werner. 2013. *Arabische Briefe auf Papier aus der Heidelberger Papyrus-Sammlung*. Heidelberg: Winter.
P.Heid.Kopt.	Boud'hors, Anne et al. 2018. *Coptica Palatina: koptische Texte aus der Heidelberger Papyrussammlung*. Heidelberg University Publishing.

P.Kratchkovski — Kračkovskaya, V.A. and I.J. Kračkovskij. 1934/1955. "Le plus ancient document arabe de l'Asie Centrale." In *Sogdiiskii Sbornik*. Leningrad, 52–90. Reprinted in Krackovskij, I.J., *Izbrannye Socineniya 1*. Moscow-Leningrad: 182–212.

P.LabartaContratosMatrimoniales — Labarta, Ana. 1983. "Contratos matrimoniales entre moriscos valencianos." In *Al-Qanṭara* 4: 57–88.

P.Lond. IV — Bell, Harold Idris and Walter Ewing Crum. 1910. *Greek Papyri in the British Museum: Catalogue with Texts. Volume IV: The Aphrodito Papyri*. London: British Museum.

P.Lond.Copt. I — Crum, Walter Ewing. 1905. *Catalogue of the Coptic Manuscripts in the British Museum*. London: British Museum.

P.MargolioughMonneret — Margoliouth, D.S. and Holmyard, E.J. 1930. "Arabic Documents from the Monneret Collection," In *Islamica* 3: 249–271.

P.Marques — Damaj, Ahmad Chafic and José Antonio García Luján. 2012. *Documentos árabes granadinos del archivo del Marqués de Corvera (1399–1495)*. Huéscar: Granada Fundacíon Nuestra Señora del Carmen Fundacíon Portillo.

P.MariageSeparation — Mouton, Jean-Michel, Dominique Sourdel and Janine Sourdel-Thomine. 2013. *Mariage et séparation à Damas au moyen âge: un corpus de 62 documents juridiques inédits entre 337/948 et 698/1299*. Documents relatifs à l'histoire des croisades, vol. 21. Paris: Académie des inscriptions et belles-lettres.

P.Mich. — Browne Gerald M. 1975. *Michigan Papyri*. XII. Michigan Papyri, vol. 12. Toronto: Haakert.

P.Moriscos — Hoenerbach, Wilhelm. 1965. *Spanisch-islamische Urkunden aus der Zeit der Nasriden und Moriscos*. Berkeley: University of California Publications.

P.Mozarab. — González Palencia, Angel. 1930. *Los Mozárabes de Toledo en los siglos xii y xiii*. 4 vols. Madrid: Maestre.

P.Qurra — Abbott, Nabia. 1938. *The Ḳurrah Papyri from Aphrodito in the Oriental Institute*. Studies in Ancient

Oriental Civilisation, vol. 15. Chicago: University of Chicago Press.

P.QuseirArab. I — Guo, Li. 2004. *Commerce, Culture, and Community in a Red Sea Port in the Thirteenth Century: The Arabic Documents from Quseir*. Islamic History and Civilization, vol. 52. Leiden: Brill.

P.Ross.Georg. IV — Zeretelli, Gregor und Jernstedt, Peter. 1925/1966. *Die Kome-Aphrodito Papyri der Sammlung Lichačov*. Papyri russischer und georgischer Sammlungen [P.Ross.-Georg.], vol. 4. Tiflis. Reprint Amsterdam: A.M. Haakert.

P.Ryl.Copt. — Crum, Walter Ewing. 1909. *Catalogue of the Coptic Manuscripts in the Collection of the John Rylands Library*. Manchester: University of Manchester Press.

P.Stras. inv. Kopt. — Boud'hors, Anne, Alain Delattre, Catherine Louis and Sebastian Tonio Richter. 2014. *Coptica Argentoratensia. Textes et documents de la troisième Université d'Eté de Papyrologie Copte (Strasbourg, 18–25 juillet 2010)*. Cahiers de la Bibliothèque copte, vol. 19. Paris.

P.SourdelMekka 1 — Sourdel, Dominique and Janine Sourdel-Thomine. 1983. "Une collection médiévale de certificats de pèlerinage à la Mekka conservés à Istanbul. Les actes de la période seljoukide et bouride (jusqu'à 549/1154)." In: *Etudes médiévales et patrimoine turc. Volume publié à l'occasion du centième anniversaire de la naissance de Kemal Atatürk 1983*. Cultures et civilisations médiévales, vol. 1. Paris: Editions du Centre national de la recherche scientifique, 167–273.

P.ThomannAlmanac — Thomann, Johannes. 2017 "A Fragment of an Unusual Arabic Almanac for 297 AH/910 CE (P.Berl. inv. 12793)." In *New Frontiers of Arabic Papyrology: Arabic and Multilingual Texts from Early Islam*, ed. Sobhi Bouderbala, Sylvie Denoix and Matt Malczycki. Islamic History and Civilization, vol. 144. Leiden: Brill, 179–196.

P.ThomannEphemeris931 — Thomann, Johannes. 2015. "An Arabic Ephemeris for the Year 931–932 CE." In *From Bāwīṭ to Marw:*

Documents from the Medieval Muslim World, ed. Andreas Kaplony, Daniel Potthast and Cornelia Römer. Islamic History and Civilization, vol. 112. Leiden: Brill, 115–153.

P.ThomannEphemeris954 — Thomann, Johannes. 2013. “An Arabic Ephemeris for the Year 954/955 CE and the Geographical Latitude of al-Bahnasa/Oxyrhynchus (P.Stras. Inv. Ar. 446)”. In *Chronique d’Egypte* 88: 385–396.

P.ThomannEphemeris1026 — Thomann, Johannes. “An Arabic Ephemeris for the Year 1026/1027 CE. in the Vienna Papyrus Collection”. In *Scientific Cosmopolitanism and Local Cultures: Religions, Ideologies, Societies. 5th International Conference of the European Society for the History of Science, National Hellenic Research Foundation/Institute of Historical Research*, ed. Giana Catsiampoura. Athens: Institute of Historical Research and National Hellenic Research Foundation, 54–60.

P.ThomannEphemeris1149 — Thomann, Johannes. 2015. “The Arabic Ephemeris for the Year 1149/1150 CE (P.Cambridge ul Inv. Michael. Chartae D 58) and the Arabic Baḫnīṭas, Greek Παχνίτης and Coptic ⲡⲁϣⲟⲛⲥ.” In *Chronique d’Egypte* 90, no. 179: 207–224.

P.ThungWrittenObligations — Thung, Michael H. 1996. “Written Obligations from the 2nd/8th to the 4th/10th Century.” In *Islamic Law and Society* 3: 1–12.

P.Vente — Rāġib, Yūsuf. 2002. *Actes de vente d’esclaves et d’animaux d’Egypte médiévale*. 2 vols. Cahiers des Annales Islamologiques, vol. 23. Cairo: Institut français d’archéologie orientale.

P.World — Grohmann, Adolf. 1952. *From the World of Arabic Papyri*. Royal Society of Historical Studies. Cairo: Al-Maaref Press.

P.Würzb. Inv. 122–127 — Wilcken, Ulrich. 1934/1978. *Mitteilungen aus der Würzburger Papyrussammlung*. Abhandlungen der Preußischen Akademie der Wissenschaften, Philosophisch-Historische Klasse Berlin, vol. 1933,6. Berlin: Verlag der Akademie der Wissenschaften. Reprint Berlin: De Gruyter.

SB I Preisigke, Friedrich. 1915. Sammelbuch griechischer Urkunden aus Aegypten. Berlin: De Gruyter and Strassburg: Karl J. Trübner.

SB XX Ruprecht, Hans-Albert. 1997. *Sammelbuch griechischer Urkunden aus Aegypten* XX. Wiesbaden: Harrasowitz.

SB Kopt III Hasitzka, Monika R.M. 2006. *Koptisches Sammelbuch* III. Vienna: Brūder Hollinek.

Index

Abd al-Raḥmān b. Subḥ 76, 81–82
Abū l-Ḥārith Ghaylān b. Uqba. *See* Dhū l-Rumma
alchemy 163–164
Alexandria 8, 173
almanac 167–170
al-Andalus 191, 202–204, 207–208
Aphrodito 4–52, 133
  tax system of 8–11
Arabic
  epistolary formulae 71–74, 78–81, 104, 112, 121
  letters (correspondence) 68–69, 72–73, 78, 81, 84, 120
  legal documents 183–186, 192
  legal formulae 185, 198, 202–204
  names 190
  paleography 90–91
  palmomantic texts 151–152
  poetry 88–90, 92, 96–100
Aragon 185, 193
Aramaic 139, 141, 153
  texts 146, 147
Ashmunayn (Ashmunein) 107, 116
astrology 162, 166–170, 173
astronomy 162, 166–174

Bactrian (language) 79
al-Birūnī 168

Cairo Genizah. *See* Genizah (Cairo)
Castille (Castilla) 191, 193–194
Castillian 184
  language mixed with Arabic 188
  law 190
Christian(s)
  in al-Andalus 183, 184, 187, 190
  in Egypt 116
  names 190
Coptic
  Arabic loanwords in 107–108, 120, 127–129, 133
  Bohairic 133
  epistolary formulae 110–113, 121
  Greek loanwords in 115, 120
  Fayyumic 105–107, 111, 113, 116, 120, 126–127, 133
  letters (correspondence) 104–105, 110–113, 120
  orthography 120
  paleography 105–106
  phraseology 110–113
  punctuation 108–110
  Sahidic 106–117, 113, 115, 126–127, 133
  tax documents 17, 30–32, 45
cryptography 165

Dēwāshtīč 68, 72–76, 79, 80–84
Dhū l-Rumma (Abū al-Ḥārith Ghaylān b. ʿUqba) 90
dioikêtês (administrater) 9, 11, 12, 20
dioikêsis (administrative district) 9, 31, 34, 38, 44, 45
divination 139, 141. *See also* palmomancy

Egypt 6–58, 71, 81, 139, 162, 170
epilechthentes (tax assessors) 9, 11–52
epoikion (hamlet) 12–16, 29, 31–33, 39–52
ephemeris, -ides 167–170

al-Fayyūm 104, 105, 116, 129
Fernando III 194
fueros 184, 189, 192–196, 199, 205
al-Fusṭāṭ 6, 8, 9, 150

Genizah (Cairo) 139, 141, 147, 148, 153, 156–157, 166
geomancy 141, 165, 175
Granada 184, 202, 207, 208
Greek
  with Coptic 29–31, 42
  tax documents 5–55
Gūrak 73–74

Hebrew (language) 139, 141, 147–149, 152–153, 157, 201
Hindi 168
horoscopes 166–167

Ibn al-Aṭṭār 183, 192
Ibn al-Mughīth 183, 192
Iran 81

Jaʿfar al-Ṣādiq 151
al-Jarrāḥ b. ʿAbd Allāh al-Ḥakamī 69, 74–75
Jews 140–141, 153, 157, 183–184, 186, 188, 191, 194
Judeo-Arabic 139–142, 148–151, 153, 186, 188, 192
Judeo-Persian 141

Khurasān 69, 70, 75–76, 173
al-Kindī (philosopher) 169

Latin
 in legal documents 184, 188–189, 192, 205
 mixed with Arabic 188
law
 Canon Law 193–195, 204
 Christian 184, 192, 195
 customary 195–196, 205–206
 formulary 185, 197–204
 Islamic (al-Sharīʿa) 201–209
 Mālikī 195–196, 199, 207–208
 Visigothic 192
logographos 16, 30, 43–44, 50–52

magic 164–165
merismos (tax assessment document) 11, 24, 26–27
Middle Persian 79, 168
Mounth Mugh 67
Mozarabs 186–189, 191, 194
Muqātil b. Sulaymān 89–90

Naqlūn 105, 113, 116–117, 122, 129, 133
Niẓām al-Mulk 207

Pahlevi. *See* Middle Persian
palmomancy 139–142, 146–147, 153
Panjikant 68, 73–74
pharmacy 163
prosopography 4–5, 16–17

Qurra b. Sharīk 12, 19, 31
al-Quṣayr (Quseir) 141–142, 153–154, 156
Qutayba b. Muslim al-Bahīlī 73–74

Romance (language) 188–189

Saʿīd b. Abd al-Azīz 76, 81–82
Saʿīd al-Ḥarashī 83
Samarqand 73–74, 79
Sanskrit 168, 173
Sogdiana 67–68, 75, 82, 173
Sogdian (language) 68, 72–73, 75–76, 78, 80–84
Sulaymān b. Abī al-Surī 84
sunna (legal custom) 183–184, 204–209
 sunnat al-muslimīn 185–186, 193, 201–203, 205
 sunnat al-naṣārā 183, 185, 192, 195, 203
al-Suyūṭī, Jalāl al-Dīn 151
Syriac 140, 164, 173

tafsīr 89, 96–97
Tajikistan 68
Ṭarkhūn 69, 72–73
tax
 assessors. See *epilechthentes*
 categories of 7
 collectors 9, 19–20, 34
 documents 11
 officials 7, 8
 structure 10–11
 taxpayers 7, 9, 15, 36
Theon of Alexandria 169
Toledo 183–209
Transoxania. *See* Sogdiana

women 6–7, 41, 189–190, 200, 204

Zoroastrians 82–83